D1260758

Judge and Jury in Imperial Brazil, 1808-1871
Social Control and Political Stability in the New State

Latin American Monographs, No. 53
Institute of Latin American Studies
The University of Texas at Austin

Judge and Jury in Imperial Brazil, 1808-1871

Social Control and Political Stability in the New State

by Thomas Flory

University of Texas Press, Austin and London

Library of Congress Cataloging in Publication Data

Flory, Thomas, 1947-
    Judge and jury in imperial Brazil, 1808-1871.

    (Latin American monographs; no. 53)
    Bibliography: p.
    Includes index.
    1. Judges—Brazil—History. 2. Courts—Brazil
—History. 3. Brazil—Social conditions. 4. Lib-
eralism—Brazil—History. 5. Brazil—Politics
and government. I. Title. II. Series: Latin
American monographs (Austin, Tex.); no. 53
Law   347.81´01   80-23447
ISBN 0-292-74015-8

Requests for permission to reproduce material from
this work should be sent to:
    Permissions
    University of Texas Press
    P.O. Box 7819
    Austin, Texas 78712

For my Mother and Father

Contents

Preface

Joaquim Nabuco, in the biography of his father which remains the fundamental book on the Brazilian empire, stated in an offhand way the paradox which underlies the present study. "One cannot make a revolution without the radicals," he wrote, "but then one cannot govern with them." Nabuco had in mind a specific situation—the forced abdication of Brazil's first emperor in 1831—but his paradox is one of basic importance for any new state and it raises questions about change and stability which this book seeks in part to answer. Just who are the men who make revolutions? If one cannot govern with them, with whom can one govern? How, finally, is a working pact forged between government and these its proper constituents?

These are general questions and this book is in one sense a general work about the building of a state and nation by a former colony.[1] As such it ranges over a broad expanse of all but trackless territory within the history of nineteenth-century Brazil. A guide is necessary in this wilderness, and one has been chosen in the theme of judicial policy, for the book is also a case study of the Brazilian inferior court system after independence. Some readers may find the study most valuable at the general level, as one example in a casebook of state-building. For reasons that I hope to make clear in the course of the analysis, however, the study of judicial policy provides more than just a structural device. The importance of judicial reform and judges in nineteenth-century Brazil is in itself a major substantive part of the story. Although the ramifications of judicial policy provide valuable insights into the construction and perpetuation of a state, the very fact of those ramifications is no less the central theme of the work.

In a preface one would like to introduce a book that is entirely self-contained and whose arguments are self-explanatory. The desire is probably an unrealizable one for an historian in any case, but certainly it is a doomed wish for a work that employs the term *liberal* as often as this one. The concept of liberalism and its variants appear frequently in these pages and require some preliminary comment. Brazilian political liberalism of the post-independence period derived equally from a philosophic commitment to localism and a reinforcing strategic commitment to decentralization. Brazilian liberalism was thus strong and well-founded, but it was also parochial in every sense. In Mexico and Argentina contemporary politicians argued over federalistic reforms to guarantee or diminish the autonomy of provinces. In Brazil they debated the autonomy of the parish, and they did so because the dimensions of this smallest administrative unit coincided most closely with their social and political thinking. Morally the parish was the family slightly enlarged; politically it was the state in remote and extreme miniature. Just why Brazilian liberalism took this form is a question central to this study. It is therefore taken up at some length and from a number of different perspectives in the first section.

A final warning in this area is necessary: until the late 1830s it is not useful to speak of formal political parties in Brazil, yet long before that time men called themselves liberals with partisan intent. For the sake of consistency I have not capitalized the term before true party formation is introduced in Chapter 9. Thereafter, *Liberal* refers to the party and its members; *liberal* alludes to strictly nonpartisan contexts. The same distinction will be observed with regard to the term *conservative*.

My approach to judicial policy is largely defined by the tension between national and local judicial needs, or, put somewhat more abstractly, public and private power. The public component of this heuristic dichotomy is by no means perfectly discrete or even well understood, but it at least displays readily identifiable markers from an early period: the monarch, his ministers, the houses of Parliament. The same is not true of the private component—local social structures and especially local elites. This book will present a body of information about local social structures and their dynamics, but it must be stated at the outset that such information falls into something of a descriptive vacuum. Little is known about Brazilian society at the beginning of the nineteenth century, and the historian does well to limit his assumptions. Here I have tried to stay close to those few basic premises that seem compatible with a society in which nearly half the population was black and enslaved and whose economy rested on export agriculture. I assume a hierarchical structure characterized by a certain rigidity between racial and class sectors. But within the free population I have not posited insurmountable social barriers, and I assume a definition of *elites* that admits considerable breadth and internal flexibility.

Social and intellectual themes are developed in each of the book's three parts, but the organizational progression of the parts derives from the standard political chronology. Part I discusses the objective conditions of economy, society, and justice in Brazil during the so-called independence period (1808-1831) and attempts to relate these to the intellectual tendencies of the time. Part II examines the judicial developments of the liberal decade (1827-1837) in their social and political contexts. Part III concludes with an analysis of the conservative reaction in the late 1830s and describes the subsequent emergence of institutionalized bureaucratic politics in the mature empire.

Acknowledgments

It is a pleasure to express my deep appreciation of the many kinds of aid and support from which this book and I have benefited. Research funding and time for writing were provided by the Fulbright-Hays program and by two National Defense Foreign Language grants. Federico Edelweiss of Salvador, Bahia, generously opened his private library to me when I badly needed it. José Antônio Soares de Souza of Niterói gave me access to the papers of the Visconde do Uruguai. The manuscript in one form or another has profited from the criticism and advice of Woodrow Borah, Maria Odila Silva Dias, Carlos Guilherme Mota, and John Wirth.

My debts to three people can only be recorded here as being of a different order and more inexpressible than the rest. Thanks to Charles Gibson for his support and confidence. Thanks to Richard Graham, who since the beginning has never been far from this project, for his contribution to the book and to the intellectual content of the years when it was taking shape. Finally, thanks to my wife, who is a professional historian and the veteran of enough scholarly ordeals of her own to get a good laugh out of any sentimentality at the end of this one.

Judge and Jury in Imperial Brazil, 1808-1871
Social Control and Political Stability in the New State

Part I. Brazilian Liberalism and Justice

in the Independence Period, 1808-1831

1. Introduction: Liberalism in a Time of Transition

Five years after formal independence from Portugal in 1822, Brazil's first generation of political leaders began to tear down the colony they had inherited and to build a state that would endure almost until the end of the century. The most intense period of reform lasted from 1827 to 1837—the heyday of Brazilian liberalism and the truly revolutionary phase of Brazilian independence. The process of destroying, building, and overhauling, however, was a dialectical one, easily overlooked because within the larger historical context of nineteenth-century Brazil this "liberal decade" presents some problems of fit. Brazil had become independent with little commotion in 1822, and by the 1840s the country was already being regarded as a model of stability in a wildly disorganized Latin America. The formative interim period is thus often obscured by what appears to be a conspicuous linear achievement of equilibrium, presumably made possible by the inflexible social requirements of a relatively homogeneous landed and slave-owning class.[1] The themes of authority and stability are so prominent in the historiography of nineteenth-century Brazil, in fact, that the country seems sometimes to have been spared the struggles that marked the period elsewhere, to have no real heritage of liberalism, and generally to have added little to the colonial period.[2] In short, to have no revolutionary content.

This retrospective emphasis on immobility or, at best, plodding gradualism, is by no means totally misplaced. Brazilian independence is indeed a story of gradualism; it was neither begun nor completed in 1822. Independence was secured formally through a series of well-spaced and circumstantial events which first shifted the colonial center from Portugal to Brazil (1808), then elevated Brazil to coequal status within the empire (1815), and finally culminated in formal independence in 1822 only as an alternative to a reversal of gains already achieved. So serene a transition was made possible by external factors: the Napoleonic invasion of the Iberian peninsula in 1807 drove the Portuguese ruler, João VI, to flee to Brazil, where he stubbornly remained until 1821. The events of 1822 likewise occurred under the sponsorship of a Portuguese monarch responding to events in Europe: Dom Pedro, João's heir, rejected a Portuguese demand for his return by declaring Brazilian independence in that year.[3] It was an independence easily won and curiously incomplete. Up through 1822 Brazilian patriots would have been in perfect accord with modern historians who find this an essentially static narrative and emphasize the preservation of old forms. But contemporary Brazilians would not have understood the application of that analysis to the period that followed. For them the dynamic point of this incomplete independence was the reaction that accumulated against it during the long period of cooptation and half-measures. They would have pointed out that this apparently serendipitous sequence of events disguised the concomitant intensification of nationalistic pressure to reform the inappropriate and expel the non-Brazilians. Their arguments would have shown a sophisticated realization of how limited had been the accomplishments of 1822, and a full romantic commitment to the concept of "independence" not merely as an event but as a universal metaphor. These men called themselves liberals; they dominated the political system between 1827 and 1837, and they give the independence period its revolutionary content.

The liberal decade is only a part of the story of what independence added to the colonial period. But it is in many ways the core of the story—the standard to which subsequent ideas about the state referred, and the context within which the colonial period was interpreted. The explanation of the liberal interval itself, however, remains unclear. To be sure, the term *liberal* suggests some general ideological correlatives in the nineteenth-century Atlantic world.[4] To some extent these intellectual contributions to Brazilian liberalism can be profitably traced to foreign sources, but the broader question of practicability in purely Brazilian terms also needs to be raised. Itself a transitional body of thought and behavior, Brazilian liberalism was in fact less dependent upon foreign models than it was a reflexive, practical response to the transitional political and socioeconomic conditions of the early national period. A brief review of these conditions suggests a thoroughly practical explanation of contemporary political liberalism, and also sketches an introduction to the Brazilian empire.

Political Transition

As the culmination of a gradual process, political independence in 1822 promised little in the way of dramatic or revolutionary change. The events of 1822 encountered no significant challenge from Portugal, and formal sovereignty was achieved all but without bloodshed. Unlike their Spanish-American neighbors, Brazilians did not face the prospect of governing themselves as a republic. A prince of the royal blood was at hand; not even a change of dynasty was necessary. Yet at the same time Brazilian dissatisfaction with quasi-colonial status was crystalized by the specific Portuguese provocations of 1821 and 1822. Nativist (anti-Portuguese) sentiments, now more prominent than ever, were not comforted by the adoption of the Portuguese-born Dom Pedro I as Brazil's new ruler. Changes in form were belied by a sameness of substance, and the question of independence persisted as if by analogy.

The new emperor was not the man to channel these pressures into something lasting, and his nine years were never more than transitional. Dom Pedro had an autocrat's temperament and wholly lacked the old king's sense of the opportune compromise. He surrounded himself with advisors of unsavory reputation and Portuguese birth. To most Brazilians his personality and milieu seemed completely out of step with the constitutional liberalism he professed.[5]

It is hard to know just what liberalism meant to Pedro I, for like many contemporaries he used the fashionable term as a symbol, without definition. Whatever his own view, most members of the Constituent Assembly of 1823 disagreed with him. In his opening address to that body, Dom Pedro set the tone that characterized the adversary relationship that existed between him and Brazilian congresses for the length of his reign. The emperor spoke condescendingly to the deputies; he tactlessly recommended that the document they were to draft be "worthy" not only of Brazil but of himself as well. The Brazilian representatives were touchy about rhetoric, and many saw in this statement an affront to their authority as the people's delegates. The delicate political atmosphere rapidly deteriorated into one of mutual distrust and accusation. Finally, provoked beyond endurance, the emperor closed the Assembly. In place of the draft that the constituents had been debating, he pledged himself to promulgate a constitution "twice as liberal."[6]

It is revealing of Dom Pedro's grasp of political philosophies that he would think it possible to multiply or divide them at will. What can be said is that the charter handed down in 1824 reflected the extremes that warred in the personality of the emperor. Within the outline of constitutional monarchy with formal separation of powers, the document held back a considerable element of personal authority for the ruler by incorporating Benjamin Constant's concept of a "moderating power." Yet the new constitution was not itself a source of great displeasure even to Dom Pedro's enemies. In some things it might not go far enough for the radicals, but most Brazilians agreed that it was a document sufficiently vague to accommodate their own ideas of a constitutional Brazil.[7]

The real crisis of the Constitution grew out of the emperor's violent intervention: closing the Assembly and promulgating the charter unilaterally. This insult to Brazilian sovereignty further aggravated resentments which had long been building against Portuguese domination. Political factions now began to coalesce in opposition to or support of Dom Pedro. Anti-Portuguese sentiments which veiled specific opposition to the Portuguese-born emperor rose to new heights, and nativism became an expression of political alignment with the enemies of the ruler. Increasingly Dom Pedro allowed himself to be placed on the defensive; increasingly he relied for advice and support upon Portuguese who hoped for an eventual reunion of the crowns. No regular session of the legislature was called until 1826, so for several years after the promulgation of the Constitution nativist tensions increased, finding an outlet in a revolt in Pernambuco, virulent press attacks, and scattered violence.[8]

By the time the new legislature convened in 1826, the animus between the emperor and opposing nativist factions foreshadowed the coming of yet another "independence" to Brazil. Even now, four years after formal political separation from Portugal, radical nativists still clamored against Caramuru, or Portuguese influence in Brazilian affairs. A less emotional but ultimately more influential group of opposition deputies based their reaction on political models rather than questions of nationality. The moderates (*moderados*) complained that the emperor's constitution was not enough. Much of the charter's promise had not been fulfilled by the executive, they argued, and the document required a liberal statutory base before it could function properly. Most of the administrative structure of Brazil remained overconcentrated, and these liberal reformers urged a decentralizing revolution in civil governance. Just as anti-Pedro as the nativists, the moderates saw their reforms as a way to diminish the emperor's power, and therefore they had no hope of his cooperation. The years of waiting and fruitless opposition had radicalized these men, too, and they pressed for decentralizing reforms with the energy of zealots.[9]

In 1827 these liberal reformers and their nativist allies joined forces to pass the first of their cherished measures—a law creating elective, parish-level justices of the peace. The liberal decade of Brazilian history may be dated from that event.[10] Such opposition-sponsored reforms provoked an emperor jealous of his prerogatives, and thus exacerbated the conflict between Dom Pedro and the lawmakers. At the same time, the parallel conflict between Portuguese and Brazilians, with its unshaded connotations of treason or national loyalty, infected the legislative process with a radical quality that precluded compromise on issues that should have had little to do with the question of nativism. Liberal reformism and revolutionary nativism had become identified.

The nationalistic attitude adopted by Brazilians was not unjustified. The emperor had designs on the Portuguese throne and probably hoped one day to reunify the dynasty. His attention focused increasingly on European politics after the death of his father in 1826. This continued Portuguese presence in government and the possibility of a resumption of the colonial relation led, at last, to the final act in the long and complex drama of Brazilian independence. In 1831 Pedro I found himself stymied. No longer able to govern against the opposition of the reformers and nativists, he returned to Portugal, abdicating the throne in favor of his son, a child of five years. Under the Constitution the boy would not be allowed to rule personally for thirteen years, so in the interim a triune regency would govern the country.[11] Brazilians finally had a native government and the long-delayed opportunity to build an empire (or republic) out of their own ideas and upon their own responsibility.

The ensuing Regency period (1831-1840) began in an atmosphere of richly dynamic paradoxes. On the one hand, a triumphant optimism projected a brilliant future for the new state, while on the other the crisis mentality that had accompanied the nativists' long struggle with Pedro I left contrasting fears of restoration and a faceless Portuguese threat. This tense combination continued to fuel the movement for reforms, now aimed, however, at consolidating the new situation and somehow preventing its reversal. A second paradox arose over the means selected to achieve these goals, because the reformers did not abandon their antipower, decentralizing measures immediately after the emperor's departure. Accustomed to being in the opposition, and not yet convinced that the danger was past, the men of 1831 thought consolidation of their regime not incompatible with the institutional fragmentation of their newly acquired power. Their reforms, therefore, were in large part negatively conceived—as measures against the emperor or guarantees against his return— and a dispersive, specifically combative form of guerrilla liberalism persisted as the orthodoxy of the day. The political arena of 1831 was completely monopolized by a party that called itself liberal partly because of ideological commitments, but more substantially because the decentralizing tenets of liberalism offered a way to combat power, discredited by long association with despotic foreign rulers.[13]

Socioeconomic Transition

(The political crisis of independence)was essentially one of institutional and national legitimacy triggered first by independence and then aggravated by the incomplete withdrawal of Portuguese authority until 1831. These political developments were paralleled and further complicated by a second crisis—a social crisis of spontaneous elite formation. The two crises are linked by the themes of colonial disability and legitimacy of rule. As a recent colony, Brazil possessed no institutional elite immediately capable of filling the political vacuum left at the time of independence. The high bureaucracy was initially disorganized and of doubtful loyalty; the church was internally divided between a conservative hierarchy and a radical priesthood; the army was split by Portuguese and Brazilian factions, had played no significant part in securing independence, and was discredited by its performance in the ignominious Argentine war (1825-1828).[14] The resulting power vacuum might logically have been filled by a coherent national socioeconomic elite, or one united by economic role or region, but the colonial heritage prevented that outcome as well, for during the independence period Brazil was suffering through a trough in the cyclical export pattern so typical of colonial economies. Without an institutional or economic foundation to support and legitimize it as a unit, no clearly articulated national elite could move into the empty space left by political independence. What we may speak of, rather, is a variety of prospective elites —agrarian, urban, northern, southern—all as yet marginal or truly parochial. For these transitional groups, operating within a restricted political arena, democratizing reforms and local autonomy offered both nontraditional claims to status and minimal interference from outside.

Certain regions, it is true, maintained more or less precarious national advantages in the early nineteenth century. Sugar, the classic colonial export, had faced foreign competition, uncertain markets, crippling price fluctuations, and generally declining production since 1650, but the long years of prosperity had left Pernambuco and Bahia, in the north, important repositories of influence. Minas Gerais, in the south, had likewise fallen from economic supremacy before the end of the eighteenth century, but its rise to regional preeminence as a producer of gold was recent and glorious.[15] In these areas, not readily thought of as marginal, the point of the economic transition is perhaps best made in the negative sense: here the inability of relatively weak traditional elites to wholly preempt the power of the independent state also prevented their obstruction of the decentralizing reforms that would contribute to the emergence of new groups.

Elsewhere in Brazil, the end of the eighteenth century and the beginning of the nineteenth was a period of economic quiescence. Occasional boomlets caused by distortions on the world market relieved the drab picture but only underscored the structural weakness of the colonial economy.[16] In effect, Brazil was doing little more than filling in world production gaps created by extraordinary conditions. Most Brazilian tropical products could be produced more cheaply elsewhere, and when prices dropped to normal levels Brazilians were left to wonder where they would turn for the next prolonged economic boom. In 1826 an astute observer expressed the economic insecurity that followed the country into the first years of independence: "I cannot predict what will become of our agricultural industry, which is the only one we have. Who will consume our exports and return us a profit now that the entire world is cultivating our products with blind fury?"[17]

The answer to the economic impasse—coffee—would become clear a few years later, but in the 1820s the question remained open. For our purposes it is enough to point out that the question was being asked insistently and had been for years before independence. The shifting Brazilian economy had reached the end of one cycle without immediately initiating another. As it sought a new orientation its condition roughly paralleled the fitful starts of the country's political development after 1808. And just as the equivocal political situation contributed to the buildup of pressures to overhaul government by the late 1820s, so the years of economic quiescence produced a generation of men ready to explore new avenues of mobility.

The social crisis of independence, then, was largely one of elite recruitment. In this sense Brazilian liberalism is to be distinguished from a more thorough conceptual challenge to the social order, its essential hierarchy, or its basic values. It should not be supposed that economic changes in Brazil have always overtaxed the adaptive resources of society; indeed, traditional families them-selves have often bridged the gap in time and place between the country's eco-nomic cycles.[18] The synthetic picture of a transitional economy is intended primarily to suggest a secondary crisis of elite instability, and to suggest reasons for the appeal of certain aspects of political thought contemporaneously re-garded as liberal. More specifically, democratic or locally autonomous institu-tions complemented a diffuse economic situation and served a consequently unsettled and poorly articulated social elite.

The partial interpretation of Brazilian liberalism put forward here has vir-tually no ideological content. It should be noted that by framing it in terms of socioeconomic variables, we have implicitly framed it in time as well. The rele-vant tenets—extreme decentralization based on localism and democratic institu-tional forms—promised to release individual energies and facilitate selective mo-bility. But once they did so, this utilitarian acceptance of certain liberal prin-ciples could not prevent more rigid patterns of social hierarchy from being re-established. Thus, in frontier areas emerging elites may have favored elective processes and local autonomy as a basis for local institutions, since this eased their own ascendancy. But with only socioeconomic motives to sustain it, this sort of liberalism could serve, at worst, as a euphemism for lawlessness; at best it was self-limiting. Once a new elite had formed, elections and localism be-came unnecessary, even undesirable, to those whose interests had shifted from gaining to protecting a position. In other words, for a rising social elite, liberal-ism offered structural advantages that would become liabilities in less than a generation.[19] It is probably for this reason that it is possible to speak, with considerable temporal precision, of a liberal "decade" in Brazil.

Combining these considerations about political and socioeconomic transi-tion, a gross practical model of Brazilian liberalism can now be described. By the late 1820s, complementary positive and negative forces sustained a demand for certain liberal reforms. The political situation contributed the negative reactive impulse. Brazilian political leaders, long in opposition, found in decen-tralization a way to attack the concentrated public power which they associated with the colonial regime and the quasi-colonial rule of Pedro I. The abdication of the emperor in 1831 left these reformers unopposed. Power withdrawn from the center had to be relocated, and the transitional socioeconomic situation provided the positive force that drew it to private hands at the local level through a liberalism of extreme decentralization and democratized intermediate institutions. Different motives inspired these two aspects of the movement, but their needs and capabilities dovetailed neatly. The result was an extremely sound practical foundation for the passage of mutually compatible reforms.

Liberal Leadership

To say that some groups of Brazilians stood to benefit from certain reforms is not the same as to say that they were "the liberals." The preceding analysis has dealt largely in generalization. Politicians and marginal, rising groups have been postulated but not named, and, to some extent, the socioeconomic analysis must remain rather nonspecific. Indeed, the multifarious transitional group, determined as much by mood, personality, and other intangibles as by social position, defies by its nature more specific identification; no organized lobby will be found here. The problem of specificity is diminished in the open political arena: political leaders are identifiable, their writings are available, and their words are transcribed in the parliamentary debates. On the other hand, the political situation itself blurred the alignments of these individuals in the late 1820s and early 1830s when "liberalism" bore a patriotic radiance that sometimes distorted the immediate interests involved. These problems stated, it is at least possible to identify and introduce the leading liberals of the day, and to sketch them in terms of our general statements about Brazilian liberalism. The correlation of socioeconomic and political flux with liberal ideology can thus be shown to be more than random even at the individual level of those who stood most conspicuously for reform. By the criteria of regional and social origin, economic connections, and profession, many of the most prominent liberal leaders of the 1820s and 1830s were new blood in a new system—transitional men and outsiders in the broadest sense.[20]

The overwhelming figure of early Brazilian liberalism, Evaristo da Veiga, provides an extraordinarily complete illustration of this apparent connection between liberalism and individual "marginality." Evaristo's very professions —printer, editor, bookseller—had scarcely existed in Brazil before 1808. Born in Rio de Janeiro, the son of a Portuguese immigrant schoolteacher and bookseller and a Brazilian mother, this classic autodidact absorbed his considerable education in his father's bookshop. After his parents' deaths he opened a shop of his own and in 1827 entered the political world with the founding of his newspaper, *Aurora Fluminense.* In 1830 Evaristo was elected to the Chamber of Deputies by the province of Minas Gerais, though he never left Rio until the end of his political career.[21]

It was as the editor and practically sole writer for *Aurora Fluminense* that Evaristo da Veiga exercised his immense influence. The publishing history of the newspaper coincides almost exactly with the years of the liberal decade, and its importance as the principal voice of Brazilian liberalism cannot be overestimated. Through it, the editor attempted to guide the energies of the reformers in the middle course favored by the moderates. *Aurora's* polemics with extreme liberals (*exaltados*) in the years after the emperor's abdication have led some writers to emphasize the "moderation" of the paper, but Evaristo stood fast on principle and no other Brazilian of his time can claim a fuller understanding or more thorough commitment to political liberalism than he. *Aurora's* strong orientation toward internal (and especially local) administrative reforms reflected the primary concerns of the liberals in the late 1820s and 1830s and encouraged their realization. Sophisticated as it was, *Aurora Fluminense* was a faithful interpreter of the practical political concerns of its time.

And so was its editor. Evaristo da Veiga seems always to have been uneasy about the economic and social position that branded him a newcomer. It is difficult to imagine a nineteenth-century Brazilian of more urban (though not urbane) background, and his writings give away a sense of puzzlement about rural Brazil, a trait Evaristo shared with many urban liberal ideologues. He was a timid orator, and his presence in the Chamber of Deputies was never marked by the bluster and eloquence of those who had received the traditional education at the Portuguese University of Coimbra. Informal evening discussions with friends across the counter of his bookshop were more to Evaristo's taste than the soirees of the well-born.[22] Yet in his power and influence he became so identified with the majority faction of liberal politics during the 1830s that the reformers were sometimes referred to simply as "Evaristos." Perhaps more revealing, however, was the lofty malice of conservatives who also nicknamed the liberals "Livreiros," or booksellers, a pun on their leader's profession.[23]

Evaristo typifies the members of new or transitional groups especially common in Brazil's cities. But we can be more specific, for he is also the prime representative of one occupational group in particular—the professional journalists—that almost always identified itself as liberal during the early years. The unsettled status of this new profession probably determined its practitioners' preference for liberal institutional reform in the 1820s, just as it opened it to talented men whose mixed blood or lack of family connections made it impossible for them to get ahead within the traditional structure.[24] In the early years of the empire the professional journalists and editors made up what can almost be termed a liberal class.

A second liberal leader, Diogo Antônio Feijó, appears superficially to have little in common with Evaristo da Veiga. In fact the two share a number of general characteristics. Born in the province of São Paulo, Feijó's family background was more obscure than humble. A foundling, he was either adopted or tacitly acknowledged by a family of some means in São Paulo. In adulthood he derived some income from what were apparently small agricultural holdings in his native province, but his professional identity was supplied by the priesthood. As a young man he combined his religious duties with the slow but steady expansion of his agricultural interests—a pattern typical of priests, whose social status was often determined primarily by their secular activities. In 1818 a personal religious crisis drove him to leave his sugar mill and travel to the town town of Itú, where he joined a group of priests who had gathered there to explore religious mysticism. Still in Itú when the denouement of independence began in 1821, Feijó found in politics a new outlet for his energies. He was elected to the São Paulo junta formed after the Revolution of Pôrto, and then as a deputy for the province of São Paulo to the Portuguese Cortes held in Lisbon. The priest and many of his fellow Brazilian representatives were shortly forced out of Portugal, and, after a brief stay in England, Feijó returned to newly independent Brazil. He was subsequently elected to the Constituent Assembly of 1823, and then to the legislature of 1826. After the abdication of the emperor, Feijó took up the important portfolio of minister of justice in the moderado government. In 1835 he was elected regent.[25]

Like Evaristo, Feijó's political importance during the 1820s and 1830s contrasts sharply with his modest beginnings and even rootlessness by traditional standards. He was also typical of other prominent liberals in his intemperate enthusiasms, which when frustrated carried him to the threshold of instability, bringing on periods of depression and despair.[26] Feijó's moods were themselves a major factor in the general political atmosphere of liberal Brazil. The troubled priest's pessimism gathered cumulatively during the 1830s, and the severity of his personality contributed to making him the strong arm of Brazilian liberalism—"the right man for a time of revolution," as Evaristo once called him.[27]

Early Brazilian liberalism had a powerful appeal for men of Feijó's profession. Anti-clericalism was not one of the active ingredients of liberal thought in Brazil, partly because of the relatively weak corporate structure of the Brazilian church, and partly, no doubt, because of the considerable participation of parish priests in liberal causes. Most priests possessed passable educations and were mainstays of the clubby atmosphere of intellectual exchange in which new ideas were often disseminated. One easily imagines them as village intellectuals loitering in bookstores (*papelarias*). If our analysis of the socioeconomic attractions of liberalism is correct, however, then the affinity of priests for liberal reforms probably had less to do with the nature of the profession itself than with the social conditions which usually led to its selection. The priesthood often represented an incomplete or marginal career solution: a poor man's professional alternative to the magistracy, or a respectable genteel poverty for a landowner's excess sons (a variation of the latter probably being Feijó's case). But it was seldom an exclusive vocation. Multiple commercial, agricultural, and political ventures also attracted priests with social ambitions that made them indistinguishable from other prospective elites. Moreover, as conspicuous figures in their communities, priests were always wellplaced to win local elections. Electoral success, in turn, predisposed them to approve of democratic institutions. For these reasons Brazil's priests often supported the early liberal reforms, at least on the abstract level, and since many were elected to the national legislature, they exercised an influence disproportionate to their absolute numbers.[28]

A final outstanding figure of early Brazilian liberalism can serve as a bridge between the type of men who favored reform and those who in later years would bring the liberal decade to an end. Bernardo Pereira de Vasconcelos was born into one of the most perfectly equivocal social situations in the Luso-Brazilian world: he was the son of a high colonial bureaucrat—a magistrate—and of a mother who was herself the daughter of a Portuguese jurist. Vasconcelos' father was serving as district judge (*ouvidor*) in the capital of Minas Gerais when Bernardo was born, and the son grew up shaded by his father's professional prestige but without roots of local wealth and tradition. Although such a situation vouchsafed the boy an education, it was with the understanding that whatever social position he attained in later life would depend on his own ambitions. These he had in abundance. Vasconcelos followed his father into the Portuguese magistracy and returned to Brazil from the University of Coimbra in 1820 to take up an appointment as county judge in the province of São Paulo. His profession was one that normally imposed great mobility, but Vasconcelos was not satisfied with his assignment in São Paulo and repeatedly petitioned for transfer back to his place of birth in Minas Gerais. Although promoted to appellate jurisdiction on the High Court of Maranhão in 1825, Vasconcelos' ambition had already drawn him to politics and he never actually occupied the seat.[29] In Parliament Vasconcelos was liberalism's orator. His education and honed verbal sarcasm made him a fearsome adversary, and his legal background made him the man to draw up legislation that incorporated the reforms favored by his colleagues.[30]

Vasconcelos' personality, like that of Feijó, requires some comment. In adulthood he suffered from chronic syphilis. The disease shows in the palsied force of his signature, and contemporaries thought they saw its effects in his unpredictability. Like Feijó, Vasconcelos seems to have been divided in the early 1830s between an idealistic enthusiasm for British constitutional liberalism and the angular realism that would mark his later years. Certainly his ideological leanings were often rendered mysterious by his very crankiness. He had a consuming horror of "anarchy," and his illiberal stand on slavery shocked many of his colleagues from the first.[31] Yet in the late 1820s and early 1830s he was one of Brazil's strongest supporters of democratic local institutions of justice and administration.[32]

This element of ambivalence in Bernardo Pereira de Vasconcelos is typical of the attitudes of many professional magistrates. Members of the judicial bureaucracy, especially the younger ones, had some of the same practical reasons for supporting liberalization of the empire that men like Evaristo or Feijó did. But at the same time they were bound by professional fears and class interests natural to men of their profession. During the liberal decade many judges joined the reformers. Their educations had exposed them to the intellectual ferment and modern ideas of Europe, and the Brazilians among them were as likely as anyone to oppose the first emperor. Judges like Vasconcelos were also outsiders in some senses: as the sons of professionals or bureaucrats they often lacked strong family or even regional identities; they were always subject to transfer and possessed driving and frequently frustrated ambitions. But they were also men with something historical to lose, and as a body they voted an allegiance to their profession and the status quo that tempered their opportunism and always gave them a fundamentally conservative sense of interests to be protected. The judges, of all the liberals, were traditionally the closest to official power. For them, therefore, the practical attractions of a decentralizing liberalism disappeared earliest. The corporate solidarity and conservatism of professional judges also tended to increase because of mounting attacks on the unpopular judicial branch of administration. And when, inevitably, some institutional reforms threatened either in theory or in practice to attenuate the influence of the professional jurist (*letrado*) elite, the magistrates would close ranks in opposition to the liberal reform movement. Nor does our example of Vasconcelos have to be abandoned here: he was among the first to turn his back on the liberals in the mid-1830s and become a founder of Brazil's reactionary party.

2. Reformist Thought and Brazilian Society

The practical model of Brazilian liberalism developed in the preceding chapter is of course incomplete, for the phenomenon did not develop without a foundation of ideas. The intellectual underpinnings of early Brazilian liberalism can be discriminated in two parts: on the one hand, it is possible to identify a formal, more or less complete philosophic commitment learned in Europe; on the other, Brazilian liberals developed their own modifications based on home-grown native views of Brazilian reality. The common bond between these two supports of the liberal movement in the late 1820s and early 1830s was the uncritical belief that a vaguely conceived European liberalism promised a categorically ideal form of government, and that Brazilian society would inevitably benefit from, and be perfected by, the introduction of good laws and institutions. Undermining the ideal construct, however, ran a current of very inconvenient questions about Brazilian social reality. Did the special characteristics of Brazilian society make liberalism (or any civilized system of thought) an inappropriate foundation for the new empire? This uneasy coexistence of theoretics and realism makes the intellectual history of the early national period a frequently contradictory one in which fragments of ideas do equivocal battle with incomplete conceptualizations. Yet the sorting of ideas, difficult as it is, does reveal intelligible basic assumptions that help to explain why Brazilians adopted a liberal approach to institutional policy.

Those who supported the reform of Brazilian administration did not have far to look for intellectual support. As in the rest of Latin America, the ideas and writings of the Enlightenment had easily penetrated the barriers of censorship erected by Portugal, Spain, and the Holy Office. Brazilians who acquired their higher education in Europe for lack of a university in the colony inevitably made at least a nodding acquaintance with Enlightenment concepts and European liberalism. The scholastic heritage of the Portuguese university, at Coimbra, was attacked in 1772, and the subsequent restructuring of the institution formally introduced the Portuguese world to modern thought, scientific process, and the concept of useful knowledge.[1] The intellectual isolation of Brazil was therefore far from complete, and as the political and economic ties of the colonial relation became obsolete and contradictory, the colonial intellectual legacy also gave way to concepts more suited to rationalizing a new relationship of colony to metropolis and of government to society. As the new century began, certain aspects of liberal thought found their way into royal policy and Brazilians appeared in the forefront of those who advocated and interpreted the new formulations. João VI's decision in 1808 to open the ports of Brazil to trade with all friendly nations, for example, owed much to the counsels and arguments provided by a Brazilian admirer of Adam Smith, José da Silva Lisboa.[2]

Liberalism, of course, taught more than commercial freedom and encouraged aspirations unrelated to immediate economic interests—it offered a whole new way of organizing knowledge. Some Brazilians were satisfied by the newly arrived king's opening of the ports, but others continued to clamor for internal improvements in administration and government. Every concession to the colony's cultural awakening sharpened colonial awareness and produced fresh demands by those inclined to question all received wisdom in the light of new ideas. A growing number of Brazilians fixed upon the possibility of applying liberal principles to the internal burdens of colonialism. Within Brazil liberalism began to mingle with national sentiment. The king's government was criticized for preserving the sclerotic modes of colonial administration and for failing to respond to the concrete, distinct needs of the colony. Royal administration was called to account, and criticism of its most vulnerable aspects—notably fiscal policy and the administration of justice—served as a stalking-horse for those whose target was the colonial system in general.[3] In the years after the opening of the ports, demands for internal reform presented a new challenge to Portuguese policy in Brazil.

After independence fashionable ideas based on principles of political liberalism did not wane, rather the contrary. The liberal press, suddenly unencumbered by virtually any administrative controls over what it printed, multiplied in an extraordinary profusion of ephemeral political sheets.[4] Accumulated discontent with royal administration combined with an untrammeled press in the years after 1822 to have a formidable impact on the as-yet-unformed political system of Brazil. *Liberalism* became by far the most articulated (if still ill-defined) political catch-phrase in the new empire—even to the point of extending its attractions to previously uninfluential segments of the body politic. In the 1830s, one conservative commentator cast his jaundiced eye on the dangers of this aspect of what he called with distaste "the Brazilian enlightenment." After noting the number of publications on sale designed to "spread" enlightened thought, he observed that "Nowadays there is no shoemaker, no barber, etc., who does not speak of the sovereignty of the People and draw fine distinctions between civil rights and political rights . . . never has there been so much mouthing of Liberalism."[5] In the 1820s those who called themselves liberals converted their ideas into an identifiable movement for civil reforms. A satiric newspaper of Rio de Janeiro described the reform fever at its height as "an incurable epidemic."[6]

The men who championed liberal administrative reforms supported their position with more than just foreign thought. If civil administration was to be reshaped, it was at least necessary to have an image of actual society against which to measure the applicability of new principles and institutions. Most reformers had a dogmatic and legalistic tendency to regard liberal institutions uncritically as a general antidote to all colonial abuses and malfeasance.[7] But as Brazilians they also nourished practical evaluations of how their ideas meshed with the country's needs and possibilities. In their campaigns in favor of internal reforms, the liberals often touched on some of the shared attitudes toward Brazil and Brazilian society that they felt made the innovations especially appropriate in their country. These optimistic images of Brazil, held so tenaciously by the liberals after independence, formed the practical intellectual foundation of the early reform movement.

At one level optimism helped maintain some distance between the Brazilian reformers and their foreign models. Brazilian liberals were prone to copy Europeans, but not to the point of self-deprecation. Indeed, one of the most powerful components of the Brazilian self-image around the time of independence was the aggressive—even utopian—belief in the young country's vast "potential."[8] In spite of the undefined economic situation of the early nineteenth century, this bright future was described primarily in economic terms. Yet perhaps because of these same circumstances, references to Brazil's potential resources were vague and defensive. Unable to pin down, much less protect, the allegedly prodigious resources that would be the new nation's patrimony, writers sometimes expressed their faith as a very modern-sounding form of economic nationalism. In 1826 the president of the province of Bahia opposed making mining concessions to foreign companies because he feared that if once they gained a foothold the foreigners would usurp all Brazil's potential resources.[9] A liberal newspaper expressed in 1833 a similar attitude in an article of xenophobic tone that criticized British interests in Brazilian agriculture, mining, and manufacturing. The article mocked "English" pronunciation of the Portuguese language with such libelous results that the British community of Rio de Janeiro forced the paper to print an apology.[10]

In promoting their institutional reforms, liberals tapped the energy generated by economic optimism. A country of brilliant prospects, they believed, deserved and required the most modern institutions. An analogy was drawn with

the United States, for many believed that Brazil should follow a course of institutional development similar to that of the North American republic. The
compliment of imitation, however, was in this case a backhanded one. Comparisons with the United States emphasized Brazil's greater potential in an effort to minimize the obstacles the empire faced in forging a liberal political system. Themselves accustomed to a boom-and-bust export trade, Brazilians took
the United States for a relatively poor country with limited economic prospects.[11] If a nation with such an inauspicious economic base could achieve its
independence and found a liberal republic, it was reasoned, then those goals
should be the easier for Brazil with its supposedly infinite resources. At the
time of the Minas Gerais conspiracy the United States inspired Brazilian plotters
with the example of a country which "with no mines other than a bit of dried
fish, some wheat and a little manufacturing had sustained so great a war."[12]

In later years, some radicals cited the abundance and diversity of Brazil as
justification for their devotion to federative ideas and to show the impracti-
cality of political centralism. What thoughtful man could doubt, wondered an
extreme federalist sheet in 1832, that given Brazil's "immense resources and
territorial capacity" she should one day be a federal republic?[13] And again,
the successful liberalism of the North American federation was cited as a valid
model if only because Brazil and the United States shared in their territorial
giantism.

It should be noted, however, that those radicals who cited Brazilian diversity as a justification for decentralizing measures were at odds with mainstream
liberal evaluations of Brazilian social reality. Although the more important
moderate-faction reformers consistently favored decentralization, they were
always at pains to play down the issue of internal diversity. Diversity was a
theoretically valid reason for democratic local institutions, of course; local conditions could best be dealt with by local officials and popular representatives.
But arguments based on the concept of diversity threatened the moderates with
unacceptable assumptions about the nation's fundamental social unity. The
benefits of decentralization were not to be confused with the evils of disintegra-
tion (referred to in contemporary shorthand as "federalism"), and the moderates avoided the association by embracing a strongly optimistic model of Brazilian society that emphasized social harmony and consensus over the diversity
and conflict posited by the extreme liberal minority. In its purest form the liberal commitment to decentralization was not institutional at all, but rested
upon an essentially subpolitical notion of organization argued in terms of behavior and social models.

The nineteenth-century reference for the belief in common social interests
was a certain reading of Jeremy Bentham. Brazilian liberals extracted from
Bentham a belief in the essential harmony of interests in rational society,

although the specific tracks of a more formal utilitarianism are all but impossible to detect. Brazilians rarely footnoted their arguments or framed them in terms of identifiable abstractions. But one senses also, in this remote tropical setting, a much earlier intellectual reference—a faint echo of the utopian moral consensus of Puritan New England. No direct influence need be sought here, for surely there was none, and the parallel is far from complete: Brazilian ideas about political unity and social consensus were articulated without religious analogy, and they were used to justify very different political institutions. The similarities seem rather to be those born of a common response by men suddenly confronted with a clean slate and taking quite seriously the idea of perfection. At their most attractive, Brazilian liberals inhabited an intellectual world halfway between the seventeenth-century ideal of organic social unity and a nineteenth-century sense of romantic individualism.[14] Their institutional thinking ultimately rested upon their faith in man and society.

The efforts of the early liberals to conceive of Brazilian civilization as a community of shared and moral interests were scarcely short of heroic. Evaristo da Veiga performed intellectual contortions. When the national elections of 1829 returned a solid liberal majority of which Evaristo approved, his newspaper typically seized the occasion to articulate its belief in the existence of a "national political conscience." Evaristo reaffirmed the liberals' belief in elections and mocked the opposition's attempts to dismiss these as the unrepresentative products of factional conspiracy and cabals. Such arguments, wrote the editor, were based on fear of democracy and disbelief in the Brazilians' ability to govern themselves. Evaristo asked rhetorically whether "such [locally] partisan issues could embrace the entire nation at the same time? Are conspiracies simultaneously held in the entire empire of isolated provinces so remote from one another?" The editor's answer was of course negative: the liberal victory was due instead to "a common principle [that] produced the same effects at the same time in this vast Brazil. . . . the love of liberty so natural to Brazilians."[15]

The moderates either denied or minimized the regional diversity that radicals on both sides posited as conditions favoring either provincial federation or authoritarian centralism. True, the moderates did advocate some decentralizing measures to assure a degree of provincial administrative autonomy. "Let the provinces speak for themselves," Evaristo urged. "They are not entombed in barbarism, and they ought to know their own interests much better than these theorists in the Court."[16] But the middle-of-the-road liberals had doubts about giving the provinces too much pwer. In 1831 Evaristo questioned whether the provincial populations had any genuine desire for federation and suggested that the issue had been concocted by ambitious radical politicians in Rio de Janeiro.[17] When attacked by the self-styled representatives of the provinces, *Aurora Fluminense* refuted the regional arguments and defended Rio de Janeiro and the southern provinces from charges that they exercised an alien tyranny over the provinces of the north. "It is a great injustice to paint the southern provinces as dominators with interests contrary to those of the north. This is not only impolitic but inaccurate."[18] The moderate liberals who dominated the reform movement believed implicitly that a liberal empire could be constructed only upon a uniform social foundation, and their own view of Brazil was therefore always one which supplied a national common denominator.[19]

When applied to Brazilian society itself, this fixation with consensus and common interests led to some remarkable follies. Liberals stretched their imaginations to the limit in their efforts to find a core of solidarity within Brazilian social structure. Luis Augusto May, one of the earliest and most important liberal editors, in 1828 justified his own belief in the appropriateness of liberal institutions with the awesome assertion that Brazilian society was in fact classless.[20] May's idea lurked in Brazilian minds for years to come. In 1839 an important Rio de Janeiro newspaper could be optimistic about attracting European immigrants to Brazil because of the "absolute absence of privilege, of class spirit, and habits of predominance" that characterized Brazilian society.[21] And as late as 1857 an imperial minister referred in the Chamber of Deputies to Brazilian society as one of "homogeneous elements" and common interests.[22]

No matter how poorly Brazilian society was understood, of course, it must have been difficult to justify the belief that Brazil's social common denominator lay in the homogeneous mass of a classless society. In cases like the last-mentioned above, such statements probably indicated simply that the elite speaker knew his audience. But the liberal thinkers of the 1820s and 1830s seemed sincere enough; perhaps they were displaying an urban naiveté about conditions in Brazil at large, for most newspaper editors were city-born and bred. Yet even in the urban context the "classless" argument seems bizarre. The point is that the classless model (and presumably others as well) did not reflect any objective judgment about society, but instead one fashioned a priori to conform to a social theory. In a desire to conceive of Brazil as a suitable environment for liberal institutions, many a liberal willingly suppressed his critical faculties for the sake of the larger argument.

In rejecting the obvious, the moderate *Aurora Fluminense* adopted an attitude less radical but nearly as problematic. Evaristo da Veiga had few illusions about the supposed absence of privilege and class and instead found a social common denominator in a middle class conceived largely in urban terms. In 1828 *Aurora* recommended that voters reject the "pompous names of great civic or military figures, or the rich businessmen whose only distinction is their luxury and wealth." In their place, Evaristo advocated the candidacy of members of the classic urban social median—the middle classes—which with their "modest merit and patriotic virtues are alone appropriate for the end which we should have in view." And, like the elite, inferior social types were also to be avoided: "it is well to note that in the more humble classes one does not commonly find the indispensable good sense and scruples."[23]

Liberals naturally thought corporate distinctions as likely as exclusive class interests to upset their plans for a harmonious democracy based on a social mean. This danger seemed especially plain in the early legislatures where "the majority of the deputies came from two classes of society . . . the clerical class and the judicial class." A very moderate commercial paper of Rio felt that the national representations should more closely reflect "the positive state of society" rather than narrow professional sectors. The *Jornal do Comércio* expressed the conviction, common to many liberals in the 1820s, that the Chamber of Deputies should be a perfect blend of the most capable citizens from all areas of Brazilian life.[24]

If Brazilian liberals were often defensive about their beliefs in the country's potential, common national interests, and social consensus, it was because of a nagging suspicion that the opposite might be the case. Negative aspects of Brazilian reality were generally overlooked in the euphoric liberal years of the 1820s and early 1830s, but they were never far from sight. Indeed, some of the idealistic assertions of liberal thinkers balanced on a thin line between simple wrong-headedness and outright self-parody. How, for example, could editor May's remarks about a classless society be taken seriously when in fact a large part of Brazil's population was made up of slaves, and certainly most Brazilians believed that race in itself was a valid determinant of class? Likewise, comparisons to the success of the United States suggested less encouraging parallels with the Spanish American republics. And the case for the existence of uniform national political interests grew less persuasive as regional rebellions began to break out in the early 1830s.

The challenge of regional unrest tied in all too neatly with more general doubts about New World liberalism. The peripheral revolts in Brazil seemed to echo the "anarchy" reigning in the Spanish American republics, and reactionary propagandists made hasty comparisons which identified liberal ideas as the common culprit.[25] In the early 1830s most liberals did their best to ignore these disturbances, but when they continued the façade began to show signs of weakening. In 1834, for example, the *Jornal do Comércio* reaffirmed its commitment to the liberal empire but worried that "American liberalism" was proving to be a "fierce and ungovernable" variety. The commercial newspaper hinted at the limits of its own liberal commitment by remarking that although Brazil had had some disturbances, they had fortunately not yet "compromised the nation's credit."[26]

But it was the ever-present challenge of Brazilian social reality that contradicted the early assumptions of liberals most disturbingly. And within Brazilian social structure, the most difficult contradiction to reconcile was certainly that of slavery and race. Some prominent Brazilians at the time of independence had recognized the inconvenience of slavery both as an economic system and as a social influence. A few voices questioned whether slave labor would even be a profitable base for the economy of independent Brazil, and their arguments gained a certain force from the transitional nature of Brazil's economy in the early nineteenth century. If Brazil's destiny were to be industrial, as some observers believed, slave labor would be unproductive and in the long run prejudicial.[27] On less pragmatic grounds, men of reflective temperament found it difficult to justify an institution which "offends the rights of humanity." José Bonifácio de Andrada e Silva, archetype of the educated colonial, hoped to see slavery gradually ended in Brazil because he was unable to reconcile the existence of a liberal constitution with a regime which in fact deprived the slave of all his "natural rights and turns him from a person into a thing."[28]

Not far behind the sweet reason and philanthropy of these arguments lay the irreducibly racist features of the slave system. Economic and ideological objections to slavery masked a more fundamental objection to the black man, whether slave or free. Negroes were accused of corrupting the customs of white society, devaluing the concept of work, and obstructing the flow of white European immigrants.[29] Terrifying news of events such as the slave uprisings in Haiti drove some jittery whites to project a racist foundation for Brazil. José da Silva Lisboa expressed a theory of white superiority and advocated the end of the traffic as a precondition to the gradual whitening and "improvement" of the Brazilian people.[30] Brazilians steeped in European liberalism not only preferred to apply their ideology to a society of common interests, they also favored a society of predominantly European descent.

Race was therefore the most powerful weapon in the hands of those who opposed a liberal solution. Reactionaries could always strike a responsive chord in white Brazilians by questioning the possibility of social harmony and popular institutions in a society divided by color. The language of diversity, intolerable to the moderates, was visually applicable to racial distinctions. Democracy thus seemed a queer and perilous form of government in a country like Brazil whose "mass of population is composed of varied [racial] mixtures, not found in any other nation and which are natural rivals." Once these elements got out of hand, warned a pamphleteer of the early 1830s, they would be "more fearsome than the lavas of Vesuvius in its greatest eruption."[31] Another sensational racist pamphlet, written in 1831 and reprinted whenever racial tensions threatened white society, linked the regional rebellions to racial holocaust. The anonymous author cited the examples of the French Revolution and the Spanish

American republics and posed the question of Brazil's fate if the people were granted "more liberty than they need." The pamphleteer's vision of Brazilian society gave the answer: race and class war was the inevitable outcome of "equality" in a society demoralized by rivalries between "the various castes of which it is composed." In vivid prose, the author described Brazilian liberalism nourishing separatist and federalist notions and eventually dividing white society into opposing factions. Now the pamphlet adopted a biblical, apocalyptic tone and built a racial metaphor on the play of light and dark. Fragmented white society would be swallowed by a "black cloud." After the extermination of whites (women excepted) by an alliance of blacks and "mestizos," the mestizos in turn would be massacred. This, warned the pamphleteer, was the inevitable fate of a nation in which the "gears of the great social machine become dislocated" by too much freedom.[32]

Racial propaganda, with its appeal to the force of social panic, powerfully defied the liberal view of Brazilian society as one with a steady foundation of common interests upon which to base popular institutions. The negative image of a country with a society of racial castes might be presented in scurrilous form, but it was not without its grain of truth. Recognizing its weakest point, the liberal press made a lame attempt to convince its readers (or itself) that racially "impure" groups shared in the common social interests of a basically harmonious Brazil. In its most superficial form, this effort consisted largely of chiding public figures or other newspapers for making derogatory references to race or engaging in discriminatory social behavior.[33] The moderate liberals made a more profound response to the dilemma of color when opposition groups seemed to be promoting racial divisions for political ends. *Aurora Fluminense* provided an analysis and a defense. Those who complained that persons of color were disenfranchised and discriminated against by the moderado government, wrote Evaristo da Veiga, were guilty of deliberately encouraging racial tensions for personal political benefit. This exploitation of what *Aurora* referred to as the "intrigue of colors" was also known in Brazil in the early 1830s as "Haitianism," and the moderado government pinned the epithet on the opposition schemes of both political extremes. The moderado press denied that *pardos* (mixed bloods) were persecuted or discriminated against for government employment. Above all, mulatto citizens were not "pariahs in Brazilian society" as left- and right-wing agitators claimed. *Aurora Fluminense* predicted that the extremists would fail to convince the pardos that their interests were distinct from those of society at large. The government newspaper forced its argument: many Brazilian blacks were enlightened and intelligent enough to know that in Brazil they did not have the same complaints as their brethren in Haiti or even in the United States. In Brazil, Evaristo continued, legal distinctions were never drawn, either in the colonial period or since independence, between free men because of their color. Evaristo acknowledged that some racial prejudices were associated with slavery but declared that independence was weakening them. Yet the liberal editor's denial of the alleged discontent of free colored groups finally rested on an argument that had to admit the threat of slavery. Since many free mulattos and blacks were themselves slave owners, Evaristo pointed out, they should share the interests of whites in preventing the spread of "ferocious Haitianism."[34]

Much of this talk of race could more accurately be seen as part of a symbolic vocabulary in which the more general question of class was debated. Brazilians who argued against slavery often pointed to the existence of a large population of (white) drifters and vagrants as one result of the slave system's degradation of labor.[35] And in their criticisms of slavery few observers could avoid expressing a pessimistic view of free Brazilian society that had little or nothing to do with race. In 1821, João Severiano Maciel da Costa described "The infinitude of families—white and colored—who vegetate in idleness, poverty and even libertinage within their homes" while a few slaves did the work. "In Brazil sloth is nobility, and laziness has erected its throne among us."[36] Padre Miguel do Sacramento Lopes Gama of Pernambuco identified vagrancy as the "dominant vice of Brazil" and wrote that all Brazilians, from the wealthiest mill owner down to the poorest day laborer, shared an irresistible tendency to lethargy—a tendency which was reinforced by the slave system. "The possession of one sad slave is enough to turn any peasant into a layabout."[37]

In the political sphere, this pessimistic view of Brazilian lassitude and indifference was frequently used as an argument against the propriety of liberal institutions. A Caramuru (Portuguese restorationist) pamphlet of 1831 held that since "the dominant characteristic of our people is laziness," authoritarian institutions were best suited to Brazil.[38] Those who thought of themselves as liberals did not go so far, of course, but when faced with obstacles to carrying out their plans, they sometimes resorted to explanations that were not very different. The *Jornal do Comércio* blamed the tropical climate for the fact that Brazilian citizens lacked a sense of political providence and displayed indifference to the popular participation that liberal institutions required.[39] Evaristo da Veiga seems to have been especially nervous about the possibility that the people might be oblivious to politics. For this reason he closely monitored election turnouts as an index of public political concern. When the elections attracted many voters he never missed the chance to proclaim that "the People are not as stupid and indifferent as some say."[40] But when electoral results or the performance of liberal institutions did not measure up to his expectations, the editor betrayed a half-conviction that the people were either apathetic or simply uncomfortable participating in politics.[41]

Some commentators believed that Brazilian apathy was inherent, but Evaristo da Veiga was inclined to blame the colonial experience. Political nonparticipation during the three benighted centuries of dependence upon Portugal, he reasoned, had left the people with a tradition of political indifference.[42] The serviceable villain of Portuguese despotism and exploitation was thus flayed once again, but the argument left a bad taste. After "three hundred years of enslavement," how much freedom was appropriate? Were Brazilians ready for "the temple of divine liberty" if they had never been exposed to "any ideas about the organization of the social body?"[43] To minimize the effect was to minimize the crime of Portugal; to maximize it was to argue against liberal reform. The solution was to mate the argument to itself: liberal institutions themselves would guide the people out of darkness and into the civic responsibility that would in turn justify the same institutions. Evaristo da Veiga was always ready to announce the "reanimation of the public spirit" because of a large turnout of voters on a rainy election day,[44] but not everyone was so sanguine. In 1833 Lopes Gama predicted flatly that "little or nothing can be expected from the present generation."[45]

The subjective assumptions which Brazilians clung to as a means of fitting liberal ideas to their own society were often simply indefensible; they carried within themselves the seeds of their own refutation. The social observations of Brazilian liberals in the 1820s and 1830s, therefore, have a probing quality of dialectic about them even when articulated dogmatically or inconsistently. They lay before us a running intramural polemic between opposing sides of the national mind, and consistency is not a virtue of such debates. Nevertheless, the basic insistence on common regional and social interests undeniably enjoyed a period of ascendancy as the prime social justification for localizing and democratizing reforms. Among the most influential members of the early liberal leadership, this ideal of consensus was firmly held as a moral precept, difficult as it was to sustain in the face of Brazilian geography and social reality. To a wider circle it had a more practical appeal, for it was the one social model with the power to reconcile the open institutions desired by men on the way up with the social order and territorial integrity necessary to consolidate gains. In this way the moral and the practical dimensions of early Brazilian liberalism reinforced one another.

Yet there was also a strictly objective side to the reformers' concern with national reality. The tension between liberal optimism and the deep-set social negativism that many Brazilians shared emphasized the fact that in reality little was known about the true nature of the Brazilian social system. Many liberals recognized the shakiness of their rationalizations, and some of them sought less subjective grounds for their beliefs about society.

As children of the Enlightenment, Brazilians of the independence period were fascinated with the possibility of using scientific methods to construct an accurate social profile of their country. In the process, of course, they hoped to vindicate their own preconceptions. Many liberals, in their efforts to isolate a social common denominator and develop institutions perfectly suited to the Brazilian situation, argued for the "scientific" study of the country. Such scrutiny would include the gathering of census data, criminal statistics, and economic surveys; it would prove the applicability of liberal institutions and reveal the weak spots where social distortions required reform. Throughout his career, Evaristo da Veiga believed that the gathering of social statistics would provide the key to creating a truly liberal empire.[46]

This strain of empiricism was a prominent characteristic of Brazilian liberalism in the early nineteenth century. Yet here too was a serious contradiction. On the one hand, imported ideas had taught these Brazilians a dogmatic commitment to theoretical liberalism—one which clearly shaped their perceptions; on the other, eighteenth-century rational experimentalism had instilled in them a contempt for "sterile theory" divorced from scientifically demonstrable reality. In this the first Brazilian emperor was not atypical of his subjects. Pedro I had expressed the antitheoretical position in his charge to the members of the Constituent Assembly in 1823. He warned the constituents against drafting a theory-bound document, for "all the Constitutions that have modeled themselves on those of 1791 and 1792 have been shown by experience to be totally theoretical and metaphysical, and therefore unworkable."[47] A few months later, however, Pedro dissolved the Assembly and eventually promulgated a constitution whose degree of liberalism he was content to describe in quantitative terms.

Attacks on theory worship were a standard weapon in the political armories of all factions. At the beginning of the reform decade, the *Jornal do Comércio* cautioned against guidance by "abstract theories" which did not jibe with social reality.[48] And in the 1830s, moderate liberals branded their radical adversaries on the left, the federalists and republicans, as excessively attached to alien "theories" unsuited to Brazil. Finally, in their turn, the reactionaries of the 1840s would accuse the moderates themselves of an unrealistic commitment to theoretical liberalism.

The brave search for a basis of social unity combined with this spirit of empirical inquiry to give Brazilian reformism its distinctly localistic administrative focus. Since most liberals subscribed to the belief that the shared characteristics of Brazilian society were more important than its diversity, the local parish (*freguesia*) unit seemed to them a kind of Brazilian microcosm. The parish could be isolated and scrutinized. Knowledge would guide reform, reform would perfect, and local perfection would radiate into the larger society. It is from the liberals' desire to analyze and serve this smallest social unit—this miniature of society and model for the state—that mainstream Brazilian liberalism gains its character as a parochial rather than provincial or federalist movement.[49]

Theory and empiricism also might be reconciled at the parish level, where administrative reformism went hand in hand with social experimentation. More than a mere microcosm, the parish could be a social laboratory. In the 1827 session of the Brazilian Chamber of Deputies, the liberal editor and deputy Luis Augusto May introduced a long-range plan to identify the dynamics of local Brazilian society while molding a liberal but "nontheoretical" plan of local government perfectly suited to national reality. The deputy diagnosed independent Brazil's major administrative problem as the continued "mystery" that enveloped the true nature of society, and the consequent "ignorance about the raw materials of administration." May described how colonial administration, particularly as represented by the legal system, had victimized the ordinary citizen —erecting barriers to his effective participation in local government, and minimizing his opportunities for interaction with the rest of "society." Unless reforms were perfectly calculated not to conflict with local conditions, predicted the editor-deputy, it would be impossible to change this pattern without risking social "convulsion."[50]

May believed that such "perfectly calculated" reforms could be developed scientifically. The heart of his plan would be the establishment of a single experimental parish in which administrative ideas could be tested empirically. May was virtually alone among liberals in his patience: his model parish plan would not be complete, he reckoned, for from eighteen to twenty years. The first years would be taken up in compiling a flawless statistical survey. Then local rivalries and conflicts would be identified, analyzed, and resolved. Eventually, through a process of trial and error, ideal governmental forms and institutions would be developed. By the end of one generation, May felt, he would have achieved a "perfect reconciliation between theory and practice." Since May joined Evaristo da Veiga and other liberals in believing in the essential uniformity of Brazilian society, the results of his single-parish experiment would be applicable to the other parishes of the empire as well. And ultimately, he believed, the lessons of the local experiment could be generalized to improve imperial administration at every level.[51]

May's scheme was too long-range to be attractive and it was defeated in the Chamber of Deputies. Its author appears to have been considered something of a crank, but his ideas, however exaggerated, were influential and almost perfectly reflected an important dimension of liberal reformist thought.[52] The intellectual spirit of experimental gradualism which had endowed May's model parish eventually found narrower expression in the proposals of more politically minded liberals who supported instead the immediate creation of untested institutions drawn from the experience of other countries. Whereas May had advocated the development of new institutions based on close observation and controlled experimentation, the politicians of the liberal decade in effect reversed the process: first introducing local institutions and then observing their effects on society. In one sense it was a case of faith in liberal theory and foreign models triumphing over organizational empiricism, but insofar as the institutions themselves were considered experimental agents, the empirical orientation remained constant.

Finally, the liberal reformers showed their practical concern for fitting reforms to actual conditions by concentrating on institutions designed to correct known grievances. The outstanding similarity between May's ideas for parochial organization and those of the men who were actually successful in passing their programs was their common focus upon judicial reforms. The impatient reformers who sought immediate decentralization and parochial reform in 1827 all tended to agree with Luis Augusto May that the Portuguese judiciary, with its administrative personality, was largely responsible for the evils of the local regime. In their legislative proposals for local government, therefore, they emphasized the renovation of the judiciary and constructed their own schemes around the locally elected parish judge promised by the constitution, the justice of the peace (*juiz de paz*).[53] This petty judicial officer was the cornerstone of plans for local government introduced in the 1820s and early 1830s; even the most nebulous proposals for imperial reorganization were predicated on the existence of the parish judge.[54] And, also like May, the institutional reformers believed that their local concerns had national validity. At all levels of administration, common grievances against the Portuguese judicial system helped shape liberal thinking and reformist policy.

3. The Judicial Legacy

It was not by chance that the reformers directed their most concerted energies toward modification of the judiciary. The ideological and the reactive arms of the liberal movement participated in different ways, but neither the meliorist reformers nor the wreckers who had merely hated colonial rule could resist the opportunities offered in this area. For during the colonial period, the judicial system was where Brazilians came closest to the regime—where they had the most influence, and also where they were most abused. After independence, therefore, justice settled precisely at the intersection of the complex push-and-pull forces that shaped Brazilian liberalism. The colonial judiciary offered both a system to reform from within and a structure of power to be dismantled.

In colonial Brazil the judicial system had acted as the handmaiden of colonial rule. The structures of justice and those of royal administration were intimately connected at the highest levels of government, where viceroy and High Court sat side by side, and outside the colonial cities the two systems were often indistinguishable. When a Portuguese monarch desired to regulate some crucial aspect of colonial life, he seldom sent troops, royal intendants, or tax collectors. More often he sent judges endowed with broad powers of administration. Inevitably the bureaucratic judiciary became identified implicitly with royal administration. Although the legal system thus shared in the prestige of the regime, it also drew the fire of native reaction against colonial rule.

This identity between royal administration and the judicial system was a conscious one in the Portuguese monarchy. Portuguese rulers since the late Middle Ages had used the legal arm to extend and solidify royal authority, first in Iberia, then in the empire claimed by the navigators. The political partnership between crown authority and the judiciary enjoyed as a philosophic justification the Iberian notion of analogy between monarch and magistrate. The king of Portugal and the Algarves cherished as his highest attribute of sovereignty

the role of supreme law-giver and judicial arbiter. By extension, the professional magistrates of the colonial empire were the monarch's surrogates, and the
force of their decisions flowed as much from derived personal authority as
from legal codifications or judicial process. The commingling and even confusion between governmental systems made problematic the concept of an
abstract, impersonal bureaucracy in the Portuguese empire. And the personalistic bonds of mutualism between the king and the magistrate further militated
to make the legal personnel—the individual judges themselves—the dynamic
center of the Portuguese legal system.[1]

Because the legal system was an important lever of colonial rule, and the
magistrates the agents of the ruler, the Portuguese legal complex became a
prime target for Brazilian reaction against the colonial regime. As Brazilians
began to anticipate the possibility of political independence they took up the
centuries-old tradition of Portuguese reform-mongers who had directed savage
attacks against the power and corruption of the legal bureaucracy. Since the
legal complex's varied administrative personality allowed it to invade virtually
every area of colonial life, these attacks and institutional complaints ran the
gamut of the abuses of colonialism.

The Portuguese structure of supreme appellate courts has been described in
detail elsewhere and need not be recapitulated here.[2] The highest metropolitan
tribunals—the Desembargo do Paço and Casa de Suplicação—were transferred
to Brazil in 1808 but remained remote institutions to most Brazilians. The
bitter and revealing reaction against the judicial system at the time of independence properly begins one notch lower, at the level of the High Court (Relação),
where direct experience and social involvement began to give the court structure a Brazilian flavor long before independence. A High Court had existed in
Brazil since 1609, with one interruption between 1626 and 1652. The original
Brazilian court sat in the colonial capital of Bahia. In 1751, after the wealth of
the colony had shifted southward, another Relação was created in Rio de Janeiro. The arrival of the royal family in 1808 led to the establishment of two
more such appeals courts, one in Maranhão and one in Pernambuco.[3] The justices of these courts, called *desembargadores,* performed circuit duties in the
rest of the colony, sat on cases sent up from the network of inferior courts,
chopped logic, and squabbled with other colonial officials.

Institutionally, the High Court was for centuries the highest tribunal in Portuguese America, and as such could be seen as a principal guardian of colonial
orthodoxy. But a less formalistic and surprisingly "Brazilian" connection between the court and colonial reality was provided by the High Court justices
themselves. Although a great majority of these jurists came from Portugal,
some were Brazilian-born and many married in Brazil. During their sometimes
lengthy tenure in the colony, many more became entangled in local society

and life through the bonds of ritual and illegitimate kinship, business dealings, and friendship.[4] Stuart Schwartz's study of the colonial Bahian High Court and its judges concludes that impersonal administrative objectives and non-formalized personal and social imperatives formed interlocking systems of organization in the Portuguese empire. Even the stodgiest level of royal administration tended to reflect the social milieu so strongly that we may speak of a "Brazilianization of bureaucracy."[5]

The lower court system of late colonial Brazil began at the *comarca* level in jurisdictional districts consisting of one or more major towns and the surrounding settlements and countryside. In sparsely populated areas of the interior these districts might be enormous and vaguely defined, while large cities or densely populated agricultural areas had comparatively smaller and more carefully delineated comarcas. The royal judicial and administrative officer at the comarca level was the ouvidor, sometimes referred to as the *corregedor*. Professionally, the post was an intermediate stop for graduates of the Coimbra law faculty working their way through a career pattern that ideally would end with appointment to one of the High Courts. These district judges periodically held court and heard civil and criminal cases in the towns of their jurisdiction; they were also charged with supervising public order in the districts to which they were assigned. Since they bore general responsibility for the administration of justice in their districts, the ouvidores also had certain powers of review over the performances of their inferiors in the judicial structure.[6]

The lowest rung on the ladder of Portuguese royal justice was the position of *juiz de fora* at the municipal or county level. Unlike the ouvidor-corregedor post, some form of which has existed in Brazil since the early days of the colony, the office of juiz de fora was introduced late in the seventeenth century. The number of such positions was increased during the eighteenth century as a part of the crown's effort to extend effective royal control to the growing and lawless towns of the colony. In towns where royal surveillance or an increased governmental presence seemed desirable, the locally selected petty judges (*juizes da terra*) were replaced by the crown-appointed, Coimbra-trained juizes de fora, whose very name (judges from outside) emphasized the importance of their links with royal government. In addition to his judicial role, the juiz de fora presided ex officio over the municipal council of the town of his assignment.[7]

The crown magistrates of the inferior courts probably became involved in nonjudicial aspects of local society to an even greater extent than the High Court judges. Royal judges inevitably acquired the ties of formal and informal relationships by which business and society functioned and function in Brazil. Such magisterial involvement in the workings of society most often came to light in complaints of avarice, corruption, or the abuse of official powers in order to further a judge's local interests or those of his cronies or relatives. An eighteenth-century ouvidor on the Mato Grosso frontier, to cite only one example, disguised his commercial ambitions to trade illegally with the Spanish Jesuit missions in the neighborhood by telling his superiors that "reconnoitering" expeditions were needed to verify the extent of Spanish penetration in the area.[8] In colonial times the crown apparently disregarded most such complaints against its magistrates as the grumblings of discontented litigants. And even when charges were well documented, considerable leniency was the rule. The profit-minded ouvidor of Mato Grosso, for instance, overcame his notorious fraternization with the Spanish enemy to end his career at the apex of his profession, as desembargador on the Relação of Bahia.[9]

Portuguese and Brazilian legal thinkers always differed in their attitudes toward such local involvements by members of the judiciary. The official position expressed in royal legislation was that magistrates should keep their distance from the snares of society. Judges were repeatedly forbidden to contract marriage or conduct business in their jurisdictions, but the repetition of the injunction only underscored the frequency of the offense.[10] Realistic observers and critics of the Portuguese judiciary recognized the fruitlessness of such prohibitions. Strict self-isolation from social involvement failed to acknowledge the transactional nature of colonial society. Judicial monasticism would not only be personally impossible in most cases, it would also weaken the judge's ability to administer justice and carry out the business of royal government. After independence, some Brazilians expressed the belief that an official policy of bureaucratic noninvolvement, where it was effective, had a detrimental effect because it assigned magistrates to places whose needs they did not fully comprehend or were indifferent to. Not understanding the dynamics of local society, politics, and economy, such judges either interpreted the law coldly, with no regard for local conditions, or they made unwise alliances which might yield momentary benefits for the transient judge but create unsettled conditions in the long run. Put cynically, the belief was that as long as magistrates were going to become corruptly enmeshed in local activities anyway, they should at least be men with a grasp of the damage they could do and an interest in preserving stability.[11] Brazilian reformers of the liberal period carried this argument for localism a step farther by demanding that local judges be locally elected—independent of the central government, not royal appointees.

It is well to note here that although anti-Portuguese sentiment was a characteristic of the Brazilian independence movement, criticism of magistrates for being Portuguese-born seldom figured in the attacks on the legal system. Indeed, by the end of the colonial period the place of birth of magistrates had become a rather meaningless concept. Brazil, like Portugal's other colonies, had no legal faculty or institutions of higher education of its own. Those who followed

the professions in the Portuguese world, therefore, were forced to acquire formal training at the University of Coimbra. There young men from Portugal, the
Atlantic islands, Brazil, and Africa were educated and socialized together from
the age of about fifteen years into their early twenties. Brazilian professional
jurists often began their careers as juizes de fora in Portuguese towns and later
were transferred elsewhere in the empire; men born in Africa or Portugal might
be dispatched for their first assignments to Brazilian jurisdictions.[12] If anything, members of the magistracy tended to identify more strongly with their
professional class than with their place of origin, a fact that did not go unno-
ticed by their critics.[13]

Whatever the socializing effect of the common education, it is also clear
that practicing royal magistrates came from a variety of backgrounds. Brazilian
nativists never consistently defended the thesis of foreign monopoly in the
judiciary because they knew it was not the case. During the last thirteen
years of the colonial period, when the Desembargo do Paço sat in Rio de Janeiro, a total of seventy-three young law graduates (*bacharéis*) were examined
by the board prior to their first assignments as judges in Brazil. Of these a clear
majority, some 55 percent, were Brazilian-born, and others came from Africa
(1) and the Azores (2), thus further diluting the Portuguese influence[14] (see
table 1).

**Birthplace of *Bacharéis* Examined by Rio Desembargo do Paço,
1809-1827**

Period	Brazil	Portugal	Azores	Africa	Total
1809-1821 (pre-ind.)	40	30	2	1	73
1823-1827	7	1	—	—	8

Source: "Livro Primeiro de Assento de Bacharéis: 1809-1827," ANRJ, Cod. 23.

The issue of national independence thus encountered neither uniform support nor opposition among the royal magistracy. Some judges were prominent
in the independence movement, but others felt that their loyalty should be to
the old king. After Dom Pedro's refusal to return to Portugal made independence inevitable, for instance, a young Bahian-born juiz de fora in Minas Gerais,
Cassiano Esperidião de Melo Matos, placed himself at the head of a pro-Portu-
guese disturbance, which earned him suspension in 1822 but did not keep
him from pursuing a career in politics after independence was achieved.[15] In
other cases, a judge's real or simply alleged lukewarmness about independence

might be interpreted as active hostility. The reluctance of the juiz de fora of the São Paulo town of Taubaté to swear allegiance to the principles of the liberal Portuguese constitution in 1821 prompted his enemies to petition the government for his removal. Eventually they terrorized him into fleeing the town.[16]

An indeterminate number of judges did leave the country as independence approached and was consummated, but the majority appears merely to have shifted allegiance from the old king to his son. Many young magistrates, fresh from their European educations, were committed to liberal constitutionalism; and even for a conservative judge to cast his lot with a Cortes-ruled Portugal was not a very attractive option. The Revolution of Pôrto had included as part of its program a thoroughgoing reform of the judicial system aimed at weakening the professional elite magistracy. And liberal newspapers in Brazil reported with approval sessions of the Cortes in which such reforms as a jury system and locally elected lay judges were discussed.[17] If such changes in the mother country gave magisterial personnel cause to question their prospective status in liberal Portugal, the constitutional subjection which the Cortes imposed on the monarch also made it difficult to argue by 1822 that support of the Portuguese government was any longer the same as allegiance to the king. Outright magisterial opposition to Brazilian independence was therefore minimal, and the transformation from colony to nation was accomplished without much obvious upset in the judiciary.

The flexibility, lack of alternative, and largely Brazilian origin of the judges combined to deliver them from the crisis of independence without serious change. Nevertheless, the institutional survival of the old legal structure even after independence aggravated national feelings that soon found an outlet in attacks on the magistracy. The reforming spirit that persisted and spread after independence included very strong opposition to the Portuguese legal system as a whole. As the demand for reform rose, Brazilian liberals attacked the unchanged colonial judiciary with criticism that ranged from the corruption of magistrates to the torpid and unwieldy character of the entire legal edifice.

The corruption of judges was one of the oldest objections to the magistracy and was prominently ventilated after independence. In 1828 a liberal sheet identified the subornation of judges as the "contagion that has been the greatest scourge of Brazil's provinces."[18] As if in confirmation, when discussing proposed reforms, magistrate-members of the Brazilian Parliament sometimes recalled, almost nostalgically, their early experiences on the bench when local potentates had tried to buy their decisions with "fifty pieces of gold for a new pair of shoes."[19] Although inferior-court magistrates were most often criticized in this way, an anonymous letter to the minister of justice attacked the entire Bahian High Court. "The more they [the desembargadores] see of a certain fine blond metal, the more they ignore the laws in order to satisfy their immeasurable ambition."[20] Foreign visitors agreed with the Brazilian reformers that the legal system rested in palms often crossed with silver. The Reverend Robert Walsh found the administration of justice to be the "greatest grievance under which the people labor" and blamed the problem on judicial malfeasance. He estimated that judges who made a salary of 300 *milreis* sometimes expended amounts of up to 10,000 *milreis*[21] and made up the difference in "the most notorious and undisguised bribery, in which there is no delicacy used and little concealment practiced." The British chaplain described the princely bribe of an English carriage made to a judge who had no qualms about "driving publicly in this proof of his corruption."[22]

The corporate spirit and exclusivism of the royal magistracy also produced bitterness in the years after independence. The judges' common experience at the University of Coimbra came to stand for magisterial oppression and arrogance in Brazil. Evaristo da Veiga seldom missed an occasion to equate attendance at the Coimbra law faculty with unjust privilege and colonial despotism.[23] Luis Augusto May combined the common prejudices against the university, and the not uncommon suggestion that Coimbra was a breeding ground of base instincts, with a generational objection to the callow and inexperienced young men who were sent to administer justice as juizes de fora. "To Brazil the magistrates literally came to spend their novitiate, exercising and venting the fiery passions of youth, and often combining this with an avarice whose origin lay in the University."[24] For these observers, colonial oppression grew out of an elite forged in a shared educational and corporate experience, not a shared place of birth. One of the most urgent demands of reformers after independence was therefore the establishment of Brazilian law schools to replace "the ancient factory" at Coimbra.[25]

If on the one hand many Brazilians felt victimized by their legal system, it was no less true that the flaws of the system depended on overloaded dockets and a good deal of public encouragement of underhanded practices. Brazilians themselves were the first to recognize what was a veritable national obsession with pursuing legal action against one another. The Pernambucan social critic Miguel do Sacramento Lopes Gama, wrote that "the spirit of contentiousness and the love of bringing suit seem to be among the dominant passions of our Brazil; I cannot believe that in any other country there are as many lawsuits filed as there are among us."[26] The clogging of the courts with trivial litigation was commonly blamed for making legal procedure sluggish and fostering judicial corruption. Officials regarded the problem as so central that the first post-independence measures to improve the administration of justice, and the first institutional reforms, were designed primarily to help clear the courts by requiring simple conciliation hearings before formal legal action could be taken.[27] Reforms of this sort were predictably unpopular among the legal parasites that

infested Brazil's courthouses, for as Lopes Gama exclaimed of the litigiousness
of Brazilians, "what an abundant mine, what a wealth of Potosí for the gentlemen of justice!"[28]

The gentlemen of justice—the courthouse crowd, as distinct from the professional judiciary—made up one of the characteristic elements of the Luso-Brazilian legal world.[29] Attracted by the venality of judges and the willingness of
litigants to trade cash or favors for advantageous rulings, the swarm of "insa-
tiable scribes, bailiffs, judges, solicitors, and shysters" turned Brazil's courts
into legal marketplaces.[30] John Luccock, who believed he could read a man's
character in his facial features, felt sure he had identified a criminal class in the
shifty-eyed lawyers of Rio. And yet he had little sympathy for their apparently
cooperative victims. "If there be among them those who promote litigation,
the people of Rio must be peculiarly open to such influence; otherwise bread
could not be found for five hundred legal practitioners, which is their computed
number."[31] *Aurora Fluminense* labeled the seamy courthouse crowd the
"interests of chicanery" and also charged them with provoking unnecessary
litigation. "We [the interests of chicanery] support ourselves through the intrigues we foment and the discord that we sow between neighbors and even in
the bosoms of families; and from this our incomes are comparable to those of
men who have attended the medical and surgical faculties." Evaristo da Veiga
estimated in 1830, some twenty years after Luccock, that from the professional
magistrates down to the lowly bailiffs, "more than two thousand people live
off chicanery in Rio de Janeiro."[32]

Once a case came to court, and the litigation mill began to turn, the parties
faced a seemingly endless series of demands by justice officials and hangers-on.
These judicial bazaars were a rich source of social satire. One Rio newspaper
ran a pointed article describing the peculiar *jeito* (knack or talent) of various
social caricatures:

> The jeito of the litigant is to scratch the back of the scribe, brighten the day
> of the court page, put up with the solicitor, suck up to the letrado, choose
> the right lawyer for the defense according to his venality or talent, offer
> favors to the judge and never spare the cash. Above all, he must be quick
> of eye and fleet of foot; keeping an open purse and a closed mouth.[33]

But comic as it might be to observe the follies of the litigants and the avari-
cious stratagems of the picaresque courthouse crowd, the system was in real
life a heavy burden to most Brazilians. Even those who could afford the expenses of justice were subject to the intolerable delays caused by overloaded
dockets. The array of unwritten procedural rules by which decisions were put
off long enough for a counterbid by the opposing party made Brazilian justice

not only expensive but sluggish in the extreme.[34] And of course, the Portuguese Cortes' proposal to return the high tribunals of Rio to Portugal would
have further prolonged the appeals process.[35] Among the major beneficiaries
of the proposed reforms of the legal system, therefore, was to be "the extraordinary number of victims that [the reforms] can yank from the claws of the
interminable and ruinous lawsuits that drive them to despair."[36] As often as
they protested judicial venality, Brazilian reformers attacked the plodding,
drawn-out procedures inherited from Portugal and cultivated by those who
made their living "singing and dancing to the sound of the groans of litigants."[37]

The legacy of bitterness against corruption, privilege, and bureaucratic inefficiency led naturally to demands for institutional reform in the 1820s. The
Constitution of 1824 itself made reference to the statutory establishment of
a new local judge for conciliations, and of a jury system to complement the
regular judicial hierarchy. Moreover, the issue of judicial reform had potentially
mighty political implications for the new government. Since judicial influence
was so pervasive and strongly felt, the reform of no other branch of government would have more immediate impact upon the majority of Brazilians. An
improvement in the conditions of justice would be a palpable boon indeed,
and a credit to the administration. The judicial question thus prompted much
official rhetoric about reform in the years just after independence. Dom Pedro
I in his yearly addresses (*falas do trono*) vied with the formal replies (*votos de
graças*) of the Parliament in professions of concern over the reform of the legal
system. Typically, Dom Pedro would exhort the legislature to take note of the
abuses of the legal system and "regulate promptly but with great care this
branch [of government] that is so important to public happiness and tranquility." Sometimes the legislators could even top the emperor's rhetoric: "[We]
are convinced that the luminous mechanism of the Brazilian Constitution cannot rotate upon the gothic gyro of the old [legal] system."[38]

The judicial reform movement had roots of long standing in popular grievances, but its proximate causes are to be found in crisis, for in the years after
independence the old Portuguese legal structure collapsed. Shopworn demands
for change suddenly became practical imperatives when the lack of professional
judicial personnel, coupled with a popular boycott of royal justice, made
reform essential.

It is impossible to determine exactly how many Portuguese magistrates left
Brazil in the aftermath of independence. As we have seen in table 1, about 45
percent of the magistrates who had begun their careers in Brazil since 1808
were foreign-born. Most of these probably stayed on, but some of them, and
some of their Brazilian-born colleagues whose main ties were in Europe, certainly returned to Portugal around 1822. Many more probably opted for an alternative route of migration: not back to Portugal, but to the new source of power

and patronage, Rio de Janeiro. Placing themselves at the crossroads of power was second nature to the Portuguese professional magistracy, and the newly independent Brazilian government offered attractive prospects for advancement. Consequently, many magistrates appear to have left their assignments or requested official leaves-of-absence in order to flock to Rio in search of connections and patronage.[39]   Still others, elected to the Chamber of Deputies, abandoned their posts and journeyed to the capital for the first sessions of the Parliament. Many judicial districts were left vacant.

The bureaucratic and administrative snarls caused by independence also contributed to the sudden shortage of judges. As senior magistrates left their jurisdictions to enter politics or return to Portugal, junior university graduates had to be funneled into the system in a hurry. But Brazil had no source of new judicial officers outside of the University of Coimbra, and independence had a disrupting effect on the flow of freshly graduated lawyers to Brazil. In addition, the old qualifying procedures also collapsed, for after 1822 the professors of the law faculty of Coimbra no longer sent to Brazil the letters of recommendation (*habilitações e informações*) that were required before a graduate could be examined by the Desembargo do Paço.[40]   Whether caused by an absolute lack of candidates or by the inevitable breakdown of formal qualifying procedures, there was a dramatic decrease in the number of professionals examined by the board after independence. Whereas in the years from 1809 to 1821 the yearly average of prospective judges examined had been an already inadequate 5.6, over the five years between independence and the abolition of the Desembargo do Paço in 1827 the average fell to 1.6 per year (see table 1).

The paucity of professional judges was keenly felt in the empire during the 1820s. In 1823 and 1824, when the minister of justice named magistrates to serve in the jurisdictions of Bahia, his instructions included frequent references to the shortage. Enough urgency was involved in filling the vacant posts to justify the circumventing of much of the regular bureaucratic forms and red tape. New judges were to be installed "immediately" rather than leave a jurisdiction any longer without a judge simply because all the paper work and ceremony had not been performed.[41]   The problem was aired in the Constituent Assembly where Francisco Carneiro de Campos drew attention to the "great lack of magistrates in many parts of the provinces" and the resulting "grave harm" to the public good.[42]

It appears also that the scarcity of judicial personnel and the run on patronage caused numerous irregularities in the filling of magisterial posts during the 1820s. The government of newly independent Brazil does not seem to have had any rigid policy about appointing magistrates to districts outside their home provinces. And with judges in short supply, the Ministry of Justice was in any event ill-situated to place many conditions on the requests of qualified magistrates to serve. As a result, judges chose their own assignments, and the districts they selected often corresponded with their own family and financial interests. Aside from the old arguments about the relative virtues of local judges versus disinterested outsiders, administrators worried about the venality of magistrates who had extensive interests in their districts. In 1826 the provincial president of Bahia complained of his difficulties in stemming the counterfeit coin industry in that province when "except for some of the desembargadores, all the present [judges] of the cities and towns are Bahians who cannot function with impartiality, especially when the time comes to correct abuses and apply force."[43]

Magisterial absenteeism further aggravated the standard grievance of ponderously slow administration of justice. Already hopelessly backed-up case loads increased still further in the absence of sufficient magistrates, and Brazil's court system, never efficient, approached chaos. The professional magistrates who remained on the bench were left to a thankless struggle with the accumulation of work and popular ill-will, both of which only tended to increase. A typical plight was that of the juiz de fora of Salvador, Bahia, Antônio Calmon du Pin e Almeida, who in 1826 reported to the provincial president that for eight months he had been forced to serve simultaneously in all the judicial posts (*varas*) in the city—probate, civil, and criminal—because of the absence of the proper magistrates. The judge faced inventories backed up from ten to twenty-five years, and civil suits continued to pile up in his court. The situation was exacerbated by the lack of popular cooperation. "I find myself in a perfect labyrinth," he wrote, "not only because of the great backlog . . . but also because of the lack of respect that exists for the constituted authorities."[44]

As the legal system with its diminished professional personnel came to a standstill, the people's lack of consideration for judicial authorities became a practical boycott. In 1828 Rio de Janeiro's English-language newspaper observed that "Every impartial observer must have remarked the miserable state to which Justice, both civil and criminal, has been reduced in this country."[45] The widely recognized collapse of the judicial system fired demands for basic reforms, and the anticipation of such reforms in turn lessened still farther the respect for the existing structure. The reform movement and the breakdown of the old legal system thus became mutually reinforcing phenomena, for the effective administration of justice depended on the prestige of judicial institutions or at least a belief in their permanence. Yet many Brazilians clearly expected that independence would bring a total institutional revolution—a scrapping of everything Portuguese. As early as 1823, a deputy to the Constituent Assembly remarked that in the eyes of the people, the new political regime implied the delegitimization of the old legal system. The popular conviction, he said, was that "the laws are no longer in force, and the magistrates have no authority."

All over the empire, the deputy reported, men gave voice to such sentiments as: "'What do I care for the worthy juiz de fora? The time of [colonial] subjection is over; now we have a Constitution whose meaning is—Liberty.'"[46]

And as the judicial system collapsed, so too did the police. Police and courts were inseparable in the Portuguese world. The powers of constabulary and magistracy always overlapped and their distinctions within the realm of "administration of justice" were blurred indeed. So in the 1820s the chaotic state of the Brazilian judiciary was reflected in the demoralization of the police. In Rio de Janeiro, where the constabulary had reached its highest point of professionalism and organization in the years following the transfer of the court in 1808,[47] law and order had become a serious issue by the late 1820s. Most of the press agreed that the incidence of crime in the capital was on the upswing. Vagrants and ne'er-do-wells from the interior formed gangs of bandits who preyed on the thriving commerce of the port city. Meanwhile, the police either connived with the criminals or stood helplessly by.[48] The Reverend Mr. Walsh reserved his harshest observations for the state of Rio de Janeiro's police in 1828. He remarked that the capital's police were not distinguished for either their temperance or their proper conduct; they were the only "natives" he ever saw drunk.[49] By the year of the abdication of the first emperor (1831), the formal system of police had become incapable of maintaining order in Rio. There were popular disturbances in the capital in that year, but the minister of justice reported that "the bureau of Police was so discredited in public opinion that it was idle to expect any good result from its employment." The minister preferred to entrust the policing of the restless city to a new reform institution —the justices of the peace.[50]

The ineffectiveness of the police and the judiciary drove private citizens to turn away from the established structure and seek private methods of solving their differences. In 1831 the minister of justice referred to the "inertia" of the judicial system and considered that it was a "marvel that each individual in society has not set himself up as a Judge of his own Rights—dispensing justice with his own hands."[51] The minister's point was suggestive, and although vigilante justice was never absent in Brazil, we may speculate that it increased in this interim period after the break with Portugal compromised the legitimacy of the traditional judiciary.

When combined with the inevitable nativist reaction against the colonial legal system, the breakdown of the courts and police in the 1820s sealed the fate of the Portuguese judicial inheritance. Reforms were necessary to satisfy national demands and as an earnest of government commitment to liberal principles. More practically, the system had to be overhauled in order to reestablish the rule of law in the empire. The reformers demanded above all the decentralizing innovations promised in the Constitution of 1824: the local justice of the

peace and the jury system. The liberal view of justice and society also promised completely new legal codes to free Brazilians from Portuguese legislation
—"absurd laws, designed for other peoples and other times."[52] The age-old
complaints of judicial oppression, and the new demands for native sovereignty,
fused in the late 1820s. As one Rio de Janeiro editor sighed, "Ah, how we do
long for the reform of the Judicial branch."[53]

Part II. Reform, 1827-1837

Contemporary rendering of a tumultuous nineteenth-century Brazilian election. The presiding justice of the peace calls for order from atop a table in the background.

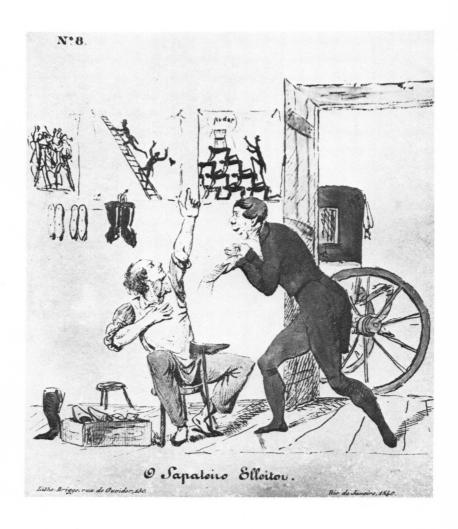

In this political cartoon of 1840, a Brazilian shoemaker gives a lesson in civic virtue and the hypocrisy of politics to a fawning candidate.

4. The Imperial Justice of the Peace

The first great reform of the liberal decade was also the first significant modification of the judicial system. The creation in 1827 of the office of juiz de paz,
or justice of the peace, marked the opening of the reform period and the proximate ascendancy of the liberals. To the modern observer the institution seems
perfectly benign; as originally conceived the Brazilian juiz de paz would be an
untrained, unpaid, parish-level magistrate, elected for a year to adjudicate petty
matters and conciliate prospective litigants. Yet almost from its conception
this seemingly innocuous jurisdiction touched off violent controversy and pol-
arized institutional thinking in Brazil. The liberal reformers made the juiz de
paz the standard-bearer of their own philosophic and practical concerns: democratic forms, localism, self-government, and decentralization. Traditionalists
and conservatives, on the other hand, saw in the local magistrate an ominous
erosion of central authority and a threat to social control in the far-flung empire. As the first step away from the colonial legal heritage, the reform acquired
a symbolic identification with Brazilian liberalism itself. The liberals defended
it passionately; their opponents attacked it without quarter. Attitudes toward
the institution thus became important factors in determining political alignments, and, as time passed, the debate over the validity and performance of the
elected judge grew into one of the major issues of the early Brazilian empire.
The history of the institution reflects the full complexity of intellectual trends
and political and social tensions in nineteenth-century Brazil. The present
chapter examines the visible tip of this institutional iceberg: its inspiration, its
creation and reception, and its formal aspects. The informal and unofficial
world of the Brazilian local magistrate is the subject of following chapters.

The law that created the justice of the peace only fulfilled a promise made
in the Constitution of 1824. Despite his lapses, the bestower of that document,
the emperor Pedro I, thought himself as much a liberal as any of his subjects;
we have already observed his pride in the degree of liberalism in the 1824

charter. The emperor's constitution specified that the judicial system of independent Brazil would eventually include such innovations as a jury system and locally elected petty magistrates to be called justices of the peace. These were significant concessions to the liberals, certainly, but not without precedents very close at hand: the Portuguese Cortes had discussed the same reforms in early 1822 and incorporated them into the resulting Portuguese constitution.[1] In Brazil, the promised institutions remained on paper until the first legislature could be convened and regulatory statutes drafted. Two years passed before the first regular session of the Parliament met, but lawmakers then lost little time in taking up the matter. On 15 October 1827 legislation ordered and regulated the establishment of local judges in Brazil's parishes.[2]

The new institution was ideally designed to function within a compatible liberal legal framework. But, in fact, the justice of the peace began its existence in isolation—without the benefit of any supporting legislation. The reformers in the first legislature had faced a choice between two options: they could attempt the sweeping elaboration of full legal codes to rebuild and modernize the country's judicial structure, or they could pass piecemeal reformist legislation with the aim of solving immediate problems. Because the second alternative was preferred, the justice of the peace was at first set adrift in the uncomplementary and hostile structure of the largely unchanged colonial judiciary. This led, swiftly and naturally, to institutional conflicts and charges of poor planning on the part of the institution's creators. The apparent oversight helps to explain much of the early turmoil that surrounded the parish judge, but it also raises the more difficult question of motivation. Why did the liberals commence their overhaul of the legal system in this manner? The answer to this question is worth detailing here, for it restates two of the major themes of the Brazilian reform movement.

First, the piecemeal approach had a powerful appeal for those reformers whose main interest had always resided simply in improving the administration of justice. New legal codes would entail time in the drafting and endless debate, but the old structure had already begun to collapse. The flight of magistrates, the backlog of litigation, and the popular boycott of royal justice were causing judicial pandemonium.[3] Isolated reforms might not be ideal, but they had the advantage of speed, and now, more than ever, immediacy seemed desirable. Those who for this reason favored the patchwork technique were the classic reformers, the judicial meliorists who thought the system susceptible to reform from within, and who may have been little interested in total structural change. One member of the Chamber of Deputies cited the urgent need to correct the notorious abuses of the colonial legal system before tackling the complicated and time-consuming task of erecting an entirely new structure.[4] Another legislator who also preferred to move from the specific to the general thought that concrete innovations such as the justice of the peace should be discussed and agreed upon independently before the more abstract legal codifications were undertaken.[5] From this point of view establishment of the Brazilian justice of the peace was a stop-gap measure. It would unclog and partially legitimize the existing legal system without totally overturning it.

Most reformers probably shared some of the attitudes of the judicial melio-rists, but more devious motives were present as well. Indeed, the very incom-patibility of the justice of the peace made the institution attractive to those reformers whose objectives were primarily political, and it could be argued that in 1827 the jurisdictional conflicts which the elected judge was sure to provoke were among the liberals' fondest goals. Pedro I's arbitrary closing of the Con-stituent Assembly, and the growing fear that he would eventually seek an ab-solutist solution in Brazil, had convinced the opposition that the time had come for an attack on his power. Since much of that power lay in the legal system, the justice of the peace offered a likely starting point. Negativism in-verted logic—the more incompatible the better. As opposition developed to the emperor, his adversaries in the legislature looked to the anomalous parish magistrate for a means of sabotaging the traditional judiciary and an indepen-dent counterpoise to anticipated despotism.

To these political decentralizers the importance of the juiz de paz lay not so much in its potential for improvement of the legal system as in its "indepen-dence." When the reformers vested significant judicial powers in the parish judge they did so in direct defiance of the emperor's traditional position as supreme arbiter of justice and source of judicial authority. In the territories of a Portuguese ruler the judges were the monarch's deputies and representa-tives,[6] but the justice of the peace was not a dependent part of the king's jus-tice in the same way as the appointive juiz de fora or ouvidor. Rather, he was an elective judge whose authority originated not with the emperor, but with an independent popular constituency. The Portuguese empire had long employed elected magistrates at the local level, but their jurisdictions (alçadas) were mi-nuscule and their responsibilities considered beneath the dignity of royal juris-prudence. The new juizes de paz, in contrast, were given authority to decide civil cases involving values higher even than those entrusted to the Coimbra-educated and royally appointed juizes de fora.[7]

In a more concrete way the principle of judicial independence added to the institution's political character. Elected locally and temporarily to serve with-out pay, the petty justice was deliberately placed as far as possible from the influence of the executive branch of government. In theory this simply guar-anteed the judge's independence, but it also served the partisan goals of the op-position by depriving the emperor of control over an important new bureau-cratic resource. To be sure, the legislative opposition had no more strings on the institution than did the emperor, but liberal deputies hoped that these local officials would share their own desires to protect the Constitution, and, in the direst of eventualities, form a line of defense against an emperor's violation of it. In short, the liberals expected democratic recruitment to produce men like themselves.[8] Seen from this angle, the justices of the peace would be local foci of liberal political support and independent units of resistance to overconcentration of power at the center. The political opposition imagined a kind of guerrilla bureaucracy.[9]

The immediate improvement hoped for by the judicial reformers was probably canceled out by the impact of this political dimension. As if deliberately to exacerbate an inevitably touchy situation, the reformers had endowed the new judge with powers that overlapped those of virtually every other institution—judicial and otherwise—in his jurisdiction. This challenge to the validity of the old system elicited an unequivocally obstructionist response from the practicing professional magistracy, whose structure had not been altered to make a place for the new official. From the first there were conflicts between the elected judges and crown magistrates, particularly the royally appointed juizes de fora, whose corporate pride was offended by having to share an ill-defined authority with elected and untrained laymen.[10]

The emperor's attitude was expressed more circumspectly, but it can hardly have been more favorable. The new institution amounted to a highly visible curtailment of Dom Pedro's judicial authority, and the monarch was not one to mistake an insult. At least one influential voice in the liberal press accused the emperor of active hostility to the elective judgeship.[11] And in his 1828 address opening the annual session of the legislature, Dom Pedro made no mention of the controversial new institution—the liberals' proudest accomplishment to date—but pointedly remarked that during the previous session the judicial branch of government had "not been improved in any way."[12] The liberals, for their part, were defiantly pleased to see power vested in an institution which they regarded as theirs in practice as well as in principle. After 1827, relations between the emperor and the legislative branch deteriorated steadily until Dom Pedro's abdication in 1831.

Whatever the intentions of its creators, of course, the Brazilian justice of the peace had an institutional pedigree of its own. The parish judge originated and evolved within a mixed framework of Portuguese precedents and modern institutional thought. The most direct and obvious of the precedents lay in the immediate colonial past: to the new judges passed the powers of three ancient Portuguese institutions that still existed to dispatch minor judicial questions in Brazil's townships and villages—the *juiz ordinário*, the *juiz de vintena*, and the *almotacel.*[13]

Before the advent of the juiz de paz, the juiz ordinário was the highest elected magistrate in the Portuguese legal hierarchy. In towns where there was no crown-appointed juiz de fora, two juizes ordinários were chosen every three years in a two-tiered indirect election. Although in theory the *homens bons* (men of substance) and *povo* (people) had a voice in the election, the final selection was made by six electors, and the order in which the judges would serve could be legally manipulated by the officer presiding over the election —usually the royal district magistrate (ouvidor) or the oldest member of the municipal council. The juiz ordinário's authority at the end of the colonial period extended to civil questions involving values up to 3 milreis in towns of over two hundred adult male inhabitants, but only to 1.2 milreis in cases involving real property. If the community had a smaller population, the juiz ordinário's jurisdiction dropped to 1.8 milreis in cases not involving real estate.[14] As we have seen, during the eighteenth century the crown replaced these local judges with professional royal appointees called juizes de fora in the more important towns of Brazil. Neither office was much beloved, and the debates over which was by nature more villainous—the juiz ordinário or the juiz de fora—did not end with independence.

In part because the juiz de paz's closest analogy in the Portuguese judicial system was the juiz ordinário, parliamentary discussions frequently referred to the latter institution, and seldom in a complimentary fashion. In the more patrician of the two houses, the Senate, where support for elective justice was weakest, comments on the reputation of the juiz ordinário were made evidently with the liberals' justice of the peace in mind. The Baron of Caeté defended the principle of professionally educated magistrates without local ties: "many of the evils that weigh upon the people are caused by the ignorance, malice, and favoritism [*patronato*] of the juizes ordinários." In the same debate, the Baron of Cairú also criticized elective recruitment of judical personnel, making a point of the abundant abuses that surrounded the elections of local magistrates.[15] Feijó, making a very different point in the Chamber of Deputies, nevertheless admitted to having witnessed "the lack of ability of the juizes ordinários who can do nothing without the advice of their secretaries."[16] Yet the generally low opinion of the effectiveness and probity of the juiz ordinário was not universally considered relevant in analogies drawn with the justice of the peace. Most contemporary criticism of the juiz ordinário issued from a nonspecific reaction against the colonial period in general and was not couched in terms of continuities or precedents. Indeed, most reformers agreed that the juiz ordinário's lack of prestige and negligible authority had trivialized the institution by the end of the colonial period, thus invalidating it for comparative purposes.[17]

A second local official whose limited judicial powers were passed to the Juizado de Paz by the law of 1827 was the juiz de vintena, or *juiz pedâneo.*

A Brazilian township or county usually included in its administrative boundaries a considerable extension of territory outside the town proper. Settlements too small to have their own municipal councils were nominally subject to the authority of the council and juiz ordinário of the county seat. But hamlets of twenty or more families located one league or farther from the county seat were entitled to have a juiz de vintena named by the council from among the local worthies. This magistrate's very restricted legal authority did not include any criminal jurisdiction or jurisdiction in cases involving real estate in any form. The juiz de vintena exercised his judicial authority only in cases involving very small sums: from .3 milreis in villages of twenty to fifty families up to 1.2 milreis in larger settlements of two hundred or more families.[18] The justice of the peace supplanted the juiz de vintena's formal jurisdiction and fully replaced him as the cardinal representative of law, order, and justice in the rural interior.

Finally, the lowly *juiz de almotaçaria,* or *almotacel,* also found his powers preempted by those of the juiz de paz. It was the almotacel's job to enforce regulations prescribed by the municipal council. A butcher cheating on his weights and measures or a housewife who allowed her pig to root in the town square might find themselves brought before one of the almotacel's weekly hearings. Apparently regarded as a distasteful job, the office was held by an individual for only one month at a time, at the end of which the council was to choose a replacement. Like his superiors, the juiz ordinário and the juiz de vintena, the almotacel enjoyed scant prestige by the time his office was absorbed by that of the justice of the peace. In 1828, in the Chamber of Deputies, the fate of the almotacel was cited as an example to be avoided by the new magistrates: a jurisdiction scoffed at and exercised only by those "who have nothing to do, or are good for nothing."[19]

It should be emphasized that the outline of local judicial administration presented here is overly theoretical and formal. Lines of authority crisscrossed and tangled in the isolated settlements of Brazil, and at no level is it possible to generalize about the way local justice actually functioned.[20] A municipal council might fail to meet for months on end, thereby leaving the town without an almotacel. A juiz ordinário who was a planter might refuse to leave his estate for any reason during the harvest. A juiz pedâneo might also be a wealthy militia captain whose word was law, not only in his tiny village, but in the whole region. It is probably reasonable to assume, however, that the status of these offices of petty justice was closely linked to that of the municipal councils, to which they were formally joined by their selection and function. And the consensus of students of Brazil's local regime is that municipal administration had reached the nadir of its effectiveness by the early nineteenth century.[21] Certainly there was little interest in resurrecting government by council in the

1820s, and the organic law of municipal councils, passed in 1828, dealt those institutions an administrative coup-de-grâce by stripping them of all their judicial functions—a measure that eliminated the appointive source of the juiz ordinário, juiz de vintena, and almotacel, though without actually abolishing the offices.[22]   Against this background of decay, the Juizado de Paz represented an attempt to revitalize local administration by salvaging the powers of three dying Portuguese institutions and joining them in the hands of a single more powerful magistrate. The relatively low incidence of conflict between the first justices of the peace and their as yet unabolished predecessors is a final indication that the new judges did not remove the traditional red and green staffs of justice from hands capable of much resistance.

With precedents such as these, associated both with abuse of power and ineffectuality, it is hardly surprising that the supporters of the justice of the peace always sought to minimize their institution's colonial heritage. And it is within this same context that we can most readily comprehend the central issue of the debates over the justice of the peace—whether the local institution should be strong or weak. The advocates of the popular magistracy saw it as the liberal institution *par excellence;* they viewed it as a political weapon and as a means of judicial improvement. For these reasons they wanted a strong justice of the peace and sought to avoid inconvenient comparisons with the remains of the old Portuguese system. Their opponents, on the other hand, delighted in such comparisons, which allowed them to use the liberals' anticolonial rhetoric against them by extending parts of it to support arguments for a weak justice of the peace. Pressed by the fact that their adversaries possessed the more consistent examples, the liberals made great efforts to repudiate the Portuguese precedents altogether. This forced them into lesser but still energetic attempts to identify their institution with foreign models. In the Chamber of Deputies, Deputy Bernardo Pereira de Vasconcelos tried to parry a proposal to limit the juiz de paz's powers by declaring, "The juizes de paz are neither juizes ordinários nor juizes vintenários, so let us have no more [talk] of the Philippine Ordinances." He went on to attack those who "propose to reduce them to the stature of juizes vintenários," and finally warned that the parish judges would not be respected or obeyed unless they were given the same powers they enjoyed in other countries.[23]

In its emphasis on small claims and conciliation, the Brazilian juiz de paz resembled the justice of the peace of revolutionary France,[24] and such foreign experiments were sometimes mentioned in the parliamentary debates. The early reformers shared the belief that foreign wisdom could be imported through good institutions of alien origin. But it was a shallow faith, for the deputies did not seem to know very much about how the justice of the peace functioned in the model countries. The Bahian Antônio Calmon du Pin e Almeida, a student of judicial institutions, ridiculed the ignorance of his colleagues and secured their attention for an extended description of the workings of justices of the peace in France, England, and the United States. Calmon's explanation made it clear that the law under consideration was not very closely modeled on that currently functioning in any of the three countries, and that much of the rhetoric about foreign models was little more than fancy labeling. His larger point, however, like that of Vasconcelos, was ultimately a contribution to the side that favored a strong local judge.[25]

In July 1827 the Chamber of Deputies sent to the Senate a justice of the peace bill much stronger than it seemed. Before the bill was sent up, Feijó expressed some revealing reservations. The civil and criminal powers of the new judge appeared to be fairly limited, he said, but the bill was so vague in its description of procedure and review that it was difficult to know whether the formal restrictions would be effective. As a result, concluded Feijó, the deceptive bill actually created a judge with no clear jurisdiction and therefore with considerable potential for arbitrary action and abuse of power.[26] Feijó's objections may help to explain why subsequent debates in the Senate did not touch on substantive matters. Perhaps the imprecision and apparent triviality of the parish judge's jurisdiction, so perceptively analyzed by Feijó, beguiled the senators into considering the bill a matter of minor import in comparison to the plans for higher courts being considered at the same time. The senators made short work of the bill, and their discussions resulted only in some minor amendments dealing principally with territorial divisions.[27] When the Senate version was returned to the Chamber of Deputies in August, the liberals put on a brief show of indignation over the amendments but nevertheless approved them all on the day they came up for discussion.[28] The emperor's approval followed, and the bill became law on October 15.

The fact that the institution could mean different things to different men is partially accountable for the widespread enthusiasm with which it was publicly received. The press in particular blared a fanfare of praise and publicity that surpassed all previous journalistic attempts to influence public opinion. The editors of Brazil's independent newspapers in the late 1820s were ideal candidates to lead public support of the justice of the peace. As we have seen, journalism was a new profession in Brazil, and those who exercised it tended to be the urban-raised sons of parents too poor or uninfluential to send their bright offspring to Coimbra for training in the traditional professions of law or medicine. Aggressiveness and persistence gained these youths an autodidact's education. Facility with words brought them into the precarious but stimulating world of journalism where they owned, peddled, and usually wrote every word of their newspapers. As the children of the middle and lower classes they were all too familiar with the way pettifoggery and magisterial corruption victimized their classes; as well-read men and polemicists they were the heirs of a centuries-old Portuguese tradition of magistrate-baiting; and as individuals they had reason to resent those of their generation whose wealth and position had won them a Coimbra education and the status of law and letters in Brazil, regardless of their stupidity or venality. The journalists were therefore natural enemies of the elitist royal magistracy, and they saw in the elective juiz de paz an inchoate meritocracy of the kind that men of their origins and talents would be sure to support.

The independent newspaper editors also had good reason to seek in the Juizado de Paz a means to contain the power of the emperor. Dom Pedro's waning commitment to freedom of the press was one of the most unsettling indications of the limits of his liberalism and guaranteed him a vocal editorial opposition. Moreover, members of the press supported the elective magistracy because they saw it as an institutional companion to the jury system, under which violations of the laws of press freedom had been tried in Brazil since 1822.[29] The press regarded jury trials with high approval, for under the new system it had proven almost impossible to obtain a conviction against a newspaper. The emperor's growing hostility to the jury system was thus correctly interpreted as further evidence of hostility to the free press. Brazil's outspoken editors had a personal stake in trial by jury that made them the one group in Brazilian society to support liberal judicial reforms because of practical experience of their benefits.

In the capital, newspapers with different points of view all saw something of their own in the justice of the peace. Luis Augusto May, the crusty oldtimer of Rio journalism whose consuming preoccupation since independence had been the creation of effective local government, wrote in his *Malagueta* that, "A strong juiz de paz is now our philosopher's stone."[30] *A Astréia,* a newspaper of pronounced nativist leanings, identified enemies of the Juizado de Paz as enemies of the nation, and prayed, "May the heavens give life and strength to this majestic tree for the happiness of all Brazilians."[31] The more aloof *Jornal do Comércio,* while sustaining a running defense of the government against its critics, emphasized the emperor's contribution by referring to the new institution as "the sweet and goodly fruit of our Constitution."[32]

If the elected magistrate's relative impact could be measured by the enthusiasm of the local press, however, it would seem that the institution had the greatest effect in the provinces. The Rio de Janeiro press, for all its lavish promotion of the Juizado de Paz, pales beside the papers that represented rural and provincial thought. *O Astro de Minas,* an ideological country-cousin of Rio's most influential liberal newspaper, *Aurora Fluminense,* filled its columns with news of the activities of specific justices of the peace, their elections, and considerations on the institution in general. For *O Astro,* the parish judge was the "most holy of institutions," and the paper hopefully chronicled the people's progress in "learning to love the new system." Juizes de paz were first elected in Minas Gerais in 1829, and a survey of the newspaper's columns in that year and 1830 shows an obsessive commitment to printing articles and correspondence related to the new officials.[33] The few truly local, small-circulation newspapers that remain from the period also support the conclusion that in all parts of Brazil the Juizado de Paz was from the first an institution of great practical impact at the local level. The newspaper of Cachoeira, Bahia, demonstrated in 1832 how completely these officials had preempted local administration and become the object of town newsmongering. One issue, probably typical, contained a few proclamations by juizes de paz, a schedule of hearing times for the judges of the town and neighboring parishes, an indignant accusation of malfeasance against a juiz de paz, and a defensive reply by an equally indignant magistrate.[34]

In addition to the flood of words printed on the subject in the periodical press, the institution gave birth to what amounted almost to a new genre for the embryonic Brazilian publishing industry—the informational tract. Public interest and the many questionable points of interpretation contained in the law created a demand for succinct summaries of the jurisdiction and duties of the judges. Lay magistrates needed plain-language guidance, and the people needed to understand the functioning of the new system. Guides and handbooks appeared almost overnight. Diogo Antônio Feijó and Bernardo Pereira de Vasconcelos were among the first to publish brief explanations of the law's provisions and give practical advice for carrying them out.[35] Such publications combined functional intent with inspirational tone. In addition to the inevitable exegesis of the juiz de paz law of 1827, most of them included sample forms of the documents a justice of the peace would be called upon to draw up. Some authors gave advice on techniques to use in conciliations or more specific directions for other eventualities. Vasconcelos emphasized the desirability of moderation by juizes de paz "so as not to make their authority hateful to the people." The handbooks were seldom complete without a florid introduction exhorting all judges and citizens to work together to regenerate the judicial system through the "blessed institution."[36]

The existence of these publications was in itself as significant as the sum of information they conveyed. Like the new institutions and the liberal press, they were part of the general reaction against the colonial past. In this case, the colonial rubric covered judicial exclusivism and what was considered, probably rightly, a conscious effort by Coimbra-trained professional judges to make the law as inaccessible as possible to the uninitiated. The liberal reformers wanted to attack this elitism by democratizing the legal structure: locally elected judges were one way; mass publicity and popularization were another.

It was the ambition of *Aurora Fluminense* at the time of the passage of the Procedural Code (1832), for instance, that all Brazilians be able to own an inexpensive compendium detailing how the system would function. Law and justice would enter the public domain, no longer to be found only in the "thick volumes unintelligible save to the chicanery artists of the courts." These "thick volumes," said *Aurora,* had been both biased and inaccurate. Moreover, their sale had constituted an exploitive branch of Portuguese commerce with Brazil.[37] No aspect of colonialism was spared.

The outpouring of publicity for the justice of the peace has been described in advance of the institution's formal structure because in Brazil public enthusiasm preceded understanding. As Feijó had warned, the administrative and judicial duties of the juizes de paz were subject to considerable doubt even after the first ones were elected. All commentators agreed that there were serious difficulties with the law; we have already seen some of the reasons why. This objective fact, plus changing circumstances, led almost immediately to plans for modifying the new judgeship. And, given the mixed motivations that lay behind the institution, it is not surprising that subsequent changes continued to run parallel to the evolving nature of the Brazilian state. An analysis of the development of the office of justice of the peace, however, must logically begin with a formal outline of the original law.

The main duty of the Brazilian justice of the peace, as the office was originally conceived, was to promote conciliations between the parties involved in potential lawsuits. Individuals planning to initiate litigation were to be summoned by the magistrate and made to argue their own cases in his presence. Lawyers and proxies were generally excluded from these hearings. Reason prevailing, an amicable solution of differences would be achieved. Although such conciliations could not be imposed upon the concerned parties, when mutually arrived at and formally drawn up they had force of law. The juiz de paz was also responsible for conciliating those involved in feuds, domestic quarrels, and community squabbles. Conflicts over local resources fell under the conciliatory jurisdiction of the magistrate: doubts about the use of private roads, river crossings, waters used in agriculture or mining, pastures, and fishing and hunting rights were first aired in his court, as were disputes over borders, dams, fences, and damages inflicted by slaves or domestic animals.[38] If conciliation failed and formal legal action was required to settle a dispute, the parish judge possessed jurisdiction in civil suits involving values of no more than 16 milreis.[39]

The town peacemaker also wore the hat of local constable and custodian by virtue of vague but potentially important police powers included in the law of 1827. When public gatherings presented a threat of disorder, it was the magistrate's obligation to disperse them; failing that, he possessed the right to call in the militia to restore order. When a crime was committed, the juiz de paz was charged with assembling the evidence (corpus delicti). He could enter other districts in pursuit of known criminals or arrest them when they entered his own district. The local magistrate could interrogate suspects and was responsible for passing likely suspects and the evidence of their crimes to the competent criminal magistrate. The enforcement of municipal regulations (*posturas*) rested on the juiz de paz, and the prevention and destruction of runaway slave communities (*quilombos*) was also specifically entrusted to him.[40]

Another responsibility of the juiz that was related to both his conciliatory and police obligations was that of community social reformer. Not only was the juiz de paz held responsible for the incarceration of the inebriated for the duration of their state, but when they sobered up it was his duty to correct their vice. The law specified that the judge should "oblige" vagrants and beggars to engage in honest work, while extracting pledges of good conduct (*termos de bem viver*) from habitual drunkards, rowdies, and scandalous prostitutes.[41]

Miscellaneous duties included the protection of public forests and the prevention of illegal timbering in private ones; notification of the provincial president when discoveries were made of useful animal, vegetable, or mineral resources; and division of the district into blocks (*quarteirões*) of no more than twenty-five families, designating a deputy in each one.[42]

It was a digressive piece of legislation that mixed the general with the specific, and the important with the insignificant. Throughout the history of the institution, for all its varied fortunes, the paradoxical image of the juiz de paz conveyed by this law remained: part respected and powerful magistrate, part yawning bumpkin; at one moment arbitrating important legal differences or commanding armed forces, the next running in drunks and lecturing whores. The law itself was vague about which image should more closely correspond to reality. Certainly it admitted a wide range of interpretation, for even where it seemed most trivial the law's apparently deliberate ambiguity might cloak sinister intent or unanticipated power: it was one thing for a judge to dirty his hands with vagrants, but what more might be said of the official who had the right to define the category? To oblige "vagrants" to work might add up to rehabilitation in one reckoning, but in another did it not simply describe the job of the labor broker?

The vastness of Brazil, the imprecision of the law, and the impossibility of uniform enforcement made the justice of the peace an institution of considerable internal variety. Country judges and city judges did things differently, and regional nuances added further complications. As the most important officials at the parish level the magistrates inevitably amassed ad hoc functions, and as elected representatives of local constituencies they often acquired illegal and semilegal functions that satisfied purely local needs. For these reasons a true picture of the imperial juiz de paz cannot be drawn from his official powers and duties alone. But an understanding of the official dynamics of the institution is nevertheless essential to understanding how and why in practice justices of the peace functioned as they did. The official attributes of the institution, and their alteration, are especially important to this study, for they reflect changing philosophical and practical approaches to the problems of municipal government, law and order, and imperial politics.

A number of government measures altered or increased the powers of the justice of the peace in the early years. Some of these measures anticipated future problems, such as the forward-looking measure of 1830 which gave the local magistrates jurisdiction over all labor contracts (*locação de serviços*).[43] As immigration and free labor became vital issues at about midcentury, this law began to take on great importance, but in the turbulent atmosphere of the 1830s more immediate concerns dominated the public mind.

In other cases, the official responsibilities of the institution changed gradually and naturally without government interference. The judge's changing role as conciliator provides a good example of a function that withered of its own accord. The juiz de paz as community conciliator, of course, was a concept adopted by the judicial meliorists to help speed justice and lessen the caseload by keeping the naturally litigious Brazilians from taking minor and easily resolved matters to court. In the first months of euphoria that followed the establishment of the parish magistracy there were frequent references to improved administration of justice because of high conciliation rates achieved by juizes de paz. The first year of the institution's existence in Minas Gerais saw *O Astro de Minas* praising individual judges for the large number of "friendly conciliations" reached in their parishes. In Rio, *Aurora Fluminense* reported in 1830 that in a single month the judge of the parish of São José had achieved nineteen conciliations, or some sixty percent of all the cases brought before him.[44] But after this early period one searches in vain for any reference to the judges' conciliatory function and its success or failure. To some degree this loss of interest is surely due to the stresses caused by the abdication of the emperor in 1831. The benign paternalism idealized in conciliation was too vague and philosophical to compete for attention with a dynastic crisis that threatened the very form of government.

Yet the office of justice of the peace never regained its prestige as conciliator, and the reason is to be found not on the national scene but in local politics, where the judgeship's conciliatory role proved incompatible with its elective character. As elected officials who owed their positions to one of two or more contending local parties, the magistrates usually lacked the moral authority of impartiality that was implicit in the concept of conciliation. Even if beholden to no one, as practical men who were magistrates only temporarily, they were not inclined to antagonize their neighbors gratuitously. Also, at least in theory, conciliation was a duty of the judge—not a power—and could not be forced on anyone.[45] Without penalty, prospective litigants could always refuse to be conciliated. For the same reason, conciliation was not a useful means of persecution—any judge had better ones available if he wished to use them. In almost any case brought before him, an active attempt at conciliation by the magistrate would probably gain him an unnecessary enemy. Too many conciliations would certainly put him on bad terms with members of the local courthouse crowd who made their living bleeding litigants. The solution found by most magistrates, then, was probably a passive one.[46] The documents certifying failed conciliations that are the cover sheets of the thousands of lawsuit proceedings that fill the country archives of Brazil must have been granted as a mere formality. Certainly the conditions conciliation was supposed to alleviate showed little improvement. Complaints of overloaded dockets and sluggish justice continued throughout the empire, and private violence was employed as frequently as ever as an expeditious means of problem solving.

One final evidence that conciliation proved ineffective may lie in the fact that there was never any statutory change in the law regarding this duty. In legislation as frequently contested as was that relating to the Juizado de Paz, only provisions which offended no one of substance were left untouched. In this case, uncontested longevity was a tribute to ineffectuality.

The other principal branch of the juiz de paz's civil authority was likewise uncontroversial and remained unchanged. By the law of 1827, the local magistrate received authority over civil suits involving values up to 16 milreis. A decree of 1833 raised the jurisdiction to 50 milreis, and in 1871, after a period of inflation, it was increased again to 100 milreis.[47] Since the judge's civil authority enveloped that of all previous local officials, there was some friction in the early years until the redundant offices and powers were eliminated. But once this was accomplished there was little conflict over the justice of the peace's civil jurisdiction. Neither the Procedural Code of 1832 nor the counter-reform of 1841 tampered with this attribute of the office, and no other legislation ever altered it seriously.

Other provisions of the justice of the peace law of 1827 that were not officially modified during the empire included the petty, the unenforceable, and the utterly uncontested. At no time during the nineteenth century was any law or decree made that would impair the judge's right and responsibility to jail drunks or unruly prostitutes. Similarly, no one openly opposed the prevention of runaway slave communities. That these duties were uncontroversial, however, should not imply that they were insignificant at the parish level. It took a carpenter's helper 63 days' labor in the Rio of 1838 to earn 50 milreis; drinking and prostitution were significant aspects of a community's social life;

fugitive slaves and their hidden communities were high on the list of popular worries. These strictly parochial aspects of the magistrate's duties, of course, also represented a large part of what the judicial reformers had wanted all along. But their effective performance was largely determined by interaction between an individual judge and his neighbors, not by statutory regulation. Once the original law had been passed, there was little the judicial meliorists could do to strengthen this side of the institution. Some legislation, like that which abolished the office of almotacel and confirmed its jurisdiction in the hands of the elected judge, could clear up conflicts between new and old officials, but ultimately the effectiveness of the judgeship in improving the administration of local justice depended upon factors outside the reformers' control. Conciliation had proved an unrealistic hope, but other aspects might not.

To some extent from the outset, however, and especially after 1831, Brazilian liberalism began to dissociate itself from this meliorist philosophy of reform. Instead, the liberals in government increasingly ignored judicial improvement as a criterion of institutional virtue, and began to apply modifications and extensions of the justice of the peace law to exclusively political ends. The influence of this political mentality upon the justice of the peace can perhaps be seen most clearly in those statutory changes which entrusted large election-time responsibilities to the parish judge. The regulatory law of municipal councils of 1828, for instance, designated the justice of the peace as the official charged with preparing lists of citizens qualified to vote in municipal elections. And the fragmentary body of instructions and legislation that passed for an electoral law in Brazil made the parish magistrate the presiding officer and head of the electoral board (*mesa eleitoral*) in all local elections.[48] These electoral powers had nothing to do with the administration of justice, but they greatly expanded the institution's political endowment and contributed to its increasing identification with the political rather than the meliorist wing of the reform movement.

Placing the parish judge in a position of electoral responsibility was a predictable-enough goal of Pedro I's opposition. After the emperor's abdication in 1831, however, the political perspective of these former oppositionists, now in government, broadened. No longer merely short-term wreckers and *provocateurs,* the liberals now found themselves responsible for building a political system of their own and at the same time maintaining effective social order; the regency government quickly identified these as the most urgent problems facing Brazil. It was to these ends that subsequent legislation radically altered the nature of the justice of the peace by increasing his criminal jurisdiction and police powers. After 1831, the justice of the peace and Brazilian liberalism began to move, together, in a distinctly new direction.

The trend toward expansion of criminal jurisdiction first became especially

pronounced after the emperor's abdication. The consternation and political
upheaval caused by that event brought to the forefront the juizes de paz with
their power to break up gatherings and their intimate knowledge of neighborhood affairs. In Rio de Janeiro, at least, the magistrates played a prominent
role, personifying the popular pressure on the emperor. Two days before the
abdication, a delegation of parish magistrates demanded, in the name of the
people, ministerial changes of the harassed Dom Pedro.[49] The French painter
Jean-Baptiste Debret was absorbed enough in the drama to depict the formal
abdication in a drawing that showed the mounted justices of the peace of Rio
assembled before the crowds to salute the child, Pedro II, in whose favor the
first emperor had stepped down.[50] As minister of justice after 1831, Diogo
Antônio Feijó extended the local judges' police powers, and, especially in areas
where there had been disturbances, the magistrates absorbed the new responsibilities naturally.[51] In the capital the parish judge emerged from the crisis
with greatly enhanced powers, prestige, and political commitment.[52]

The 1832 Code of Criminal Procedure completed this expansion of the justice of the peace's criminal jurisdiction. The Procedural Code, as it was usually
called, was the fullest expression of judicial philosophy produced in the liberal
decade, and in greatly expanding the powers of the juiz de paz it was in part a
reaffirmation of liberal commitment to independent local justice.[53] In effect,
however, the Procedural Code signaled a very basic shift in the administrative
emphasis of the parish institution. The original law of 1827 had created a
magistrate of primarily conciliatory and civil jurisdiction who nevertheless carried a certain coercive potential to mobilize local resistance to an absolutist
threat. The Procedural Code reversed the order of precedence, deemphasizing
the civil jurisdiction of the justice of the peace in favor of his criminal and
police powers. After 1832 the juiz de paz possessed authority to arrest wanted
criminals in his or any other jurisdiction and to judge crimes for which the
maximum penalty did not exceed a fine of 100 milreis ($77) and six months in
jail. More important, the Code gave the magistrate responsibility not only for
assembling evidence but also for determining cause for arraignment, arrest, and
the bringing of charges (*formação de culpa*) in all criminal proceedings. As the
official responsible for bringing formal criminal charges, the parish judge stood
at the base of the entire system of criminal justice. Even in cases that exceeded
his own jurisdiction his role was crucial, for in drawing up the formação de culpa, he was responsible for organizing and presenting the evidence by which a
higher magistrate or jury would try the case.[54]

Other official or semiofficial duties complemented the new powers granted
by the Procedural Code, for to some extent the elected magistrate had become
a policeman even before the Code was passed. We have seen how the parish
judge gained some constabulary powers of an ad hoc nature in order to deal

with political conflicts and riots after the abdication of the emperor. These powers tended to become institutionalized with time because they suited the liberals and because the empire possessed no organized police force to contest them. But other powers had also been vested in the first justices of the peace that would facilitate their ability to exercise a measure of social and political control over the populations of their parishes. Chief among these were duties related to local statistics. Although no such responsibility was explicit in the law of 1827, the magistrate's intimate contact with his community soon made him master of human statistics, while his role as clearing house for rumor and gossip kept him up-to-date on newcomers, foreigners, and drifters. In the act of breaking his district up into blocks and naming inspectors for them, a judge was obliged to have considerable knowledge of the geography and residential patterns of his parish. And in preparing lists of those qualified to vote in primary local elections he was required to know something of the amount and nature of his neighbors' incomes.

Not all justices of the peace were as zealous as the one in Feira de Santana, Bahia, who in 1843 was keeping a civil registry of births and deaths in his parish and succeeded in having a municipal regulation passed requiring all citizens to register in his book.[55] But provincial and national authorities did expect the juizes to elaborate local censuses upon request. The chief of police of Rio de Janeiro conducted local censuses of the city through the parish judges in 1834 and again in 1838.[56] The provincial president of Rio did the same thing province-wide in 1840.[57]

The passion of educated Brazilians for empirical study of their country in the early nineteenth century caused a proliferation of schemes designed to improve government by collecting exact statistics. In every case the juizes de paz were designated to be the local operatives of such plans. Some of the schemes were elaborate indeed, and all of them were conceived as instruments of social management. O Astro de Minas recommended in 1835 a law that would force the justice of the peace to begin each year by carrying out a census of the inhabitants of his district. The count would include information on "sex, age, parents, birthplace, occupation, marital status, health, possessions, income, etc." O Astro saw such a census, not only as a means of ascertaining population figures, but also to measure "the moral level of the people."[58]

In practice, the average justice of the peace was very remiss about supplying formal statistics. And as such counts came to be increasingly identified with taxes and conscription in the later 1830s, most people also found it expedient to dodge them if possible. Whatever the motives of a provincial president in ordering a statistical survey, the parish judge and his constituency usually had locally valid reasons for falsifying it.[59] The point, however, is not the local judges' inefficiency as official information gatherers, but the universal and correct assumption that they possessed such information, essential to the performance of police and criminal duties. Based upon this assumption, the Ministry of Justice made frequent requests for local magistrates to carry out surveys or licensing schemes whose objectives were ultimately disciplinary. Bahian judges in 1829 were instructed to identify and issue passports to all free blacks in their districts; in 1832 juizes in Minas were to do a complete survey of their districts with the aim of identifying and prosecuting all vagrants; Rio's magistrates were to gather political intelligence on all foreigners in their parishes in 1833.[60]

Even more than the original justice of the peace law these modifications brought by the Procedural Code reflected the political stresses of the day. In the aftermath of the emperor's abdication, Brazilian liberals feared both a restoration attempt and internal agitation by Portuguese loyalists. By further strengthening the hand of local authorities, it was hoped, serious consequences might be avoided. Furthermore, the weaknesses of the new regency government underscored the lack of government authority or effective control outside the provincial capitals.and large cities. The situation called for an urgent remedy, which could not be provided by creating a new intermediate authority. The justice of the peace already existed and in many cases had even accumulated unofficial powers similar to those proposed in the Procedural Code. Then too, the judges' performance at the time of abdication had earned them a reputation for liberalism in the capital, confirming the reformers' belief in the link between elective recruitment and political orthodoxy. Liberals had only to extend their faith in elective justice to include elective police, and the constabularization of the Juizado de Paz seemed a logical step. And yet the reformers still had no real control over the institution. The central government's right to suspend justices of the peace was confirmed in 1831, but it cannot be argued that this made the local judges "police agents of the government" after that date.[61] This may have been what the liberal government desired, but in fact the elected magistrates continued to enjoy nearly complete de facto autonomy. Magistrates suspended by the Ministry of Justice were seldom convicted of wrongdoing by the local juries that they themselves had helped to choose.[62] And, of course, after the passage of the Procedural Code the juiz de paz had a near monopoly on local enforcement of government orders, a fact which made government suspension an empty threat. After the early years the Ministry of Justice seldom even bothered to use this statutory control over the parish magistrates.[63] By 1832, then, the justice of the peace had evolved into an institution of portentous internal contradiction: an elected official with virtually unlimited official powers at the local level but essentially uncontrollable by the government which created him.

The liberals' extraordinary faith in the loyalty and fairness of elected authorities did not prove to be justified in many cases. Eventually the question of reasserting control over the parish judges grew into a major political issue. The conservative reaction which set in on the heels of the Procedural Code was relentless in this regard. Finally in 1841 the Conservative Party succeeded in reforming the discredited Procedural Code—taking most criminal and police powers (and especially the responsibility for drawing up criminal charges) out of the hands of the justice of the peace and giving them to government-appointed officials.[64]   These changes, generally seen as part of a reversal of ideals, are discussed at length in Part III.

Yet the institutional development outlined here already suggests the inadequacy of an analysis couched only in terms of ideals, for very practical forces shaped the juiz de paz's institutional growth from the outset. True, liberal ideals and a strong current of disinterested judicial reformism had figured importantly in the development of the elected judgeship. Conciliations would streamline the court system; citizen judges would demystify and break the strength of the professional magistracy; locally elected officials would comprehend local needs and conditions. But it is equally true that in cumulative fashion the original regulatory law, the Procedural Code, and intervening legislation also reflected persistent efforts to use the magistrate for more or less ephemeral political ends. An elected judgeship would weaken one of the emperor's most traditional sources of authority; an independent but presumably liberal magistrate would mobilize opposition to an absolutist threat; a police officer would keep his watchful eye on social unrest and political subversion. For a time these twin forces found a common conceptual ground in the justice of the peace's "independence." But the ideals of judicial independence meshed with the dual goals of the liberals only as long as they were in the opposition. After they came to power in 1831 and expanded the judge's criminal and police-related powers to deal with immediate political and social problems, the liberals discovered that "independence" might better be translated as "irresponsibility" where their crucial political interests were concerned. The peculiar institutional development of the justice of the peace had at last laid bare the ultimate jurisdictional conflict of the Brazilian empire—one not specifically contemplated in 1827—that of private versus public power. With the identification of this problem in the early 1830s, the distance between Brazilian liberalism and conservatism begins to close.

The internal contradictions of the juiz de paz gave heightened importance to the judge's unofficial personality. The institution's formal aspect, while necessary to an understanding of the way in which the Juizado de Paz developed, provides only the sketchiest outline of the local and informal importance of the elected magistrate. In his parish, the justice of the peace was a flesh-and-blood personality whose powers were defined as much by individual and community pressures as by statutes and decrees. Moreover, because he was such a central figure and such a creature of his milieu, to describe the imperial juiz de paz is, in great measure, to describe the political and social life of the Brazilian parish community. Such a description would be valuable in itself; local life in imperial Brazil is not well understood. But it is especially appropriate in the present context to seek some understanding of the Brazilian grass roots by examining the performance of the justice of the peace, for that is what Brazilian politicians, thinkers, and lawmakers did in the 1830s.

5. Judicial Personnel: The Justice of the Peace

The institution which the liberals fashioned from a mixture of ideals and pragmatism in Rio de Janeiro took shape in the Brazilian parish (*freguesia*) as an individual citizen-judge with ideals, interests, and a personal identity of his own. Soon complaints about the institution began to focus narrowly and often with personalistic virulence on the shortcomings of individual judges. More abstract charges showed a related concern with the broader problem of popular recruitment. A standard critique in this vein emphasized the alleged inability of untrained laymen to understand the law or of private citizens to devote enough time to their judicial duties. As the veneer of liberalism and the election of officials began to wear thin, many critics noted that the juizes were, after all, men with other professions and interests which they could not be expected to sacrifice for the sake of spending a year as model magistrate. Such commentators suggested that professional magistrates would be better suited to exercise the complicated powers held by the lay judges. The accumulation of these and less charitable observations led in short order to a reversal of the liberals' positive stereotype: by the later 1830s the elected magistrates were increasingly depicted as uniformly incompetent and corrupt. All justifications of this negative stereotype recognized the recruitment of judicial personnel as a central problem but never systematically explored the questions that interest us here: Just who were the justices of the peace? What sort of men were actually elected to administer justice to their neighbors? How faithfully did the chosen men reflect the political and socioeconomic forces that created Brazilian liberalism? And finally, how did the novelty of democratic recruitment fit the traditional structures of established Brazilian society?

These questions are not easy ones to answer. Since the justice of the peace, as a local institution, was responsive to local circumstances, its character varied with changes in place and time. The following discussion attempts to recognize this variety by including data on magistrates who acted in the capitals of the provinces of Bahia and Rio de Janeiro, and on their counterparts in the rural interiors of those provinces. A second difficulty is the absence of even the most fundamental data required to identify the early judges. After the year of their installation there are no comprehensive lists of the justices of the peace of the capitals of Rio and Bahia until 1844, and no such lists exist in any year before 1847 for the parishes of the interior.[1] For the purposes of this study, fairly complete compilations of names have been assembled from signatures and textual references contained in official correspondence—a technique which skews the sample in favor of the most active judges and includes those *suplentes,* or alternates, who actually occupied the judgeship.

Only occasionally does the magistrates' official correspondence give a clue to their private occupations and local status. Biographical data on the local judges are scarce, save in the exceptional cases of individuals who went on to achieve national or at least provincial political prominence. More than nominal identification of these local officials finally depends on the distillation of data picked out of local notarial records, wills, and inventories. An attempt at this has been made in the cases of the capital of Bahia and the rural township (*município*) of Cachoeira in the Recôncavo, a sugar-producing area on the shores of the Bay of All Saints. A certain percentage of judges remain unidentifiable, though in itself the absence of information in such local sources suggests some conclusions about the individuals for whom we have only a name. The available facts and the educated guess justify a number of preliminary generalizations.

The typical justice of the peace of the liberal decade was neither the philosopher-king heralded by the institution's most vigorous supporters nor the shifty ne'er-do-well of the detractors. He was usually not the wealthiest and certainly not the poorest citizen of his parish community. In cities and towns where merchants, professionals, master-craftsmen, and the like made up something resembling a middle class, the juiz usually came from among its members. Urban judges were usually prominent enough to be familiar to most voters but not so established as to be without aspiration to higher social prestige. As a group the urban magistrates were characterized by youth and ambition—they were the kind of upwardly mobile, transitional individuals who personified Brazilian liberalism. In rural areas with reduced "middle sector," the judges came from among the landowning families that saw in the parish judge a valuable official extension of their own local ambitions. Extended families maneuvered their younger members into elective office, while newcomers and sons-in-law also sought the official consecration and practical facilities of judgeship. The burdens of the office and its electoral nature may have made it less than attractive to the cream of the elite. On the other hand, the judge's powers and prerogatives could not be regarded with indifference and appear to have been disputed especially by youthful, rising elements among the socially privileged.

Both in the cities and the countryside, lay judicial personnel tended to combine the dynamism of transitional groups with the values of a traditional elite.

Bahia

For the purpose of constructing social profiles of Bahia's urban justices of the peace, two of the largest and most populous parishes of the Bahian capital have been singled out. In the larger of the two, the centrally located Freguesia da Sé, ten different men occupied the post of juiz de paz in the ten years between 1828 and 1838. Research in local records and more traditional sources revealed relevant social and economic information in five of these ten cases. Two magistrates of the Sé achieved high political distinctions in their lifetimes, and information on them is therefore available in published biographical sources. The others were locally prominent men, but their economic profiles can be reconstructed only from records of local transactions. The second city parish is that of Santo Antônio Além do Carmo, a large freguesia which included the urbanized northern portions of the capital. Of the eleven men who served as parish judge in Santo Antônio between 1828 and 1838, six can be positively identified (see table 2).

Table 2.

Occupations of Early Justices of the Peace of Salvador, Bahia, 1828-1836

Freguesia da Sé

1828: João Ladislau de Figueiredo e Melo	apothecary/suburban landowner
João Gonçalves Cezimbra	merchant/distillery owner
1831: Francisco Gonçalves Martins	sugar mill owner/professional judge
1832: José Mendes da Costa Coelho	lawyer/merchant
1835: Caetano Vicente de Almeida	
Galião	suburban landowner/merchant (?)

Santo Antônio Além do Carmo

1828: Pedro Rodrigues Bandeira	merchant/sugar mill owner
Justino Nunes de Sento Sé	suburban landowner
1831: José Jorge dos Santos	sugar storage (*trapiche*)
Lázaro José Jambeiro	officeholder/suburban landowner
1832: Lázaro José Jambeiro	officeholder/suburban landowner
1834: Lázaro José Jambeiro	officeholder/suburban landowner
1836: José Pedro de Souza Alcamim	merchant/suburban landowner
João Batista Viana	merchant/suburban landowner

The most individually prominent citizens ever elected to the office of juiz de paz in the Bahian capital were those chosen in the first elections, held in 1828.

Enthusiasim for the new institution and the tendency to vote for the most visible citizens combined to elect some members of Bahia's highest socioeconomic and political elite in the first years. The outstanding example of this phenomenon was the election of Pedro Rodrigues Bandeira as the first justice of the peace of Santo Antônio Além do Carmo. Bandeira has been described as one of the wealthiest men of his day in Brazil—his financial position in Bahia was probably unrivaled.[2] He administered a fortune made in commerce, shipping, and the slave trade and invested in at least half a dozen sugar mills in the Recôncavo and numerous cattle ranches in the interior.[3] Bandeira was not active as local magistrate; he probably avoided service altogether by alleging precarious health and passing the post to his alternate. His very election, however, is eloquent testimony to the early prestige of the new institution.

Another member of the Bahian elite was elected to serve as alternate in the Freguesia da Sé in 1828. João Gonçalves Cezimbra, 48, was one of the province's outstanding businessmen, and his economic stature was complemented by political ambitions. Cezimbra was elected to the municipal council in 1829,[4] but refused the post in order to serve as provincial vice-president in the early 1830s. Twice, for short periods in 1830 and 1831, he was acting president of the province. Elected to the national Chamber of Deputies for the 1834-1837 session, he served for only two years before returning to Bahia to devote himself full time to his rum distilleries and business interests.[5] In 1840 he became the first president of Bahia's newly formed Commercial Association, and his business partner and son-in-law, Antônio Plácido da Rocha, succeeded him as head of that organization in the following year.[6] Cezimbra, in partnership with his son and son-in-law, owned the commercial house of Cezimbra e Filhos in the capital. Esteemed as he certainly was in Bahia, his business was not exempt from hardship. In 1839 the partnership was forced to mortgage all its assets in order to borrow the large sum of 20,000 milreis in working capital from a local convent, and three years later Cezimbra e Filhos was unable to pay its dues to the Commercial Association.[7] It is unclear whether, as alternate, Cezimbra ever actually exercised the post of parish judge in the Frequesia da Sé, but it is again significant that a man of his position and political drive should have been elected to the new office in 1828.

Another judge of high status was elected in the Frequesia da Sé in 1831. Unlike Cezimbra and Bandeira, however, Francisco Gonçalves Martins is known to have actively exercised the post, and apparently he derived personal benefits from it as well. In this he seems a figure of transition between the first semi-ceremonial elite officeholders like Bandeira and the more modest and active judges of later years. Gonçalves Martins was just twenty-four years old in 1831 and on the verge of a truly exceptional public career in imperial politics. Born to a mill-owning family in the traditional sugar município of Santo Amaro, he had been destined by his wealthy father for a career in the magistracy. Gonçalves Martins returned to Brazil with his Coimbra law degree in 1830, dabbled in journalism, made political contacts, and was elected justice of the peace while waiting for his first appointment as crown magistrate. In 1833 he was elected to the Bahian municipal council;[8] in the same year he received imperial appointment to the coveted post of district judge (*juiz de direito*) of the Bahian capital. Two years later he became the provincial chief of police. Elected as an alternate to the legislature of 1834-1837, he served in the place of João Gonçalves Cezimbra for the last two years of his term, and from then until he was made senator in 1850 he was never without a seat on the Bahian delegation in the Chamber of Deputies. He was twice president of his province and until his death in 1872 was Conservative Party leader in Bahia. As a magistrate he rose to the High Court position of desembargador.[9]

It is not likely that Gonçalves Martins viewed his term as justice of the peace as the beginning of his judicial career. But neither is it credible that a youth of his background and ambitions would seek election to an office he regarded as beneath him. Probably in 1831 the politically-oriented Gonçalves Martins wanted visibility in the important Freguesia da Sé. The direct political leverage of the judgeship might also have been attractive: 1831 was the year of the creation of the National Guard in Brazil, and parish magistrates presided over both the preparation of lists of those qualified to serve and the controversial elections of officers. A clever judge could easily parlay these powers into political currency, and it does not seem that Gonçalves Martins missed his chance.

Gonçalves Martins' family connections and education were certainly more important to his subsequent success than his early election as parish judge in Bahia. The typical urban juiz de paz, however, came from more humble stock, for which election as judge could represent a direct step toward the realization of social and financial ambitions. Most of Bahia's magistrates came from a middle level of men with some access to capital through commercial, professional, or family resources. A striking number invested in urban real estate and suburban farm lands. Perhaps as much out of thirst for traditional social prestige as for financial gain, they often acquired sugar lands near the city. Although not unquestioned members of the elite, they possessed the aspirations of the upwardly mobile and found in the elected judgeship an accessible slot in the traditionally exclusivistic judicial and administrative complex. For these city dwellers the local magistracy must have seemed attractive because it conferred the prestige as well as the practical benefits of official power.

The first justice of the peace of the Freguesia da Sé fits neatly into this general pattern of socioeconomic status. The apothecary João Ladislau de Figueiredo e Melo owned a pharmacy (*botica*) adjoining the centrally located Santa Casa da Misericórdia and was probably one of the best-known residents of the parish. In the same year that he became magistrate of the Frequesia da Sé, he was also elected overwhelmingly to the provincial council.[10]   João Ladislau could also be technically considered a *senhor de engenho* (sugar-mill owner), but socially and economically he was far removed from the great potentates of the sugar lands of the Recôncavo. His single sugar mill was situated in the parish of Brotas, well to the east of the city in an area given over primarily to farms (*roças*) on which foodstuffs—especially manioc and fruit—were cultivated for consumption in the city. A sugar mill was something of a rarity in this part of Bahia, and João Ladislau's was probably a small one. The juiz de paz also owned at least one attached cane farm, and appears to have owned roça lands in the adjoining district of Cabula as well.[11]   His suburban holdings most likely represented the investment of overflow from his professional career, and, in fact, this sort of modest diversification seems to constitute an identifiable economic pattern among men of João Ladislau's social station in early nineteenth-century Bahia. The 1830s in particular appear to have been years of intense but relatively low-cost land development to the east of the city. A road was opened into the area shortly after independence, and growing urban demand evidently added to the rapid valorization of farm lands in Cabula and Brotas. Then, in 1827, the lifting of restrictions on sugar-mill construction led to the building of numerous small mills in the same area. Most of these farms and mills were owned as a sideline by men like João Ladislau for whom land in the Recôncavo had long been inaccessible.[12]

Another professional with investments in real estate succeeded Francisco Gonçalves Martins as parish judge of the Sé in 1832 and served again in 1835. Though certainly not in a class with Gonçalves Martins, José Mendes da Costa Coelho does appear to have been financially comfortable. A lawyer by profession, Costa Coelho borrowed the moderately large sum of 3,200 milreis in 1834 against a four-story building he owned in the commercial district of Bahia. The loan was to be paid off in four years, but Costa Coelho did so in only one, liquidating the debt in the same year that he served as parish judge.[13]   The ownership of such a large building in the lower city is all but a certain indication that Costa Coelho's law practice was supplemented by an involvement in commerce. Costa Coelho also was evidently one of the men sought by Gonçalves Martins as political allies in 1831. In the following year, juiz de paz Costa Coelho presided over his ubiquitous young predecessor's election as lieutenant colonel of the all-important First Battalion of the National Guard, responsible for maintaining order in the central city.[14]

The last justice of the peace of our sample for the Freguesia da Sé, Caetano Vicente de Almeida Galião, served in that parish's second district in 1835. Economically he can be grouped with the first magistrate of the Sé, João Ladislau de Figueiredo e Melo. He too owned a small suburban sugar mill and farm land in Brotas but resided in the city. Like the apothecary, he appears to have held the land more as an investment than as a means of livelihood, and it is probable that his primary occupation was commerce. Clearly he was speculating when he bought a small sugar mill northeast of the city for 12,000 milreis in 1839 and sold it three years later for 16,000 milreis in cash and in land. The land he acquired in this transaction was a truly large farm in the district of Brotas, val-valued at 9,000 milreis.[15]

By 1835, when Galião became justice of the peace, the novelty had worn off the office and the institution had gained a routine and character of its own. Galião identified some features of the transformation in a letter outlining his own reasons for accepting election in spite of bad health: "with the intention of showing my gratitude for the consideration of my voters, and of proving that this job was not created for the persecution of the people, as is widely said." Yet this well-meaning citizen who wished to vindicate a liberal institution was shocked at the obstacles that faced him as judge. He informed the provincial president in a dismayed tone that "in this city there are certain 'privileged' streets into which [the juiz de paz's] police patrols are not allowed to enter."[16] This is not the place to discuss these aspects of the operating judgeship, but because the persecutions and privileges were the work of the magistrates themselves, we can read Galião's complaint as a clue to the type of personnel who were now occupying the office. By the mid-1830s men like Galião could still see the ideal side of elective justice, but as an institution the Juizado de Paz had clearly made its compromise with a society that included many a darkened back street.

The remaining judges of Santo Antônio Além do Carmo closely fit the patterns of economic activity that we saw emerging among the magistrates of the Freguesia da Sé. The man elected to succeed Pedro Rodrigues Bandeira, Justino Nunes de Sento Sé, also appears to have been a member of a prosperous middle class with enough capital to invest in farm and sugar lands near the city. Sento Sé owned a sugar-cane farm in the Cabula area to the east of Bahia and in 1834 was building a mill on it. By the next year the mill was functioning and Sento Sé became a member of the suburban class of sugar-mill owners to which two of the magistrates of the Freguesia da Sé sample also belonged.[17] Like many of the first judges, Sento Sé interpreted his mandate in a willful and arrogant manner and his public refusal to obey an order of the provincial president earned him suspension in late 1828.[18] Nevertheless, he went on to serve on the municipal council from 1829 to 1832.[19]

One juiz de paz of the sample from Santo Antônio, Lázaro José Jambeiro, served in three different years: 1831, 1832, and 1834. Like many of his counterparts, Jambeiro was a respected urban professional with money to invest in land. As scribe of the Port Authority (Escrivão da Mesa Grande da Intendência da

Marinha), Jambeiro had held a high, lucrative position in the royal bureaucracy of Bahia since 1825. He was elected to the municipal council in 1829.[20] His first investment in real estate appears to have been the purchase of a farm near the city in the same year of his appointment as Escrivão da Mesa Grande. Over the next fifteen years he bought, sold, and mortgaged other farms and a small sugar mill on the peninsula of Itapagipe, just north of the city. In his wheeling and dealing, Jambeiro overextended himself; when he died at an early age his estate was insufficient to cover a 3,000 milrei debt to his father.[21]

Another man who served as justice of the peace in 1831, José Jorge dos Santos, belonged to the same general social sector as Jambeiro but lacked his financial exuberance. Santos' family owned a *trapiche* or sugar warehouse and loading dock called Trapiche dos Coqueiros located on the Bay at Agua dos Meninos. Trapiche ownership and operation was almost always a family enterprise and could be quite profitable, but the Trapiche dos Coqueiros was evidently a small operation hard-pressed to compete with the four or five great sugar warehouses of Bahia. Santos also owned some town properties, but the family seems always to have been dangerously near financial ruin.[22]

The last two judges from the sample served in 1836 in the first and second districts of the recently divided parish of Santo Antônio.[23] Both were merchants. José Pedro de Souza Alcamim, justice of the peace of the first district, mortgaged urban real estate in 1832 in order to secure operating capital for what appears to have been a large retail business. He also owned a cane plantation in an unspecified location and repeatedly bought and sold farmlands of considerable size in Cabula throughout the 1830s.[24] Alcamim's counterpart in the second district, João Batista Viana, is almost a mirror image. He too used his urban properties as collateral for the operating capital his business required and invested overflow in farmlands just north of the city. Batista Viana seems to have been a more established merchant than some of the others who served as justice of the peace; as early as 1822 he owned commercial properties in the business district that included a three-story edifice with shops and warehouse space that sold for over 7,000 milreis. In the late 1830s, Batista Viana followed a pattern observable in many members of the urban merchant class by acquiring land—first a large farm, then a sugar mill in Bomfim da Mata ten leagues from the capital.[25]

Examples from other urban parishes tend to confirm the social and economic homogeneity of the parish judges of Bahia. The man most often justice of the peace in the capital, Francisco Eduardo Nunes do Reis, who served in São Pedro Velho parish for five years in the 1830s, owned a large retail dry goods business and acted as sugar commissary for mills in the Recôncavo.[26] In the parish of Pilar another warehouse owner was twice justice of the peace—André de Carvalho Câmara, owner of the great trapiche Quinta Prensa.[27] Men such as these were not among the most powerful or political men of the province, but it should be noted that their interests were often similar to, or even entwined with, those of Bahia's true social titans. The parish of Vitória, for example, was dominated utterly by the Cerqueira Lima clan, but a member of that elite family served only once as justice of the peace, and that, predictably, in the early year of 1831. More representative of the institution as it matured by the mid-1830s was another magistrate of the same parish, José Augusto Pereira dos Matos, who served in 1834 and 1838, owned a fair-sized distillery in his district, a third interest in farmlands east of the city, and was an intimate of the Cerqueira Lima household.[28]

Bahia's justices of the peace were usually men with the high visibility and large clienteles that made them natural candidates for elective posts: merchants, professionals, bureaucrats, an apothecary. Within their middling social group they were more or less well-off financially but too young or ambitious to hoard their capital. Anxious to diversify and with the nerve to speculate, they invested money in farmlands because in early nineteenth-century Bahia both cash-cropping and land speculation could yield big profits. The acquisition of land also constituted part of a more conservative process by which urban social climbers had long converted mere wealth into social currency. Although the profit motive was probably paramount and is certainly the more tangible, the frequency with which these magistrates bought or built modest sugar mills is suggestive of a continued aspiration to the supremely traditional title of senhor de engenho. Whatever his motives, serving as justice of the peace was one way for an ambitious man to enlarge his circle of influence and secure an advantage over neighbors beholden for the many favors at a judge's disposal. The dark corollary of this equation of course lay in the persecution that the judge could bring to bear upon a rival or enemy. Put in a general way, the men who served as justice of the peace in urban Bahia usually belonged to the socioeconomic sector for which the office could most easily act as an extension of private ambitions.

In the interior many of the same forces worked to determine what kind of men held the office of justice of the peace. At the same time, however, differences in the structure and values of rural society, together with the factor of distance from administrative centers, gave both the office and the men who held it special characteristics not typical of the urban judge. The importance of the magistrate's police and military powers, for instance, was always accentuated in the interior. Most rural magistrates bore high patents in the citizen militia or, after 1831, in the National Guard. The prevalence of justices of the peace who displayed their militia rank suggests a second relevant characteristic of rural society. Militia officers and judges—indeed, all local figures of authority—were chosen from the same preselected population, and the extent of their overlap is an indication of how very restricted that population was. It is an oversimplification to describe rural Brazil as a two-class society of masters and slaves, but latifundia, monoculture, and slave labor did limit the number and types of individuals who were likely to be entrusted with authority of any kind. As a result, we will not find the same occupational diversity as in the urban judges; nor can we speak of a "middle sector" in quite the same way.[29]

Given these differences and limitations, some similarities are readily observable between the judges of the capital and one man who held the post in the Recôncavo town of Cachoeira for four years from 1829 until 1832. Francisco Antônio Fernandes Pereira, like the great majority of Cachoeira officials, was born into the sugar culture as the son and brother of cane planters (*lavradores de cana*) who owned lands near Cachoeira. But Fernandes Pereira made his fortune in the town by engaging in the same kind of diversified and large-clientele enterprises that characterized justices of the peace in the Bahian capital. Fernandes Pereira was Cachoeira's largest tobacco buyer and most of the tobacco produced in the município entered his warehouses before being shipped to the great merchants of the capital. The justice of the peace owned rural property too—cane farms and other small holdings (*roças sítios*)—and when he died his real estate holdings in town comprised seven two-story buildings. He held the rank of captain in the militia, but it is appropriate that with his commercial connections the judge served the local regiment as quartermaster in charge of supply. Fitting another pattern of elected magistrates in small communities, Fernandes Pereira also operated a tavern in Cachoeira.[30]

Fernandes Pereira was ideally suited to serve as justice of the peace in his community. Probably no man knew the town and its people better than he, and the tobacco-buyer-cum-tavern-keeper was active as local judge—energetically guarding and extending his prerogatives through disputes with the juiz de fora, the town almotacels, and the commander of the militia battalion.[31] Any active magistrate earned resentments, however, especially in his own parish, and Fernandes Pereira was no exception—he was a notorious partisan of one of the local political factions, or *partidos*. As defender of the general interests of his fellow parishioners, on the other hand, he attracted the attention of the provincial government, who suspected him of protecting local counterfeiters from the vigilance of the juiz de fora.[32]

For the remainder of the 1830s, the office of justice of the peace of Cachoeira was dominated by a cabal which illustrates other characteristics of office-holding peculiar to the interior. The central figure in the cabal, Colonel Joaquim José Bacelar e Castro, was a member of the traditional sugar aristocracy of the Recôncavo. In 1833, when he was elected juiz de paz of Cachoeira, he had just achieved military distinction by occupying the nearby town of Feira de Santana on the occasion of a small "federalist" uprising that had begun in

Cachoeira and threatened to spread.[33]   As an active senhor de engenho he had no time for the judicial post but was reluctant to relinquish control over it. He therefore passed it on in succeeding years to what can be termed the "bureaucratic" arm of his extended family. Bacelar e Castro never sired any children of his own, but in marrying a widow he had gained a stepson trained in the law at Coimbra, João José Espínola. The young lawyer set up practice in Cachoeira and married into a local family. His wife's brother, João Xavier de Miranda, succeeded Bacelar e Castro as parish judge in 1834 and two years later served in Cachoeira's first district as well. In 1839, apparently in preparation for a bizarre maneuver designed to catapult the lawyer Espínola into the office of probate judge, the two brothers-in-law were each serving as justices of the peace —one of the first district and the other of the second district of Cachoeira.[34] Such mazes of influence were common in the interior, where the agricultural elite sought to reinforce its advantage by establishing official ties with administration, particularly through the magistracy.[35]

It should be remembered that Cachoeira was a town of some size which was affected by its rural surroundings but also exhibited characteristics found in the provincial capital. The historical stereotype of the justice of the peace, however, has been drawn almost exclusively from completely rural parishes, where the lack of social diversity lent a kind of inevitability to the men who held the official posts of authority. A key rural sugar parish with numerous mills located in it, for example, would almost unavoidably have a mill owner or member of his family as juiz de paz. The Cachoeira parish of Iguape, with its sixteen working mills in 1827, was typical in electing the owner of one of them, Manuel Ignácio de Lima, repeatedly in the 1830s and 1840s.[36]

The sort of family domination that we observed in the town of Cachoeira was even more prevalent in the outlying parishes. A report of attempted electoral fraud provides an example. In 1841 a messenger carrying a sealed ballot-box containing the votes of the parishioners of one of the districts of Santa Ana do Catú parish was laid up overnight in a nearby mill by a bad case of hemorrhoids. When he prepared to set out again the next morning he was confronted by a column of over fifty armed men, whom he suspected of planning to steal the ballot box. At the head of this unbidden escort rode the justices of the peace of the fourth and fifth districts and a major in the National Guard. Their names, respectively: Joaquim Gonçalves de Araújo Góes, Paulo de Araújo Góes, and Major Manuel Joaquim de Araújo Góes. The courier refused to go with this menacing force and wrote to the provincial president and the secretary of the Electoral Board requesting instructions. The next day the officials reappeared with more men and the justice of the peace of the third district as well, Paulino de Araújo Góes, but were apparently not willing to violate the mill where the messenger had taken asylum. Finally a subterfuge got the messenger and his ballot box to their destination intact.[37]

Another family-ruled parish in the Recôncavo was that of Outeiro Redondo in Cachoeira. The mill-owning Vieira Tosta family dominated that parish and elected three of the four justices of the peace chosen to serve there from 1844 until 1848.[38] There is every reason to believe that most previous juizes de paz likewise belonged to the Vieira Tosta clan. The administrative arm of this *engenho* family reached farther than most. One son who never served as parish judge, Manuel Vieira Tosta, took his law degree in São Paulo in 1831 and in 1833 was named judge for the judicial district of Cachoeira—a post he held until 1842.[39] Manuel Vieira Tosta's political and magisterial career took him far beyond the office of juiz de direito of Cachoeira, but the example illustrates the degree to which powerful families sought to strengthen and protect themselves by controlling the administration of justice in their areas. With a member of the family sitting as elected judge in their parish, and another as imperial judge of the entire judicial district, it is unlikely that the Vieira Tostas felt very threatened by anything short of acts of God.

Rio de Janeiro

The sheer size of urban Rio de Janeiro makes an accurate socioeconomic analysis of that city's judges unfeasible, but in general, what is true for Bahia seems to hold for Rio de Janeiro. The political roles of judges in the imperial capital were perhaps more visible, if only because the stakes were higher in crucial Rio. There, by virtue of the importance of their electoral duties, the parish magistrates were often prominent political leaders. In the early years, Rio's press sometimes reported elections for justices of the peace as important votes of confidence in the government, and the fall of at least one cabinet was predicted because of the election of hostile juizes de paz in the parochial elections.[40] This heightened political role also accounts for the existence of semiprofessional magistrates in Rio's large urban parishes—men who occupied the position year after year as a kind of ward boss.

The parishes of the interior of Rio de Janeiro province also show patterns of justice of the peace recruitment similar to those of Bahia. In marginal parishes and small settlements where no one was very rich, the office tended to fall into the hands of innkeepers or tavern owners.[41] In the coffee country of the Paraíba Valley, on the other hand, planter (*fazendeiro*) families usually dominated the Juizado de Paz.

The *Almanack Laemmert* of 1847 and 1848 clearly shows such a preponderance of coffee interests holding the office in the municípios of the Paraíba Valley.[42] The dominance of coffee planters was nearly total in the rural parishes, and town parishes showed only a few exceptions to the rule. Of the four justices of the peace elected to serve over a four-year period in the

Table 3.
Occupations of Paraíba Valley Justices of the Peace, 1846-1850

	coffee planter	"capitalist"	shop-keeper	inn-keeper	lawyer	priest	unknown
Piraí (town)	4*						
Arrozal	3						
Dores	3			1			1
Rezende (town)	2		1				
S. Vicente	4						
Campo Belo	3					1	
Santa Ana	4						1
Vassouras (town)	2	2					
Paty do Alferes	4						
Sacra Família	4						
Valença (town)	2						1
Santo Antônio	4						
S. João do Príncipe (town)	2		1				1
Rio Claro	3						
Passa Tres	4						
Barra Mansa (town)	3						
Espírito Santo	3				1		
	54 (82%)	2	2	1	1	1	4

Source: *Almanack Laemmert* (Rio de Janeiro, 1847-1848), pp. 38-44, 128-229.

* After 1832 justices of the peace were elected in sets of four once every four years in order to avoid over-frequent elections.

município of Vassouras, for example, those of the town parish included two categorized as "proprietors and capitalists" but whose families were linked directly to coffee interests and two who were classified simply as coffee planters. In the Vassouras rural parish of Paty do Alferes, all four magistrates were planters, and three of them were members of the same family. Likewise, the parish of Sacra Família had a full complement of four planter judges.

Of seventeen coffee parishes of the Paraíba Valley for which economic activity can be matched with holders of the office of justice of the peace between 1846 and 1850, 82 percent of those who served were positively identifiable as coffee planters. Of the remaining judges, 7 percent were unidentifiable, probably due to oversights and lacunae in the *Almanack*, and the rest included one innkeeper, two storekeepers, one priest, and one lawyer. The two categorized in Vassouras as "proprietors and capitalists" were almost certainly adopting a fashionable title whose grandiosity was meant only to proclaim their position at the pinnacle of the coffee elite.[43] Surely the real percentage of planter-judges was not less than 85 percent in the Paraíba Valley (see table 3).

These data about Rio's rural justices of the peace are limited and should be understood with qualifications. The very definition of the term *fazendeiro* can be placed in doubt, and the sources reveal nothing of the status of the planter-judge within this group of men who called themselves or were known as fazendeiros. Certainly we should be prepared to encounter considerable disparity of social status within the general category.[44] Other questions arise that cannot be answered by the recruitment data alone. How many of these judges actively carried out their duties? Were some mere figureheads or puppets created to represent local factions not mentioned in our sources? It may be that among the rural elite generational differences were as important a factor as occupational or status distinctions in the cities; the sources do not elucidate whether in Rio those most likely to hold the judicial post represented the youth and in-laws or the mature, established branches of planter families.

It does seem clear that the typical justice of the peace—whether rural or urban, from Bahia or Rio de Janeiro—was a man of substance in his parish. Although the data reveal certain differences between country and city judges, they more emphatically underline the broad prestige of the early Juizado de Paz and uniformly give the lie to the stereotyped caricature of the juiz de paz as a rustic half-wit. On the contrary, men of stature and ambition were chosen as magistrates in their communities. The result was an institution with a dimension of power and position that it could never have gained through statutory provisions alone. And yet, if this is so, what accounts for the negative stereotype? Why did Brazilian elites and emerging elites eventually fail in their support of an institution they dominated?

The answer to this question seems to lie in nuances of social structure that can only be inferred from the recruitment data we possess. The type of personnel elected posed no menace of fundamental social dislocations, but it does not necessarily follow that the institution was perfectly compatible with Brazilian social reality. It is also necessary to consider the finer question of whether the justices of the peace represented primarily "class" solidarity or intraclass rivalries. The data suggest that they probably represented both. Even a modest sugar planter or coffee grower doubtless shared with the true magnates of his category a basic set of social assumptions and instinct for class preservation. Urban professionals and merchants probably subscribed to the fundamental social beliefs of the status groups to which they aspired. And a more tangible pressure favoring solidarity came from below; it is significant that no reference has been discovered to the existence of a black justice of the peace. On the other hand, rivalries within the elite, however petty, were bound to find expression and extension in local elections, and there is overwhelming evidence that victorious factions regularly used their control of the judgeship to harass opponents and perpetuate rivalries within their general social stratum. The institution thus worked to undermine the very solidarity that it seems to express in terms of personnel.

Any explanation of this paradox must center on the mode of recruitment. Elections favored those who controlled the electorate, so the dominant social groups were served; well-to-do urban types were elected in the cities, and planters and mill owners were chosen in the countryside. Yet the elective recruitment process itself entailed potentially destructive social costs if elections led, as they often did, to violence, or if harnessed constituencies were armed and pitted against one another by ruling class factions whose local prestige was on the line. The elections unerringly returned prominent men and their lackeys, but tensions generated at election time were not likely to subside precisely because the social groups to which the juizes most commonly belonged assured the institution of the status-conscious and energetic personnel who would fully realize or even overstep its statutory potential. If, as much of the data suggest, the juizes were often elected from among the upwardly mobile men who formed the social base of Brazilian liberalism, then their driving use of the office may have been viewed with alarm by more established elite members who felt threatened by the newcomers. Indeed, ambitious and motivated judges often pushed their authority far beyond the boundaries of local harmony, and factional conflicts frequently became institutionalized around the office. In sum, the judges as a whole may well have represented the interests of dominant social groups, but within those groups their authority was almost always contentious. While the local institution might square with general class needs, the early enthusiasm for it soon soured under the attacks of local opponents who worried about the pernicious effects of elections or simply could not stomach individual officeholders. Such local opposition, combined with fierce institutional conflicts, swiftly converted the parish judge's world into one of near-perpetual conflict.

6. The World of the Justice of the Peace

The elective judgeship occupied an ambiguous position at the parish level that in some ways mirrored its internal contradictions as a nationally conceived instrument of reform. It is probably fair to say that no other innovation brought by independence had a comparable impact upon the way Brazilian neighbors dealt with their common affairs. But just as the liberals' early devotion to localism was quickly found to have serious drawbacks as national policy, so the consignment of local matters to private hands did not prove entirely satisfactory even at the local level. The new institution had an unsettling effect upon the communities it served, and it produced an expressive array of disruptions and opposition. Conflict seethed around the institution with an intensity that helps to explain the later conservative reaction, and in patterns that reveal certain structural features of life and power in small Brazilian communities. In the early history of the Brazilian state, public and private interests intersected in the justice of the peace.

The earliest conflicts faced by the justices of the peace were the natural consequences of their superimposition upon an existing and incompatible judicial structure. Such clear institutional conflicts as resulted from jurisdictional overlapping between the parish judge and his colonial predecessors, the juiz ordinário, juiz de vintena, and almotacel, however, were among the most easily resolved. As we have seen, the local offices were too weak to be capable of effective obstruction, and the immediate visibility of these disputes made them the objects of relatively speedy clarification. Such conflicts were typical only in the first months of the new judgeship's existence.[1]

Less easily managed were the inevitable clashes between the elected judges and the Coimbra-trained professional magistrates. The most conspicuous early antagonists among the professionals were logically the juizes de fora, the clarity of whose jurisdictions had been deliberately clouded by the creation of the new magistrates. No clear lines separated the jurisdictions of the two offices, and elective lay justice fundamentally challenged the corporate spirit and career aspirations that the juizes de fora absorbed along with their professional educations.[2]

In general, the regular administrative hierarchy sided with the professional magistrates in cases of institutional conflict. Provincial presidents in particular were inclined to favor the career judges. The presidents themselves were typically men with legal training and often had risen to their positions through the traditional magisterial hierarchy.[3] They therefore shared a certain corporate solidarity with practicing crown judges. The provincial president of Bahia in 1829 wrote to the minister of justice about a typical dispute between the juiz de fora and the justice of the peace of Santo Amaro. He admitted abuses of authority on the part of the juiz de fora but tried to portray the professional judge's behavior as justifiable given the provocations he had suffered from upstart local magistrates who "have interpreted the law of their creation in the broadest way possible, thinking themselves sovereign and independent. They have committed errors and whimsical iniquities like these that provoked [the crown judge] to exceed his jurisdiction."[4] Such incidents added to the strain already present in Brazil's overlapping jurisdictions, and contributed as well to defining a basic conflict of interests between professional and lay judicial personnel.

Provincial presidents also sided with professional judges because they believed the local magistrates to have essentially different administrative interests. The presidents and juizes de fora, after all, occupied somewhat analogous rungs on the administrative ladder. They represented public power. They regarded the elected and "independent" justices of the peace, on the other hand, as representatives of the private power of local interests.[5] Crown juizes de fora, for instance, were often assigned by provincial presidents to carry out specific administrative tasks in the interest of provincial governance. When this public interest did not coincide with particularistic local interests, conflict became inevitable and the crown judge's job was made more difficult. There was nothing new in this, except that in the 1830s local resistance usually formed (and with unprecedented effectiveness) around the elected magistrate. The frequency of conflicts of this sort quickly induced the professional administrative hierarchy to view the independence of the justice of the peace as something akin to "renegadism." In the first year of the new judges' existence, the provincial president of Bahia expressed such a concern to the ministry. The bad examples of some of the parish magistrates, he wrote, would surely cause others to "regard themselves as independent and with the right to define their jurisdiction as they see fit."[6]

An example of what the president feared occurred in Cachoeira, Bahia, in 1829. Cachoeira had by the first years of independence grown into a center of counterfeit coinage operations that continued to be a headache to the government until well into the 1830s.[7] In 1826 the provincial president sent an energetic juiz de fora to Cachoeira with instructions to break up the bogus coin industry. The crown judge, Antônio Vaz de Carvalho, met resistance from all quarters and gained numerous powerful enemies. Vaz de Carvalho maintained a precarious control of the situation only because his status as agent of the provincial government in a problem area gave him ready access to regular troops. These he used both for carrying out raids on counterfeiters and for stifling his critics. Resentment and opposition to the juiz de fora continued to increase, however, and it is probably not coincidental that his transfer was announced not long after the election of the first justices of the peace in Cachoeira. The news of Vaz de Carvalho's transfer touched off what was officially termed a riot, led by Cachoeira's juiz de paz Francisco Antônio Fernandes Pereira.[8] Those who were glad to see the departure of the "strong-willed and arbitrary" juiz de fora ran through the streets of town, set off fireworks, and rang the church bells long into the night. An effigy of Vaz de Carvalho was buried in the town square by torchlight, and the impromptu celebration concluded at the house of the justice of the peace who invited the participants in for "refreshments."[9]

The locally elected judges could do a great deal to harass and obstruct crown officials, although they found them to be formidable adversaries, possessing resources unavailable to the parish magistrates. While the justices of the peace had to rely on strictly local support, the appointed magistrates could mobilize allies in every branch and at virtually every level of imperial administration. Many higher judges, desembargadores and ouvidores, naturally agreed with the juizes de fora that the traditional prerogatives of the royal magistracy should not be jeopardized by nonprofessional officials, and the imperial government was permeated by members of the professional magistracy, the letrados. The interests of the administrative establishment were thus reinforced by the corporate interests of the professional magistracy. One symptom of this alliance was very effective letrado obstructionism from the outset.

Both in Rio de Janeiro and in Bahia, letrados and their allies in government were accused of delaying execution of the justice of the peace law, and then of trying to sabotage and discredit the institution once it was established. José Carlos Pereira de Almeida Torres charged in the Chamber of Deputies that when the regulatory law arrived in Bahia, in 1828, it was "murdered" by the authorities who allowed the elections to be held in such a way as to compromise their legality.[10] The following year, Lino Coutinho accused Bahian provincial officials of hostility toward the Juizado de Paz and gave examples of provincial presidents illegally "deposing" local judges with the connivance of the professional magistrates. The Bahian deputy also insinuated that a conscious attempt had been made to hold the new institution up to ridicule. When elections were held for justices of the peace in the município of Santo Amaro, Bahia, he said, confusing or misleading instructions sent from the capital led to the election of magistrates in every chaplaincy as well as in every parish. Since any rural agricultural establishment of any size had its own chapel, this meant that every sugar-mill complex in Santo Amaro elected its own juiz de paz. Lino Coutinho reckoned the resulting number of juizes in Santo Amaro at a ludicrous 300.[11]

In the imperial capital, where the election of the first justices of the peace was delayed until 1830, observers quickly singled out the letrados as those most responsible for depriving Rio of the benefits of elective justice. As early as 1828 vigorous protests in the Chamber of Deputies accused the government of toadying to the interests of the professional magistracy by postponing the elections for justices of the peace in the capital. When the emperor criticized the legislature in 1828 for failing to improve the administration of justice, deputies acknowledged the chaotic situation but blamed it on the fact that professional judges did not honor the existing laws. Lino Coutinho asked pointedly why the government had not yet forced the execution of the juiz de paz law in Rio and concluded that if the administration of justice had not improved it was because crown magistrates did not want it to.[12] Bernardo Pereira de Vasconcelos was even more specific. Repeatedly he baited the government and his letrado colleagues for foot-dragging in the matter of justices of the peace for Rio while the institution was already functioning in other provinces. If Rio still had no parish judges, said Vasconcelos, it was because the professional magistrates opposed the institution.[13]

Much of the press concurred in this analysis. *A Astréia* wrote in 1828 that "those who feel their supremacy diminished" by the elected judges were trying actively to discredit the institution by interfering with elections, "as if it were not enough that the [same] Srs. Magistrates, out of a misplaced corporate spirit, should have declared themselves congenital enemies of the paternal magistracy of the justice of the peace." This liberal sheet nevertheless predicted that no amount of interference could discredit an institution "already idolized by the people."[14] Luis Augusto May sized up the situation in much the same way but was not so optimistic about the outcome. "It is sad to see how [Rio's] affluent classes have been successfully turned against the institution of the justice of the peace. All the magistrates, with a very few exceptions, agreed to make war on this institution." The editor hinted at the collusion of interests between magistracy and administration: "so great was the pressure of the magistracy and the government [*ministério*] . . . that it was not until the end of the third year of the Legislature that the law . . . of the Juizes de Paz was passed." May then went on to describe the difficulties that lay ahead of the elected judges because of their powerful opponents in the government and professional judiciary.[15]

The acrimony of the debate had an effect on Brazilian political formation that overshadowed any mere jurisdictional conflict between the professional judges and the justices of the peace. By 1831, when the emperor abdicated, even the moderate reformists among the liberals had convinced themselves that most of the remaining letrados were extensions of the fallen government and therefore prone to treason. The letrados, for their part, had been pushed into an even more defensive and compact corporate spirit than before; many were about to stop calling themselves liberals. The parish magistracy was caught in the crossfire of this most portentous polarization in early Brazilian politics.

Another group connected to the Brazilian court system that viewed the justice of the peace with trepidation—though on a smaller scale—was the overgrown network of courthouse employees and hangers-on.[16] The liberal press and other supporters of the Juizado de Paz anticipated that the new institution with its powers of conciliation would choke off the livelihoods of pettifoggers and chicanery artists by resolving petty differences before they reached the litigation stage. In 1830 *Aurora Fluminense* claimed that in the short time they had been active, the justices of the peace had indeed "clipped the wings of chicanery" in spite of "incomparable effort being made by certain shyster lawyers . . . to discredit the new magistrates."[17] Nevertheless, the existence of legal parasites did not end with the creation of the juizes de paz. The value of the justice of the peace as a conciliator proved ephemeral, as pointed out earlier, and litigation continued to jam the courts throughout the empire. To judge by the unabated flow of complaints, the lawsuit mill continued to operate and flourish rather conspicuously, and the ambulance chaser and his retinue continued to be a familiar social complex.[18]

The whole array of bailiffs, shysters, and expediters persisted, but the *escrivão,* or legal secretary and scribe, displayed the most creative adaptation to the new institution. Because the local magistrates served for limited periods of time and frequently passed the position to alternates in order to tend to their own affairs,[19] the scribe assigned to the juiz assumed the great responsibility of maintaining continuity. After serving for years, it was often the scribe who instructed short-term elected judges in their duties and the procedures for carrying them out. Since he prepared the docket of the parish court, the scribe was able to delay judicial action or hasten it; as controller of all paperwork he was in a position to fabricate evidence or make it disappear. If the magistrate was involved in some lucrative but illegal activity connected to his official responsibilities, it was almost necessarily in partnership with his legal secretary.[20] Contrary to the hopes of the judicial reformers, the influence of these legal auxiliaries was transmitted intact from the old system to the new.

The creation of Juizado de Paz hardly gave reason to abandon the old refrain:

Quando vires um Juiz	Whenever you see a Judge
Muito unido ao escrivão	In cahoots with his scribe
Franze a testa; isso é sinal	You can bet that his justice
Que a justiça anda em leilão.[21]	Is the price of a bribe.

Many local institutions felt their prestige and prerogatives threatened by the justices of the peace, but it was the municipal councils that protested most regularly. The justice of the peace law of 1827, together with the law of municipal councils passed in the following year, left the traditional municipal governments of Brazil with no judicial powers and dependent for their income upon petty fines levied by the juiz de paz. Then the Additional Act of 1834 completed the humiliation of the local councils by subjecting all their regulations and expenditures to the approval of the provincial assemblies—reducing them to the level of one municipal council that felt it necessary to report to the Bahian assembly the purchase of four wood-screws needed to repair the bed of the circuit judge.[22]

In some places, to be sure, the councils and justices of the peace functioned in harmony. Justices of the peace and council members (*vereadores*) were elected at the same time and in the same way; they represented similar social classes and sometimes individuals would hold the two posts simultaneously or consecutively. The recruitment data for Salvador, Bahia, show a number of such cases.[23] But the collective body had no real control over the magistrates in its township and this was a bitter reversal. The juiz de paz was a living symbol of the municipal councils' decline into ineffectuality.

The councils were in fact so weakened by the laws of 1827 and 1828 that it is difficult to speak of clashes between them and the new magistrates over official powers—the councils were left with virtually none. The few administrative areas in which the Juizado de Paz and the municipal councils did have formal contact, however, were frequently the scenes of friction: a justice of the peace might refuse to enforce local regulations passed by the council, or a council could deny confirmation of the magistrates' choices for block inspector or scribe. But such petty hostilities were as often the symptom as the cause of bad relations between municipal councils and juizes de paz. More important, probably, was the question of who would retain the prestige—however symbolic or impotent in practice—of community guardian and advocate.

Especially in the turbulent early 1830s, justices of the peace assumed the municipal councils' traditional political (and rhetorical) functions to a surprising degree. The exaggerated protestations of loyalty and patriotism that the councils had produced in moments of crisis at the time of independence and before were supplanted in 1831 by the same kind of document penned by the justice of the peace: descriptions of speeches, proclamations, and paternalistic soothing of community tensions; fierce attacks on the ex-emperor and reassurances of local solidarity and adoration of the new ruler. The parish magistrate acquired almost overnight a political status that was physically depicted by the seating arrangement of the Thanksgiving Mass held in Rio in 1831 to celebrate the abdication of the emperor Pedro I. The city justices of the peace, decorated with "civic laurels," were seated just beneath the child-emperor and regents, along with the most favored senators, deputies, and generals. The members of the council were nowhere to be seen.[24] It became common for the elected magistrates rather than the council to relay news of political and economic problems to provincial authorities. Citizens with a grievance no longer took their petitions to the municipal council but preferred to secure the support of the justice of the peace and make their requests, through him, directly to higher authorities.[25] The elected judges, then, absorbed both the councils' official powers and the traditional unofficial ones—those of civic booster, proxy, and figurehead.

Only the humiliation of the kind of administrative living-death that the Juizado de Paz dealt the municipal councils can account for the levels of ferocity the institutions reached when they did collide. Seemingly, all of the many local protests lodged against justices of the peace were supported, if not led, by the local council, and vice-versa. In Cabo Frio one juiz de paz entertained the audience at one of his weekly hearings by referring to the councilmen as a "gang of jackasses," who were collectively good for nothing but drinking rum and laughing at each others' jokes.[26] And in Bahia, the council of Belmonte, after two of its members were physically assaulted by the parish judge, called him "the Caligula of our time" and reported that he kept a mulatto slave for the sole purpose of murdering personal enemies.[27]

Another local institution that existed in a near-permanent state of conflict with the Juizado de Paz was the militia, or, after 1831, the National Guard. Many justices of the peace also held posts of high rank in these civilian forces, but while serving as parish judges they were seldom able to avoid collisions with the active militia commanders. The "Second Line" (Milícias and Ordenanças), and later the National Guard, had their own hierarchy of rank, of course, but the citizen military was also nominally subordinate to the juiz de paz.[28] Moreover, after 1831 the judge held responsibility for qualifying men between twenty-one and sixty for service in the National Guard and for granting exemptions in the cases provided by law.[29] Disputes soon arose over this mixed authority. Juizes frequently complained that militia or National Guard units entered their parishes without permission, while the commanders of the units protested that no such permission was necessary. When parish judges arrested

National Guardsmen or officers, their superiors often contended that this violated some vaguely conceived military privilege (*foro militar*) that in fact did not exist in any de jure sense.[30]   In retaliation, National Guard commanders sometimes refused to furnish armed forces when the magistrates requested them, or even instructed their soldiers not to testify in local court hearings. In extreme cases it was not rare for particularly irascible officers to use force to obstruct the juiz de paz in his police or judicial duties.[31]

At first glance it would seem that in a power struggle between the two institutions, the decisive advantage would lie with the militia because of its number and military aspect. Yet to assume that the National Guard automatically monopolized local power through force of arms is to entertain a false premise. In fact, militia officers faced large and sometimes insurmountable difficulties both in recruiting and in equipping an effective force. One reason for this was the chronic shortage of arms even in the most critical areas. Militia requests to the government for firearms were constant but unattended, and the same pattern continued after the creation of the National Guard.[32]   A more important reason for Guard ineffectuality, however, was the prevalence of exemption from service. Although all male citizens with the low minimum property qualification were formally required to serve in the Guarda Nacional, a large number of these—professionals, students, teachers, foremen, for example—were exempt from active service and were usually placed in the reserve.[33] This made commanders dependent upon the relatively reduced population of small free farmers, artisans, and other interstitial economic types for legitimate active duty. Citizen soldiers of this class, moreover, were among those who could least afford to drop their labors whenever a superior officer called, and they were notoriously immune to the persuasions of civic and patriotic cant. To some degree, most commanders faced dilemmas similar to that of the Guard captain of Penha de Itapagipe parish in Bahia who could not police his district at night because all his guards were fishermen who were at sea between dusk and dawn.[34]

The rub between justices of the peace and the National Guard developed because the magistrate had several means of keeping a Guard commander's active force at a bare minimum. The most radical solution was adopted by those judges who simply refused to organize the National Guard in their districts. This was often easier than it might seem, for the National Guard law of 1831 itself shared some of the socially dysfunctional characteristics of other liberal legislation by its introduction of a democratic chain of command: officers were to be elected by majority vote of those qualified to serve as soldiers. The law thus conformed to the early liberals' antipower preferences by largely removing the militia from the government's patronage area, but in doing so it also displayed a fine disregard for the traditional analogy between social structure and military hierarchy. Local magistrates sometimes reacted strongly against the institution because it extended the principle of democratic recruitment too far. In this they only articulated officially the reluctance of all local elites to associate on an equal basis with clear social inferiors, since if a local potentate were not elected officer he would still be obliged to serve as a common soldier. The possibility of such an extreme social dislocation was a theoretical fear, never verified in practice, but it was a real fear nonetheless, and instrumental to judges who had no desire to see a strong competing force in their parishes. From the Bahian hinterland, one juiz de paz reported that he had not followed orders to create the National Guard in his district because he could not bear to see the "few good men mixed indiscriminately with the hundreds of bad men ... who are totally unacceptable and lack the moral qualities, color, and everything else that should be characteristics of such a respectable force."[35] A Rio judge wrote that election as officer conferred no prestige and that men of substance consequently poked fun at the new authorities.[36] Over and over again provincial governments reported that the National Guard was no more than a name in the interior.[37]

Where the Guard was organized, the justice of the peace still could trim its personnel through exemption. In the annual preparation of lists of those eligible to serve, a juiz might excuse from active duty his friends and employees and those of his cronies. Reluctant citizens could also secure exemption by suborning the judge. One observer in 1840 estimated that some four hundred individuals in urban Rio alone avoided service by making monthly payments to their juizes de paz.[38] There was certainly an economic advantage to be gained from being placed on the reserve list because active service in the Guard could take a man away from his livelihood for days at a time. Some Brazilians even went so far as to claim Portuguese citizenship (and automatic exemption), evidently believing that nativist persecution was a lesser evil than serving in the National Guard.[39]

The most common way a parish magistrate granted exemption from Guard service, and the one which generated the keenest resentments, was by naming block inspectors (*inspetores de quarteirão*). By law the magistrate had the right to divide his district into "blocks" of less than twenty-five families and to name a deputy in each one. Since the law stipulated no minimum population per block, there was theoretically nothing to prevent a judge from deputizing every male citizen in his parish, thus exempting them from the Guard. Although there is no conclusive evidence that juizes named more inspectors than the spirit of the law allowed, their numbers did vary widely even in parishes of comparable population.[40] And even if a judge named fewer than one per twenty-five families he might be making a sizable dent in the number of men most desirable for service. The scant information that is available on the block inspectors themselves also indicates that they were taken largely from the groups most eligible to serve in the National Guard. In 1836 the inspectors of the Freguesia da Sé (Bahia) were principally drawn from the city's petty middle class: clerks, book-keepers, small businessmen, one notary's assistant, and one musician. One-third of the total were classified as mixed bloods.[41] Even taking into consideration the social limitations imposed by the small authority of the block inspectors, they must have been chosen to some extent for their personal qualities. The post could be arduous and dangerous—above all it required a man whose stature and prestige among his neighbors gave him the presence necessary to command and arrest. Men like this were at a premium in the National Guard, and their exemption for service under the juiz de paz was demoralizing to the militiamen themselves and potentially threatening to their commanders.[42]

For whatever reason, there can be no doubt that the officers of the National Guard were especially irritable about the exemptions granted to block inspectors and that justices of the peace were especially jealous of their right to name individuals as inspectors. Conflicts over the issue were many, and most Na-tional Guard commanders seem to have shared the feelings of the commander of the battalion of Cachoeira who wrote to the provincial president in 1834 complaining of difficulties facing the National Guard "from which some of the civil . . . authorities exempt those individuals best able and qualified to serve by appointing them to unnecessary posts."[43] But when, in 1836, the Bahian provincial government recognized the seriousness of the situation by ordering an investigation of the office of block inspector in Bahia, most magistrates truc-ulently refused even to furnish lists of their inspectors, alleging that the pro-vincial government had no authority over their appointments.[44]

In spite of the difficulties that a guard commander could encounter in mus-tering an effective force, the stereotyped image of the Brazilian National Guard "*coronel*" riding at the head of formidable armed forces may not be entirely erroneous—at least in rural areas. In such cases, however, it seems that the irregular soldiers were only rarely legitimate members of the National Guard. More often a commander's individual power and prestige were more effective than his institutional rank in gathering armed followers taken from among his own dependents and the marginalia of Brazilian society: tenants, squatters, drifters, even fugitive criminals and hired guns.[45] Yet, even if threatened with such a force of irregulars, a justice of the peace had indirect means of contain-ing the military powers of a guard commander. One of the duties of the juiz was that of conscription—the feared and hated "*recrutamento*" by which troublemakers, vagrants, political enemies, and other "undesirable elements" could be captured and sent in chains to serve in the regular army or navy. Forced conscription was one of the most arbitrary and abused powers in the Brazilian empire, and it is certain that many juizes who dispatched "idlers, va-grants, and criminals" to their provincial capitals for conscription were consciously limiting their rivals' military capabilities by so doing.[46]

For the purpose of examining local power structures, conflicts are perhaps more illuminating than harmony—for one thing, they produce more documentation. But it should be noted that if two local institutions were usually mutually antagonistic, they could also combine forces. Indeed, many extra-institutional factors in Brazil's parishes could positively predispose justices of the peace and guard commanders (and others as well) to cooperate. Foremost among these factors were challenges to interests held in common by members of a single social stratum and to family administrative networks.

In rural parishes with very high slave populations, for instance, nothing produced institutional solidarity more quickly than the prospect of slave uprisings. In the Vassouras (Rio de Janeiro) coffee parish of Paty do Alferes in 1838, over one hundred slaves escaped from the estate of an important coffee planter, and local officials swung into action to recapture the valuable slaves. The justice of the peace of Paty do Alferes, José Pinheiro de Souza Werneck, requested a contingent of National Guard from the district guard colonel, who responded immediately with a force of over 160 men. Under the circumstances the common threat precluded petty obstructionism, but it will also be noted that the colonel, Francisco Peixoto de Lacerda Werneck, was the juiz de paz's cousin. The 160 guards were divided into four units, each of which was jointly commanded by an officer of the guard and a block inspector deputized by the judge. After a march of six leagues the column overtook the slaves and, after hearing "energetic" speeches delivered by the colonel and the parish judge, recaptured a number of them. While this operation seems exceptional as a model of cooperation between magistrates and militia commanders, it is evident that the cooperative aspect was largely determined by nonbureaucratic factors: race-fear and kinship. An undercurrent of institutional friction is nevertheless observable in the rather forced division of command between guard officers and the juiz de paz's block inspectors. Note also that although in their official reports the two Wernecks recounted the details of the operation similarly, each claimed that ultimately the command of the operation had been his alone.[47]

A final local figure who felt his influence in the parish menaced by the Juizado de Paz was the parish priest or chaplain. Probably no single individual was more central to a community's social life than the priest. He had the ear of all his parishioners, heard their confessions, and gave them advice; perhaps he taught their children as well. The analogy between the original conception of the paternalistic conciliatory justice of the peace and the parish priest spiritually overseeing his flock is compelling. Brazilian liberalism did not include aggressive anticlericalism, and religious freedom was never even much of an issue,[48] but it is difficult to believe that some of the proponents of the Juizado de Paz did not envision the institution as a kind of democratic civil priesthood.

Even the territorial boundaries of the judge's jurisdiction were basically ecclesiastical: the parish and the chaplaincy.

The analogy does not seem to have been lost on parochial voters. In the
first year of the judgeship's existence, especially in parishes of the interior,
many priests were elected to serve as local magistrates.[49] The ease with which
priests fell into the new judicial posts was immediately noticed by the church
hierarchy. The archbishop of Bahia, who was also a member of the Chamber
of Deputies in 1829, stated that in theory he did not oppose the idea of the
padre-judge as long as the chief function of the judge was that of conciliation.
However, objected the archbishop, the duties of the juiz de paz had already
been so expanded from that original ideal that the job was no longer compatible
with the duties of parish priests. He worried that Brazil's all-too-worldly priests,
if they were charged with enforcing regulations, collecting fines, and arresting
criminals, would forfeit the spiritual respect of their communities. Then too,
he argued, in the interior priests were spread thin already and were barely able
to carry out their religious duties.[50] Others disagreed. Feijó and the bishop of
Maranhão argued that parish priests were in fact among those best qualified to
occupy the post.[51] But the position of the Bahian prelate was more persuasive
and in 1829 national legislation declared parish priests (*párocos*) ineligible for
the office of justice of the peace.[52]

Catholicism was the state religion, of course, and priests who were appointed
and paid by the empire had been expected to perform certain secular duties for
the state long before the coming of the justice of the peace. The priest's traditional role as keeper of local statistics, for example, made him a key political
figure after independence when lists of voters were required in a hurry so that
elections could be held. Voting districts were inevitably divided along parish
lines, and since the municipal councils could not supervise elections in all the
parishes of their districts, the local priests were often the only agents the government could use in outlying areas. Priests invariably sat on electoral boards and
were called upon to evaluate which citizens were qualified to vote. The number
of electors in each parish, too, was usually determined by the priest's estimates
of his parish's total population. In other ways the provincial and national governments conferred highly important election-time powers on parish priests after
independence. In Bahia, for instance, when the first general election was held
in 1824, the presiding officers of parish elections were to be chosen from current and former council members, but in each parish the parish priests were also
assigned to sit on the electoral boards and were designated as the official keepers
of the instructions sent out by the government.[53]

The priests, then, not only had an important say in deciding which of their
parishioners could vote, they could often interpret election instructions as they
pleased. Since they were not without ambition, it is not surprising that in the

elections that led up to and followed independence priests frequently were chosen to serve their parishes as electors. In the rural parish of Angra dos Reis, Rio de Janeiro, the primary elections of 1822 returned priests as six of the twelve electors to which the parish was entitled by its population. And in other rural parishes the number of priest-electors seems to have been limited only by the number of priests residing in the parish.[54] High percentages of padre-electors resulted in a similarly high proportion of priests in more important elective offices. The first legislature (1826-1829) counted twenty-three clergymen sitting in the Chamber of Deputies—a higher total than that of any other single group and rivaled only by the seventeen professional magistrates.[55]

Thus, in the first years of the empire Brazil's priests had become important components of the political system—both formally through electoral functions and informally by virtue of their community stature and influence over decisions made by their parishioners. The 1827 law and subsequent legislation promised to change this by transferring some of the official powers to the lay magistrate and dividing others between the priest and the judge. Most official statistics became the preserve of the juiz de paz, and the same logic that made the priest necessary on electoral boards now worked for the inclusion of the parish judge. Electoral laws soon placed the magistrate in charge of parish elections, though the local priest continued to sit on the board and have a voice in qualifying citizens to vote.[56] When parish priests were made ineligible for the judgeship in 1829, the ill will caused by the forfeiture and sharing of these electoral powers immediately rose to the surface. Priests reluctant to give up any of their election-time influence began sermonizing their voting preferences on Sundays, and some used their remaining powers to elect justices of the peace whom they felt they could trust. An anonymous letter published in *O Astro de Minas* in 1829 described how the first justice of the peace election in a parish of Minas Gerais was falsified by the priest in favor of an elderly militia captain because of the priest's conviction that the juiz de paz should be a descendant of "those accustomed to governing."[57] After they were excluded from election as juiz de paz, most politically active parish priests turned to conservative allies and began to think of themselves as the representatives and defenders of traditional political structures in their parishes.

There was more to the antagonism between priests and magistrates than jealousy over official responsibilities. Fernando de Azevedo has described the close relations between agricultural elites and the local priest or chaplain in the sugar-growing areas of Brazil in terms that could be applied equally well to the juiz de paz after 1828.[58] A single individual like the magistrate or the priest could serve as a liaison between the agricultural potentate and the community at large: an invaluable source of information on rivals and rumors, as well as a strategically placed ally at election time. The multimember municipal council was unwieldy to influence, but a priest or parish judge could be a son, nephew, or other member of the family; often he could be bought. Probably it was by largely usurping the priest's unofficial position as the most desirable ally of local elites that the juiz de paz most often gained the clergy's enmity. In 1830 *Aurora Fluminense* reported that in many parishes the priests had openly declared their hostility to the new magistrates, "perhaps because the new institution promises to wrest from them a predominance to which they were accustomed." The paper claimed that some priests instructed their parishioners not to seek conciliation in the juiz de paz courts, and generally spread negative propaganda about the institution. "Possibly they are not ready to forget the time when the district commanders entrusted them with the most secret orders and when they had a say in all the business [of the parish]."[59]

The introduction of the elected judgeship in parishes where power was contested by factions eventually led to an institutional expression of local rivalries: one faction would control the juiz de paz and the other the parish priest. At election time in such parishes, with both the magistrate and the padre sitting on the electoral board, elaborate subterfuges were employed to tip the election in one direction or another. A magistrate who impeached the right of a citizen to vote might find himself in a shouting match with the priest if the prospective voter happened to be a supporter of the latter's faction. In one parish of the province of Rio, the parish priest was accused of bringing to the parochial election bundles of falsified ballots hidden under his cassock. As the election progressed he furtively substituted these for the legitimate ones and left the election with his vestments full of opposition votes.[60] In extremely troubled parishes, the judge and the padre might seek to avoid each other's influence altogether by illegally presiding over separate elections (*duplicatas*) and then taking their chances with which election the provincial assembly would recognize as legitimate.[61] It is probable, too, that priests were sometimes responsible for the extremely frequent disappearances of ballot boxes locked overnight in churches.

Ultimately, however, the priest had only the power of his few electoral duties and whatever personal influence he could exert on his parishioners to trade for the patronage of local potentates. Especially after the expansion of the parish magistrate's criminal jurisdiction by the Procedural Code of 1832, the priest became a less important figure in his parish's political and social life. The outcome was what appears to be a generalized resentment among clergymen of a magistracy that usurped their growing political powers in the first years of the empire, and in so doing usurped the sources of their local standing as well.[62]

Although we have here been concerned primarily with what might be called the "abrasion factor" of local judges, it should be noted that for each local enemy the parish magistrate made, he was also quite likely to gain a local ally. Institutionally the Juizado de Paz was too potent not to excite considerable opposition, but, in many ways, the Juizado de Paz was indeed compatible with local needs. Although the judge could seldom satisfy all the influential elements in his parish, to a certain extent his interests were by definition those of his community, and by law he held the power to promote those interests in a way that no municipal council or juiz ordinário ever could. Equally important, his elective status assured him the local support of a group of neighbors who had chosen him—the community prestige that made his official powers operative.

In the process of translating his official powers into effective local authority, however, the justice of the peace once again attracted the attention of Brazil's lawmakers. Soon after the emperor's abdication, imperial politicians had a variety of reasons for wishing to reverse the concentration of power in the hands of local officials. The most compelling argument against the earlier belief in localism was that the excessive decentralization of the Procedural Code was endangering the uniformity of the rule of law in the empire, and thereby jeopardizing the social and political integrity of Brazil. Alarmists began to portray the locally elected judge as an administrative renegade—a petty satrap who violated the law in his parish more than he enforced it. These criticisms, of course, ultimately revolved around changing concepts of the nature of the law—whether it should serve private or public power in the developing empire. By the mid-1830s this question was at last being sharply defined, and the debate over it, as it related to the parish magistracy, centered upon the two great issues of impunity and electoral fraud.

The charge that justices of the peace were not vigorous enough in their prosecution of criminals was a constant refrain of the critics, especially after the passage of the Procedural Code. In parishes where the juiz de paz was supported by a faction, his adversaries would customarily charge that the judge gave his supporters carte blanche to engage in illicit activities. Less partisan observers noted that the temporary nature of the magistrate's tenure, and his dependence on the community, led many judges to avoid antagonizing their neighbors if they could, even at the expense of failing to enforce the law.[63] During the 1830s, however, the extent of powers held by the juizes made it difficult for an elected judge to play a passive role in his community. To the claims of passive impunity, then, were added cries of active persecution of political enemies. At the same time, the connotations of the word *impunity* were enlarged from the local context to include situations which the national or provincial governments found intolerable—specifically, the protection of illegal enterprises by parish magistrates who had the power to block the application of justice to such activities within their jurisdictions.

In a country the size of Brazil, the variety of illicit operations that were lucrative locally but offensive to the government was practically limitless. In Cachoeira, Bahia, for instance, counterfeiting was a prosperous business presumably supported by sugar producers who paid off their debts to the merchants and brokers of the capital in bogus coin. In order to stem this local industry, the provincial government was forced to rely on crown judges because justices of the peace protected the counterfeiters. Even if individual juizes disapproved, they could seldom be counted on to carry out active measures.[64]

One illegal activity—contraband—was widespread enough to engage the connivance of the justice of the peace in virtually every parish of the empire. And of the varieties of smuggling that affected Brazil in the 1830s, one overshadows all the rest: slaves. Clandestine slave landings after the cessation of the legal traffic (1831) became identified in many minds with local magistrates. The Englishman George Gardner, in his account of travels in the interior of the province of Rio de Janeiro, described seeing columns of from twenty to one hundred Africans marching inland for sale. "There is no secrecy made of their movements, nay, magistrates themselves are very often the purchasers of them. It is likewise well known that the magistrates of those districts where slaves are landed, receive a certain percentage of them as a bribe to secrecy."[65] A parody of the empire's Procedural Code, published in 1841, included special instructions for preventing the importation of illegal slaves: "whenever news is received of a landing of Africans, the juizes de paz shall . . . create a general alarm, carrying out investigations to the north when the landing is to the south, and vice-versa." According to the comic document, which appeared in newspapers in the capital, the penalty for importing slaves was to be "ten percent by value, payable to the juiz de paz."[66] As early as 1835 the official report of the Ministry of Justice referred to the complicity of parish judges as the main reason that the laws against importation of black slaves could not be enforced. "It is generally said that in several parts of the empire and in this province most of the juizes de paz aid and protect that contraband by marking out disembarkation points and sites for public sale."[67]

Bringing illegal slaves ashore and whisking them into the interior was an uncomplicated task in the parishes of the rural coastline. Africans disembarked on the beaches south of Rio de Janeiro sustained the exceptional coffee boom of the 1830s, and in aiding this traffic the juizes de paz were the agents of the great coffee planters. Most planters, it is true, had more modest operations than Joaquim José de Sousa Breves, who kept semiprivate deep water ports at Mangaratiba and Marambaia in the bay south of his vast upland coffee holdings in Piraí. To ensure a smooth flow of blacks from Mangaratiba to his plantations, Sousa Breves and his commercial representative on the coast controlled the local parish judges, who in turn prevented opposition by keeping potential adversaries permanently under indictment.[68] In 1841 the government commissioned a ship to patrol the Rio coastline as a deterrent to contraband activities. But the illicit slave business had become so important that in Parati, not far from Mangaratiba, the town juizes de paz called the people together and, telling them the ship was a "pirate," managed to capture it—impounding the boat and imprisoning its commander.[69]

Even when slave ships were captured and brought into the great ports of Brazil for impoundment and trial, the justices of the peace of the urban parishes often succeeded in averting total losses of the human merchandise. With his procedural responsibility to establish the existence of a crime and then formulate charges, the judge was first to go aboard captured vessels and gather evidence.[70] The opportunities for corruption were all but irresistible, and for this reason the parish judges of the port parishes of Bahia were always key links in the smuggling chain.

The case of one slaver that landed in Bahia in 1834 shows how blatant the cooperation between justices of the peace and the slave trade could be. A brig carrying 230 Africans was captured just outside the Bay of All Saints after spending several days cruising up and down the coast, apparently searching for a place to unload. The juiz de paz of the port parish of Conceição da Praia was called in to carry out an inquest and bring charges against the offenders. When the judge was slow to produce formal charges, the provincial president applied pressure but succeeded only in hurrying the magistrate's decision that the capture had been made illegally and that the ship and slaves should be returned to their owner. The president was outraged and ordered the case appealed, but since the same justice of the peace had prepared the evidence to support his own contentions, the jury confirmed his illegal-seizure decision. Both ship and cargo were returned to the owner who was ordered to pay court and maintenance expenses and did so "grudgingly."[71] The juiz de paz had probably saved the owner in the neighborhood of 100,000 milreis ($77,000). No wonder the value of the Juizado de Paz of Conceição was generally quoted at around 8,000 milreis per year.[72] Similarly, in the capital of the empire, men got rich by inspecting ships as juiz de paz of Santa Rita parish—winking at small shipments or deliberately committing procedural errors that would invalidate the charges against captured smugglers.[73]

Other forms of contraband also relied on the cooperation of the justice of the peace. In Alagoas, judges sold illegal licenses to cut Brazilwood or simply worked in cooperation with smugglers of the protected dye-wood. The provincial president was virtually helpless to stop the trade because even if his own authorities made arrests, the juiz de paz would refuse to draw up the charges necessary to begin proceedings.[74]

The contraband industry, especially that involving slaves, provides an example of the elected parish magistrate as a tool of private interests—reconciling local needs with disagreeable laws imposed from without. The cessation of the slave trade was primarily a British concern and excited very little support at any level in Brazil at this time. Hence the widespread violation of slaving laws and the relatively minor interference by the Brazilian government. The juiz de paz, as he enriched himself, could help to bring in the labor Brazil needed, while furnishing the government with a scapegoat to present to angry British consular officials.[75] In the extreme case of the contraband slave trade, the imperious demand for labor led to a complete vitiation of the law at the local level.

Presumably, many government elements favored local circumvention of the British-imposed slave laws. Impunity for slavers was therefore an acceptable impunity. The same was only relatively true in the case of the local judges' interference in the electoral process. A central government concerned with making its authority effective in the whole empire could view only with ambivalence the facile lawlessness of local officials, even in a common cause like slave smuggling. But in the case of electoral fraud, uncontrollable local judges were an immediate threat to the internal peace of the empire and an insurmountable barrier to creating a rational political system. Election-time manipulation, like slave smuggling, responded to certain local needs, but unlike the slave trade these were contested needs that were not universally agreed on. The man who performed such manipulation made enemies locally and nationally, and that man was usually the justice of the peace.

The means by which elections were fixed and falsified in Brazil will here be treated only incidentally. So many generations of Brazilians have been fascinated by the ingenious and amusing methods of fraud employed by their ancestors that the cataloging of these techniques approaches the status of a historical subgenre.[76] It is enough for our purposes to recall that the juiz de paz presided over the electoral boards that verified a citizen's credentials to vote, received his vote, and then counted it along with those of his neighbors. Outside the election itself, the magistrate controlled major forms of intimidation and persuasion: conscription, police, and an array of favors. Beyond all this, most parish judges were involved in local family rivalries or institutional conflicts. In any contested election the justice of the peace was bound to be a central figure, even if not necessarily a victorious one.

A brief description of elections that took place in the Bahian Recôncavo from 1840 to 1842 gives a kind of composite picture of the variety of misadventures that could befall a parochial election. In 1840 the justice of the peace of Iguape parish in Cachoeira awoke on voting day to an altogether typical scenario for a contested election. The church where the election was to be held was surrounded by a rag-tag army of men from a sugar mill belonging to the township's National Guard commander, a personal enemy of the juiz de paz. As the judge pondered his alternatives, the commander himself rode into town with the parish priest, also a political enemy of the magistrate. The two posted themselves at the door of the church and defied the magistrate to preside over the election there. The judge declined the challenge and led his supporters out of town to his own sugar mill, where they proceeded to hold an election of their own while the priest and guard commander held a duplicata election in the parish church. The election improvised by the National Guard commander and the priest was subsequently declared invalid by the provincial government.[77]

In another parish north of the Bahian capital a fistfight broke out between the justice of the peace and the parish priest over disagreements about the eligibility of certain citizens to vote for the parish electors. Similar problems in a parish nearby prevented completion of the election in a single day, and the ballot box was locked overnight in the parish church. The next morning it was found broken in a pasture, with its contents torn and scattered over the countryside. Undaunted, the local judge, without the knowledge of the parish priest, produced a list of electors "the majority of whom were his relatives."[78] In the township of Jaguaripe, where the control of local officials was divided between factions, a justice of the peace of one faction simply indicted all the municipal councilmen, magistrates, and National Guard officers of the other faction for imaginary charges of sedition. The members of the faction under indictment (and thereby disqualified from political participation) then convinced the juiz de paz of a neighboring município to bring like charges against all *their* adversaries. In the end no elections were held in Jaguaripe because all the local officials were under spurious indictment for sedition.[79]

Nor were such bizarre proceedings isolated or exceptional. A coffee planter serving as judge in the interior of Rio de Janeiro left the parish priest and voters waiting at the church in 1835 while he and a priest who belonged to his household held an "election" secretly at the *casa grande* of one of his estates. In the imperial capital in 1833, the entire liberal faction of Santa Rita parish marched out of the election when the juiz de paz, with the aid of thugs, refused to seat any of that faction's representatives on the electoral board. And in 1840 the magistrates of Glória parish in Rio qualified over three times as many citizens to vote as they had in 1836, making up the difference with minors, slaves, and imaginary names. Most observers agreed that Antônio Pereira Rebouças that "a justice of the peace is worth 40 to 50 electors in his parish."[80]

Government spokesmen complained a great deal about electoral abuses, but not out of their devotion to the elective principle. Fraudulent practices by justices of the peace were generally exposed as part of a reaction against *private* control of elections. Indeed, the eventual conservative reaction would seek reforms not so much to attenuate the illegitimate influence of the juiz de paz as to force him to share that influence with a government-appointed official. Far from protecting the interests of democracy, this official usually represented only the government's desires to control elections for its own ends. It is possible that some election-time violence may have been avoided by this decision to entrust elections to public rather than private interests, but fraud certainly persisted and may even have increased because the involvement of nonlocal interests upset whatever balance existed between parish rivals. Although the principles of pure democracy were ill-served either way, democracy's rhetoric was broadcast loud and long by the opponents of the Juizado de Paz in an effort to discredit the institution. The perversion of democracy was, of course, not the real issue, but in the end the elected magistrate did become linked with sharp electoral practices in the popular imagination. And since the political critics of the institution only offered more of the same, the meliorist tenets of localism and popular participation themselves were ultimately the victims.

Among the most provocative aspects of studying a grass-roots institution like the justice of the peace is the insight it can offer into the social existence of small communities. Contemporary Brazilians seem to have shared our curiosity about their society, and the juiz de paz quickly came to the attention of Brazil's social critics and satirists. Sometimes the clown, more often the comic foil, the parish judge entered Brazilian popular literature almost as soon as the first ones were elected.

One of the earliest works of Brazilian literature after independence was a one-act farce entitled *O Juiz de Paz da Roça* (The Country Juiz de Paz). Written in 1833 by Luis Carlos Martins Pena, a gifted comic dramatist, the play is notable for the acute observation of local customs. It is a comedy of manners in the best sense. Although partaking of two ancient Portuguese comic traditions—magistrate heckling and ridicule of rural ingenuousness—it is in content a completely Brazilian, native drama. The plot: Manuel João, a modest manioc farmer and member of the National Guard, is called upon by the justice of the peace's scribe to escort to Rio a man recently "recruited" by the magistrate for induction into the imperial army. Manuel João cannot easily afford to leave his farm, but the magistrate has threatened to have him arrested if he refuses. Since the village has no jail, the reluctant draftee is to be kept under guard at Manuel João's house overnight. The core of the play is a circuslike scene in the court of the juiz de paz. To a stream of complaints and arguments presented by his rustic neighbors, the magistrate tosses off a stream of arbitrary and self-serving decisions while his scribe accepts the "gifts" of those who hope for the judge's favor. At one point a Negro appears bearing a bunch of bananas and a cringing note addressed to "Mr. Judge, Mrs. Judge, and all the little judges." When confronted by a serious case involving land boundaries, the juiz begs off, and when the injured party insists that the magistrate is required by the Constitution to investigate his claim, the juiz de paz declares the Constitution temporarily suspended.

The play ends when the recruit turns out to be the true love of Manuel João's daughter. She frees him during the night and the two are hurriedly married. Married men were legally exempt from conscription in Brazil, so the magistrate is obliged to countermand his order. In the final scene the juiz de paz invites the community into his house to dance a *fado* in honor of Manuel João and the young couple, and the cast dances about the stage singing nonsense couplets in praise of their parish judge.[81]

The success of *O Juiz de Paz da Roça* spawned a number of imitations by much lesser dramatists. Although serious drama usually meant the ponderous French romantic melodramas of the age, no evening at the theater in Rio was complete, it seems, without at least one *entre-actes* farce lampooning rural life in Brazil. The same conceits and devices were used so often that by 1840 audiences in Rio were weary enough of them to hiss the farce *O Juiz de Paz Abdicando* (The Justice of the Peace Abdicates) for its exaggerated affectation of countrified speech and the tired old gag of bringing live animals onto the stage as presents for the venal judge.[82]

Juiz de paz jokes became a comic genre. Satiric publications multiplied in the 1830s, and they rarely missed a chance to laugh at the foibles of country people and country magistrates. Even the sober journals of Rio sometimes filled out their columns with humorous (and probably apocryphal) descriptions of the absurd and trivial cases brought before parish judges by jealous husbands, shrewish wives, and the like.[83]

Although such publications exaggerate and occasionally disfigure the parish magistracy in the interest of humor, they generally make a point that is worth taking. The closest study of the institution only reinforces the impression that in many parishes the justice of the peace actually did serve as a kind of social director, in a surprising number of cases acting as an entertainer and figure of diversion. In one city parish of Bahia the juiz de paz issued licenses for a *batuque,* where blacks, whites, and pardos danced together to Afro-Brazilian drum rhythms.[84] And the weekly hearings in the magistrate's court, airing as they did domestic quarrels and petty local squabbles, appear to have been as well attended and savored by gossip-mongers as by the interested parties. Many judges used such occasions to hold forth, entertaining their neighbors with personal prejudices and advice in much the same way parish priests did in their own precincts. Certainly many magistrates made election time a festive occasion in their parishes. On the eve of a parochial election in one parish of Minas Gerais the juiz had the inhabitants illuminate their homes while a band "circulated" through the town, playing patriotic music to the assembled population of the tiny hamlet. In many parishes juizes exploded fireworks at election time inside the parish church election-site to antagonize the priest and in the streets to delight the crowds. The elaborate hoaxes and stratagems used by local judges to win elections or achieve other objectives can only have been conceived as crowd-pleasers.[85]

The ideal of effective local self-government has been frustrated and denied to Brazilians by successive governments from 1841 until the present day. And the particularly oppressive centralization of the present has bred nostalgia for supposedly simpler times when communities resolved their problems without government interference. Lately, the office of the imperial justice of the peace has even enjoyed a measure of retrospective celebrity, in part because it seems to furnish proof that Brazilians are historically capable of self-rule.[86] Interpretations of this sort, oversimplified as they are for political purposes, are perniciously attractive, and this study is filled with too much nineteenth-century political rhetoric not to be respectful of that of the late twentieth century. But such an interpretation of the Brazilian justice of the peace can be adopted only in contradiction to much of the data presented here, and confronts us therefore with certain paradoxes. Modern concepts of popular participation, for instance, must be sharply qualified when the recruitment data show that only a relatively small segment of elite and elite-fringe population ever had realistic access to the elected judgeship. Then, too, the ideal of harmonious local self-government is hard to reconcile with the panorama of conflict that seems to provide the institution's backdrop. And it is necessary to reponder, finally, the emergence of negative stereotypes because, whatever their inaccuracies, they found support at the local level as well as at the national. All these considerations seem only to reinforce the conclusion suggested in the preceding chapter: even for those who controlled the Juizado, its drawbacks may have outweighed its benefits.

One readily sees this as paradoxical because it sits uneasily with one of the oldest stereotypes of Brazilian history—that of a rural elite firmly in control of its own sociopolitical environment—and also with a newer theory, Raymundo Faoro's idea that landed elites unanimously desired localistic institutions because they preserved local autonomy against the intrusions of the centralized, patrimonial state. Within the transitional sociopolitical time of early national Brazil, however, the paradox seems less stark and perhaps anachronistic.[87] It is true that, insofar as we may broadly conceive of a Brazilian elite, members of that group did control the Juizado de Paz and in cases like that of slave-smuggling the common goals of the group may have actually been met by the elected magistrate. But the amount of conflict between the judges and other local individuals or institutions that represented similar social groups prevents us from assuming any unanimity in support of the local magistracy. On the contrary, the institution seems to have been a major factor in fostering local factionalism among those who aspired to the judgeship. Not everyone could control the office, and its formal powers made it an ideal vehicle for persecution of rivals or enemies. Local elites who did not enjoy the favor of the juiz de paz or his patron had little choice but to seek the position for themselves, and factions soon developed for this purpose. But the peculiarities of the post and the understood limits imposed by the social system made "out-faction" access problematic. The benign resolution of factional aspirations through the electoral process was usually impossible because the sitting magistrate had the most important say in controlling local elections and, hence, his own succession. Any realistic attempt by an "out-faction" to gain control of the institution would be at the probable cost of bloodshed, feuding, and the consequent stirring up of social elements whose mobilization endangered all elites regardless of their political affiliations. At this point the state-builder's concern with social control becomes a shared concern of paramount importance for both local and national political elites. In frontier or transitional areas where elite formation was just taking place, local tumult might be instrumental in establishing the status of the most powerful or clever. But in an empire that tended toward authoritarian stabilization, as even the frontier areas eventually did, the elected magistrates promoted an instability just as threatening to those who controlled the institution as to those who did not. Factional interests sustained the institution in the short run, but in the long run the social costs of elections and "factionalism" itself could only erode the Juizado de Paz's class support.

A somewhat similar convergence of interests can be seen between local and national elites over the question of political control. It is not incorrect to frame the institution in terms of private versus public power, so long as absolute distinctions are not drawn between the two. In a state-building context the dichotomy is not likely to be perfect; a relationship is being worked out that will eventually be called the political system, and we can anticipate considerable give and take between its public and private components. So it is incorrect to suggest, as Faoro does, that local elites uniformly favored the Juizado de Paz because it allowed them to insulate themselves from the influence of the central government.[88] While the judge's power at the parochial level made the post of undeniable importance locally, it should not be forgotten that the juiz's political "independence" rendered him virtually powerless as a liaison between those who controlled him and the central government. Historically the Portuguese "dependent" magistracy had long performed this crucial political function; the links of crown justices with central administration on the one hand and local society on the other had served as important two-way conductors of powers and demands. Popularly elected magistrates, however, were deprived of this historical role by the lack of any direct lines to higher administration and government. In effect, the new institution isolated the parish from central government and vice-versa. The anti-Juizado de Paz position eventually taken up by the central government and crown bureaucracy who wanted a voice in local politics through control of the magistrates could therefore validly be turned inside-out and used by local elites who needed a voice in national politics which the juiz de paz could not provide. Although this factor was not a divisive one like factionalism and election-time violence, it certainly predisposed many elites —especially in stabilized or stabilizing areas—to accept with alacrity counterreform institutions based on the old "dependent" administrative chain, and to shed whatever allegiance they may have had to an institutional policy that emphasized local autonomy. In the end the Juizado de Paz, in spite of its accommodations and adjustments, remained a transitional institution in Brazil, and after the first years its wisdom was questioned even by those who appeared to benefit most from it.

7. Legal Codes and the Jury System

Brazilian liberals continued to press their advantage in the years immediately following the creation of the Juizado de Paz. More than just an end in itself, the parish judge announced the comprehensive overhaul of the entire Portuguese judicial system. Nationalistic reaction entered into the desire for new laws and codifications, but there was also reasoned agreement that anything would be an improvement over the old system. No one saw much good in the body of Portuguese law and procedure. At best it was thought to be an obscure and contradictory accumulation of the centuries; at worst the draconic and repressive product of a colonial regime. Certainly it was antiquated by the lights of the nineteenth century.[1] The 1824 constitution had called for the codification of laws and judicial structures more suited to Brazil, but like the law creating the justice of the peace, the two great imperial legal codes were not introduced and debated until the end of the 1820s. The Criminal Code of 1830 and the Code of Criminal Procedure of 1832, along with the Juizado de Paz, completed the liberals' reform of the judicial system.

The Criminal Code

It is an indication of the general political climate of Brazil in the late 1820s and early 1830s that the Criminal and Procedural Codes, though attacked viciously by conservatives in later years, were passed in the most desultory fashion —without extensive debate or serious opposition. In the first regular session of the legislature of 1826, the subject of legal codification was introduced and a resolution discussed that would offer a prize to the author of a suitable civil and criminal code.[2] By 1827 two model criminal codes had been submitted: one prepared by Bernardo Pereira de Vasconcelos and one by José Clemente Pereira. A special committee named to study the two proposed codes found the liberal Vasconcelos' preferable for discussion and reported it out in August of 1827.[3] Nevertheless, it was not until 1830 that the bill was openly debated by the Senate and the Chamber of Deputies.

Most of the debate over this proposed Criminal Code centered on the issue of capital punishment. Within the specific subject of discussion, however, more general and even ulterior concerns can be detected. For one thing, the lengthy discussions over whether or not the death penalty should be retained in the new code provided the perfect emotional platform for attacks on the cruelty of Portuguese criminal legislation embodied in the major codification of Portuguese colonial law, the Philippine Ordinances.[4] Legislators seized the occasion to reaffirm their commitments to liberal principles and to reassert their rejection of the colonial past. And as occurred in the earlier debates over the justice of the peace, these attacks on the Portuguese judicial system in general often bristled with resentment toward the magistracy in particular. *Aurora Fluminense* typified this facet of the liberal position when it hailed the final passage of the new Criminal Code in terms that identified magisterial misconduct with Portuguese law. "The barbaric and shameful *Livro Quinto* [the criminal portion of the Philippine Ordinances] will cease to exist, and with it the free hand with which the desembargadores manipulated and modified in practice this code of blood."[5] In the end the death penalty question was resolved by compromise,[6] but not before the attendant airing of grievances had betrayed the political complexion and antipower bias of the new code.

Superficially, the Criminal Code was an uncomplicated document. Its role in the legal system was to define crimes and prescribe reasonable penalties. In most cases any innovation would be a simple lessening of punishments—a modification of degree rather than of substance. Thus, as with capital punishment, in other provisions also the Criminal Code softened the ancient laws of the Portuguese empire. Penalties attached to abuses of freedom of the press and speech were diminished, and the old injunctions against moral offenses such as concubinage were simply eliminated.[7] Observers noted the influence of foreign models (particularly British) and the thought of Bentham, and though most agreed that it was a document "worthy of the nineteenth century,"[8] there were some misgivings from the outset. The contemporary English historian John Armitage felt that the authors of the code had been blindly influenced by foreign legal formulations that were incompatible with Brazilian needs. He found many crimes to be vaguely defined and was worried by the mildness of some penalties that seemed "in certain cases . . . to have been rather in favor of the criminal, than of society at large."[9] Brazilians would soon echo Armitage's doubts.[10] Their early approval of the code's mildness, however, is partly to be explained by political factors.

The penal provisions of the Criminal Code were in part engineered to suit the political goals of the emperor's opposition. Like the law that created the justice of the peace, the code had a practical as well as an ideological side, and if its intellectual roots anchor it in the liberal decade, its political dimension situates it squarely in the antipower phase of Brazilian liberalism that immediately preceded and followed the emperor's abdication. Indeed, nothing better reflects the tension between the congressional opposition and Pedro I in 1830 than the vastly liberalized provisions in the Criminal Code relating to the definition and punishment of political crimes. Under cover of revising the inhumane laws of Portugal, the liberals who opposed the emperor and wished to curtail his power to persecute political enemies (among whom they counted themselves) did so by weighting the Criminal Code overwhelmingly in favor of political dissidents and revolutionaries. Capital punishment and forced labor (*galés*) were rejected as penalties for political crimes, and in cases of sedition or revolt only "leaders" could be brought to trial. The code's definition of leadership was in turn cast so vaguely that it could be legally established only with the greatest difficulty. Those who would challenge an established government by force had the law further stacked in their favor by yet another impractical definition. In this case the existence of "rebellion" would be established by the assembly of over 20,000 persons bent on overthrowing the government.[11] Armitage commented that the code made punishment of the crime of rebellion "altogether illusory."[12]

The emperor was less than five months from abdication when the Criminal Code was passed. Probably he was already contemplating the move, and the piecemeal but steady erosion of his juridical authority by statutes passed since 1827 must have had a part in forming his decision. By stripping away the crown's traditional judicial prerogatives—first by creating an independent local magistracy, and later by codifying laws that placed the emperor's opposition outside the grasp of even the conservative superior courts—the liberal opposition had legislated the emperor to an administrative standstill. From his vantage point outside the fray, Armitage wondered why the emperor had not refused to sanction the code unless its "noxious clauses" relating to political crimes were rendered acceptable. The historian concluded that Dom Pedro's counselors had committed a "criminal imprudence," or at best "showed themselves lacking in all intelligence" by not recommending an imperial veto of the section on political crimes.[13] But the emperor did not obstruct the code. Whether he had such an option in 1830 might be debated, but certainly the Criminal Code contributed to the demoralization of his government and further compromised his authority at a time when political agitation was on the increase. Hemmed in by a hostile legal structure, Dom Pedro may have felt he had no alternative to abdication.

The Procedural Code

The other great imperial legal code, the Código do Processo Criminal, or

Procedural Code, was a mixture of reformism and politics like the Criminal Code, but its innovative structural departures and political significance easily transcend the earlier document in importance. Because it was passed in 1832, after the abdication of the emperor, its political orientation was somewhat less combative and more directed toward the political and judicial structure over the long run. In this it conforms to the state-building chronology we have outlined: by 1832 the liberals, now in power, could afford a half-turn away from their antipower posture. A new phase had begun in which the securing of political and social control would be foremost. A strong legacy of guerrilla liberalism remained, fueled by the real fear of a restoration attempt, but it coexisted with a more positive overall orientation. The Procedural Code could now do what there had not been time to do in the late 1820s. It eliminated the formal remains of the Portuguese legal system and described a structure of judicial organization. It established the last of the long promised and awaited institutional reforms—the jury system. The new code also strengthened existing liberal institutions such as the justice of the peace. It was rightly considered the very embodiment of the liberal legal philosophy.[14]

The Procedural Code came to be law in an even more perfunctory fashion than the Criminal Code. A proposal for a Procedural Code had been presented back in 1829, but its failure to include the creation of a jury system had outraged liberals and kept it from being directly debated in Parliament. The period of uncertainty that preceded the abdication of Pedro I prevented the devotion of much attention to the question in late 1830, and it was not until July of 1831 that a new version, drafted largely by the liberal Manuel Alves Branco, was brought before the Chamber of Deputies. The lower house passed it rapidly —by "acclamation," it was later described—and the Senate debated sporadically around the measure for a few days in 1831, then returned to it and finally passed it a year later.[15] The delay in the Senate can be attributed in part to the objections of professional magistrates who found organizational flaws and perceived the political importance of the measure, but the weakness of this opposition and the lack of discussion in the Chamber of Deputies are nevertheless hard to account for.

Historians have given no very satisfactory reasons for the relatively frictionless passage of the Procedural Code through the Brazilian legislature. To a certain extent the lack of initial controversy must be taken as another measure of the approval that liberal legal reforms still enjoyed in the early 1830s. It is surely impossible to minimize the importance of the code, and profitless to conjecture on the insensitivity of Brazil's lawmakers to what was a landmark event in their country's administrative history.[16] In some ways, however, these speculations all beg the question, for in fact the law was the object of violent attack, though the controversy did not begin until after passage. In effect, the provisions of the Procedural Code were debated after the fact, and those debates continued practically without let-up until the document was finally reformed in 1841. Nor was the battle joined only in the press and the unofficial political world. The year after passage, the minister of the empire established a joint committee to examine and revise the new Procedural Code, even before it had been fully implemented.[17] This inversion of the normal order of the legislative process suggests some insights into the way the bill was perceived by contemporary lawmakers. Clearly urgency was still a major factor in 1832, but if what we have said about the changing priorities of the liberals is correct, then we would expect that urgency to serve more positive goals after the emperor's departure.

And indeed, whereas reforms like the Juizado de Paz and the Criminal Code had been partly conceived as ways to remove support from the emperor, the 1832 document was regarded more as a means of building and managing support for the new government. In the Senate the Marquis of Caravelas tried to stimulate his colleagues into laying aside their disagreements and passing the code immediately as a bid for popular political support.[18] He relied on the familiar argument that the codes were actually what made the Constitution operative.[19] Without them the empire was in the paradoxical position of retaining procedure "developed by an absolute government in a time of the greatest ignorance," within a regime of constitutional guarantees that were diametrically opposed to what this antique legal system practiced. Caravelas sweetened his argument by suggesting that when the Procedural Code was passed the people would at last grasp the benefits of the Constitution and identify those benefits, not with the ex-emperor who had promulgated the Constitution in 1824, but with the government which had made it function by passing the Procedural Code in 1832. The Marquis submitted that "the people go by their experience ... and when they see fair trials and judgments they will say 'this is the consequence of the Constitution, therefore this government is good—much better than the other one'."[20]

The Marquis of Caravelas' views were shared by many who hoped to consolidate the empire in a liberal mode during the Regency period. A new procedural organization, it was assumed, would improve the lot of the people dramatically enough to gain their support for the new government and whatever reforms it chose later to impose.[21] Here were grounds the judicial meliorists and the political builders could agree on. Perhaps even more important than the popular support that might be created with the new code, however, were the more selective loyalties that could be bought through patronage. In reorganizing the inferior courts and police, the code provided the new government with jobs that could be filled by its own appointees. Here was a more tangible source of leverage, for patronage supplied the government with a network of obligations and, at least in potential, a means of enforcing the uniform authority of the state throughout the vast empire.[22]

Finally, by linking the Procedural Code with the Constitution, the senator also tapped a vein of reaction against the deposed emperor. There is an unmistakable analogy between the emperor's Constitution and the liberals' Procedural Code. Just as the date of abdication in 1831 must share the honors of independence with the break from Portugal in 1822, so the Código do Processo passed in such a hurry in 1832 resembles the Constitution summarily promulgated in 1824. The comparison is not exaggerated even in retrospect, for the Procedural Code and its later modifications, because of the way that it deployed the government's agents of civil coercion (the police and magistracy) came to be regarded by some of the empire's most acute observers as the practical political charter of the regime.[23] Symbolically, then, the code of 1832 was the liberal's constitution—a native contribution, unsullied by the imperial fiat, to the philosophic and organizational foundation of the country. Like any constitution, it played a legitimizing role for the regime that introduced it, another fact that may partially account for its rapid adoption.

In the chronology of Brazilian reformism, the Procedural Code was a transitional document. Power was not yet trusted in 1832; indeed, the emperor might not even be gone for good. Yet there were now practical, in-power considerations to be made regarding political support and social discipline, and these goals seemed to require a government that could make its authority felt in the entire empire. Then again, among the moderates there persisted a sincere preference for local institutions, elective officials, and independent justice; or, seen from the in-government perspective, fragmentation of power. So although their immediate goals perforce changed dramatically after the emperor's abdication, the liberals were not yet ready to abandon their earlier commitments in pursuit of these goals by 1832. As a result, for all its managerial intent, the Procedural Code was an unwieldly instrument of control. The major coercive potential of the new code, for instance, was to be found in the sections on criminal jurisdiction and police. But as a previous chapter has described, the code entrusted the most basic steps of criminal procedure to local justices of the peace, thus greatly expanding their powers. Under the Procedural Code of 1832 the juiz de paz became the cornerstone of the imperial judiciary. The liberals had recognized the need for a certain uniformity of control, but then, paradoxically, delegated the responsibility for it to an uncontrolled institution.

The moderados' abiding faith in popular participation could also be seen at work in the higher levels of the judicial structure created by the code. At the county level the juiz de fora was replaced by a magistrate called the *juiz municipal* who was chosen by the provincial president for a three-year term from a list of three names presented by the local municipal council. The municipal judge's principal duties were substituting for his immediate superior, the juiz de direito (district judge), during his absence and the execution of the district judge's orders, sentences, and injunctions. The extent of the powers already granted to the justices of the peace made the juiz municipal's actual jurisdiction a minimal one, but since municipal judges were by statutory preference selected from among the recent graduates of the imperial law schools, the position quickly came to be regarded as a proving ground for aspiring professional magistrates—a kind of three-year clerkship under the district judge.[24]   The right to name municipal judges thus provided the government with a substantial, though qualified, new patronage power at the local level.

The same process of selection from lists submitted by municipal councils was was also employed to fill the post of *promotor público,* or county prosecutor. This office also served as a feeder for the ranks of the professional district judges.[25]

The one purely appointive imperial magistrate established by the Procedural Code was the juiz de direito, who replaced the colonial ouvidor or corregedor in the next higher administrative division, the comarca or district. The juiz de direito closely resembled his colonial predecessor. Like the ouvidor, he was to be a letrado—a law-school graduate and professional judge with some prior experience. His duties according to the code were those of circuit court judge and chief of police, though the latter title carried no substantial authority.[26] His main formal responsibilities were to preside over jury trials in the county seats of his district and to apply the terms of the Criminal Code to offenders convicted by jury panels.[27] The formal procedural duties of the juiz de direito, however, are only the thinnest expression of his real significance in the dialectic of Brazilian administrative development. The juiz de direito's direct patronage links to the central government, his powers to supervise the activities of local judges, and his sense of corporate identity made him the classic alternative to the independent magistracy embodied by the justice of the peace.

The Jury System

The idealists showed their tenacity by clinging to the justice of the peace, but for them the real heart of the Procedural Code lay in the jury system. The jury was the logical culmination of the principle of popular participation as applied to the judiciary. Even more than the Juizado de Paz it embodied the ideals of judicial self-rule and localism; like the Juizado de Paz it threatened the professional magistracy directly and tested basic assumptions about Brazilian society. When critics later assailed the Procedural Code and the liberal reforms in general, they often found a common point of aim in the jury system. And by making conspicuous the failures of the jury, they were often successful in discrediting the very fundaments of early Brazilian liberalism.

The jury system had been an issue in Brazil since before independence. In 1821 the Portuguese Cortes had instituted a limited jury system to deal with infractions of the freedom of the press laws, and in the following year the Cortes established the institution in Brazil to deal with similar cases.[28] The Brazilian version was watered down in comparison to the law in effect in Portugal——for one thing, in Brazil the jurors were named by crown magistrates (corregedores) whereas in the metropolis they were locally elected. The new system nevertheless met with great approval in the colony.[29] After independence, in 1823, one of the first laws passed by the Constituent Assembly reaffirmed the competence of juries to judge matters regarding freedom of the press, and when the Assembly was dissolved prematurely, this law was executed by decree.[30]

There had also been discussion in the Constituent Assembly about extending the competence of the jury system to decide criminal and even civil cases. The ill-fated draft constitution of 1823 included among six basic "individual guarantees" the right to trial by jury.[31] These guarantees were missing from the Constitution of 1824, but both the legislators' draft constitution and the emperor's version described the ultimate authority of the judicial branch of government as vested exclusively in "judges and jurors." Some cautious members of the Constituent Assembly warned that it would be a mistake to include the creation of a jury system specifically in the constitution before new legal codifications could be passed to modify the "inhumane criminal laws" of the Philippine Ordinances. Other representatives, concerned with the format of the constitution itself, thought that specific procedural matters such as trial by jury should be taken up by subsequent legal codes and left out of the constitution.[32]

Another group opposed the jury system on practical grounds because they feared it was inappropriate for Brazil. One deputy alluded to the total "ignorance" of the majority of Brazilians and recommended that the jury be put into effect gradually and only in those areas where the level of civilization seemed commensurate with the responsibilities of jury duty. He proposed an amendment that would permit the jury system only in the larger cities and towns (by this he meant only in the provincial capitals). The amendment was not seconded.[33] Another view that found little support in this early period but prefigured a whole school of later conservative criticism was expressed by the Bahian José da Silva Lisboa. He called for the education of the people before the institution was established. What good was the jury system, Silva Lisboa questioned, if the people who were to be the jurors could not understand the laws or the principles behind the institution itself? Silva Lisboa's arguments for education included something more than just literacy. Certain characteristics of Brazilian society, he argued, were presently incompatible with the jury system and invalidated the entire concept of the "jury of peers." Since most crimes

were committed by slaves and free blacks, he suggested (erroneously), relations
between the jury and the defendant would be reminiscent more of master-slave
relations than those defined by legal codes.[34]

True to the pattern of debate we have witnessed over other liberal reforms,
however, most representatives merely grasped the opportunity to turn the debates into another attack on the Portuguese magistracy. Once again the corruption and plain stupidity of crown judges were laundered in the halls of Brazil's
Parliament. Favorite tales of judicial venality were brought out and traded.
Orators heralded the jury system as a "celestial institution" that would protect
the dignity and fortunes of Brazilians from the powerful, grasping magistrates
of the crown.[35] Speakers struck the theme so often that at some point the
original issue—the jury system—became secondary. Silva Lisboa observed his
bitter colleagues and commented trenchantly: "In the debates that have been
held in this assembly, so much acrimony and invective have been piled upon the
magistracy that it seems that these entreaties for the introduction of a jury system are founded less on the excellence of that institution . . . than upon rancor
and hatred against the established judiciary."[36] Had the Constituent Assembly
not been dissolved, the combination of considered support of the jury as an institution and rancor against the professional judiciary would probably have been
sufficient to create a jury process in criminal actions even before regulatory
legal codes could be passed. The Constitution of Pedro I was more conservative on this point: although it specifically foresaw the creation of the jury system, it made its eventual establishment contingent upon the dispositions of the
as-yet-nonexistent legal codes.[37]

The creation of the jury system paralleled that of the Juizado de Paz in wid-
ening the split between the professional magistracy and the liberals. Like the
local magistrate, the jury system constituted a frontal attack on the elite judiciary. Jurors were customarily referred to as judges in their own right—*juizes
de facto,* or judges of the facts. They might even be illiterate, but in theory the
professional judge who presided over their meetings was unable to modify their
decisions. Evaristo da Veiga appreciated the threat that the jury posed as a
"political institution destined to temper the unbounded preponderance of a
class [the professional magistrates] that would otherwise dominate everything."[38]
And the letrado judges, for their part, reacted much as they had against the
juizes de paz: criticizing and sabotaging the institution in hopes of discrediting
it. One liberal newspaper parodied the indignation of the magistrates who by
the creation of the jury system now found their powers and prestige diminished:
"'Judgments by jurors who never went to Coimbra! A shoemaker can be a
judge by this Code . . .' say those of the Coimbran school for whom nothing is
any good if it can't be found in the Ordinances of the Realm of Portugal."[39]

The professional magistracy's opposition to the jury system did not prevent it from being received with public enthusiasm that fell only a little short of that accorded the Juizado de Paz. Publicists who had anxiously anticipated the inauguration of the jury system in Brazil since the days of the Portuguese Cortes now waxed eloquent about the new institution in the bloated rhetoric and religious metaphors that were apparently reserved for liberal innovations.[40] The spate of manuals and informational tracts that had accompanied the justice of the peace also complemented this latest procedural change. In 1835 a single publisher's advertisements in the *Jornal do Comércio* offered five titles directly concerned with the problems and the promise of the jury system. A citizen interested in studying the history, theory, or practice of the jury of peers could purchase the two-volume Portuguese translation of *Sir Richard Phillip's Golden Rules for Jurymen.* Also available were guides, manuals, and outlines written by Brazilians for the instruction of potential jurors. At the same time, a conservative political opposition was beginning to coalesce in Brazil, and a noteworthy attack on the government and the liberal judicial reforms thinly disguised itself as one of these tracts and irreverently characterized the jury system as a "sacred cow."[41]

The only formal qualifications necessary for a citizen to serve as a juror were good sense, probity, and eligibility to serve in second-degree elections (i.e., as an elector). This last qualification only excluded Brazilians under twenty-five years of age and those who earned less than 200 milreis per year—a poor wage in Brazil at the time.[42] Justiniano José da Rocha wrote that the only persons effectively excluded from serving on jury panels were "women, children, and the village idiot."[43] As if to reaffirm the democratic principles behind the jury, the law specified that the lists of those eligible to serve be prepared by a board of three men presided over by the elected magistrate, the justice of the peace. The parish priest and one of the members of the municipal council were to sit with the judge on the qualifying board, and the lists of eligible citizens would be publicized, either in the press or by public display on the parish church door. These parish lists of prospective jurors would be revised each year and sent to the county seat where they would once again be scrutinized and finally entered in the general roll of jurors for the township. The listed names would then be transferred to individual slips of paper and kept locked in a box in the meeting rooms of the municipal council.[44]

When the district judge decided to call a session of the jury in one of the townships of his jurisdiction, he notified the municipal council of his intentions. In most counties, jury sessions were supposed to be held twice annually; in provincial capitals the law provided for three yearly sessions, and in Rio de Janeiro and the capitals of Bahia, Pernambuco, and Maranhão, six sessions were prescribed by law. On receiving orders by the juiz de direito, the council assembled to choose sixty names at random from the box containing the prospective jurors.

The chosen sixty were then notified of the dates of the upcoming jury session. Witnesses and defendants out on bail were called in and the local justices of the peace were charged with publicizing the approaching session in their parishes.[45]

At the opening of the session, with the juiz de direito presiding, the sixty jurors were divided into two groups. The first twenty-three names chosen at random by a small boy formed the Primeiro Conselho de Jurados, or grand jury, also known as the Jury de Acusação. In secret, this body elected its own president and secretary and, still behind closed doors, deliberated over each of the cases prepared by the juizes de paz of the county for presentation at that session of the jury. If the grand jury found sufficient evidence of the existence of a crime and its perpetrator, it would return a formal accusation; if not, the defendant, witnesses, and public prosecutor could be admitted to the jury room to make necessary clarifications. If the jury still found no grounds for accusation, the case would be thrown out.[46]

In cases that the grand jury felt justified in bringing to trial, the defendants were arraigned before a second body of twelve jurors, the Segundo Conselho do Jury, or the Jury de Sentença, chosen at random from the names remaining in the box. This petit jury reviewed the formal charges, the depositions, and the legal status of the case before hearing direct testimony and the arguments of the prosecution and the defense. At the end of the courtroom proceedings, the district judge read a summation of the testimony presented in the case and charged the jurors with five specific queries regarding the existence of a crime, the guilt of the defendant, the degree of his guilt, and whether indemnification was called for.[47] The answers to these questions were determined by an absolute majority of the jurors voting in secret session. If the jury found the defendant guilty, the juiz de direito was called upon for sentencing—virtually his only direct role in the whole procedure.[48]

The structure was a rather complex one that depended on an exceptional amount of cooperation and the mobilization of a great many people. Unlike the Juizado de Paz, the jury system was hard to justify as a means to eliminate legal bottlenecks or to speed the administration of justice. Defendants arraigned by the grand jury in one session normally had to wait for their day before the petit jury until the next session (usually at least six months). When the jurors did meet, the sessions were not short; by law they lasted at least two weeks and could be extended for up to one more week depending on the work load. Deferred judgment was especially inconvenient because it meant that prisoners would be incarcerated for extended periods, thus increasing costs as well as the likelihood that suspects would escape from Brazil's inadequate jails.

For the reformers, however, all these drawbacks were overshadowed by the concept of judicial independence, which the jury system symbolized even more perfectly than the justice of the peace. The jury system was no new issue, and over the years the arguments in its favor had come to be as little questioned as the wisdom of the institution itself. Judicial independence had been the prominent arguing point for the jury system since the first debates in the Constituent Assembly in 1823. Nicolau Pereira dos Campos Vergueiro, a liberal representative from São Paulo, based his support for trial by jury (in both criminal and civil proceedings) on the need to set local justice free of the pernicious influence of the dependent professional magistracy. He submitted that it was vain to hope that any government would make a serious attempt to reform the corrupt district magistracy or hold it responsible for its abuses. Therefore, the only way to assure judicial independence was to create popular institutions like the jury with no ties to the dependent district magistracy. Vergueiro apparently harbored some doubts about how the jury system would work out in practice, but in spite of his reticence he saw no alternative to the institution, if only to "attenuate the abuses" of the professional judges.[49] Another advocate of the jury system stated flatly in the same debates that "only [jurors] can be called truly independent judges."[50]

The jury's role in guaranteeing judicial independence was described by the newspaper *Nova Luz Brasileira,* whose analysis in 1830 made clear that the chain of oppression that had traditionally linked the government to the higher magistracy was still as much an issue as ever. "The jury weakens the influence and lessens the weight of the magistrates and tribunals upon civil society, and diminishes the power of the government." Professional magistrates came in for special criticism as "panderers to power," dominated by personal interests and passions and possessed by a dangerous corporate spirit. "Jurors, on the other hand, are much farther from the byplay of the passions, influences, bribery and the intrusions of power. They are an almost infallible means of obstructing the effects of despotism and tyranny."[51] *Nova Luz* was a radical sheet with great acuity of social observation. Eventually it went the extra step and, instead of merely calling for the jury as a buffer against the letrado representatives of "power" (government), began advocating the application of elective principles at all levels of the Brazilian judiciary. Such a reform would guarantee the genuine independence of the entire judicial arm of government, and additionally make Brazil "the envy of old Europe."[52]

The principle of judicial independence that was exalted in the jury system and the Juizado de Paz, then, was applied negatively against the professional magistracy. And here is one of the central contradictions of the transitional document that is the Procedural Code. At a time when the harmonious coexistence of dependent and independent magistrates was not thought to be possible (there was, after all, the evidence of five years mutual belligerance between justices of the peace and professional judges), the new code prescribed just such a mixed system. Then, instead of promoting the unity of the system, the

Procedural Code delegated relatively greater responsibilities to the popular and "independent" institutions—the jury and juizes de paz—at the expense of appointive, and therefore "dependent," judges at the district level. In doing so, it drove still deeper the wedge of bitterness that divided these two extremes of the judicial branch; and by implying the superiority of one source of authority over the other, it bred internal incompatibility in the legal system it created. The sociologist-historian Francisco José de Oliveira Vianna has described this contradiction in his broader analysis of the political system of the empire. Sovereignty in Brazil, he has written, not only rose upward from a popular base in a democratic fashion, but also descended from the emperor through his power to appoint high officials. The result was collision and conflict at the point where these two sources of sovereignty met. Oliveira Vianna never specified the exact point of contact, but in the period discussed here at least one such collision site was in the heart of the judicial system—where the "independent" jury/juiz de paz complex met the "dependent" juiz de direito.[53]

In the liberals' preference for extreme judicial independence, then, lay the political blunder of the Código do Processo. The code did create the cadres needed to guarantee political and social control: a network of trained professional judges whose jurisdictions covered all Brazil and who were responsive to the government that appointed and maintained them. But it simultaneously weakened and alienated these potentially valuable agents by dividing their traditional powers and prestige between largely uncontrollable institutions like the the jury system and the Juizado de Paz. It is unlikely that many liberals in the early 1830s gave much thought to currying the favor of the letrado class of magistrates. Most of them, to be sure, advocated the opposite—"tempering the preponderance of that class," in the words of Evaristo da Veiga—and preferred to cast their lot with the more democratic institutions. But they were mistaken in thinking they could clip the wings of the centuries-old and socially influential class of professional judges simply by restricting their jurisdiction as the Procedural Code did. The result of their attempt was the near institutionalization of animosities between the letrado group and the liberals. And from a purely practical standpoint the code became unmanageable because the two extremes of the judicial system it created were so often mutually hostile. Magisterial, and eventually Conservative, criticisms that the system established in the Procedural Code was unworkable in Brazil became self-fulfilling prophecies as disgruntled district judges made life difficult for their inferiors or, demoralized, shirked their own meager duties and turned to opposition politics.[54]

The Procedural Code of 1832 not only promoted judicial disunity and hard feelings against the government, but also exacerbated some of the very judicial problems it was meant to correct. All the judicial reforms of the liberal period were at least partially justified by the assumption that the colonial judiciary had been an overgrown, unwieldy, and sluggish apparatus. Reforms like the Juizado de Paz and the jury system were designed to streamline and rationalize the legal system. But the Código do Processo, with its emphasis on neighborhood magistrates and popular involvement, only ballooned the judicial structure outward until there were no longer enough citizens to fill all the offices it created. The situation became ludicrous in the sparsely populated and backward provinces of the north and the interior. A communiqué from the northern province of Ceará to a Rio newspaper in 1835 stated in exasperation that Ceará could muster neither the personnel nor the material resources needed to rearrange provincial justice in accordance with the Procedural Code. The writer calculated that even without counting lawyers, block inspectors, and the like, some three thousand persons would be required to fill all the judiciary entities that were established by the code. A province twice as populous and four times as educated, he said, would be unable to fill so many posts.[55]

In many rural counties the problems of assembling sixty respected men for two weeks of jury duty were simply insurmountable. Like the soldiers of the National Guard, eligible jurors could not afford to leave their crops or businesses and virtually always sought excuses to avoid serving. A virulent Bahian critic of the entire liberal judicial structure described the workings of the code in rural areas in colorful terms that were probably not far from the truth:

> In the interior there are places where only four or five men know how to read and write; these are immediately snatched up for justices of the peace (a worse plague than the cattle tick), council members, etc., etc., and in the end there is no one to serve on the jury. And if with great difficulty some are successfully rounded up for the sessions of the jury, what a sorry lot of poor devils these jurors are! ! ! [56]

Even if personnel were available, however, no dramatic increase in efficiency was accomplished by the new code. The jury system that went into effect in 1832 was faced with a huge backlog of cases to be tried and a rather ponderous two-stage mechanism for dealing with them. One session held in the city of Rio de Janeiro in 1838 handled fifty-six different trials, forty-one of which involved crimes committed twenty to thirty years before.[57] A district judge who wished to keep up with the incoming load of contemporary cases confronted the alternatives of simply ignoring the backup or instructing the jury to throw out the older cases. In cities it was sometimes possible to hold special sessions to help catch up with long-pending cases, but in outlying areas this was clearly impracticable. In the interior the difficulties of gathering sixty men for jury duty often prevented regular sessions, thus contributing to the case backlog.[58]

Still more ironic than the way in which the Procedural Code hampered the administration of justice was the mockery that it made of the concept of judicial independence. The most common complaints about the lack of jury independence, however, were not directed against the traditional judicial subservience to the central government that had concerned the reformers, but toward the control that local magnates exercised over both the formation and the decisions of the institution. Critics noted the vices of the selection process for jurors which was highly suspect anywhere that local offices were dominated by partisans. After all, the jurors were the "legitimate children" of the juiz de paz, the parish priest, and the president of the municipal council.[59] Padre Lopes Gama, Pernambuco's most sensitive social observer, claimed that in all the towns of the interior a certain number of powerful figures chose the members of the jury and then fixed its decisions for their own ends.[60] And as early as 1834 even the minister of justice recognized that the juntas responsible for qualifying prospective jurors used their discretionary powers to eliminate men whose political opinions differed from their own.[61] In their haste to make the jury independent of government and letrado influence, the liberals had created an institution that was open to illegitimate pressures from all sides.

The reasons for the jury's vulnerability to outside influences lay in the Brazilian jury's popular structure and the nature of Brazilian society. It seems that in most places persons with the social standing to be "independent" usually found a way to avoid jury duty, leaving the task to the social classes who were most susceptible to the temptations of bribery, the nagging of old obligations, and the voice of authority. Contemporary critics pointed out that for such citizens—often illiterate and bewildered by the complexities of jury duty —the very concept of independence had no meaning. When they were not told what to do by their employers or protectors, they took their opinions from lawyers or the presiding district judge.[62]

Elites shirked jury duty because it was a time-consuming burden, but their absence on jury panels was also due to the class-crossing aspects of jury selection. The kind of men who might seek the authority of the Juizado de Paz did not relish this more unsavory duty of participatory government. The presence, or even the potential presence, of humble citizens on jury panels was evidently enough in itself to make the members of a local elite ill-disposed to serve as jurors, and as they sought exemptions the domination of Brazil's juries by socially dependent classes became a self-reinforcing phenomenon. Not long after the creation of the jury it had become axiomatic that the "better quality" of citizens always avoided duty. "Many sober, well educated, and conspicuous citizens flee from this duty so as not to find themselves in the hard necessity of rubbing shoulders in the courtroom with insignificant nobodies—some of them fools, others stupid, and many extremely crude."[63] Those who saw this boycott by the better classes as the main flaw of the jury system argued for higher

property qualifications, literacy requirements, and smaller numbers of jurors to
be required to hold sessions (e.g., thirty instead of sixty).[64]

The combination of ponderously slow administration of justice and suscep-
tibility to influence at the local level was responsible for the major charge
brought against the jury system in the nineteenth century—that of indulgence
of criminals, or, as it was more often stated, impunity. In Brazil, wrote Padre
Lopes Gama, only the smallest fry of the criminal world was likely to be convicted by the jury. A competent thief, he argued, would be financially capable
of buying the indulgence of judge and jury; and it was a rare offender who
could not find a *padrinho* or protector that subservient jurors did not wish to
displease.[65] Humble jurors were especially influenced by fears of reprisals by
those they convicted. Indeed, the most dangerous cutthroats seemed to be the
ones who escaped from jail most often after conviction. Brazilian jails were extremely insecure, and breakouts were a regular event in municipal life. Even in
Rio de Janeiro, where prison security was much superior to that of the interior,
the district judge reported that the Aljube jail was broken out of on an average
of once every two months.[66] And, of course, when intimidated jurors failed
to convict, equally fearful witnesses refused to testify, and impunity became a
vicious circle.[67]

Another major reason for impunity was the relative ease with which bail
was granted under the Procedural Code. Suspects out on bail found it easy to
disappear in the isolated and badly policed interior of the country. Even without jumping bail, defendants who could go their own bond or find someone to
do it for them seldom came up for trial. The large caseload and limited prison
facilities forced most district judges to prepare their dockets in such a way as
to give the swiftest possible hearing to suspects in jail—partly to forestall their
escape and partly to clear the jail for new occupants. Suspects out on bail
were given second priority under the system, and many never came to trial at
all. In 1836 the minister of justice described the situation as a chief cause of
impunity and noted that the granting of bail had come to be considered tantamount to acquittal.[68] In Rio, juiz de direito Eusébio de Queiroz tried to con-
jure the problem by holding a special session of the jury in 1838 exclusively
for the defendants out on bail. The jury handled sixty cases and returned more
convictions than acquittals. The district judge reported that the session's primary significance was to "convince those out on bail and their bondsmen that
putting up bail is not the same as being pardoned. I am certain that from now
on it will not be so simple for criminals to find men to post their bond."[69]

The Criminal Code shared the blame for the problem of impunity. Almost
invariably those who deplored the jury system's bad conviction record also
thought that the laws were too soft even when they were applied. As we have
seen, crimes with political implications were the objects of special leniency

under the Criminal Code, and the notorious timidity of juries where political matters were concerned made convictions in such cases doubly rare. At worst, when crimes of rebellion or sedition were at issue, the jury became merely another bone of contention between local partisans who tried all means to pack the panel with dependable jurors. Local judicial proceedings thus provided a new arena of conflict, aggravating and perpetuating the very causes of the crimes they were to judge. The central government, with its developing interests in the prosecution of subversive elements and the preservation of public order, would soon recommend the removal of political crimes from the competence of the jury system.[70]

The impunity question forced many Brazilian legal theorists into evaluating judicial effectiveness by percentage of convictions. The jury system, however, made high percentages all but impossible to achieve. An extremely active district judge with a strong personality could sometimes get a fairly high conviction rate out of juries chosen in the imperial capital, but outside Rio de Janeiro juries were notoriously passive, lenient, or cowed. In 1835, to cite a typical example, jurors who met in the Ceará counties of Sobral and São Bernardo acquitted all the defendants brought before them out of what was described as "indifference" and an "ill-conceived spirit of bonhomie."[71]

Where political tensions were for any reason heightened, the conviction rate usually fell out of sight. The Rio province coffee county of Piraí, for instance, was one such troubled area in 1841. Rivalries that had arisen in Piraí over the elections of the preceding year had not been resolved, and groups of armed men who owed allegiance to the different local factions still roamed the township in 1841. Land disputes were involved and the provincial government described the tense climate in Piraí as the result of "disunion and misunderstandings between the prominent families of that area."[72]   Finally, in April 1841, the justice of the peace of Arrozal parish arrested an insignificant supporter of the opposing faction, thereby touching off a jailbreak attempt in which one man was killed and several were wounded. The district judge, typically on leave in the capital at the time, was dispatched by the provincial president along with a force of police to restore order in the county of Piraí, and several of the unruly elements allegedly responsible for the jailbreak were arrested. With the arrival of the juiz de direito and the approaching session of the jury at which those involved in the Arrozal jailbreak were to be tried, pressures were brought to bear upon the judicial structure and the climate of opinion in which it was to operate. Some forms of pressure were less subtle than others: in the two months preceding the trial, four murders thought to be linked to the chain of events that had begun with the elections of the previous year were committed in Arrozal parish alone. One local observer commented that "this trial has been trampled [atropelado]. The judge has been threatened and terrorized, people armed, forces of thugs and vagrants mustered. All in order to intimidate and win by fear."[73]

In the session of the jury that was held in Piraí in October, the specific techniques of intimidation and the general atmosphere of stress that had reigned for so many months resulted in across-the-board acquittals, which outraged the district judge. The two defendants charged with homicide, jailbreaking, and assault in connection with the April incident were not even indicted by the grand jury, although the charges were properly prepared by the juiz de paz, there were several eyewitnesses, and one of the defendants had even confessed. Murder suspects in two other cases were indicted by the grand jury but acquitted by the petit jury. In each case, reported the district judge, there was abundant evidence and in one there was a confession. Moreover, in cases of swindling and slave theft apparently unrelated to the jailbreak, the jury acquitted defendants in the face of ample proof and confessions.[74]

If the problem of impunity bedeviled the central government, it also robbed the jury system of local support. Unlike the justice of the peace, who enjoyed a measure of practical compatibility and community support precisely because he could be actively used to advance factional interests, the jury's contribution to the byplay of local power could only be a passive one. Interested parties could usually make a jury exonerate a suspect in spite of overwhelming evidence, but convictions could not be forced as long as there was any lobby at all for acquittal. Since the social circumstances we have described loaded juries with timorous jurors afraid to convict (in contrast to the energetic and often prosecution-happy juizes de paz), the jury was an impossible vehicle for the harassment of rivals. In other words, because the jury system served up impunity for everyone, it served no one. For this reason the institution never attracted the factional support that cultivated and sustained the Juizado de Paz because of its value in local disputes. After the first years local support for the jury system all but vanished.

All the legal reforms of the late 1820s and early 1830s exhibited the marks of Brazilian liberalism. Reaction against the colonial experience and public power, admiration of foreign models, eighteenth-century experimentalism and nineteenth-century romanticism all played a part in motivating the reforms of the liberal decade. In no case, however, did the reforms function in reality as they had been designed to do ideally. The Juizado de Paz was arguably compatible with local needs, but only in a rather anarchic way that seemed to skirt or corrupt the basic principles involved. The jury system was even more disappointing, for here the guiding principles of popular participation and localism themselves undermined the institution's local prestige and effectiveness. The failures of the jury system were especially painful for Brazil's liberal theorists to rationalize because this institution came closest to reflecting their ideals in pure form. Philosophic and social implications could be dodged in criticizing the Juizado de Paz by concentrating on more or less specious *ad hominem* arguments, but to attack the jury system was to impugn the competence of Brazilian society to police itself. Some critics did essay lame attempts to discredit the jury system on theoretical grounds.[75] But most of Brazil's thinkers accepted on faith, as did Caetano Maria Lopes Gama in 1823, that "The intrinsic goodness of [the jury system] is such that to find it inappropriate in Brazil it is necessary to discredit the nation."[76] Years later a Conservative jurist, José Antônio Pimenta Bueno, repeated that "The goodness of [the jury system] is above all question. Attacks on it are in the last analysis attacks on the moral status of the country."[77] The jury system's poor performance in Brazil thus set in motion a relentless process of logic. Since the ideals behind the institution were never really questioned, the blame for its failure could only fall upon the country's "moral status"—the culprit by default. The liberal idealists were especially vulnerable to the terrible implications of this deduction, because by the mid-1830s they had lost the practical support for decentralization that had earlier been provided by their movement's oppositionist character. The inadequacies of the reforms and the changing exigencies of the emerging state therefore began to tear away at the liberal movement's intellectual foundations. Hardheaded theories of control now began to emerge as the political orthodoxy of the day, and a new set of ideas was required to justify them. Seeking an explanation for the failure of its cherished institutions, the intellectual side of Brazilian liberalism furnished those ideas by turning furiously on Brazilian society itself.

Part III. Reaction and the Counterreform,

1837-1871

8. Reactionary Thought and Brazilian Society

Brazil's foremost conservative publicist, Justiniano José da Rocha, believed in a dialectic. History, he thought, was an eternal struggle between the values of authority and those of freedom. Within this struggle he discerned a three-stage pattern: periods of "action" were followed by periods of "reaction," and when both these stages were completed, the historical process concluded with a time of compromise and consolidation of gains which he called "transaction."[1] From a vantage point around mid-century, Rocha readily identified the liberal decade (1827-1837), with its radical innovations and departures from tradition, as preeminently a period of action. The years that followed fit his theory equally well, for after the mid-1830s an abrupt reversal of liberal trends led to a resurgence of conservative thought, the calling of a conservative-minded ministry in 1837, and a period of intense reaction in Brazilian institutional policy. Although they lacked Rocha's hindsight and elegant schema, the contemporaries of this conservative rollback were also acutely aware of what was taking place. They discussed it at length in newspapers and political forums. They gave the phenomenon a businesslike name—clipped and practical like the movement itself, a contrast to the gassy rhetoric of the theory-bound liberals—Regresso or Return, a retreat from the ideals and achievements of the liberal period.

The ideological turnabout originated, took shape, and triumphed during the Regency period (1831-1840), years that have long been recognized as crucial to the political formation of imperial Brazil. The very form of government appeared to be in doubt, for when the first emperor departed in 1831, it was not certain that the interregnum would end with the ascension of his minor son. The political field contained a sizable contingent of republican radicals, and thirteen years separated the child emperor from the age at which he would constitutionally be permitted to rule. Many of the radicals of 1831 clearly hoped to create a consensus in favor of a republican form of government and prevent the accession of a new monarch altogether. Joaquim Nabuco thus saw the Regency as a republican experiment—one that failed—and recent historians have adopted his thesis.[2] In fact, however, the radicals' thwarted hopes for a republic were of minor importance when compared to the disillusionment of the majority moderates. Viewed in the whole context of the reform movement, the republican failure can best be seen as part of a larger test in which the ideological tenets and political strategies of Brazilian liberalism were tried, found wanting, and ultimately rejected. The reasons for this reversal are to be found in the same factors that had determined the liberal ascendancy itself. Changing political and economic conditions lay at bottom, but the pressures these changes released were once again manifested in dissatisfaction with the legal system.

Like the liberal period, the Regresso unfolded in a context of precise events that help to explain it. For reasons that had nothing to do with law, society, or economics, the fear of restoration vanished when the deposed emperor suddenly died in Portugal in 1834. From the date of his abdication until the confirmation of his death, rumors that Pedro I was planning to reclaim his throne had abounded in Brazil, and the large Portuguese-born population was suspected of fifth-column activity in support of such a restoration.[3] It should be recalled that all the liberal reforms from the Juizado de Paz to the Procedural Code were in part justified as instruments of defense against just such a vague Portuguese menace: the Juizado de Paz and Criminal Code to foil an emperor's thirst for absolute power, the National Guard to counter the Portuguese-dominated army, the Procedural Code to solidify support for the liberal Regency in the face of possible restoration. The death of Pedro I relaxed once and for all this crisis mentality that the liberals had traditionally taken advantage of—or possibly cultivated—and in doing so removed one of the practical stays that had supported their reform program from the beginning. Moreover, as long as the Portuguese absolutist (Caramuru) threat could be maintained convincingly as the monolithic danger on the right, legitimate conservative opposition within Brazil had tended to become confused with it and to find its own message tainted by the unpatriotic connotations attached to the supposed Portuguese faction. Here was another weapon that the liberals could no longer use against their conservative opponents after the death of Dom Pedro, and a "patriotic" right-wing opposition emerged immediately. The end of the restoration scare in 1834, by invalidating the liberal government's claim to be protecting native Brazilian institutions from an external peril, thus opened that government and its institutions to more serious internal challenges.

The old devil of semicolonial authoritarianism, personified by the first emperor, was replaced in the 1830s by a series of regional demons which threatened the integrity of the state. In the extremities of the empire, provincial interests went the liberals one better and expressed their dissatisfaction in outright insurrection against central and provincial authorities. Revolts in Bahia, Pará, and Maranhão in the north, and Rio Grande do Sul in the south, undermined the liberal government's posture as the guarantor of provincial interests and dramatized the Regency's inability to enforce its authority in all areas of the empire. The disturbances were by no means inspired by uniform grievances. Restorationist sentiment was an issue in the Cabanos War in Pernambuco; federalism and secession were goals of the Guanais Mineiro and Sabinada revolts in Bahia and the Farroupilha in Rio Grande do Sul; racial or caste tensions played a part in Pará, Maranhão and Bahia; and local power struggles seem to be at least partly responsible in all these rebellions.[4] But whatever their origins, they weakened the government by their persistence and coincidence. Newspapers hostile to the government filled their pages with distressing notices from the outlying provinces.

The regional revolts proved to be an embarrassing test of the state's authority. The moderate government was helpless to end the violence, and the uprisings dragged on for years. The regular army was itself suspected of absolutist sentiments after abdication, and its uneasy garrisons were involved in the regional disturbances on more than one occasion.[5] The liberals' own institution, the National Guard, was a double embarrassment, because far from remedying the situation by providing a loyal and ready militia, the Guard was seldom effectively organized and its factional origins frequently contributed to the unrest. The government found itself master of no armed force or police power capable of maintaining order in the empire: a disastrous military state of affairs, and one which drastically undercut the liberal Regency government's prestige in Brazil and abroad.

A momentous development in the Brazilian economy by the 1830s raised the political stakes and made the liberals' failure to maintain order a fatal one. Brazil's cyclical export economy had been on the downstroke ever since the gold mines had begun to play out in the second half of the eighteenth century, but in the early 1830s coffee trees began to bear abundant fruit in the rich cherry-red soils of Rio de Janeiro's Paraíba River Valley. During the decade coffee became Brazil's first export, accounting for 44 percent of total export earnings over the period. The volume of coffee shipped from the port of Rio jumped from 539,000 *arrobas* (1 arroba = 14.69 kilos) in 1820 to nearly two million ten years later, and to almost five million by 1840.[6] The result was a dramatically raised level of revenues in a country that had been struggling to finance its first independent years with foreign loans.

At the head of this agricultural surge stood a newly emerged elite—the plantation owners of the coffee zone.[7] As a group they were aware of their importance in making the empire's customshouses produce a fresh flow of income for government coffers, and they were quick to make their own imperious demands heard in the chambers of the state. As the owners of coveted tracts of land rendered precious by investments of time, capital, and human life, the planters required a government that could guarantee their investment and if possible increase its yield. As the owners of gangs of slaves that sometimes mounted into the hundreds, they could brook no social unrest nor tolerate delays or incompetence in quelling it where it did appear. Finally, the political status of all Brazil concerned them because their own prosperity often depended on the state of Brazilian credit in foreign markets.

The coffee planters of Rio de Janeiro province therefore constituted a potential nucleus of powerful opposition to the liberal government. Insofar as the liberals and their reforms were perceived as responsible for regional unrest and political fragmentation, this newly established elite found them intolerable. When the external threat of restoration was removed in 1834 and the internal threat of disorder reached dangerous levels, this group—quickly dubbed "the oligarchy"—formed the core around which the conservative opposition party coalesced.[8]

The liberals proved unequal to these new challenges because of the damage that internal disillusionment was causing their movement by the early 1830s. Interwoven with all the circumstantial changes caused by the death of the ex-emperor, the regional disturbances, and the rise of coffee, was the demonstrable failure of the new institutions to improve the quality of life. More than that, many observers noted an active deterioration of the conditions of politics and justice in Brazil as a direct result of the liberal innovations. It was not only easy but at least partially valid to attribute the centrifugal tuggings of peripheral rebellions to the federal reforms of 1834; to link widespread electoral fraud with the local magistrates who presided over elections; to blame the problem of impunity on the jury system; or to find the causes of anarchy in the disorganized National Guard. To a certain extent, emerging conservative groups played upon these failures in a partisan attempt to discredit the men who had passed them, but the failure of the liberal institutions was real enough to be acknowledged grudgingly even by their most ardent supporters.

We have already described some of the objective flaws in the liberal reform institutions. In the 1830s Brazilians were aware of these more or less specific weaknesses, but their subjective criticisms ranged wide and gave voice to more general preoccupations as they explored the implications of the liberal interval and tried to find reasons for its poor performance. Just as an objective study of the functioning of the Juizado de Paz or jury system is in some ways an excursion into a Brazilian parish, so the study of changing Brazilian attitudes toward those institutions gives an intriguing glimpse of the national mentality and evolving self-image before mid-century.

Although the native conservative reaction did not get fully under way until

after the death of Pedro I in 1834, the sentiments of the underground Portuguese party, the Caramurus, had long foreshadowed it. Antinativist pamphlets
and broadsides that appeared after the abdication warned Brazilians against
"republican" institutions imported from other civilizations and stressed that
Brazil was essentially a monarchical country. Most of these baleful documents
singled out liberal legal institutions for particularly concentrated attacks. Justices of the peace who abused their powers to the point of becoming like "mon-
sters in human figure," and the "raving demagogues" who were seated on Brazil's juries, symbolized the nation's drift away from its true monarchic destiny.[9]
Such reactionary propaganda drove home its point by predicting the dissolution
of the empire and civil war as a result of decentralizing reforms and by blaming
the leniency of the legal system and the spineless National Guard for foment-
ing the disruption of society and obstructing social control. A favorite theme
was the allegedly larger number of "vagrants, thieves, and . . . murderers . . .
that nowadays infest our cities, villages, and countryside." And the dread fear
of slave rebellion was invoked as the ultimate consequence of foreign ideas and
liberal excesses.[10]

The earliest of the liberal legal reforms, the Juizado de Paz, was always the
most vulnerable to criticism because individual judges so often abused their
powers, made enemies, or found themselves the central figures in local disputes.
Local political rivalries and bickering soon came to revolve around the local justice of the peace, and while such conflicts were usually more personal than institutional, the sheer amount of friction seemed to require some explanation.
Supporters of the institution responded by regretting the role of local factionalism in juiz de paz elections and blaming political influences for the disappointing performance of magistrates in some parishes. *O Astro de Minas* presented
an apology for the transgressions of the judges of Minas Gerais in 1836 by pointing out that they had been elected during a "revolutionary period" (1833) and
therefore chosen more for their political opinions than for their level-headedness.
"This is why there is a clamor against the juizes de paz. But when the public
spirit is more tranquil we will see judges who have not been elected in the midst
of political passions; then we will make our judgment."[11] *Aurora Fluminense*
accepted the political nature of the local magistrate but only underscored the
problems of an elected judiciary when it complained bitterly of the election of
restorationist-faction magistrates in Rio de Janeiro in 1833.[12]

But if die-hard liberals were at pains to discover simple temporary reasons
for the difficulties that their institution was encountering, an emerging conservative press expressed opposition sentiments in language that harked back to
the colonial tradition of attacks on the magistracy. In 1834, Padre Lopes Gama
of Recife wrote that Pernambuco's parish judges strutted about arrogantly like
"little Sultans." To Lopes Gama the judges were "the most intolerable little

despots of Brazil . . . who in their capriciousness and weight-swinging are as bad as the most wild-eyed governors of the old regime."[13]   Even the generally liberal *O Sete de Abril* ran an article in 1833 chiding the juizes de paz for their "well-known stupidity, pedantry, and foolish pride," and accusing them of "wanting to be the Pashas and despots of Brazil as long as they have some party or person of respect behind them."[14]

After the Procedural Code greatly enhanced the police and judicial powers of the elected magistrates, criticism began to focus more on institutional shortcomings than on individual judges. It was remarked that the heightened responsibilities of the Juizado de Paz had rendered the post incompatible with short-term tenure by laymen. Many commentators worried that citizens of the better sort would avoid the onerous burdens of judgeship, leaving the office in the hands of less competent individuals who might have received "one or two votes only."[15]   Even if serving as parish magistrate were not considered undesirable, on the other hand, some critics doubted that many of Brazil's parishes contained enough men of sufficient intelligence, learning, and probity to exercise the jurisdiction successfully if a different man had to serve each year of the four-year period between elections. While the man with the highest or second highest vote might be acceptable, they reasoned, in a small parish little could be expected from those who placed third or fourth.[16]

All these concerns reflected a growing disbelief in the ability of popular discernment to choose men to serve in a judicial capacity. Implicitly, objections to the temporary nature of the Juizado de Paz, doubts about the ability of most men to serve competently, and distrust of the elective process of selection led right back around to the colonial notion of an exclusivistic and specialized elite magistracy. The hand of the professional judges and the mentality that had made them so powerful during colonial days were transparently present in all criticism of this type. Juizes de paz were scoffed at as too uneducated to exercise the jurisdiction, and the mysteries involved in gathering evidence and drawing up charges were exaggerated to make them seem thoroughly outside the ken of the uninitiated. Such criticism was especially pernicious because it seemed so reasonable—sympathetic to the overworked and befuddled lay judge who was saddled with a job "the performance of which is far beyond his capabilities." After all, even the liberal press had to agree in part that many juizes had too much to do after the Código do Processo increased their responsibilities.[17]

Closely related to these views was the attitude of the central government. Regardless of their ideological commitments, governments both liberal and conservative shared common objections to the Juizado de Paz. Because, at least in theory, it was the government's responsibility to see that the administration of justice proceeded fairly and efficiently, widespread dissatisfaction with the legal system reflected directly on the ministry. This held especially true for the liberal administrations that followed the abdication of Pedro I, because the re-formed legal system was so much their own creation. And for these administra-tions the problem was the more acute because the nature of their creation de-prived them of any control over it. The emperor's abdication had vaulted the liberals into power where they, like the emperor, were handicapped by an un-responsive local magistracy precisely when they most needed control of the imperial bureaucracy and police to stifle civil disturbances and consolidate their own position.

The first liberal ministries instantly appreciated the predicament.   One month after the abdication of Dom Pedro, the liberals' minister of justice re-ported that juizes de paz were trafficking in "conciliations" and often became too dependent on local bosses. Running counter to all the ideals of judicial independence that had been influential in creating the local judges, the minister suggested that justices of the peace be given a salary by the government in order to make them independent of local elements.[18] This startling recommendation to put local judges on the government payroll to assure their "independence" would have been considered a contradiction in terms by the liberals just one month before it was made. It is indeed a striking example of how quickly a statesman's point of view could change when he moved from opposition benches into the government.

Other liberals in the justice ministry remained truer to the founding principles of locally elected justice, but all of them struggled with the problems of govern-ing without any direct control over local justice and police. In 1832 Diogo Antônio Feijó acknowledged that the government's hands were tied, and yet, "The juizes de paz who are exclusively entrusted with [the police] . . . cannot always give the time necessary to their work . . . nor do all have the necessary intelligence and circumspection." Feijó, whose hatred for the professional magistracy was unrivaled, nevertheless suggested that government-appointed judges ("upright and intelligent") be assigned to oversee the local magistrates, share some of their powers, and "give the government some way of [assuring] tranquility and public security." Otherwise, said the minister, "without any unified means of action, the government cannot assume any responsibility."[19]

But the situation was not remedied, and the momentum of the reformers in Parliament defied the pleas of the ministry. By 1835 the state of regional "an-archy" and unrest had reduced the liberal government to desperate straits. Min-ister of Justice Manuel Alves Branco, the very man who had presented the final version of the Procedural Code to the legislature back in 1831, declared that "next to Religion . . . the Police is the most important factor in the tranquility of nations." In his frenzy to get constabulary authority separated from the elected magistrates and restored to the hands of government appointees, Alves Branco stated that the police should be the "first and most efficacious auxiliary of the Government and the courts," which, "without any doubt demand a class of operatives who have no other cares, or tasks—especially in states which find themselves in the circumstances of our country." The minister went on to compare the present police structure, under the parish judges, unfavorably with even the chaotic police system of the colonial period. Finally he showed how far the liberals had been pushed from their original ideals by the hard realities of four years in government: he requested that the legislature give the government the right to appoint juizes de paz.[20] The last liberal justice minister of the 1830s, Antônio Paulino Limpo de Abreu, while still recommending reforms, looked backward wistfully. "In the beginning the institution of the Juizado de Paz was greeted with loud applause and eulogies, but afterward came the time of its decadence."[21] Liberals and conservatives seem essentially to have agreed with Limpo de Abreu's analysis of the sorry state of the Juizado de Paz by the mid-1830s. As early as 1834, when deputies critical of the judgeship read examples of malfeasance into the official record of the legislative debates, few voices were raised in defense of the institution.[22]

When the conservatives came to power in 1837, then, their official attacks on the Juizado de Paz did not differ substantially from those of their predecessors. Under the Regresso cabinets the call for reform rose more stridently, however, and the elected judges were the objects of stronger and more colorful language. One minister of justice asserted that many juizes de paz in the interior "should be in our prisons doing penance for their long careers in crime."[23] In his yearly reports, first as provincial president of Rio de Janeiro and later as minister of justice, the Regresso mastermind Paulino José Soares de Souza, avoided the shopworn complaints that had become such commonplaces and instead jolted his listeners with grisly stories of mutilations, disembowelments, and multiple murders in order to dramatize the need for effective police control. Paulino's especially gruesome report as minister of justice in 1841 certainly did his cause no harm, for the sweeping reforms he sought were passed later in that year.[24]

The conservative governments of the late 1830s used the discredit of the elected magistracy to taint other liberal ideals and institutions as well. The minister of justice serving in 1840, in criticizing the parish judgeship, indirectly registered a blanket indictment of the electoral principle in times of distress. "In all countries there are times when passions dominate society and produce a large number of crimes. This vice invades the population and affects the election of judges who therefore represent the passions and vices of the election itself instead of symbolizing the image of the Law."[25] And because the liberal institutions were interconnected, the discredit of one naturally implicated the others. Since jury panels were qualified by the juizes de paz, for instance, corruption in the judge presumably led to like corruption in jury formation.

Attacks on the parish judge could also be parlayed into political capital. Regresso spokesmen in government manipulated the juiz de paz question to cur-
ry favor with the professional magistracy, especially with the district judges
who had been offended by the institution of elected local magistrates. Regressista politicians repeatedly demanded the return of the powers of drawing up
charges (*formação de culpa*) to the professional district judges who could understand legal subtleties, and they lamented the waste of talent that the lessening
of letrado authority since 1827 had caused. Paulino José Soares de Souza, himself a professional magistrate, interpreted the frustration of his class with the
liberal judicial system: "If the elections do not return an active and intelligent
juiz de paz, then the actions of the district judge are worthless . . . and his functions are limited to sterile recommendations."[26]   Such statements by government officials reflected the high percentage of professional judges in conservative political circles as much as they betrayed a policy of recruiting others into
the emerging party. But either way the implications were clear: the decline of
liberal institutions would be paralleled by the reascension of the professional
magistracy.

After the Juizado de Paz, the most controversial of the liberal legal institutions was the jury system. The petty judge and the jury were considered to
share responsibility for the problem of impunity, but critics attacked the institutions from different directions. By 1835 the Juizado de Paz had grown and
been modified into a *sui generis* institution whose police functions gave it a
highly political character which divorced it from most of the early ideals of impartial neighborhood justice and opened it to wide-ranging criticism. But the
jury system, unlike the local magistracy, remained something of a sacred cow
in Brazil.[27]   Because the jury as an institution was never larded with the extra-
neous responsibilities that transformed the Juizado de Paz, it retained its original conceptual purity. And yet juries did not perform well in Brazil, and their
uniformly ("as if by common instinct") high rate of acquittals was thought to
be a major factor in perpetuating civil unrest in the country.[28]   The apparently
successful performance of juries in other countries made the institution difficult
to attack from a theoretical point of view; its anonymous nature exempted it
from the kind of individual smears that damaged the entire institution of the
Juizado de Paz; and its lack of direct police and political powers spared it the
full measure of government criticism. While the jury's failures were demonstrable, then, expressions of dissatisfaction had to go deeper than those aimed
at the Juizado de Paz. Critics therefore sought explanations for the failure of
the jury system more in the nature of Brazilian society than in the institution
itself.

Attacks on the conceptual or intrinsic goodness of the jury system were very
rare, for as Justiniano José da Rocha sarcastically observed, "to doubt its good-

ness—almost its infallibility—is a sacrilege."[29]   Rocha was virtually alone in his skepticism about the fundamental wisdom of the jury system. In his essay on the flaws of the liberal judiciary, published in 1835, Rocha did try to demonstrate that the jury also functioned poorly in other countries (he mentioned France and England). As for the Brazilian version of the institution, the journalist was especially critical of the juror's responsibility for finding law. Jurymen should be judges of the facts of a case, he argued, not of the law or its applicability; but Brazilian juries were required to determine whether the defendant's actions constituted a crime—a question of law, not of evidence.[30]   Rocha believed that the Brazilian jury system was thus robbed of its "essential character," but his argument, by far the most sophisticated advanced by any critic, had little popular resonance.[31]

A more potent and common complaint about the jury system grew out of the question of impunity, especially of political criminals. In ordinary criminal proceedings the jury's role lacked the immediacy of that of the justice of the peace, and tempers had time to cool before the jury could be empaneled— usually a matter of months after the fact. But in the political cases that often became *causes célèbres* in the provinces, tenaciously held political convictions assured that the performance of juries would be closely scrutinized. When jurors acquitted those involved in political disturbances they furnished local and national elites with an explanatory link between the jury system and the regional rebellions.

The prosecution of the Sabinada rebels of Bahia is illustrative. The Sabinada revolt of 1837 was a federalist uprising that succeeded in capturing the capital city of Bahia province for a few months in 1837-1838. When the rebels were finally driven out, those civilians captured were tried by jury in public court. The trials extended over two years, and although two revolutionary chiefs were sentenced to death, many others were acquitted.[32]   The *Correio Mercantil*, Bahia's foremost conservative newspaper and the political organ of the provincial government, interpreted the Sabinada as a class war, vigorously protested the "impunity" of the rebels cleared by the jury, and launched a campaign to discredit the lenient institution. Everything about the jury system galled the editor of the *Correio* (a professional magistrate by training):[33] it was slow to meet, its proceedings dragged, its members were taken from inferior and irresponsible social strata, and it affronted the pride of the professional judges as a class. But most of all, Bahian juries did not share the editor's vindictive attitude toward the rebels of the Sabinada. The *Correio Mercantil* railed against "the philanthropy of our time" that absolved known revolutionaries and placed political crimes under civilian jurisdiction rather than that of military tribunals. The newspaper, representing the most influential conservative circles of the province, strongly advocated that political crimes be tried in military courts and that the jury's competence in such matters be curtailed.[34]

Problems of civil unrest, exemplified by Bahia's Sabinada, brought the attention of the embattled central government to rest on the jury system as one factor responsible for the activity of subversive elements. By the mid-1830s some observers were suggesting the possibility of removing "the most delicate" matters from the competence of the jury;[35] and after the outcry created by the Sabinada revolt, legislative proposals surfaced for either turning political offenses over to military courts or for creating "special tribunals" to prosecute political cases.[36] *Aurora Fluminense,* in 1838, deplored this campaign to circumscribe the jury system's authority and denied that the institution was to blame for many provincial rebellions.[37]

Sniping at legal fine points in the jury's powers and suggesting alternative procedures for judging political crimes were in themselves minor weapons in the Regresso attack on the jury system. As long as the principles represented by the jury were widely sanctioned, as they seem to have been, the blame for its failure had largely to be placed outside the institution. The principal energies of the campaign to discredit the jury system, therefore, were directed not against flaws in the institution itself but against shortcomings in Brazilian society that prevented the successful functioning of the new system. It was around the jury system issue, then, that discouraged liberals and the emerging conservatives hatched the most pervasive and long-lived of Brazilian arguments against liberal institutions—that which held liberalism inappropriate in Brazil because of the country's "inadequate level of civilization."

The argument that Brazilian citizens were not civilized enough to exercise wisely the responsibilities of jury duty began at the level of the individual juror. The Constitution of 1824 and the Procedural Code had included a property qualification, of course, but it was clearly not high enough to keep the humble off Brazil's juries. One Rio newspaper complained that the 200 milreis annual income requirement opened the jury to "individuals of the lowest class, ignorant and accessible to all kinds of seductions, whose only interest in society is its disruption." Even if the requirement were raised to 300 milreis, continued the newspaper, it would still not exclude "the black street vendor and the most moronic and miserable workman."[38] In Pernambuco, *O Carapuceiro* also supported a more exclusive policy that in addition to raising the income requirement to 400 milreis would demand literacy and reduce the number of jurors per session from sixty to thirty.[39]

If the inadequate-level-of-civilization argument could be applied selectively to the poor and the uneducated, it could also be fitted to more general regional and rural-urban prejudices. One of the most popular proposals for reform involved the withdrawal of trial by jury from the rural counties of the interior which seemed to be least civilized and most backward. In noting that almost no one in Minas Gerais any longer had a good word for the jury system, *O Universal* nevertheless did not doubt that "some parts of Brazil are already in circumstances to receive the Procedural Code, as we should expect from an enlightened and moral people—but in the empire as a whole it is certainly not practicable."[40] Most Regressista or conservative commentators thought that the jury system could only be "practicable" in the provincial capitals and large cities of the empire because, as Justiniano José da Rocha reminded, "There is more to Brazil than Rio de Janeiro."[41]

The discovery of this incompatibility between much of Brazilian society and liberal institutions naturally implied a reevaluation of the usefulness of foreign models in framing institutional policy. Even if the imported institutions had been successful, however, some form of reaction to the Anglophilia of the liberals was probably inevitable, as the constantly invoked examples of the English, French, or United States experiences had lost much of their persuasiveness by the mid-1830s. Statements like that of *Aurora Fluminense* in commenting on proposals for special courts to try political crimes ("the very mention of exceptional tribunals would cause an Englishman's hair to stand on end")[42] seemed increasingly irrelevant and even undignified in the face of real Brazilian problems. In an article that was reprinted in the Rio press, the Pernambucan Padre Lopes Gama identified the distinctive characteristic of Brazilians as "a taste for aping the worst things about foreigners." Since England and France had a jury system, chided Lopes Gama, Brazil had blindly emulated those countries without any regard for the diverse conditions of their own.[43] A Bahian newspaper insistently belittled the jury system as a "fashion,"[44] and in Rio someone was moved to verse:

> We are not yet France or England.
> We are the newborn Brazilian people,
> And the jury will be the ruin of our land.[45]

Growing objections to the justice of the peace and the jury system soon brought the entire legal system under fire and led to full-scale reevaluations of the practicability of the liberals' reform program. Even the most stalwart liberals began to waffle on their commitment to liberal institutions. A turning point was reached in 1835 when the soon-to-be regent Diogo Antônio Feijó wrote an article that was reprinted in *Aurora Fluminense. Aurora,* liberal journal *par excellence,* seemed to be publishing an admission of defeat as it analyzed the "anarchy that reigns in all Brazil." Among free peoples, said the article, the strength of the state and the assurance of individual security rest on two institutions—justice and the citizen militia—but in most of Brazil "the National Guard and the Jury . . . seem to have been aborted at birth." The National Guard was in many places so discredited that some wanted to reestablish the old militias. The juries of the country were dominated by the idle, who were in turn dominated by those with specific interests in their verdicts.[46]

The paper that had so fervently supported the elected judgeship now referred to the local magistrates as "a scourge upon the people who elect them." Feijó's article criticized the adoption of British or North American institutions inappropriate to Brazil, and charged that the most serious problems of Brazil derived from the fact that recent legislation was "ill-suited to our habits and customs, and designed for a superior civilization." The Brazilian people did not understand either their rights or duties under the new system and "show that for centuries they were educated in Absolutism and that fourteen years are not enough to regenerate an entire people."[47] The tone of the article was one of the profoundest personal discouragement and melancholy, for Feijó, its author, and Evaristo da Veiga, the publisher of *Aurora Fluminense,* were old liberals who had fought for the very institutions that they here denounced. Their extraordinary confession of doubt caused a sensation in political circles,[48] and while neither man allowed the spirit of self-criticism to lead him into the Regresso camp, their published ruminations of 1835 illustrate the pervasive nature of liberal disillusionment that made the reactionary movement so many converts after the middle of the decade.

As the Regresso movement gathered steam, a conservative political press emerged whose editorial policy focused sharply upon the failure of the legal reforms and the weaknesses of Brazilian society. Some of these newspapers accepted subsidies from the political arm of the Regresso,[49] but others were independently skeptical of the wisdom of the liberal reforms. The popular and much reprinted *O Carapuceiro* of Pernambuco, whose priest-editor Miguel do Sacramento Lopes Gama had begun his journalistic career as a radical liberal, now lampooned the new institutions on every occasion. The Juizado de Paz, the jury system, and the National Guard were favorite targets, and the perverse, insubordinate, and deceitful nature of most Brazilians was found to bear the blame for their failures. Padre Lopes Gama now saw Brazil's problem as "having wanted to race up the giant steps of civilization three at a time."[50]   In his nastier humors, Lopes Gama ascribed all of Brazil's current ills to the liberal principles and institutions introduced since independence. Upon surveying the panorama of regional uprisings he exasperatedly declared in 1838 that "the people of Brazil are as likely candidates for democracy as the Moslems are to recognize the authority of the Pope."[51] The chief curmudgeon of the Brazilian empire had found in the Regresso a congenial political home.[52]

Lopes Gama was not alone. Following the Sabinada rebellion and the failure of the Bahian jury to punish severely enough its participants, the *Correio Mercantil,* formerly a dry collection of commercial notices, launched an attack on the liberal legal system so furious that charges of sedition were eventually brought against the paper, and its campaign was heatedly discussed in the national Parliament.[53] The "Lavrador do Recôncavo" series, begun in 1838, featured the rustic vernacular wisdom of a mythical Cachoeira sugar planter who in reality was probably the letrado editor of the paper, João Antônio Sampaio Viana. The immensely popular "communiqués," which appeared roughly at two week intervals, interpreted events and institutions from an authoritarian, intensely reactionary point of view. The Lavrador do Recôncavo scoffed and railed at the liberal legal institutions and singled out the liberal press for having spent "eight years nibbling away like an epidemic at this emaciated giant, the Empire of Brazil." The Lavrador expressed nostalgia for colonial days and blamed the legal codes, the jury system, and the Juizado de Paz for "laying Brazil out with her legs in the air."[54] Between communiqués, the *Correio Mercantil* pursued an editorial policy which held that "the single origin of our troubles is ... our judicial organization." If the impunity fostered by the Procedural Code was necessary to assure "liberty," then the newspaper could do without that blessing, "preferring instead the natural state of society, where at least the strongest was always the most respected."[55]

After the mid-1830s, the liberals had no defenders in the press who could match the popularity of the *Carapuceiro* or the Lavrador do Recôncavo. The attacks on the reform institutions and the moral quality of Brazilian civilization had become general, and a government spokesman stated as early as 1836 that "there is not a single liberal institution that does not have many enemies dedicated to its discredit and destruction."[56] Even the liberal government was finding fault with the juizes de paz, and the classic liberal newspapers now admitted that the great reforms had been largely disappointing. It was a remarkable reversal of the consensus, and one that depended very heavily upon acceptance of the proposition that Brazilian civilization was in an early stage of development. Such an abrupt and thorough about-face demanded a more synthetic explanation than had yet been developed, and in the late 1830s and early 1840s many observers searched for it in national character and public morality.

One of the most commonly mentioned reasons for the inadequacy of Brazilian civilization was the lack of education—the ignorance—of the people. Formal education, to the Brazilian mind, conferred an almost mystical distinction upon those who possessed it, and vice versa. Back in 1829, during the discussions of the Criminal Code, one liberal newspaper had accepted the argument that capital punishment was probably "indispensable" in Brazil because "presently not all of our people can acquire a primary education."[57] Similarly, general education or the lack of it was held by many to have the same global effect for good or evil that was often thought to be a property of the legal system. In the course of the debates that centered around reforming the Procedural Code in

1841, one deputy minimized the effectiveness of reforming the legal system and instead advocated general education as a cure-all for Brazil's woes. "It is not so much the reform of our Codes as that of our customs that will suffocate anarchy."[58]

Yet formal education of the people (*instrução*) was seldom mentioned specifically as a tonic for the ailments of the liberal legal structure. More often, the question of education kept closer to the colloquial and classist Brazilian definition of the word *educação*, with its connotation of manners, breeding, or cultural background. Critics who worried about illiteracy in juizes de paz or jurors seldom suggested that more people be taught to read; instead, their objectives were to limit judicial responsbiility to those with a suitable "educação." Literacy and good breeding overlapped only incidentally.

To liberals fighting in defense of their legal reforms, "educação" meant the reform of all those characteristics of Brazilian society—irresponsibility, dependence, indifference—that made liberal institutions perform poorly. "The people are now used to hearing only the sonorous words 'equality and liberty' without seeing the duties that go along with them," wrote the editor of *O Astro de Minas* in 1836. He argued that Brazil's problems derived from a rapid adoption of the rights of freedom without a simultaneous acceptance of its obligations. Still in the early stages of disillusionment, the newspaper was optimistic but vague about the future: "[Give us] morality, [good] customs, and *instrução*, and we will become able to enjoy all these institutions."[59] But where, if not through formal education, was this anticipated moral development of the Brazilian people to come from?

One source was obviously supposed to be the popular guides and handbooks that had sprung up to explain the reforms and show the way to good citizenship. Another, hoped liberal journalists, would be the osmotic effect of political discussion in the press. Liberal newspapers took to heart this role as reformer and political guide of the "people." Frequent articles outlined how to make wise decisions as well as which decisions to make in specific instances such as elections.[60] But the most important of all the factors in the moral education of Brazil was seen to be time—precisely the commodity in shortest supply from a political point of view. When the jury system was under attack and threatened with crippling modifications in 1838, for example, *Aurora Fluminense* pleaded only for time: "The jury has still not had time to put down roots in the soil of our nation; only time can provide the political education of societies."[61]

In the last analysis, however, the doctrinaire liberals were intellectually unprepared for even a partial failure of their institutions, and were therefore unable to defend them effectively. The remaining idealists could observe that the institutions were not working well; they could accept that the people were ignorant, immoral, even perverse; but still they could not qualify their categorical assumptions about the transcendent wisdom and innate practicability of their reforms. Arguing that time, education, or propagandizing would make Brazilians able to enjoy the fruits of liberalism was therefore beside the point for men like Evaristo da Veiga whose reasoning ran in circles around the central goodness of the liberal institutions. Ultimately *Aurora Fluminense*'s strongest defense of reforms like the jury system remained one that, while acknowledging the need to "educate" and moralize the people, supported the institutions themselves as educating agents. "The jury system should be regarded as a powerful means to educate the people for liberty," wrote Evaristo in 1835.[62] And as late as 1838, his newspaper printed that "the jury system is more than a guarantee; it is a civilizing influence like all free institutions."[63]

Issues such as formal education and public morality eventually came to rest on the doorstep of the church, although lay observers tended to blame the shortcomings of Brazilian civilization less on the representatives of organized religion than on the people's disinclination to heed the church's teachings.[64] In the early 1830s, pamphleteers of the Portuguese restorationist party had warned that irreligion and liberalism went hand in hand. Such Caramuru publications argued that liberalism weakened religious faith and that irreverence bred liberalism; they prophesied a grim future for a Brazil that was turning away from monarchy and religion in order to embrace a set of false, modern principles.[65] After the disillusionments of the 1830s, Regresso conservatives accepted irreligion as a fact, and in their effort to discredit the liberal administrative structure, they updated the Caramuru argument by questioning the practicability of democratic institutions of self-government in a society where "moral precepts are as good as dead, and religious precepts are totally forgotten."[66]

Liberals also believed that the people had abandoned their religion, and adopted a sophisticated version of the argument as an explanation for the failures of liberal institutions. For *O Astro de Minas* and *Aurora Fluminense* in 1839, the analogy was between irreligion and the civic irresponsibility that many liberals saw as the major obstacle to liberalism. Both conditions were caused by the average Brazilian's cynical lack of faith and personal commitment, whether to the church or to political ideals. As the liberal press saw it, this "political, moral, and religious skepticism" pervaded Brazil because, since independence, the country had been nurtured exclusively on eighteenth-century French philosophy: "essentially irreligious, sensual, and the enemy of all forms of authority." *Aurora* wrote that in this sense Brazilians were "still eighteenth-century Frenchmen . . . one hundred years behind the times."[67] Brazilian commentators all concurred that the people's immorality and lack of religion were linked, and regardless of their politics they tried to enlist the faith on their own side of the administrative question.

Liberals and conservatives also agreed that many of the reasons for "our

miserable state of corruption and degradation" lay in the colonial experience.[68]
In its early stages, this argument grew naturally out of the anti-Portuguese
nativism of the abdication period and was closely related to concern over the
"educação" of Brazilians. According to the *Carapuceiro,* Brazil's problems of
government derived from the "incompetent tutelage and terrible customs which
we received from the defunct absolutist regime of the Kings of Portugal."[69] In
Rio, a liberal newspaper singled out the period after 1808 for creating the "critical circumstances" in which Brazil found herself. "The prolonged stay of two
depraved Kings and their demoralized Courts implanted the most damaging social vices and corrupted our customs."[70]

In the late 1830s, cooler analyses pointed out the effect of the colonial
period on institutional success or failure. Padre Lopes Gama cited Brazil's overnight transition from an "almost Turkish administration [as Portugal's colony]
to the most refined heights of the Representative system for which we had . . .
not the most fleeting shadow of preparation."[71] Feijó recognized the stubborn
persistence of colonial behavior even long after political independence had been
secured. "[The people] obey out of habit, and more in deference to the authorities themselves than to the Laws . . . just as was the case under the absolutist
regime."[72] Evaristo da Veiga also saw in ingrained attitudes and habits the
prime obstacle to a liberal empire, and called for individual and public efforts
to "emancipate ourselves from the despotism of these old evil habits, as we
freed ourselves from the despotism of power."[73]

On the other hand, "anarchy," immorality, and revolt in the empire darkened the image of the colonist as well as the colonizer. The United States, for
example, could now be seen as an inappropriate model for Brazil because that
country had been "peopled and tutored by philosophers," whereas colonial
Brazil was settled by "criminals, exiles, and vagrants."[74] This type of exaggeration became so prevalent under the first Regresso governments that a liberal
newspaper protested that to judge by government rhetoric, "one would think
that the Brazilians had only yesterday crawled up, naked, out of the rivers—
abandoning a nomadic existence to try Society for the first time."[75]

It should be noted that few of the reasons given for the low level of Brazilian civilization and morality were advanced in the spirit of raising that level.
Aurora Fluminense might call for time, and an occasional individual might propose a long-term program of formal education, but for the majority of observers, and especially for the Regresso political faction, the lesson of disillusionment was simply the negative one. Brazilians were too uncivilized to govern
themselves. Contemporary thinkers concluded not that ways should be sought
to bring the Brazilian people up to the level of nineteenth-century liberalism,
but that the organizational and philosophical foundations of the Brazilian state
should be modified to suit the notion that the people could not be trusted.

During the troubled 1830s, therefore, a distinctively conservative philosophy of politics and government, history, and society took deep root in Brazil—eventually supplanting the idealistic liberalism of the early years of independence and marking all subsequent Brazilian history with its assumptions and reasoning.

Although the conservatives frequently referred to themselves as "monarchist" in philosophy, in fact their movement was more simply a negative reaction against the liberal reforms. If any principle underlay the Regresso, it was an opportunistic empiricism—opportunistic in that the liberals had performed the experiments from which the conservatives drew their conclusions. Experimentalism had long been called for by liberals, too, who believed that the country should be scrutinized closely and scientifically in order to identify its needs and perfect its institutions. The liberals had hoped, for instance, that justices of the peace would gather exact statistical information in their parishes. And when the failure of many liberal reforms became evident, the phenomenon was often blamed on insufficient study and understanding of Brazil's distinct characteristics. The Regressistas, while not pretending to have independently gathered the expertise to perfect Brazil, claimed a shaky empirical superiority over their predecessors by simply espousing a program different from the liberal program that had failed.

Conservative empiricism was conscientiously identified with a "good sense" or "common sense" approach to government. Liberals were criticized for their devotion to theories, and the practical aspects of administrative experience instead claimed the admiration of conservative spokesmen.[76] For Paulino José Soares de Souza, legislation itself was a science which should obey the "severe and exacting methods employed in the natural and physical [sciences]." The collection, coordination, and divulgation of facts, he declared, would be the conservatives' weapon against the "vagueness and rhetoric ... with which Social Science has become so hallucinated in the vast dominions of optimistic imaginations."[77] As minister of justice in 1841, Paulino played on fears of "anarchy" by giving as an example of the "scientific" approach to administration the collection of crime statistics for the entire empire. Such a collection of "facts" would enable the government to monitor the "moral progress" of the people. The minister of justice had pioneered this technique for "measuring the underdevelopment of civilization" when he served as president of the province of Rio de Janeiro in 1839, and the statistical approach to resolving the law-and-order issue became a conservative standby after 1841.[78]

The critical conservatives drew a number of conclusions from a revisionist analysis of Brazilian history since independence. In their reexamination of the recent past, Regressistas identified Brazil's political problems as lack of governmental prestige and radical departures from tradition. As early as 1832, Diogo

Antônio Feijó had foreshadowed this aspect of the coming reaction when he
sought the reasons for the weakness of the new liberal government in the historical circumstances surrounding the abdication. After independence, said Feijó,
the country was kept together only by the "habit of obedience, the fear of a
return to absolutism, and the prestige of a powerful monarch." When Pedro I
abdicated, however, all this disappeared and "the Prince was succeeded by citizens taken from the midst of society without any prestige except that of their
probity and patriotism." Hence the social unrest of the Regency period and
the constant attacks that weakened the government.[79]

The later Regresso interpretation of the early history of the Regency period
exaggerated this liberal view in order to exalt the inherent prestige of the monarch. By extension, the acephalous liberal years were portrayed as a time of
governmental irresponsibility and weakness which encouraged social dissolution.
Nine years after Feijó, Paulino José Soares de Souza sat in the same chair and
gave the conservative view of the abdication and Regency period: "Only a short
time before [the abdication] we had left a colonial regime. We were too dis-
trustful and fearful of authority, and we avidly embraced the vague and rhetorical doctrines of an exaggerated freedom."[80] For the Regressistas, this
exaggerated freedom, along with an imprudent drive toward precipitous progress, were the misguided objectives of the liberals in 1831. "The ideas of absolute progress" lay behind the abdication of the emperor in 1831 and brought
to power those who wished "to carry Brazil immediately to a state of absolute
perfection," went one article printed in *O Sete de Abril* in 1838.[81] *O Sete*
had begun its existence in 1833 as a liberal sheet but had followed its patron,
Bernardo Pereira de Vasconcelos, into the conservative camp two years later.
Vasconcelos was the most prominent of many liberals who abandoned the
party during the mid-1830s to become the founders of the Regresso movement.
In 1837 he gave a personal analysis of the events of the early 1830s as a justification of his political conversion.

> I was a liberal [in 1831]. Freedom was new in the country then; it was part
> of everyone's aspirations, but it did not exist in the laws or in practical
> ideas—[central] power was still everything, so I was a liberal. Now, however,
> society presents us with a different aspect: the democratic principles won
> the day and in many cases have been prejudicial. Society was then menaced
> by power and authority, now it is threatened by disorganization and anarchy.[82]

The conservative historical interpretation was most fully expressed by Justiniano José da Rocha, the chief conservative publicist, in his articles in *O Brasil*
and eventually in his pamphlet *Ação, Reação e Transação*. Rocha believed that
the Regency period had had great potential as a time for Brazilians to acquire

experience in self-administration and the practical business of government. But instead of realizing that potential, the "democratic experiment" had only bred disrespect for leaders and intemperate criticism of authority. The resultant political struggles of the Regency therefore made Brazilians "forget the true principles of monarchic stability" while depriving them of their opportunity to "master the complicated workings of public service." Out of this frustrating experience, thought Rocha, had come an irresistible tendency toward Monarchism, "just as in 1831 there was an inclination toward republicanism."[83]

To the Regressistas of the chaotic late 1830s and early 1840s, a return to the principles of monarchy meant reinforced government authority to restore order in the empire. Indeed, before it adopted the Conservative Party label, the Regresso movement had referred to itself simply as the "Party of Order." Order, of course, meant social control. The irresponsibility, low level of civilization, and immorality of the people had been among the prime lessons of the liberal decade, and the first Regresso governments openly sought greater authority to repress the outstanding manifestations of Brazilian untuliness. But there was another side to the question of order. The beneficiaries of the orderly empire promised by the Regresso, for instance, were presumably distinct from the savages who had proven that liberalism was inappropriate in Brazil. During the initial period of reaction against the liberal government and its institutions, critics had tarred the Brazilian people indiscriminately for their inadequate degree of civilization, but after the conservatives came to power they began to develop new, more sophisticated evaluations of society which exempted their own clientele from the blanket slurs of the 1830s. Fully formed, the conservative image of Brazilian society rested heavily upon a corporate social analysis and regional prejudices that reflected both the political disillusionments and the economic triumphs of the 1830s.

In the most general sense, the segments of society who were to benefit from and support orderly government were those who enjoyed material prosperity. For the Regressistas this general goal of material progress took the place of the institutional or "absolute" progress of the liberals. "We now have enough freedom in our Institutions," a newspaper had printed in an early (1836) version of this argument. "What we need now is security in which to enjoy this freedom and our prosperity."[84] Two years later the voice of the Regresso in Bahia asserted that there was too *much* freedom in Brazil's institutions and espoused "material progress" as "more useful than these utopias."[85] Not only would "order" guarantee prosperity, but industry and hard work would reinforce political stability. "Among us political institutions have not received the material consecration of industry," wrote Francisco de Sales Torres Homen in *O Despertador*. Torres Homen believed that the liberals' mistake had been their failure to "make industry the foundation of the political edifice." The turmoil of the Regency period therefore resulted from "unchanneled activity and public energies undirected toward useful objectives."[86]

The general goals of order, prosperity, and industry gradually became confused with the more narrow, class-bound aspects of political support. The revival of authority thus depended especially upon the support of those who had the greatest material interests in the preservation of order. The rest of society —the people—would be put to work in order to keep their energies channeled and "accustom them to obedience."[87] Vasconcelos' newspaper, *O Sete de Abril,* spun a new interpretation of recent Brazilian history in 1838 that showed how class-conscious the reactionary movement had become. Brazil, like all countries, went the article, had a "Conservative Class" of capitalists, men of industry, and businessmen whose fortunes reflected the status of the nation. From 1808 until independence, the efforts of this conservative class had given Brazil a prosperous time of "progress in order." From 1822 until 1831 the seeds of disorder germinated in Brazil, culminating in the liberal period when "we launched ourselves in a career of speculation—not mercantile, but political." During these years the conservative class had been forced into what was described as a "contemplative existence," and had only reemerged with the triumph of the Regresso.[88]

The reactionaries' "empirical" reevaluation of Brazilian society led them to attempt a more detailed analysis of the components of this conservative class. The result was a confused social model that mixed economic and corporate distinctions according to what the conservatives saw as the political roles of different groups. The empire's professional groups, for instance, were immediately identified as an important social category chiefly because of their access to and potential influence upon less well-delineated economic groups and society at large. Hence the teachers, priests, journalists, and professional judges of the empire—men whose work touched many lives and whose influence reached into most other sectors of society—were analyzed in terms of their "social force" and then cajoled into supporting the Regresso. Theirs would be the task of building a nationwide power base out of the more elusive "productive" or "conservative" classes.[89]

Of the professional groups that thus attracted conservative attention, the magistracy took precedence. Much as royal government had done during the colonial period, Brazil's reactionaries regarded the professional judges as the ideal political intermediaries. Themselves social composites drawn from all the responsible classes, the judges were situated pivotally between the central government and local sources of power throughout the empire. Power could be channeled through them in either direction. Writing in *O Cronista* in 1837, Justiniano José da Rocha noted the "incalculable strength" of this "little apprehended and seldom analyzed" social force. Rocha concluded that the magistracy, because of its "corporate spirit and general close-knittedness, its independence of character and means," was the most powerful "social force" in Brazil. The independence Rocha referred to was an extra-official independence derived from the power to employ "inertia in resisting the desires of the other powers . . . and the dictates of the law." The editor compared the strength of the professional magistracy to that of a cork "which because it is soft and flexible appears insignificant, and because it appears insignificant is indestructible."[90]   Bernardo Pereira de Vasconcelos' newspaper showed a similar fascination with the professional judges. "The Magistracy . . . is the one Body in society . . . that has within it the strength to retard or advance Society on its road to happiness." Like Rocha, the author of this later article saw the public authority of the judges as inextricably linked to their social composition. "All the interests of society can be found interconnected [in this group], and that is why the Corps of Magistrates is the strongest constituted power in the State."[91]

The class interests that conservatives most hoped to tap through the professionals, and the magistrates in particular, were those of the rural landed elite. The Regresso's glorification of Brazil's landowners—the fazendeiros and senhores de engenho—had evolved naturally from the initial uneasiness displayed by many city liberals who had feared the hostility of local bosses to liberal institutions like the Juizado de Paz. At first these liberals had recommended men of the "middle class"—not the elite—for the new elective positions.[92]   But later, in 1833, when Caramuru candidates were elected in the parishes of the capital, the liberal papers had acknowledged the political support of the rural voters (Eleitores do Campo), whose overwhelmingly antirestorationist vote had saved the province of Rio from being represented by a coalition of left- and right-wing extremists. Cautiously, *Aurora Fluminense* began to express its gratitude to the landed classes and even suggested that the "landowners and planters" would be the best candidates for the provincial elections of 1834.[93]

The Regresso represented the logical political culmination of these earlier flirtations with the landowners. Just as the coffee boom brought new prosperity, it also brought an apparently identifiable economic elite that could provide a "class base" for a political system or, even, a national myth. As civil unrest threatened the peace of Brazil's countryside, the landowning classes of the interior began to exercise a powerful fascination on the public mind. In 1840 the drama critic of the *Journal do Comércio* criticized a new play's superficial characterization of a coffee planter and expressed his own enthusiasm for the landowner:

This social type [the fazendeiro] needs to be well understood and well studied in order to be properly interpreted on stage. Only a Walter Scott

would be able to present all the almost imperceptible gradations of this varying character who tries to join the traditions of the past with the modifications of the present, who is a combination of openness and cunning, pride
and courtesy, affability and that certain gruffness of character that is the
inseparable companion of the man whose wave of the hand governs hundreds of slaves.[94]

While the interest in rural landowners was often expressed generically, the
prime example was always the coffee planter of Rio de Janeiro province, the
fazendeiro de serra acima referred to by the drama critic. The reactionary
movement of the late 1830s sought to identify itself most closely with this
group, and in times of political adversity fell back upon its support. When a
liberal faction came briefly to government in 1840, the newspaper of the Party
of Order protested the liberals' firing and removal of hostile public officials, including district judges, in the province of Rio de Janeiro, but cockily told its
readers that "We can guarantee that the influences that the government should
fear cannot be moved. Let us see if the cabinet can dismiss and transfer the
planters from their estates."[95]   The increasingly close ties between the Regresso
and the coffee interests of Rio province earned the party a sarcastic description
by liberal Antônio Pereira Rebouças in 1843: "a party whose head is in Rio de
Janeiro, but whose sinuous tail wraps around all the other provinces."[96]
Given that the Regresso fawned so assiduously on Brazil's rural landowners,
it might seem paradoxical that regional and antirural prejudices strengthened
during the period. By the late 1830s national politicians were indeed losing
their enthusiasm for the hinterlands and localism, but because their enthusiasm
for the rural elite simultaneously soared it is obvious that the apparent antirural bias was in fact part of a growing sense of class conflict that better accounts for the systematic vilification now directed at (poor) country people.
Outside the coastal strip from São Paulo to Recife, ran the rhetoric of the post-
liberal period, "men in isolation become brutish or forget the social regime and
the subordination that it necessitates."[97]   Speaking for the Conservative Party
in 1841, Paulino José Soares de Souza showed how combative the regional
prejudices had become. The people of the interior and isolated areas, said Paulino, were imbued with dangerous and undigested ideas of freedom and took
neither law nor authority seriously. "[This population] constitutes a part of
Society distinct from that of our littoral and many of our towns and is characterized principally by barbarous customs, acts of ferocity, and horrible crimes."[98]
The reactionaries' analyses were heavily value-laden, but they were predicated on an essentially static model of Brazilian society. What most distinguished
the conservatives from the liberals, even the staunchest of whom now agreed
that Brazilian society needed radical reform, was the belief that the country's

problems could be solved by manipulating or even accentuating what the conservatives complacently regarded as the fixed characteristics of its social structure. Many a conservative hoped to institutionalize formally some feature of
Brazilian society that seemed especially attractive. "The productive classes,"
or some part of them, for instance, might become "a hereditary class of nobles."[99]

The Regresso's most elaborate full model of society and the state belonged
to Justiniano José da Rocha. In a series of four articles entitled "Let Us Look
to the Future," Rocha gave Regresso thought about government, class, and Brazilian society its most complete and revealing formulation.[100] Rocha began by
repeating that because of the disillusionments of the liberal years, the one remaining positive base of political faith in Brazil was the central image of the
monarch. The most pressing political tasks of the 1840s, therefore, were to
consolidate the principles of monarchy and to buttress the prestige of the new
emperor himself. In unfolding his plan for achieving these goals, Rocha presented a total vision of free Brazilian society and its workings.

At the bottom of the social pyramid that Rocha described were the poor
free folk of Brazil. The journalist combined the predictable generalizations
about the people's low level of civilization so common in the late 1830s, with
the specific class prejudices of the 1840s in summarily dismissing this group as
a positive participant in the political process: "without any moral beliefs, without religious faith, without love of work, what kind of belief can they have in
politics?" Unfortunately, this "seminomadic" group had proven in the unrest
of the Regency period that it was a threat to government authority. In order
to stabilize the empire, government had to have some means of effective control over the free poor, to whom the standard goads of "material progress" and
even the blandishments of reason meant nothing: "they are [proletarians] because of the indolence that prevents them from pursuing wealth, the child of
work. . . . So here we have our proletarian, still a primitive being who obeys
the first twinges of his passions." One special characteristic of the Brazilian
"proletariat," Rocha noted, was that unlike the European industrial proletariat
which flocked into the cities, the Brazilian variant was overwhelmingly rural.

The perils that this unprincipled rural proletariat posed to the monarchy
called for the loyal support of offsetting social groups. Rocha considered but
rejected the urban "middle classes" for the counterbalancing role. The petty
commercial sectors, the artisans, and the bureaucrats were more civilized and
moral than the free country population, he reasoned, but they had been profoundly disillusioned by the unrest of the 1830s and could not be depended
upon to support a system of which they were skeptical.

One urban group that caught Rocha's eye was the top layer of urban "productive" society—the large merchants. The role of the great merchants in controlling the rural proletariat would be an indirect one carried out through the

merchants' influence over the agricultural magnates of the countryside. "The first rank of our commerce is in constant contact with . . . the rich landowners of the interior," and commercial correspondence would lead to an exchange of ideas. Therefore, a government which secured the support of the great commercial interests would have achieved "more than a little to guarantee internal tranquility."

At the pinnacle of Justiniano José da Rocha's social model, then, stood the rural landowners. Their support of the monarchy was essential because they alone could govern the dangerous free population. The journalist described how the rural proletariat depended upon the landowners for asylum and sustenance and therefore clustered around the plantations of the interior like European proletarians gathered in the cities. "These citizens [the landowners] living as they do, almost like Kings . . . have an almost absolute power over a large part of the population. The people follow the lead of the landowners who are therefore in a position to answer for public order, guarantee respect for the Law and the authorities, and frustrate the criminal activities of the ambitious." Rocha advocated that the landowners be linked to the government as closely as possible and by any means necessary. They would be lionized, patronized, and flattered with titles: "It is well that these citizens make up a kind of aristocracy; let us regulate and bind to the throne this aristocracy that already exists by the very nature of things and because of the overwhelming influence of large landholdings and wealth."

Ultimately, Rocha urged, the planters and their "correspondents," the large merchants of the cities, should be involved in the more formal workings of government by increasing their classes' representation in the Brazilian Parliament. The journalist lamented that so few great merchants had shown interest in active political participation, but predicted that when the landowners and merchants were "called" to Parliament, their positive and practical contributions would more than offset their lack of theoretical sophistication and rhetorical skills. Ideally, the landowners would dominate in the Senate, while commerce would be best represented in the Chamber of Deputies.

Over the long run, Rocha even had a plan for institutionalizing class control over the rural proletariat while instilling in the free poor that love of work which they so conspicuously lacked. Rural landowners would stabilize the drifting free population of the interior by settling them in villages or sharecropping colonies where, under the fazendeiro's tutelage, they would be "educated" in the virtues of labor. Such a scheme would also strengthen the ties between the landowners and his colonists, because the "colono's" gratitude to the landowner for having called him to a "higher condition" would result in "lasting bonds between the colonists and the founder of the colony." Bonds of loyalty and obedience would also be created and reinforced, supposed Rocha, by the colonists' regular payment of rents on the land they worked for the fazendeiro. The government would reward the landowners for their initiative with imperial titles of nobility which would in turn stimulate others to establish similar colonies.[101] Rocha denied that he was calling for a "new feudalism."

It is hard to imagine ideas more dramatically at odds with those that had been used to justify the liberal reforms. In the late 1820s and 1830s liberals had conceived of Brazilian society in terms of its common interests, and had studiously avoided class- or region-oriented images of their country. Innovations like the jury system and the elected judge had to some degree been predicated upon the existence of a social common denominator that would validate popular participation in the judicial system. Thirty years later Aureliano Cândido Tavares Bastos observed that "the Procedural Code imagined a nation with a standard level of civilization and morality, respect for law, and aversion to crime." By the time this spokesman of a later generation wrote, the flaws of this notion seemed obvious—it was a "generous conviction," Tavares Bastos admitted, discreetly echoing the language of emergency that Rocha took from the frightening disappointments of the liberal experiment.[102]

For as their institutional superstructure collapsed, the reformers' conceptual framework was crushed beneath it. Brazilian society was now blamed for lacking a measure of "civilization" sufficient to make popular institutions work. The social common denominator supposed by the liberals had proved to be too low. A deepening of interest in the outline of society and an analytical concern with its parts eventually raised the question of whether a social common denominator existed at all. In their attempts to isolate the troublemakers and identify the responsible elements of society, Regresso thinkers developed a fragmented and categorized vision of Brazilian society that mixed class, corporate, and regional distinctions like so many apples and oranges, and which dismissed out of hand the existence of social harmony or common interests. The most immediate effects of this reevaluation of society were to be found reflected in the cynical philosophies of government developed in the conservative 1840s, attempting as they did to identify government symbiotically with the interests of selected social groups. Justiniano José da Rocha foreshadowed this brand of Regresso political thought with his plan for synchronizing government and class interests by literally parceling the country out in fiefdoms to the rural aristocracy. Thus Rocha proposed to ensure rural stability and guarantee a dependent labor force, while at the same time fortifying the principles of authority and the legitimacy of the monarchy. These were the supreme values of the reactionaries of the 1840s; upon them they would build a Conservative Party and a political system for imperial Brazil.

9. Justice, Police, and Patronage, 1834-1841

The Marquis of Maricá spent his time assembling shallow dicta for use as filler in Brazilian newspapers. In 1839 one of his maxims made a precise political statement. "The people," he wrote, "are better off under a government of scoundrels than under a government of fools."[1] Consciously or not, the Marquis had furnished a motto for the hard-nosed and practical conservatives who dominated Brazil's second generation of politicians—men who did not think of themselves as scoundrels but who were sophisticated enough not to be offended by any label used to set them apart from the liberal ministry they opposed. The new conservatives regarded the handiwork of this "government of fools." In spite of all their reforms, the liberal idealists had failed to improve the administration of justice at the individual level, and in that failure had demonstrated that their evaluation of Brazilian society was naively optimistic. The pragmatists among them, on the other hand, had shown their inability to fashion a state; they had succeeded only in alienating and abdicating control over much of the judicial bureaucracy, thereby forfeiting the political power that traditionally flowed both ways between the government and its agents in the legal system. By 1837, with the country in a state of turmoil, the Liberal Party found itself with a vanishing intellectual foundation, little administrative leverage, no military strength and no clear corporate- or class-based support—in short, no state system at all.

The conservative opposition which formed after the mid-1830s observed all this with dismay and offered "order" as an alternative. In 1837 the Conservative Party put a formal end to the liberal decade when it captured the ministry and a parliamentary majority. Under the Conservatives, the mixture of ideological and political motivations which had inspired the liberal reforms was largely purged of its ideological component, and the practical political aspects of institutional policy now became foremost. Yet an important strand of continuity connected the goals of the Liberals to those of the Conservatives who followed them: in both cases crucial political objectives were to be achieved through manipulation of the judicial system.

The Additional Act (1834)

As we have seen, the rhetoric of the transitional 1830s indicated some fundamental rethinking, and certainly it emphasized conflict between political groups. The discontinuities of the period, however, are perhaps less important than the continuities, for the practical problems of government had been forcing the executive branch of the liberal movement to the right ever since 1831. Liberal legislators or publicists might continue to defend the democratic institutions and the decentralized judiciary, but liberal ministries soon threw up their hands in despair at trying to govern with no control over local justice and were quick to seek more practical reforms. Just as liberal ministers of justice proposed plans to harness the elected justices of the peace, then, their colleagues in the Ministry of the Empire recommended the creation of vaguely defined "secondary agents" of the government to stand between the municipal councils and the provincial presidents in the administrative chain.[2]

It is possible to interpret the celebrated Additional Act of 1834 as the first institutional expression of this liberal desire to recentralize administration. Traditional historiography has cast the Additional Act in precisely the opposite role—portraying it as the crowning achievement of Brazilian liberalism because of its concessions to provincial autonomy at the expense of central authority.[3] But in fact, many of the powers delegated to provincial authorities under the Additional Act were not previously vested in the central government at all. Rather, they were the prerogatives of local government—particularly of the municipal councils. Champions of local government in Brazil therefore have a very different perspective. For all its pretense of decentralization, they point out, the Additional Act sacrificed local autonomy to the provincial capitals.[4] Under the Additional Act, most of the traditional powers of the municipal councils passed into the hands of the newly created provincial assemblies which subsequently became responsible for ruling on everything from municipal expenditures and local taxes to the naming of doormen, jailers, and other petty local officials.[5] The effect of the Additional Act, therefore, was not all centrifugal; at the local level it had a centralizing influence that deprived the already decadent municipal councils of their remaining authority.

The same trend toward centralization can be observed in the Additional Act's effect on provincial administration of justice. Stripping the municipal councils of their powers had little practical significance, for much of their influence had already been removed by the liberal judicial innovations—notably the justice of the peace and the municipal judge. But the Additional Act also gave the provincial assemblies an open-ended and tantalizingly vague power to pass legislation governing the creation, suppression, and appointment of all municipal and provincial employees. In the judicial area, provincial and municipal posts were defined as those offices below "High Courts [*Relações*] and superior tribunals" —a definition that was ordinarily interpreted to include all posts beneath that of desembargador.[6] Thus, the Additional Act gave the provincial assemblies the authority to regulate the judicial personnel established by the Procedural Code —even to the point of abolishing or creating offices. Just as vague and no less important was the Act's provision giving the assemblies the right to legislate on municipal police.[7]

To confer such powers on provincial governments could only be regarded as a decentralizing measure if the central government had held those powers previously. Yet the legal system established by the Procedural Code was already extremely localized—parochial, not provincial—and its autonomy had been a major complaint of every government since 1831.[8] Provincialization would therefore have the net effect of an intermediate centralization, placing in the hands of provincial assemblies powers previously held at the municipal or parish level. If the liberal structure of courts and police had scattered the administrative powers of the central government, then, the Additional Act gradually began the task of reclaiming them.[9]

Provincial Counterreforms

After the Additional Act made it possible, Liberal ministries often encouraged provincial assemblies to pass modifications of the judiciary and police structures which they themselves could not enact on a national basis because of lack of parliamentary support. In 1835 the legislative assembly of São Paulo created appointive administrative officials in the municipalities of the province and entrusted them with some of the powers previously vested in the justices of the peace. Feijó so admired the reform that he recommended it to all other provinces in a circular of that same year.[10] A liberal Pernambucan, Luis Cavalcanti, tried unsuccessfully in 1833 to convince the Chamber of Deputies to pass legislation stripping the parish judge of many of his powers. When his proposals were rebuffed in Rio he took them to the assembly of his home province where they were accepted and served as the basis for the reform of Pernambuco's local police in 1836.[11] These provincial administrative reforms served as models for similar legislation elsewhere in the empire. Most of the affected provinces called the new appointed agents *prefeitos,* or prefects, and the reforms came to be known generically as the *leis de prefeitos.*

The prefect laws addressed themselves to the general problem of regional unrest, and to the specific problem of autonomous and uncontrollable justices of the peace, for the two matters were seen to be connected. The distribution and relative potency of the reforms reflected these concerns. In peaceful provinces the prefect laws were moderate, if indeed they were introduced at all; in São Paulo, for instance, prefects were specifically charged with carrying out orders of the provincial government but shared only minimal powers with the juiz de paz. In effect they did little more than create a symbolic government presence in the towns and villages of the province. Of the provinces of the center-south, São Paulo alone established a prefecture.[12] In provinces threatened by internal disturbances, on the other hand, prefect laws were almost universally adopted, and often were radical reversals of the ideals of local justice and police embodied in the liberal Procedural Code. Ceará's appointed prefects not only accumulated some of the criminal jurisdiction of the parish judges, but the law of their creation also modified the election process used to select the magistrates —giving the provincial president the right to choose juizes de paz from lists of three presented by the parochial voters. Pernambuco's law of 1836 went even farther. It established prefects and sub-prefects and divided between them all the criminal and police functions previously held by the justices of the peace, leaving the elected judges with little more than their original conciliatory jurisdictions. Not content with anything less than a thoroughly provincialized system of courts and police, the Pernambucan assembly also abolished the office of juiz municipal, gave the prefect the district judge's title of chief of police, restricted the number of juries to one per comarca, and trebled the property requirement for jurors. Alagoas' law of prefects created officials responsible for vigilance over drifters and ne'er-do-wells in their districts. Some form of prefect law was also passed in Sergipe, Paraíba do Norte, and Maranhão.[13]

Although Bahia never passed a prefect law, in 1838 Antônio Pereira Rebouças introduced a comprehensive plan to unify the provincial police and judiciary under a provincial police chief with agents called "police magistrates" in each comarca and "magistrates of criminal procedures" in each town. The latter would completely supplant both the judicial and constabulary responsibilities of the juizes de paz. Bahia's conservative *Correio Mercantil* strongly endorsed the centralizing plan and urged the provincial government to commit a large slice of the province's budget to funding it "because police without money is like a candle without a wick."[14]

The powers which the Additional Act gave the provinces were also used to unify authority over nonjudicial resources and bring them into the political network. Many provinces, for instance, seized the opportunity to make National Guard officers appointed rather than elected. Such legislation not only proposed to avoid the local disturbances that were so often blamed on Guard elections, but it also gave the provincial governments another important power of patronage. São Paulo's provincial president received the right to name Guard officers in 1836, Pernambuco soon passed a similar law, and other provinces followed their example.[15]

The political potential inherent in the provincial appointment of Guard officers could occasionally make such reforms a cause rather than a solution of local factional disturbances. In 1838 the provincial assembly of Bahia passed a law de-democratizing the National Guard and making all local officers appointive. In the interior town of Palame the first provincial appointments apparently displeased the local magnates who dominated the elective National Guard, and for three years they succeeded in preventing the execution of the new law. In 1841, a concerted attempt by the juiz de paz and other authorities to swear in the new Guard officers triggered a violent reaction by over one hundred armed men who threatened the magistrate, shot the windows out of his house, and shouted *vivas* for the old law. In his report, the district judge informed the provincial assembly that the events were caused by "the most lowly people of [Palame], at the instigation of some of the most important individuals of that place."[16]

The homegrown provincial plans for securing unified control over police, justice, or the militia probably did little to remedy the petty despotism of local officials. Pernambuco's Padre Lopes Gama reported that as far as corruption was concerned, in his province the prefects and sub-prefects had simply taken over where the juizes de paz left off.[17] In many cases, no doubt, the prefects and parish magistrates were the same people. But to conclude from this that the provincial reforms were a failure would be to miss their point. There was no ideology implied nor meliorism intended in such laws as there had been in the creation of the elected judges or Guard officers. Thoroughly pragmatic, often harsh in their effects, the prefect laws and militia reforms had only two goals: the quelling of social unrest and the weaving of a firm political fabric by connecting the most important local bureaucratic influences to a central source of authority. In this they foreshadowed the Regresso.

There is some circumstantial evidence that the provincial police laws did have a positive effect on stemming regional disturbances. The important upheavals of Pernambuco, Alagoas, and Ceará all preceded the passage in the mid-1830s of provincial prefect laws. In Bahia where no such law was passed, on the other hand, serious manifestations of unrest persisted throughout the Regency.[18] But in general, and surely from the point of view of the central government, the provincial laws were a case of too little too late. The truly threatening rebellions, like those of Maranhão, Pará, and Rio Grande do Sul could not be handled by provincially appointed officers of police and justice if only because the provincial governments themselves were riven by the same factional splits that sparked these long-term rebellions. In such circumstances, the appointed police became factional agents, not representatives of order, and only contributed to broadening the basis of conflict.

The further exacerbation of factional divisions thus became one of the most serious political consequences of the patronage powers which provinces delegated to themselves by centralizing key areas of administration. At the local level, factions became either "in" or "out" as a function of their relations with the provincial governments, and the recipients of patronage favors tended to perpetuate themselves locally through application of bureaucratic leverage. The linking of hitherto independent local officials to the centralized power of provincial governments was of course an important step in building a hierarchically responsive political system; the liberals themselves had encouraged that step by passing the Additional Act and subsequently advocating measures like the "prefect laws." But if the central government and the provinces essentially agreed on issues like law enforcement, they could only go so far together on politics. Outside of its right to name provincial presidents, the Rio government possessed no firm control over provincial politics under the Additional Act, and when faced with a hostile provincial legislature the central government was as helpless to promote its interests as were the local "out" factions.

In the first years of the Regresso, therefore, conservatives argued persuasively, and many liberals agreed, that the provincial laws passed under the Additional Act were an intolerable invasion of the basic sovereignty of the monarchy. Some of the prefect laws virtually abolished the Juizado de Paz, and others made the office appointive or otherwise changed the method of its selection. The elected magistrate's existence, however, was provided for constitutionally, not merely by statute, and its essential modification by the provinces was therefore of doubtful constitutionality.[19] Moreover, although the Additional Act undeniably gave the assemblies the right to pass legislation affecting provincial magistrates, many observers were appalled at the radical structural modifications that some provinces made in the theoretically uniform imperial legal system. As early as 1836 the fear was expressed that Brazil would soon have eighteen separate Procedural Codes—one for each province.[20] In their enthusiasm, the provincial legislatures had also offended the central government by regulating everything from ecclesiastical patronage to the structure of the imperial Army. They created banks, tinkered with fiscal policy, and levied local taxes that interfered with national revenues. "In a word, they invaded everything, decentralized everything, and were destroying the empire."[21]

But unquestionably the most influential argument against the Additional Act and the provincial laws was one which pointed out the degree of independent power which provincial governments were developing through their control of patronage, courts, and police. Paulino José Soares de Souza described the politics of provincial autonomy in terms calculated to dismay anyone troubled by the problem of guaranteeing order in the empire.

Let us say that one of the provincial factions won the elections and a majority in the provincial assembly. The faction could then proceed to set itself up in power: for example, after naming its own men to the posts of the National Guard, it could make laws giving those officers life-tenure. Thus the faction created obstacles to keep the other side from being able to govern in the future.[22]

Most ominous to those who wished to build a national political system were the reforms which gave provincial governments a line to every level of the judiciary: "The faction made its own people juizes de paz and put them on the municipal councils. These authorities, in turn, made up the jury panels and indirectly [by proposing lists of three] named municipal judges, probate judges, and prosecutors."[23]

Such thoroughgoing provincialization of the judicial bureaucracy left the central government, regardless of its politics, helpless in the provinces. If the provincial president, as the only administrative authority named by the central government, did not go along with the "faction," he would find his opponents "armed with the means of a vigorous resistance—one with the appearance of legality and legally insuperable." In this way the provincial interests that controlled the legal system "built themselves into a [political] fortress—impregnable not only to the oppressed [provincial] faction but to the central government as well."[24] Such political analyses combined readily with the regional prejudices and social pessimism of the Regresso period to form a solid foundation for a program of administrative centralization.[25] The spokesmen of the Conservative Party, whose emergence corresponded with the passage of the provincial police laws, believed that nucleating political power in the capital of every backward and unproductive province of the empire was as dangerous as entrusting the selection of local officials to the dubious judgment of the people.

The Reform of the Additional Act (1840)

Empiricists that they were, the reactionaries of the Regresso period had learned a great deal from the experiments of the "government of fools" that preceded them. By 1837 the major political lesson of the liberal decade was clear. A government that lacked control of the judiciary, the police, and the legal personnel could not govern. Conversely, and more cynically, a government that kept a tight institutional grip on the judicial bureaucracy, as many provinces had demonstrated after 1834, could entrench itself in power, reward its friends, and repress its enemies. In short, the Conservatives were convinced that local officials should be harnessed, but equally convinced that provincial governments should not be handed the reins.

The reins of course were patronage. The provincial reforms had shown that a patronage-based system could encourage local factionalism and lead, in some cases, to disorder; but centralized control over the police and courts would at least give the government the strong local presence which it lacked under the liberal system. Then too, since Conservatives tended to identify their political position closely with certain strata of a society which they imagined as divided horizontally along class or semicorporate lines (e.g., "the productive classes"), they expected opposition, too, to be class-based and controllable by the inherent nature of the static social system they posited. Vertical factionalism, which divided class and corporation internally, they identified with the social distortions caused by democratic institutions in a society unprepared for them. The Conservatives thus saw no disadvantage in a policy of harnessing the empire through patronage, and they set out to make it possible. They proposed first an "interpretation" of the Additional Act—instrumental legislation designed to free provincial employees from the patronage area of provincial governments as a preliminary to shifting them into the national patronage area. The personnel of police and justice would be most affected. Justiniano José da Rocha believed the most important aspect of the Interpretation law to be that which "regulated the relations of dependency in which magistrates were placed by the Additional Act."[26]

In fact, proposals to modify the Additional Act, like those which recommended reform of the Procedural Code, had appeared almost as soon as the Act passed into law.[27] But it was not until 1837 that the interpretation project in its final form began its journey through the Brazilian Parliament. Discussions were heated in the Chamber of Deputies, where the bill was not finally approved until 1838. The measure encountered stiff opposition in the Senate also, and debate lasted through twenty-eight sessions. Final differences over the Interpretation bill were only resolved in a special joint session of the Chamber and the Senate held in 1840, the year of the measure's promulgation.[28]

When finally enacted in 1840, the long-debated reform restricted the right of provincial assemblies to alter the nature and duties of provincial and municipal employees whose offices had been created by uniform imperial law. Thus the inviolability of the judicial structure of the Procedural Code was reasserted. The new law also forbade provincial legislation in matters of "judicial police," or more specifically, the all-important duties of preparing criminal evidence and bringing charges. No longer could provincial assemblies suspend or discharge magistrates summarily as they had been allowed to do under the Additional Act.[29] The interpretive legislation cleared up the vague and easily abused language of the Additional Act, and while it did not undo all that the provinces had done before its enactment, it reestablished the principle of uniformity in the legal system and national bureaucracy.

The Interpretation of the Additional Act was discussed in blunt and practical terms. From the very introduction of the bill in 1837, it was clear that patronage was the basic issue and that control over the judiciary was the specific goal of the bill's sponsors. Paulino José Soares de Souza explained to his colleagues in the Chamber of Deputies that under the terms of the Additional Act, the provinces controlled all the inferior courts of the empire. He conceded the need for a measure of provincial autonomy in the immense country, but submitted that national officials and the general laws of the nation should not be subject to radical modification or even suspension by provincial governments. Paulino made much of the point that individual magistrates, whose positions were created by national laws, could nevertheless be uprooted, transferred, or even dismissed by the provincial governments.[30]

Some of the debaters flayed the provinces' misuse of the Additional Act in language that betrayed the Conservatives' own ambitions in the patronage question. The magistrate Antônio Luis Dantas de Barros Leite, representing Maranhão in the Chamber, suggestively described the political reasons for provincial laws to govern the legal personnel:

> What the [provincial] administrations want is the opposite [of public works and improvements]. They want to appoint prefects, pay them a thousand milreis, and have municipal judges and prosecutors with fat salaries. In other words, they are for anything that tends to increase their clientele. . . . Look at Pernambuco, for example. On every corner there's a prefect, a civil magistrate [juiz municipal], and a district judge.[31]

Such observations about clientele politics were expressed with disapproval, but they tell more about the strategies of the Conservatives than about their value systems. The Interpretation of the Additional Act was precisely such a clientele-oriented bid for the support of the professional magistrates, and, voting in a block for the first time, that group was largely responsible for the bill's passage in the Chamber of Deputies. In 1839, when the Interpretation bill reached the Senate, its supporters tried to hurry it through on the grounds that it had been mandated by a solid majority of fifty-six votes in the Chamber of Deputies. The priest-politician José Martiniano de Alencar of Ceará immediately took issue with those who claimed that this high vote reflected the measure's popularity. Alencar denied that the vote in the lower house reflected anything but the corporate interests which the Conservative Party cultivated. Without mentioning the magistracy by name, Alencar pointed out that of the fifty-six deputies who voted for the Interpretation bill, forty-three were "members of one class, and only thirteen represented other classes." Therefore, he argued, it was specious to say that a large majority of the Chamber of Deputies favored the measure when in fact it had been passed by a "class" which only coincidentally could swing a majority in the lower house. The only valid conclusion to be drawn from the fifty-six votes was that "the bill is desired and valued by one class of Brazilian society. That cannot be denied."[32]

Alencar opposed the bill because he had long believed that the provinces should have some police and judicial powers of their own.[33] He charged that the alarmist rhetoric about the imminent dismemberment of the empire as a consequence of the Additional Act was merely a Regresso tactic to build an authoritarian political system upon a panic, and funnel power into the hands of a few. No one apprehended the political content and the corporate base of the reactionary reforms better than he: "It seems to me that the idea of this bill [the Interpretation], and that of some others[34] . . . is to establish a completely new political system—and a system which is certainly not unfavorable to one of the classes of society which will derive great advantages from it."[35] In questioning the representative validity of parliamentary votes bought by appealing to the dominant class or corporate interests within the Parliament itself, Alencar was among the first to perceive the political trends of the 1840s.

José de Alencar's observations raised the Senate debates over the Interpretation to a more general level of political discussion than was usually achieved in haggling over legislation. Alencar's class reference to the magistracy was thinly veiled, and class-conscious professional judges in the Senate rose to the defense of their corporation.[36] Feijó, always ready to contribute to a session of magistrate-baiting, explained the apparently paradoxical behavior of professional judges who voted for reforms that would put their appointments and "independence" in the hands of the central rather than provincial governments. He observed that men who were deputies only temporarily but magistrates permanently and by profession hoped to trade their political support of centralizing reforms for choice appointments—perhaps even the coveted seats on Brazil's High Courts—by a grateful government after their terms were complete. As a result, concluded Feijó, the political activities of magistrates were seldom disinterested and always suspect.[37]

Nicolau Pereira de Campos Vergueiro, a liberal Paulista landowner, explored the implications of corporate politics. He acknowledged that most citizens naturally wanted their class interests represented in politics, but warned against runaway corporate dominance in the houses of Parliament: "The class of magistrates is absorbing the other powers of State. There can be no doubt of this: the fact that there are forty-three members of this class in the Chamber of Deputies shows that [the magistrates] have almost absorbed a branch of the legislative power." Vergueiro recognized what he called the "preponderance" of the magistrates as a class, and predicted that they would continue to dominate for some time to come. In mock self-effacement, the planter-politician said he was looking forward to the day when agriculturalists would "shine" like the judges, "so that I can amount to something."[38]

Returning to the floor, Senator Alencar expressed his doubt that the magistrates would soon relinquish their hold over the legislative branch. He reiterated that more was at stake than the professional ambitions of a few judges, because the legislation being considered to interpret the Additional Act and reform the Procedural Code would only reinforce the legislative "magistocracy." Alencar claimed that 80 percent of the members of the lower house were magistrates[39] and that if the Conservative counterreform legislation were passed the next legislature would be completely made up of judges "because the bacharéis [are] scattered over the whole of Brazil as municipal judges, probate judges, and prosecutors, to say nothing of the district judges. No elector will deny his vote to his judge, nor will there be any judge who does not want to be a deputy."[40]

Political Events

The Interpretation of the Additional Act was so often mentioned in conjunction with other Conservative reforms because it was widely recognized as merely the first step toward realization of a sweeping counterreform program. The Interpretation was necessary in a mechanical sense to allow other reforms—in themselves more substantial—to function properly by protecting them from the interference of provincial legislatures. The proposed reforms of the Procedural and Criminal Codes being debated simultaneously with those of the Additional Act were clearly of greater importance; indeed, they were direct reversals of the liberal ideals of independent justice and localism. And even more than the Interpretation of the Additional Act they enjoyed the support of the professional magistracy. When the passage of the Interpretive law demonstrated the legislative potency and corporate allegiances of the Conservative majority, the subsequent passage of these other legal reforms became a virtual certainty.

Menaced by political extinction if the Regressista majority succeeded in centralizing administrative authority in its own hands and perpetuating itself politically through patronage, the Liberals made a desperate bid to return to power and break the impetus of the counterreform movement. Only two months after the passage of the Interpretation bill, a group of Liberals led by Antônio Carlos Ribeiro de Andrada engineered a coup d'état by "sponsoring" an unconstitutional early majority for the adolescent emperor, Pedro II. The youth dismissed the Conservative cabinet and on 24 July 1840 formed a new ministry representing the Liberal minority. New elections were called for the end of the year, but the Chamber of Deputies with its Conservative majority was not dissolved.[41]

The new ministry, though nominally Liberal, was not very reminiscent of the liberalism of the 1830s when men like Feijó and Evaristo had dominated the party. The outstanding members of this ministry, Antônio Carlos and Aureliano de Sousa e Oliveira Coutinho, shared the political pragmatism of the

Regresso. They were experienced parliamentary maneuverers and inveterate pullers of strings. The Party of Order had no more practical men in its ranks, nor better candidates for a "government of scoundrels." The political instincts of Antônio Carlos and Aureliano were indistinguishable from those of men like Conservatives Paulino José Soares de Souza or Bernardo de Vasconcelos, but as leaders of the parliamentary minority their tactics were perforce different. Once again in government, and faced by the prospect of institutionalized Conservative hegemony if the counterreforms were passed, the Liberals' only recourse was to the electoral system. They therefore applied every pressure at their disposal in an effort to rig the parliamentary elections of 1840 to return a Liberal majority.

The election of 1840 is instructive as a tumultuous, awkward model of the sort of political fixing that the Regresso faction would eventually institutionalize for its own benefit through the authoritarian counterreforms. In the province of Rio de Janeiro and elsewhere in the empire, the Liberal minister of justice transferred partisan district judges and replaced them with trustworthy or at least neutral magistrates before the elections.[42] Although such transfers were not made public by the government, newspapers kept their own informal lists of disgruntled district judges who had been transferred for political reasons. A Conservative newspaper of Rio de Janeiro charged the new Liberal ministry with "removing" over forty district judges.[43]

In most provinces the Liberal government also named new presidents and supreme commanders of the National Guard. In both Rio de Janeiro and Bahia, for example, new provincial presidents were appointed within a month after the formation of the Liberal cabinet.[44] The *Correio Mercantil* of Bahia protested the government's dismissal of Conservative officials as a "politics of vengeance." The newspaper was especially outraged by the dismissal of the supreme commander of the National Guard in the comarca of São Francisco, an act it regarded as a gesture sympathetic to the Sabinada rebels, whose lenient treatment by the São Francisco jury the commander had vigorously opposed. Closer to home was the transfer of the *Correio*'s outspoken ex-editor, magistrate João Antônio Sampaio Viana, from his comfortable post as district judge in the capital to that of the isolated backwater comarca of Caravelas in southern Bahia.[45]

The naming and shifting of provincial presidents, Guard commanders, and, to a certain extent, district judges, were all powers the central government enjoyed under existing laws. But if elections were to be fixed, local officials needed to be controlled as well, and the Liberals tried with varying degrees of success to reach them through the provincial laws passed under the Additional Act. In Bahia, for instance, the provincial law of 1838 giving the government the right to name officers of the National Guard was employed wholesale to assure Guard support for government candidates in the coming elections. One

Bahian deputy complained of "terrible transactions" made between the government and local officials over political support. He was especially critical of the use of National Guard posts as a payoff for electoral favors. He noted that in Bahia the number of National Guard units had lately proliferated greatly but that most such units existed in name only. Suddenly there were more officers than guards in the Bahian militia: "There are many colonels and a multitude of other officers [hear, hear]; and for what reason? To serve as advance guards . . . for the future elections." From the floor an unidentified deputy confirmed that Bahia's was not an isolated case. "This is a nation-wide evil," he shouted.[46]

The Liberals' own institution, the Juizado de Paz, was perhaps the most crucial factor in deciding the elections of 1840. The old ironies remained in effect, however, for the local judges were still the least accessible to government influence. Most localities still elected their juizes, and though their police or judicial powers had sometimes been restricted by provincial "prefect laws," the elected judges continued to preside over primary and secondary elections. Unable to dismiss or transfer these local agents, the government resorted to intimidation or bribery in order to enlist the juizes' connivance at election time.

Predictably, the ministry had the most success in the national capital where its resources of persuasion were most concentrated. Soldiers from the Rio Army garrison and sailors on shore leave received payment in tobacco and cane liquor for imposing government supporters on the parish election boards. The Conservative opposition reported that these men from the Marine Arsenal and the Army quarters were joined by "workers giving off a vile miasma of cachaça and cigarette smoke, armed with clubs [cacêtes] and wearing yellow neckerchiefs, [who] went from one parish to another composing the electoral boards."[47] The all-important formation of electoral boards could usually be decided by a shouting match, so the government toughs were hired as much for their lung power as for the menace of their cudgels.[48]

In Conservative parishes, the government's "infernal mob" arrived at the church election-sites early and either prevented the access of opposition voters to the church or seated their own members by force on the electoral boards. In Santa Ana parish the justice of the peace, collaborating with the ministry, delayed the beginning of the election until the mob arrived. The exceptionally strong-minded juiz de paz of the parish of Santa Rita, on the other hand, resisted a violent challenge by the government supporters and was ultimately called to the imperial palace, where an interview with the minister of the empire and the minister of justice at last convinced him to yield to the government faction.[49] These attempts to control the city elections resulted in a virtually complete victory for government candidates. Handpicked electors obediently voted for the government ticket.

But the ministry was unable to overturn the Conservative machinery of the interior of the province of Rio de Janeiro. The coffee planters identified polit- ically with the Conservative Party, and, as we have seen, selected their juizes de paz from among their own ranks. Despite persistent rumors that the Liberal Party would attempt to "buy off" some of the wealthiest landowners, the inte- rior of Rio province voted overwhelmingly for Regresso candidates. In fact, the vote from the interior was sufficient to offset the rigged elections of the capital, and the Conservative press rejoiced that of the ten deputies selected for Rio, six were members of the Conservative opposition. Even more gratifying, three of those elected were the leaders of the Conservative Party whom the ministry had pledged itself to defeating: Paulino José Soares de Souza, Joaquim José Rodrigues Torres, and Eusébio de Queiroz.[50]

Nevertheless, in the rest of the empire the strong-arm tactics of the Liberal government yielded the expected majority. And everywhere the atmosphere of corruption and constraint in which the elections of 1840 were held earned them the sobriquet *"eleições do cacête"* (the elections of the bludgeon).

The notoriety of the Liberal abuses, however, played into the hands of the defeated Conservatives, who seized the occasion to launch a vigorous attack on the electoral system in Brazil and add momentum to their counterreform pro- gram. The Conservatives' analysis of the elections of 1840 grew out of and con- firmed the regional and class biases of the Regresso. For Conservative observers, the heroes of the elections were the landowners and coffee planters of Rio de Janeiro. They alone had resisted the goads, threats, and bribery with which the government had fixed the elections elsewhere. The outlying provinces, on the other hand, had been most permeable to government corruption. The Con- servative press described the provincial elections in the same alarmist style they used to report and editorialize on regional rebellions. The elections of 1840, they suggested, had set class against class and even threatened to spark race war. Bahia's Conservative sheet reported that in elections held in the interior of that province, "certain masters armed their slaves for these elections. Slaves armed by landowners against landowners!!! Utter aloud, if you dare, what must follow."[51] In Rio de Janeiro Conservatives harped on the lowly social origins of the gangs who had guaranteed the formation of pro-government elec- toral boards in the capital. Justiniano José da Rocha coined a happy term that perfectly married the Conservatives' class prejudices to their scorn for the hypo- critical idealism of the Liberals. The form of government offered by the Liber- als, said Rocha, should be called a *canalhacracia* ("mobocracy").[52]

Just beneath the partisan motivations of such attacks lay the real distaste of many Conservatives for active electioneering across class lines. The elections of 1840 were Brazil's first taste of a clearly partisan election with high stakes, and the idea of electoral success depending on candidates "prostrating themselves day and night before the ballot box" upset the Bahian newspaper *Correio Mercantil.* Bahia's Conservative press could not understand the vote itself apart from the "quality" of the voter, and found it "nauseating to see the indignity and villainy with which men who fancy themselves vote-getters go right up to the shoemaker, the butcher, and the bricklayer to beg them for a vote!!!"[53]

To the Conservatives, the abuses of the elections of 1840 and the turmoil that had accompanied them reemphasized the need for centralizing reforms. At the same time, however, the electoral success of the Liberals made the passage of those counterreforms problematic. Because of internal divisions, the Liberal cabinet fell in March 1841, only a few months after the elections, and was replaced by a ministry of Conservative sympathies (Paulino José Soares de Souza was minister of justice), but the newly elected legislature that was to convene in 1842 would be overwhelmingly Liberal. The Conservatives had less than a year to pass the remainder of the counterreforms; if they were held up until the next session they would be blocked indefinitely by the men elected in 1840.

Faced with this prospect, some Conservatives advocated the invalidation of the corrupt elections of 1840. Even before the elections were tabulated the Conservative press had called for their nullification in the capital, and as the overwhelming victory of the Liberals in the rest of the empire became clear, Conservative spokesmen began to advocate the eventual dissolution of the entire Chamber of Deputies elected in 1840.[54] But dissolution depended upon the emperor, still something of an unknown quantity; a more reliable course of action for the Conservative legislature would be to pass the counterreform legislation before the seating of the new Liberal majority in 1842. Justiniano José da Rocha repeatedly drew attention to the oppositionist makeup of the coming legislature and the impossibility of getting the reforms through after it convened. "In 1842 we will have an invasion of Vandals in the legislative branch," he warned. Rocha recommended energy in the passage of the recentralizing measures before the incoming legislature left the country "to the discretion of the disorganizers."[55] The legislative session of 1841, therefore, saw the successful effort by the lame duck Conservative majority to pass the most important of the reactionary counterreforms. By hurriedly reforming the Liberals' Procedural Code, the Conservatives simultaneously restructured the legal system and wrote their own ticket to continued political power.

The Reform of the Procedural Code (1841)

The reform of the Procedural Code, known more commonly after its passage in 1841 as the "Law of December 3," did not overtly dismantle the Liberal judicial structure. Instead, it made appointment the dominant mode of selection for judges of Brazil's inferior courts, rendering those judges dependent upon the central government in much the same way that the crown-appointed judges had been during the colonial period. Buttressing this system, and neutralizing the troublesome justice of the peace, whose elective status was guaranteed by the Constitution, the reform also created a parallel hierarchy of appointed police officials. This new network of local police would in turn be responsible to provincial chiefs of police carefully selected from among the professional magistrates by the central government.

According to the proposed reform, municipal judges and public prosecutors were no longer to be named by provincial presidents from a field of three candidates proposed by municipal councils. Rather, municipal judges would be named for four-year terms by the emperor (in practice, the minister of justice made all appointments). The post of local prosecutor likewise became an imperial appointment. Both these county-level officials were to be named from among the graduates of Brazil's new legal faculties; in other words, they would most often be fully indoctrinated, aspiring professional magistrates. At the district level, the naming of the juiz de direito was entrusted exclusively to the central government, reversing the practices of some provinces under the Additional Act. The revived district judge would exercise broad powers of supervision over every level of legal procedure from the parish officials through the municipal magistrates. If he discovered irregularities in the bringing of charges or the judgments made in inferior courts, he held the right to charge the magistrates involved with malfeasance.[56]

Alongside this judicial structure, the Conservative reforms of the Procedural Code strung a series of police officials with considerable judicial prerogatives. From the provincial capitals, police chiefs named by the minister of justice appointed high sheriffs (*delegados*) in each county or municipality. On the recommendation of these sheriffs, the chief of police then named a deputy sheriff (*subdelegado*) and six substitutes at the parish level. The police powers and criminal jurisdictions which had been accumulated by the justices of the peace were transferred to this centralized chain of police.[57]

Just as one of the primary objectives of the Liberals' 1832 Procedural Code had been the strengthening of the juiz de paz, then, a major goal of the Conservatives' counterreform law of 1841 was the humbling of that local official. The new law parceled out the powers of the parish judge to the new appointive officials of police and justice, effectively reducing the elected magistrate to its original role as a conciliator. Most important, the power to draw up the formal charges that were the foundation of all criminal court proceedings was completely withdrawn from the justice of the peace and entrusted to either the appointed professional magistrates or the sheriffs. The radically shrunken authority of the parish judge led in turn to the abolition of the *junta de paz*, the local panel of appeals formed by a number of juizes de paz meeting jointly.[58] The

Juizado de Paz was virtually cut out of the imperial legal structure. In effect, the Conservatives had replaced this elected local judge with extensive police functions by an appointed local police officer with extensive judicial functions. While under the Law of December 3 the Conservative fixation with police and social control took precedence, the traditional mixture of police and judicial powers persisted in the hands of the imperial sheriffs.

The reform of the Procedural Code also fundamentally altered the nature of Brazil's jury system. Indeed, no other facet of the reform illustrates more fully the nature of Conservative thinking about the relation of the legal system to society. The most important changes in the jury reflected the Conservatives' class and regional prejudices.[59] Whereas the liberal Procedural Code had made qualification for jury duty contingent simply on the 200 milreis yearly income needed to serve as an elector, the Conservative reform introduced a literacy requirement, raised the stipulated income, and qualified the source of that income to favor landed groups. After the new law went into effect, the minimum annual income for jurors in the major cities of the empire was 400 milreis. In secondary cities the requirement fell to 300 milreis, and in villages and counties of the interior it was pegged at 200 milreis. These income minimums were only valid, however, if they derived from the salaries and emoluments of public employment or from real estate. Men who made their livings in commerce or industry faced an income requirement exactly double that demanded of landowners and public servants.[60] In this way, the Conservative legal reformers sought to ensure that most juries would be dominated by the landowners whose interests they sought to articulate, or by public employees whose links of dependency to the central government were obvious. And the higher qualification for merchants betrayed the Regresso's preference for "the great commercial interests" that Justiniano José da Rocha had described in terms of the mutual interest and influence they shared with the agricultural elite. Here, in fact, were all the values implicit in Rocha's scheme of Brazilian society, perfectly reflected in the elitist reform of the jury system.

Although limiting participation on jury panels to the responsible sectors of society would presumably put an end to impunity, the Conservatives also reinforced direct government controls over Brazil's juries. Among the powers taken from the justices of the peace, for example, were those relating to drawing up the lists of qualified jurors. Under the new system, appointive county sheriffs became responsible for deciding which citizens met the requirements for jury duty. Recourse from these decisions by the sheriffs could be had to a review board consisting of the district judge, public prosecutor, and the president of the municipal council. In other words, the selection of jurors was at every level determined by government appointees.[61] Finally, even the decisions of the jury could be overturned by the appointive judicial hierarchy. Unlike the original Procedural Code, the law of reform gave the presiding district judge the right to appeal jury verdicts which he found "contrary to evidence."[62] Justiniano José da Rocha summed up the new system with approval: "thus the district judge and the High Court—the magistracy, in a word—exercised over this popular institution a kind of inspection and tutelage."[63]

The broad outline here presented is one of a legal system forged to conform to a distinctly nonliberal philosophy of law and society. In it the Conservatives reestablished control over the nation's magisterial network and emphasized the importance of police in a country whose major ill they diagnosed as a lack of order. At the same time, they discarded democratic principles in favor of an exclusivistic and elitist approach to the institutions of justice—one which closely matched their own evaluations of Brazilian social reality. But the legal and philosophical importance of the reforms of the Procedural Code cannot be separated from the measure's political significance. Through its expansion of patronage and its potential for coercion, the Law of December 3 also made the Procedural Code the controversial blueprint of Brazil's political system for the rest of the century. The staid *Jornal do Comércio* was not referring to philosophical discussion when it described the debates over this reform as "the most bitterly fought struggle ever heard in our Parliament."[64]

The Conservatives' reform was politically motivated in both the long and the short run. By tying the judicial system more closely to the ministry it was supposed that over the long term a measure of political responsibility could be instilled in the empire. Diverting attention from the wrecking job which their centralizing reforms did on the principles of locally elected justice, the Conservatives invoked the ancient Iberian notions of the identity of magistracy and royal sovereignty by linking their judicial schemes to their stated goal of enhancing the monarchy's prestige. In this sense, they argued, the reform of the Procedural Code could be understood as a mechanism for political consolidation along monarchical lines. After the law was passed, Rio's Conservative newspaper saw no need to hide the political connection. "We do not consider [this] law . . . as a law of judicial organization, but rather as a political law . . . and it is as a political law that we proclaim it one of the first measures of social reorganization according to the principles of monarchy."[65]

In the immediacy of the short run, of course, the reform of the Procedural Code had the virtue of saving the Conservative Party from being turned out of power by the Liberals' rigged elections of 1840. When it became clear that the reform would pass before the end of the 1841 session of the legislature, Liberals who grasped the political impact of the new law protested its passage not on grounds of judicial theory, but politically, as a coup d'état. With the appointive powers included under the new reform, the party that controlled the Ministry of Justice controlled virtually the entire imperial bureaucracy, a fact which would undercut the Liberal parliamentary majority's authority and possibly lead to dissolution of the Chamber.[66] Again *O Brasil* gave the Conservative Party view using abstractions such as "anarchy" and "order" to disguise the partisan political aspect. "The elections of 1840 set us up for a terrible struggle between anarchy and the spirit of order in 1842 . . . [but] Providence, watching over the fate of Brazil, gave us on 23 March [date of the formation of the Conservative cabinet] a year of truce during which to prepare our defense."[67] The reform of the Procedural Code was the defense which the Conservative Party, cloaked as the spirit of order, prepared in its own behalf. Even more than the Liberal reforms before it, the new outline of judicial organization was a weapon of political combat.

Because the transfer of the justice of the peace's powers to appointed officials was such a prominent part of the reform, the debate over the new constabulary structure revolved around many of the old criticisms of the locally elected judges. Liberals, who by 1830 were in virtually unanimous agreement on the need to reform some aspects of the Juizado de Paz, objected to the continued mixture of judicial and police functions in the new appointed sheriffs. Padre José Antônio Marinho of Minas Gerais warned that civilized nations would "never admit such a thing" as this confusion of police and judicial duties in one official.[68] A Liberal Bahian deputy emphasized the manifest inconvenience of mixing the powers. The lessons of the parish magistracy, he pointed out, should have taught Brazilian lawmakers that one man could not single-handedly be responsible for arresting, bringing charges, deciding guilt or innocence, and passing sentence. Rather than working any improvement, then, the Conservative reform would only mean "a simple change of words; what in the old days was given to the justices of the peace is now given to the sheriffs and their deputies."[69] The Conservatives parried even the most reasonable objections of Liberals by throwing the discredited Juizado de Paz back in the faces of its creators. How could Liberal deputies protest that police and justice were immiscible if they themselves had created an institution that joined the two? A typical exchange took place between the Liberals Francisco Álvares Machado and Padre Marinho and the Conservatives Honório Hermeto Carneiro Leão and Antônio Luis Dantas:

Álvares Machado: . . . and will this legislature be the one to hand Brazil over to an army of cops?
Carneiro Leão: That's very strong language.
Dantas: And what about the juizes de paz?
Marinho: The juizes de paz cannot be compared to the sheriffs.[70]

As the bill moved inexorably toward passage, tempers flared and the Liberals gave voice to more immediate concerns. One difference between the sheriffs and the justices of the peace escaped no one: the police-magistrates were all to be named by the government. Attacking from a legalistic posture, the Liberals objected to the cavalier reversal of all their ideals of judicial independence by a bill which proposed to create "a new magistracy, one unforeseen in our Constitution, temporary and dependent upon the government."[71] But from a practical point of view the minority worried about a government using the "dependent" police and courts to persecute political enemies. Álvares Machado feared that the reform would enable the government to bring charges against its adversaries at election time, thereby disqualifying them from political participation. The deputy recognized the unlimited possibilities for applying political leverage by manipulating "the immense clientele with which the government will be armed."[72]

The Liberals' trepidation about multiplying government clientele and the uses of patronage was well founded. All the new legislation tended to expand and strengthen the professional dependent magistracy whose members so permeated the Conservative Party. While the reforms of the Procedural Code were being debated in the Senate, for example, the lower house had concerned itself with a bill creating two new High Courts and increasing the number of posts on them. Many Liberals thought the bill had been fashioned as a reward to those magistrates in Parliament who had contributed to the passage of the Interpretation of the Additional Act. The Liberal press saw the law as "one which is of greater interest to the magistrates who want to be desembargadores than it is to the country."[73] One deputy pointed out the dangerous precedent of a magistrate-dominated Chamber of Deputies passing legislation that narrowly benefited that class. He predicted that the establishment of the new High Courts would only "create new candidates for deputy and senator . . . all [the judges] will end up here, and we will have a Parliament made up entirely of magistrates."[74] Some members of the Liberal minority saw the expansion of Brazil's system of appeals courts as part of a political strategy of the Conservative government to buy the support of the nation's professional magistracy. *O Maiorista* described the measure as an effort to "broaden the sphere of the [government's] cronies,"[75] and one deputy urged his colleagues to "speak plainly, this bill has only one objective: opening the door to ministerial patronage."[76]

This political fear of the growing identity between government and magistracy was a marking characteristic of the debates over the reform of the Procedural Code. The increased powers of the professional magistrates—especially the municipal judges and the district judges—and the government's control over their appointments, transfers, and careers, made the reform seem to consummate the government-sponsored "magistocracy" that Liberals had feared since the Interpretation of the Additional Act. In the Senate, Holanda Cavalcanti described the change from the Liberal Party's earlier distrust of the professional judges to the Conservatives' glorification of the magistracy:

> Gentlemen, it is extraordinary that nowadays no one wants to make a move without the magistracy. In the old days the cry went up: no more magistrates! Down with the judges! Organize a Procedural Code and bring on the jury system! But now everyone else is excluded and the magistrates are the provincial presidents, members of the Parliament, and chiefs of police. In short, they are everything.[77]

Holanda Cavalcanti recognized that the district judge was the pivotal element in the Conservative scheme, but the proliferation of appointed municipal judges and police officials (sheriffs and deputies) also drew Liberal fire. The press and politicians of the opposition repeatedly pointed out that the reforms would endow the government with an "army of judges in whose hands alone rest the fortunes, honor, security, and liberty of all the people."[78] José Bento Ferreira de Melo, a priest from Minas Gerais, identified the tendency of the time as "the enslavement of all Brazilians by the magistracy." Another senator predicted that the swarm of municipal judges, as the dependent local representatives of the central government, would "do more damage to Brazil than the locusts of Egypt."[79]

Such objections identified a conscious Conservative Party policy of expanding the legal bureaucracy. Here was another continuity, for the new reform only exaggerated a trend begun by the Liberals in 1832. Yet there were differences of substance between the increased number of government jobs under the 1832 Procedural Code and the bureaucratic proliferation accomplished by the Conservative reform of December 3, 1841. The Liberals' expansion of the legal system had been in the sense of popular participation—prosecutors, municipal judges, and justices of the peace were locally chosen and unpaid. The Conservative structure of 1841, by contrast, put most of these officials on the payroll and converted them from a local to a national bureaucracy by appointing them from Rio. To a certain extent the change in approach from unpaid to salaried magistrates reflected a change in the financial state of the empire. It is possible that the Liberals had created so many unpaid posts in part because in the troubled 1820s and 1830s the government could not afford to pay a national bureaucracy. The coffee boom had presumably given the Conservatives this ability to pay by 1840, but it was their desire for a "responsible" legal system that had made them aware of what a salary could be expected to buy.

Whether or not they believed that magistrates should be paid by the government, a great many observers of all political faiths agreed that the Law of December 3 was excessive in its creation of new posts. In theory the law virtually doubled the number of legal officers by establishing a system of police that paralleled the legal hierarchy of the Procedural Code. The total number of justices of the peace and municipal judges in the province of Rio de Janeiro under the Procedural Code had been 108. The Law of December 3 added another 96 sheriffs and deputy sheriffs.[80] Hidden beneath these figures was the immense number of substitutes (6 for each deputy sheriff, high sheriff, and municipal judge) that the regulatory legislation allowed the government to name. Finally, the law made the established jobs of municipal judge, district judge, and prosecutor more attractive by raising their emoluments and enhancing their powers.[81] In the Senate, Paula Sousa insistently called attention to the "legions" of judges and the "hordes" of police whose appointments depended on the government under the reform. He predicted that the new paid officials would cost the empire at least one million milreis more per year, and predicted a "rush" on the many jobs created by the law—particularly the new openings for "paid letrado authorities."[82]

To old Liberals, and even to some critical Conservatives, the new system seemed a throwback to the bureaucratic burdens of the colonial period. It filled Brazil with an oppressive number of government officials, gave the ministry virtually unlimited powers of patronage, and encouraged the growth of what would later be termed *empregomania*—the preference for unproductive bureaucratic sinecures rather than useful employment.[83] Reactionary though he was, the satirist Miguel do Sacramento Lopes Gama found these aspects of the reform law as hard to stomach as the Liberal code had been. Shortly after the passage of the December 3 Law he composed an acerbic mock "Criminal Code" which skewered the multiplication of bureaucrats and judges. The basic conceit of law behind Lopes Gama's "code" was that all acts contrary to the government's wishes constituted crimes, and all critics of the government were criminals. He portrayed the judicial structure itself as a corrupt pyramid of self-seeking magistrates.

> The magistrates will be judged by other magistrates: in general rascals and crooks will be judged by their own kind! . . . in each parish there will be a High Court whose desembargadores will spend most of their time on leave, on vacation, or on special assignments. . . . there will be as many comarcas as there are streets in our cities, villages, and settlements. In each comarca—that is, in each street—there will be a district judge for criminal matters and another for civil suits. And every back alley will have a municipal judge.

Lopes Gama calculated that the salaries of this judicial plague would amount to triple the present revenues of the government; the difference would be made up out of taxes imposed on, among other things, "breathing-air and the circulation of the blood."[84]

The final Chamber of Deputies vote on the momentous reforms of the Procedural Code was tumultuous. Defeated, the Liberals vented their fears and indignation in sarcasm. One deputy remarked that it was too bad that the session had not been held the day before—the Day of the Dead—because the *dia dos finados* would have been an appropriate date to pass "the bill that does away with public liberty."[85] In a last attempt to forestall the promulgation of the new law, Liberals circulated petitions requesting that the bill be quashed by imperial veto. But this tactic failed also and on December 3, 1841, the reform law received the emperor's sanction.[86] In the terms of the Marquis of Maricá's aphorism, Brazil's transition from a government by fools to one of scoundrels was complete.

Political Events

The single hope of the Liberals after December 3, and also the single obstacle now faced by the Conservatives, was the Chamber of Deputies elected in 1840. The approaching legislature of 1842, fruit of the corrupt elections of 1840, might be able to stall execution of the new law or even annul it. The lame-duck Conservative ministry, however, found itself in a position of considerable strength after passing the controversial procedural reform, and now pledged all its prestige to persuading the young emperor to dissolve the incoming legislature. The abuses of the notorious Liberal elections of 1840, claimed the Conservatives, had made a mockery of the electoral process and the rule of law. And their arguments were compelling, for even the Liberals were hard pressed to justify the validity of the election of 1840. Under the circumstances, the Conservative ministry had little difficulty in persuading the emperor to dissolve the incoming Chamber and schedule new elections in the following year.[87]

The Conservative cabinet prepared for the new elections by transferring judges and filling the new table of organization with political supporters. A typical case was that of Minas Gerais where the Conservative provincial president gerrymandered parishes "with his intentions and eyes fixed only on the future triumph at the polls." A contemporary observer charged that in Minas all the appointments of sheriffs and deputy sheriffs were decided politically. All over the province men who had served as justice of the peace for many years were suddenly confronted with centrally appointed deputy sheriffs whose sympathies lay with the Conservative government.[88] The new deputy sheriffs were ideally situated to tilt the coming elections in favor of the government because in the election of 1842 they were to sit with the juiz de paz and the parish priest on the electoral board responsible for qualifying citizens to vote and be chosen as electors. Since the juiz and the parish priest rarely represented the same side of local factions, the allegiances of the sheriff would usually determine the political coloring of the junta.[89] The Liberals were witnessing the creation of a system in which they had no apparent access to power.

Faced with this prospect, the large Liberal contingents of Minas Gerais and São Paulo rose against the centralizing Conservative government. In spite of the participation of old firebrands like Feijó in São Paulo and eloquent representatives of a new generation of Liberals like Teófilo Ottoni in Minas, however, the rebellions were quickly suffocated.[90] The Conservative cabinet interpreted the outbreaks as further evidence of the subversive nature of Liberal "demagogues" and continued to set up their new legal system in preparation for the elections of late 1842.

The specific mechanics of this new judicial-electoral system can best be seen at the level of the justice of the peace. In parishes where the elected magistrate represented a faction disagreeable to the government, an opponent of that faction would be named deputy sheriff and charged with promoting government candidates in the election. The deputy's legal and police powers, together with his influence in the matter of local conscription, could usually swing an election. In parishes like those of Rio's Paraíba Valley, on the other hand, where most juizes de paz were convinced supporters of the Party of Order, the government rewarded the elected judges by naming them deputy sheriff also. A similar duplication of office-holding also occurred at the county level, where the duties of municipal judge and high sheriff were sometimes combined in one individual.[91] As a rule, in parishes and counties whose politics pleased the government, the new police structure simply overlay the old judicial system of the Procedural Code; but in parishes which presented political problems or potential conflict, the police hierarchy could be applied as a parallel and counterbalancing influence and a rallying point for local factions supporting the government. The election of 1842 set a pattern for the future, so that although the elected judgeship had lost much of its original power, the magistrate himself remained an important figure in the political system. Eventually the distinction between juiz de paz and deputy sheriff became so thoroughly a function of politics and elections that casual observers of the legal system could not tell the two apart. Around mid-century two North American travelers trying to describe Brazilian legal structure and procedures claimed that the deputy sheriff was the Brazilian equivalent of the justice of the peace. If there was an institutional difference between the justice of the peace and the deputy, they were not aware of it.[92]

Like the turbulent elections of 1840, then, the elections of 1842 were fixed, and in much the same way. But in the interim the Conservatives had institutionalized the fix with their centralizing reform of the Procedural Code. Now the government could choose local electoral officials in most places, and the voting in 1842 proceeded in peace and utter predictability. An overwhelming Conservative majority resulted, evidence that imperial Brazil had at last devised a workable political system.

10. The Politics of Justice, 1841-1871

The Conservative reform of 1841 and the defeat of the Liberal rebellion in the following year brought Brazil to a kind of equilibrium. The political men responsible for the change viewed their achievement with both serenity and fatigue. In 1848 the provincial president of Rio de Janeiro assured the central government that news of the revolution in France would "die on the shores of our land." Brazil, he wrote, had paid in full its "tribute of blood on the fields of civil discord, and now, weary of struggling and chasing after political reforms, [the country] seems to be concentrating the lion's share of its vitality on the exploitation of the abundant resources of its soil and in the development of its material interests."[1] Privately, politicians adopted a more existential interpretation of the new mood, though they often favored the same imagery, which ran to the fiscal after the Conservatives came to power. Referring to a proposed reform, the forty-two-year-old Ângelo Ferraz declared in 1854 that his reformist days were over: "I have paid that tribute of youth." Now he took other counsel from "the burden of the years."[2] João Maurício Wanderley, whose career would span the empire, was similarly drained at age 39: "old age has made me leery [of reform] and a partisan of the hot compress."[3] These faintly ridiculous allusions to old age by men far from their dotage underscore an important aspect of the transition: the change was felt at the heart; it was one of attitudes and generations, not merely of political parties and institutions.

Former Liberals like Bernardo Pereira de Vasconcelos now flocked to the Conservative Party, and new faces appeared for whom affiliation with the conquering Conservatives in the 1840s seemed as natural as affiliation with the Liberals had been in the 1830s. The party's unofficial charter, and the true political constitution of the empire, was the reformed Procedural Code: it made it possible to rig elections, and the Conservatives rigged and won them; it increased the government's area of patronage, and the Conservatives used the new power to good effect. This much is true, but the model as it stands is inherently suspect, for it is the perfect antithesis of the earlier liberal system and thus an ideal construct based on the supremacy of public power. As such it cannot accommodate conflict or change in the later history of the empire; it cannot account for its personnel or their recruitment. Important questions remain unanswered about the reconciliation of public and private interests in imperial Brazil.

Perhaps the most obvious question regards the survival of the two-party system. The Law of December 3 and the centralizing legislation that went with it were all part of a blueprint for a single-party system. The goals of the Conservatives could hardly have been different. The men of the Regresso distrusted elections and democratic forms. They lamented but accepted the backward state of Brazilian civilization that required a stable source of authority. Their view of Brazilian society was one which assumed the ultimate victory of elite class and corporate consensus. Political opposition, for the Conservatives, was hard to distinguish from social threats; hence the fear of the mob and the often-expressed worry that an opposition party would try to build a following among blacks, workmen, or other socially disreputable elements.[4]   The centralizing laws would presumably make this impossible by uniting the "responsible" or "conservative" classes in a union of self-interest.

Two factors, however, prevented the Conservative Party from establishing a single-party politics. First, to the Conservatives' surprise, the clientele- and patronage-based system forged by the centralizing laws divided imperial politics sharply along factional rather than class lines. In Brazil's parishes, rival elites —planters, mill owners, cattle barons—vied for government favor and the titles and powers of office holding. Far from articulating class consensus, the new laws of bureaucracy encouraged factional splits and the formation of "in" and "out" partisan rivalries. Community rivals, whether divided by family feuds, litigation, or economic competition, all sought the support of the bureaucracy and local out-group grievances translated directly into opposition politics at the national level.

A second reason for the survival of the Liberal Party was the partial survival of those characteristics of transition that helped to explain Brazilian liberalism in the 1820s. Although the rise of coffee soon created entrenched interests that the Liberals would find difficult to overcome, the advance of this new crop along an economic frontier which originated in the Paraíba Valley of Rio de Janeiro and progressed gradually into São Paulo, constantly replicated at its leading edge the earlier formation of frontier elites. These emerging elites of the coffee frontier—to say nothing of marginalized groups in less-favored areas, or grasping middle groups in the cities—continued to prefer the autonomy that localistic institutions like the justice of the peace gave them. While established "oligarchies" of the populous littoral provinces such as Rio de Janeiro, Bahia, and Pernambuco dominated the Conservative Party, then, the Liberal Party continued to find support for its oldest beliefs among rising groups in São Paulo, Minas Gerais, the cities, and other socially fluid or peripheral areas.[5]

The stubborn persistence of a political opposition raises other questions about the undeniable success of the Conservatives' political reforms, since, at least on paper, they appear intolerant of faction. If the Conservative system served only certain groups and provinces, in what sense can it be said to have forged a Brazilian state? How did political give-and-take function in fact? What was the new structure's role in the political integration and stabilization of half of a continent? The answers to these questions lie beyond the official table of organization or the force of statute. They must be sought in the extra-official contours of imperial government, and these are obviously difficult to describe. Indeed, Conservative mastermind Paulino José Soares de Souza found it hard to refer to these practical aspects of the Law of December 3 without mixing metaphors. It was a sensible, benevolent law, he explained, not a political "fortress" but a "flexible spring" which could be used by either party.[6] It is this unelaborated theme of flexibility that is of interest here, and one key to its explanation is to be found in judicial personnel. The Law of December 3 was, after all, a law of judicial as well as political organization, and the essential flexibility of its politics was provided by the men who occupied the bench.

Critics of the Law of December 3 had displayed a great deal of concern over the imperial judiciary ever since the bill was introduced for debate. Most critics, it is true, phrased their considerations in the familiar vocabulary of judge-baiting, but more thoughtful observers probed the two major problems they saw growing out of the Law of December 3: first, the now-more-powerful government's ascendancy over the professional magistracy; and second, the likewise more powerful professional magistracy's ascendancy over local interests.

Liberals were conceptually certain of their abhorrence of the magistracy's growing dependence upon the executive branch, but they were not really comfortable with the realities of the Brazilian case, since the corrupt union of the professional magistracy and public power had long been a convenient shibboleth. For purposes of polemical simplification, the two branches had become rhetorically indistinguishable, but to argue against judicial dependence supposed the possibility of their separation. In the Chamber of Deputies a member fumbled with the argument. "Everything will be subject to the judicial aristocracy," he shouted instinctively. Then, reconsidering, he amended, "or rather, to the government, for this reform subjects the judiciary to the [ministry]."[7] The Liberals of 1841 seemed unable to decide which entity—the "government" or the judiciary—would ultimately be responsible for oppression, and they were especially hesitant to separate the two since to blame one would be to exonerate the other. This ambivalence had roots in more than rhetorical fictions, but these can only be appreciated after some attempt is made to effect the separation which the early critics shunned.

The 1841 law did indeed create a professional magistracy dependent upon the central government. The law's political essence derived from the coercive ties of dependence—primarily the power of appointment—that bound the magisterial network to the government and gave the ministry ultimate control over its judicial representatives. Put simply, in return for his appointment and salary, the magistrate would represent and make palatable the authority of his patron, the central government. This was dependence in the ideal sense, since it had no necessary partisan content. Our evidence of the relationship, however, is often of a partisan nature, for Brazil's two-party political system made the judges' function as a dependent agent of the government most clearly visible in the partisan juggling of appointments. The existence of national parties made a ministry's choice of personnel crucial, not only to the long-run authority of the central government, but also to the short-term fortunes and electoral success of the party-in-power. Manipulation of judicial personnel, therefore, became an infamously partisan activity, and while the partisan aspect was only a variation on the government's basic right to control its own agents, such party maneuvering does suggest the extent of the judiciary's dependence as well as its politicization.

The Constitution forbade dismissal of professional magistrates, so the mechanics of judicial manipulation centered in the use and abuse of the power of transfer (*remoção*). Since at first most judges sympathized with the Conservative Party, the Liberals were ironically forced to use remoção most blatantly. When the Liberals held power briefly in 1840-1841 and again from 1844 to 1848, for example, their transfers of judges and dismissals of inferior officials rearranged the bureaucratic personnel of the entire empire. These ministerial transfers were apparently not a matter of public record before 1855, but newspapers in the capital kept their own lists and their estimates usually tallied. In eight months in 1840-1841, the Liberal minister of justice transferred forty-three district judges, causing chaos in the judiciary by sending some to comarcas that were already occupied. When the Liberals returned to power in 1844, some fifty-two district judges (at the time there were 116 comarcas in the empire) were transferred in preparation for the parliamentary elections.[8] The Liberals' desperate attempt to break the power of Conservative judges in the critical province of Rio de Janeiro in 1844 can be traced in the provincial president's correspondence with the minister of justice requesting a complex series of transfers and switches designed to get "frenetic opposition" judges out of the province or relocate them where their "opposition would cause little harm."[9] The practice of rearranging magistrates soon became the norm, and when the Conservatives returned to power in 1848, the new minister of justice made over seventy transfers in a single year.[10] The party on the outs invariably protested this practice of "inversion," but, in private, most politicians shrugged at the periodic "contredanse of judges."[11]

Because a judge's political affiliation was a prime condition for appointment by partisan ministries, it was necessary for the minister of justice to know where the potential district judge stood on party matters. At first this was facilitated by the relatively small number of professional magistrates in the empire—approximately 150 district judges at mid-century—and the assumption that most of them were Conservative. But as time passed, younger and more opportunistic magistrates began to mount the Liberal bandwagon, and a judge's sympathies could no longer be taken for granted. Conservative and Liberal ministries apparently kept (and destroyed) political records, which included information that could not be allowed to fall into the hands of the opposition. The magistrates themselves sometimes showed a selected amnesia about past service. When in 1849 the Ministry of Justice asked for career résumés from the juizes de direito of Rio de Janeiro the district judges were remarkably vague about their professional histories, sometimes forgetting the year of an assignment and almost uniformly failing to mention political and administrative offices held between judicial posts.[12]

The political account books which do remain to us—probably by accident—are revealing documents. The Liberal ministry of 1847 undertook one such survey of its judicial support in the provinces, and the result, albeit fragmentary, showed at once how spare was Liberal support among the judiciary in that year and how assiduously anti-Liberal magistrates had been exiled to remote, and electorally insignificant, comarcas. In the northern province of Ceará, for example, fully seven of ten juizes de direito were actively hostile to the Liberal ministry, and in the northeastern province of Paraíba, four out of five judges opposed the government. The judges appointed for five of the six comarcas of remote Piauí had not even taken office, and the single magistrate active in the province was an oppositionist. Apparently the Liberals had concentrated judges of their own persuasion in the more important provinces of the center-south. No data were given for Rio de Janeiro, but of the fourteen judges of Minas Gerais there were "only two political complaints," and in São Paulo at least two of the seven district judges were overt supporters of the party in power.[13]

As the number of eligible letrados in the empire increased and it became less possible to assume that a judge would favor the Conservative Party, political head-counts had to be carried out at the level of the municipal judge—the proving ground for graduates of the Brazilian legal faculties, and anteroom to appointment as district judge. One remaining ledger of "classified information" on municipal judges, which was begun in 1846 and kept unevenly thereafter, gives fairly complete political information on the municipal judges of Piauí province in 1862. The entries, supplied by a provincial president, sometimes referred to the judges' competence or intelligence, but their true purpose was to provide an accurate guide to the politics of the young magistrates. A succinct entry might include simply the information that the judge was "Conservative. Good judge. Intelligent and knowledgeable. Above party intrigues." But in other instances the president would elaborate: "I do not know his politics, but by his family I would expect him to be Liberal." Only three of the twenty-four judges listed were identified with neither party, and one-third of the total was classified as "political," that is, actively involved in elections. One was called a "committed and frenetic Saquarema (Conservative). He is ruled by his political passions." Another Conservative was described as "an eminently political judge. Serves as party boss in the district. Protects his friends and gives no quarter to his political enemies." A Liberal involved in partisan activities was said to be "influenced by his father, who is party boss in Paraíba."[14]

The government's need and ability to transfer judges reinforced their tendency to be openly partisan, for political service was one of the few bargaining points the judge had in the assignment and transfer process. To be apolitical was a liability, for as one deputy put it, "If a district judge doesn't involve himself in politics he loses the regard of the public, and there is always another one whose political inclinations please the government of the day. Let us bid the former farewell; his transfer will make way for the latter."[15] Influential relatives or contacts might win a desirable first assignment for a young law-school graduate, but thereafter a judge's willingness to serve the ministry was usually the determining factor in making the best assignments. Most conventional letters of recommendation seem to have been routinely ignored and, especially after mid-century competition stiffened for the coveted posts in the magistracy, a young letrado's progress was usually determined by his ability to promote party interests.[16]

From a judge's point of view, of course, an inopportune transfer to a remote comarca might be tantamount to dismissal. A magistrate could sometimes refuse the post and settle down to await something better, but for men with families, arbitrary government transfer for political reasons was an onerous burden. The reshuffling of judges that followed each change of government deposited a fresh contingent of disgruntled magistrates at the café tables and ministry doorsteps of Rio de Janeiro. And at such times the official correspondence of political leaders swelled with the pleas of those who were unhappy with their new positions ("Here I find myself, for my sins, in Rio Grande do Norte"), or whose expectations had been dashed because "the minister had a son-in-law to place."[17]

For the most part, however, the empire's career judges acquiesced in the considerable inconvenience posed by political transfer. Their Portuguese heritage included no alternative tradition of disinterested appointment by merit;

and in Brazil the belief that judges might be appointed for reasons other than political ones does not appear to have been widely held. When, in 1854, one federal deputy protested another's cynical view on this matter, saying that if he were minister, "I would choose according to merit," his remark was met by the "prolonged hilarity" of his colleagues.[18]

The professional magistrates also tolerated their dependence on the executive because the potential stakes were so high. And here the critics of the 1841 law identified the second point of their argument—the excessive power of the resurrected letrado magistracy at the local level. In order to make the magistrate an effective political deputy, the government was forced to invest the official with virtually all the powers of the state. A district judge exercised immense power in his comarca, and observers quickly and accurately interpreted that power in political terms: as a means to coerce local support. In the debates over the law one Liberal senator gave a concise evaluation of the role the magistracy would play in creating a political system. The law, he protested, would set up a judicial elite "charged with going out to make deals with local potentates."[19]

Certainly the reactionaries of 1841 had proposed to give judicial personnel ample currency for making such deals with the landed elite. One article in their bill would have entrusted to the government-appointed municipal judge the sole right to judge crimes of contraband, including the illegal importation of African slaves so important to the coffee planters of Rio de Janeiro. A liberal newspaper called the proposal "a sword of Damocles suspended above the heads of all the most powerful people of Brazil."[20] The article was omitted from the final bill. Another source of leverage over landed groups concerned the role of magistrates in establishing legal title. In 1841 the minister of justice referred to the municipal judge's responsibility for conducting surveys and validating land claims as justification for making these officials appointive and salaried. Disingenuously he made the point that the unpaid, locally selected municipal judges of the previous system could hardly be called upon to leave their private jobs to go into the forest for months at a time to carry out surveys. How much better it would be to professionalize these judges, give them a salary and larger emoluments, and have the ministry name them without interference from local municipal councils.[21] The minister's unspoken point was not lost on the Chamber of Deputies: through its appointed magistrates, the Conservative government hoped to extend its rural power base by trading political allegiance for preferential treatment in title validation.

The new patronage powers that the government acquired by virtue of the 1841 law would also be brokered by the professional judges in such a way as to reinforce or create a political clientele at the local level. The new police post of deputy sheriff, and the plethora of substitutes named to fill possible vacancies, soon came to be granted honorifically in recognition of service to the government or simply as a means to pay court to local elites whose support was desired. In 1842, for example, many such posts were distributed to planters who supported the government against uprisings in São Paulo and Minas Gerais. A district judge serving as chief of police in western Rio de Janeiro related to the minister of justice the means by which, with promises of deputy positions, he had wheedled one wavering family into supporting the government at this moment of crisis: "The Freires," he reported, "were annoyed with the government for not having named them deputy sheriffs or alternates . . . in spite of their being the richest planters of the area." The judge invited the head of the family to dinner, and the accompanying promises of patronage were so well received that the patriarch "offered supplies for the troops and assured me that the government could count on his person and his fortune."[22] For the rest of the decade members of the Freire clan dominated the appointive post of deputy sheriff in their parish.[23]

Again a rather fine distinction must be drawn between the political interests served by judges primarily as servants of the central government—any central government—and those they defended as party agents. In the case just mentioned, the Conservative judge's partisan affiliation might lead him to suppress the rebels because they were "Liberals." On the other hand, his bureaucratic identification with the regime simultaneously made upon him more general, nonpartisan demands associated with political integration; that is, the preservation of stability and the strengthening of the entire political fabric against a challenge. His support could thus be enlisted against a threat to the system rather than in behalf of a narrow partisan manifestation. In this case a combination of motives probably lay behind the judge's actions. The Freires were no doubt enlisted primarily in the name of the monarch's interest in avoiding disorder, and only incidentally to the political advantage of the Conservative Party.

The judges' local leverage found its most usual expression in the matter of elections. By a careful balancing of favors, threats, or fraud, the partisan judge could normally get local elites to turn out the vote for government candidates. Conflict was avoided by offering positive inducements to the elite, and reserving cruder tactics for the inarticulate and powerless voter. Before contested elections, for example, judges often invoked their prerogative of forced conscription into the imperial Army or Navy. To the humble voter this was perhaps the most feared weapon of intimidation at the judge's disposal. The very threat of being uprooted and subjected to the execrable conditions prevalent within the Brazilian armed forces was sufficient to make a man vote as the local judge and police desired; indeed, rumors of an impending round of conscription could send virtually all the opposition underground. This technique was thus especially favored because it balanced partisan electoral goals against government interests in stability by limiting the potential for violence among local factions. When, in 1841, fighting threatened to break out in some of the parishes of western Rio, for instance, the provincial president ordered the district judge to begin "rigorous conscription of the ne'er-do-wells who infest the area, in order to diminish the opponents' potential following."[24]

Contrary to the fears of Liberals in 1841 that the judges would use their powers to coerce support and bully opposition, relationships between judges and local elites were distinctly transactional. Even in the course of their normal duties on the bench, imperial magistrates preferred to deal themselves the cards of the bargainer, doing judicial favors that could be repaid at election time, or indulging opposition groups just enough to involve them in tacit recognition of the give-and-take of imperial politics. During the 1840s the Liberal Party led two regional rebellions—as noted in Minas Gerais and São Paulo in 1842, and in Pernambuco in 1848. In both cases the rebels were tried by highly political Conservative judges. The judge who presided at the trial of the first group of defendants also directed virulent newspaper attacks against the Liberals of Minas Gerais. Yet the Liberals implicated in that revolt were uniformly acquitted by juries, and there is no evidence that he or any other judge tried to override the jury verdicts as was the district judge's right under the Law of December 3. In Pernambuco, José Tomás Nabuco de Araújo, the Conservative judge who presided over the political trials of the Liberal rebels of 1848, was also intimately involved in the politics of the province and had political grievances against the very defendants who came before him. Although the Pernambucan juries did vote to convict the leaders of the revolt, Nabuco himself appealed the conviction in one case and apparently allowed the others to stand only because the customary process of granting amnesty had begun even before the trials ended.[25]

Ironically, the judges' very dependence on the central government also imposed certain limits on their political activism at the district level, and it may be that judges sometimes tempered their partisanship for professional considerations. Political journalism, for instance, was second nature to a partisan judge, and, especially in times of stress, magistrates often combined their formal duties with political writing for the local press. But they paid a price, and others may have been warned away by their example. While sitting as presiding judge in the trials of Liberal political rebels in Minas Gerais, Firmino Rodrigues Silva openly contributed to two Conservative newspapers, one of which was pledged to "centralizing and giving direction to our party, and beating down the audacious rebels." And the vicious attacks on the Liberal Party by editor-magistrate João Antônio Sampaio Viana in the troubled Bahia of the late 1830s won that letrado a comfortable post as district judge of Salvador when the Conservatives returned to power. But a judge's overt collaboration in partisan journals was a delicate gamble. Such service might consolidate his reputation within his own party, but the more a judge advertised his politics, the more he had to fear when his party left power. Firmino Rodrigues Silva was transferred by a subsequent Liberal government to the isolated, Indian-infested southern comarca of Santa Catarina. And the return of a Liberal ministry likewise yanked the urbane Sampaio Viana out of the Bahian capital and sent him to the comarca of Caravelas in the south of Bahia, where life was later described by another luckless judge as "insipid . . . no one takes tea and there is not a single piano."[26]

In the long run, the judges' sensitivity to the needs of the regime, together with their professional and political insecurity, appear to have made the magistracy a factor in the preservation of the political peace of the empire after the 1840s. Stability was one of the government's prime goals, of course, and local factional conflict reflected badly on the ministry's judicial representatives. Whatever his party, a judge who had achieved the prestige of a desirable appointment was more likely to use his power to conciliate than to persecute. A peaceful comarca meant predictable elections and prolonged tenure for the judge; a turbulent comarca gained the judge enemies, caused contested, violent elections, shortened the life of the ministry and earned certain transfer. Opposition judges exiled to faraway assignments, on the other hand, might agitate more openly because they had less to lose, but rarely to the point of promoting local discord.[27] More often the banished magistrate's bureaucratic fatalism and professional insecurity led him to wait peacefully for a change of ministry or spend his energy on securing a leave-of-absence. Regardless of his party, it was ordinarily in a judge's interest to minimize local frictions and at least passively perform his function as government representative in his district. The result was a measure of stability in a highly partisan political system.

This constructive role as political mediator, unforeseen by the critics in 1841, was mirrored in the social ties judges established with the landed elite. The lack of comprehensive graphical data on professional judges makes impossible a complete analysis of their social origins. But information available on some of the most prominent professional magistrates of nineteenth-century Brazil does indicate that relatively few could claim family elite status backed by land. A sample of the judges who were also eminent political leaders in the 1840s and 1850s seems to bear this out: Paulino José Soares de Souza was the son of a physician, while Eusébio de Queiroz, Bernardo Pereira de Vasconcelos, and José Tomás Nabuco de Araújo were all the sons of magistrates. Honório Hermeto Carneiro Leão and Aureliano de Sousa e Oliveira Coutinho had military fathers. Only Manuel Vieira Tosta and Francisco Gonçalves Martins were the sons of prominent landowners.[28] The sample is no more than illustrative, but it is not reasonable to imagine that judges who attained less in their careers, and on whom we have no biographical information, would have come from more privileged social situations. Nor is there any historical discontinuity here, for in range and even distribution of social background, this small sample bears comparison to Stuart Schwartz's findings for colonial magistrates.[29]

To this mixed group of individuals a legal education was the ticket to administration, politics, and social enhancement. The legal education at Coimbra had long been a heady introduction to the Portuguese conception of the empire and its governance. Similarly, attendance at the two Brazilian law schools, which opened in 1828, was an intensive preparation for political and administrative involvement in the newly independent nation.[30] Among the students, political journalism seems to have occupied more time than instruction, and in this unique gathering of youths from different provinces and social backgrounds a premium came to be placed upon ambition and social skills. The cultivation and exchange of contacts was pursued obsessively. Long after their careers had ended, aging judges would recall with clarity their first encounters—perhaps on the boat to Lisbon or in the gaming houses of the university town—with the other youths who would later help secure a desired appointment or ask such help for themselves.[31] Like the Portuguese university, the Brazilian institutions appear to have instilled a corporate spirit and solidarity in their graduates that largely overcame the advantages or stigma of origin and gave the judges a kind of wild-card status in the social system.

Brazil's rural elites and these young magistrates had much to offer one another. Graduation from the legal faculty assured a young man of contacts throughout the empire and an entrée at most levels of government; investiture as a professional judge made the letrado a man of considerable official and extra-official power. For planters and landowners who were inevitably somewhat isolated in the interior and usually embroiled in litigation, these were invaluable qualities. Most judges, for their part, were quite susceptible to the attractions of local sponsorship by the socially privileged. Such association made a magistrate's tenure immeasurably more pleasant, and, after all, close identification with the landowners seemed implicit in the political goals of the government. Certainly a judge whose father had been an itinerant crown bureaucrat or middle-level professional could be swayed by the attentions of landed clans. Professionally, too, close ties with the empire's social elite could go far toward advancing one's career; conversely, it was known to be hazardous to ruffle the influential. Albino José Barbosa de Oliveira, just out of law school, took up the comarca of Cachoeira, Bahia, in 1832 and shortly thereafter displeased one of the richest men in the province in a case of land litigation. The callow judge's decision may have served justice, but it also won him a hasty transfer to a less desirable comarca, where he was more careful not to alienate the powerful.[32]

Usually it was understood that a magistrate's local relationships only complemented his professional ties to the crown and his political ties to the ministry. A renegade judge was of limited use locally, for much of his power there lay in his corporate and government identity. Nevertheless, in times of tension or in areas of ironhanded clan rule it was not unheard of for a magistrate to completely "go over" to the service of a local patron. Such was the case in 1845 of the municipal judge of Cantagalo, who had been personally "recruited" in Rio de Janeiro by a county political boss who needed a judicial puppet.[33] Another satrap of Rio de Janeiro province, Comendador Joaquim Breves, openly subsidized the municipal judge who lived without charge in one of Breves' houses along with two of the planter's personal lawyers.[34] And in the interior of Bahia, where in the 1840s the central government lost control after a bloody feud broke out between families, the judge of Pilão Arcado sported sidearms as he turned out spurious criminal indictments against his patron's enemies.[35]

More often, magistrates served as conduits between local and national interests. Such a judicial articulation of private interests can be seen at a very high level in the composition of the famous "oligarchy" of Rio de Janeiro that was so instrumental in creating the Conservative Party in the late 1830s and early 1840s. The so-called oligarchy was a group of three extraordinary men who represented the emerging coffee interests of Rio de Janeiro province, and is usually described simply in terms of its origin in the Rio province planter aristocracy. Yet a closer look reveals that only one member of this "oligarchy," Joaquim José Rodrigues Torres, was himself a coffee planter. The other two, Paulino José Soares de Souza and Eusébio de Queiroz, were young career magistrates who had had no ties with Rio de Janeiro before adulthood. Both were the sons of professionals—a physician and a judge, respectively—and had been raised elsewhere. In fact, neither was even a native Brazilian: Paulino had been born in Paris, where his father was studying medicine, and Eusébio in Angola, where his father served as crown ouvidor. Rodrigues Torres's plantation near the town of Saquarema in Rio province may have given the Conservative Party its popular name, but the true organizers of the party appear to have been those two talented outlander judges adopted by the provincial coffee aristocracy as their representatives in the capital.[36]

That ambitious judges were alive to the possibilities of professional and social self-advancement through extra official involvements with Brazil's agricultural elite is patent in the very concept of the "good comarca." The desirability of a judicial district was determined mainly by its political and economic potential. In 1831, for example, Albino José Barbosa de Oliveira chose São João d'El Rei, in Minas Gerais, as his first magisterial position, on the grounds that, of the sixty vacancies offered, this comarca was the home of the most federal deputies. Later in the 1830s, after the coffee boom had begun in Rio de Janeiro,

Albino (and most of his colleagues, it should be noted) lobbied for an assignment there.[37] Some letrados preferred positions near their own homes and
family interests, but most district judges accepted the forced mobility of judgeship with a good grace that seems curious in a country where regional and family ties were strong. The reason lies in the dual origin of a judge's power and
the need to maintain balance. Just as surely as these professionals kept strong
their links with the locus of formal power in Rio de Janeiro, they also sought
to establish informal and social links with the shifting loci of socioeconomic
power in the empire. We may generalize that the "best" comarcas of the empire lay along the cutting edge of the economic frontier.[38]

The interplay of sociopolitical and legal transactions between the judge and
the elite clientele of his district was often formalized by matrimony. Time and
again promising young magistrates were brought into the families of the landed
classes as sons-in-law. By thus incorporating a judge, the bride's family enhanced
its standing in Rio de Janeiro and greatly expanded its contacts within the government and central bureaucracy. And of course, to choose from the pool of
talented letrados represented a unique opportunity for a planter with a marriage-
able daughter to entrust at least part of his inheritance to proven ability without sacrificing social appearances.[39] To the judge, of course, such a marriage
brought an array of blessings. It strengthened his bargaining position with the
central government and gave him the financial and regional security of which
he was deprived by his profession. For magistrates of middling social background, such marriages represented "arrival" in the most traditional sense, and
may even have been a powerful reason for entering the magistracy in the first
place.

The frequency with which judges contracted advantageous marital alliances
would seem to support such speculation. Paulino José Soares de Souza formalized his political bonds with the Rio de Janeiro oligarchy by marrying the
daughter of one of the principal planters of the sugar-producing lowland areas
near the capital. The bride was also the sister-in-law of the planter and political
leader Joaquim José Rodrigues Torres, on whose rural property the ceremony
was performed. Thus in one stroke, this judge, son of a doctor and raised in
Maranhão, gained kinship links to both the coffee and sugar aristocracies of
Rio de Janeiro. Another magistrate, Albino José Barbosa de Oliveira, has left
in his memoirs a joyful account of dodging the matrimonial designs of planters
and their daughters in the districts where he served. Albino's reluctance seems
to have been strategic; in any event it paid off handsomely when he was at
length sought out as a likely son-in-law by the head of one of the greatest landowning clans of the São Paulo coffee frontier, the Sousa Queiroz. The prospective bride's immense fortune, and her family's extensive political influence, overcame the modest Bahian judge's hesitancy, and he accepted the match without

so much as a glimpse of the girl. As a final example, we may mention Firmino Rodrigues Silva, who married in his judicial district of Minas Gerais the daughter of an influential and traditional local family. The marriage propelled Firmino's political career, and the schoolteacher's son from Rio de Janeiro eventually became an imperial senator.[40]

As the empire took form, then, it sometimes became difficult to tell which source of power—public or private—was truly responsible for judicial dependence. This was the genius of the system and the source of its flexibility. Yet for the judge-intermediaries themselves there was a third possibility which casts light on the early Liberals' inability to imagine the judiciary as a discrete branch of the state. As brokers who dealt extensively in proxied powers, the magistrates derived independent leverage of their own. Those who married locally became planters as well as judges; and the political expression of such mergers at the national level led naturally to a similar blurring of lines between the magistracy and the government itself. The privileged position the judges held as beneficiaries of the support of both the local elites and central government, for example, made them nearly unbeatable if they chose to run for office. As a consequence, judges were elected to the national legislature in such numbers that they sometimes made up as much as 41 percent of the Chamber of Deputies. Thus the letrados gained a measure of direct control over the system that they already manipulated indirectly.

The high percentage of magistrates in the legislative branch was a touchy subject because, at least in the 1830s and 1840s, most judges were Conservatives. The highly partisan character of the debates over judicial reform that culminated in the law of 1841 made the magistracy a political issue and reinforced the political activism of its members. So the newly emerged Conservative Party, which had hoped to resurrect the professional judges as an integrative and centralizing element in a diffuse empire, also found in them a formidable corporate base for a political party. Conservative theoreticians, many of whom were career magistrates themselves, believed that the judges were the key to creating a stable political system, and it was a short step from cultivating their support of the government to enlisting them in the party. Conservative publicists wrote seductively of the "social force" of the magistracy, and party leaders applied their flattering corporate analysis of Brazilian society to the task of enlisting the judges.[41]

Figure 1 shows at a glance the effectiveness of this Conservative policy of lionizing the magistracy. Most graphically, the peak years of magisterial participation in the Chamber of Deputies all came in the aftermath of political crises —the Liberal revolts of 1842 and 1848 and the ministerial crisis of 1868—that temporarily turned the electoral machinery over to the Conservative Party.

The at-first overwhelming party imbalance within the magistracy explains

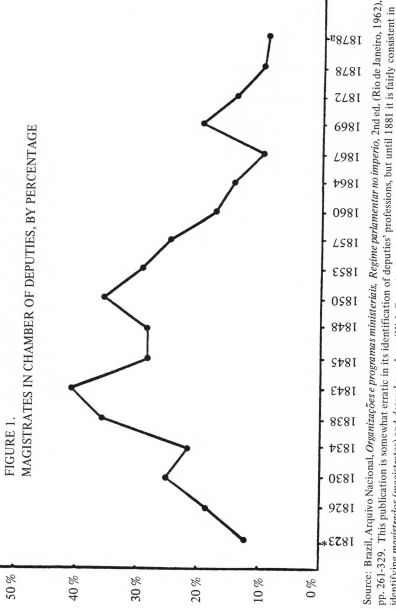

FIGURE 1.
MAGISTRATES IN CHAMBER OF DEPUTIES, BY PERCENTAGE

Source: Brazil, Arquivo Nacional, *Organizações e programas ministeriais. Regime parlamentar no imperio*, 2nd ed. (Rio de Janeiro, 1962), pp. 261-329. This publication is somewhat erratic in its identification of deputies' professions, but until 1881 it is fairly consistent in identifying *magistrados* (magistrates) and *desembargadores* (High Court justices), with increasing completeness after 1860. The failure to include the professions of titled nobility before 1860 has been partly corrected by including the titled judges mentioned in the text.

* Constituent Assembly

the continued antijudge posture of many Liberals long after the system of judicial brokerage forged by the Law of December 3 had shown its amenability to manipulation by either party. Even the most vehement critics of 1841 soon came to realize that the law they opposed was too valuable to the party in power to make its reform plausible. And the Conservatives were fond of pointing out that the Liberals "never changed so much as a comma."[42] But for many years after 1841 the Liberal Party had excellent practical reasons for fighting judicial dominance in the legislative branch. To comment, as many did, on the prospect of "a Parliament made up entirely of magistrates" was the same as to warn of a legislature made up entirely of Conservatives.[43]

As figure 1 illustrates, the fear of judicial monopoly of the legislative branch was sometimes not much exaggerated. Repeatedly during the empire the Liberal Party proposed reforms to make professional judges ineligible to hold political office or to retire them from the magistracy if they were elected. Liberals cited the constitutional issue of separation of powers, and also argued forcefully that the political interests of judges prejudiced the administration of justice: "for a year before the election there is no justice because [the judge] is setting up his machine . . . and for a year afterward there is no justice because he is paying off his votes."[44] But class opposition by the magistrates in Parliament made reform impossible, and debates over eligibility usually degenerated into furious, sterile sessions of name-calling between the pro- and antimagistrate factions. The only eligibility law passed during the empire was the provision in the 1855 electoral law that forbade the election of juizes de direito from their own judicial districts. The restriction, however, was substantially offset by simultaneously converting to representation by districts rather than provinces, making it a simple matter for a judge to trade his district's support for election from an adjoining district. In practice the law was regarded as ineffective and was spare comfort to those Liberals who continued to lobby in vain for "absolute ineligibility" of magistrates.[45]

Yet the Conservatives themselves had reason to be ambivalent about the judicial faction in the Chamber of Deputies. For one thing, it was soon clear that party alternation in power and the steady production of new letrados by the legal faculties would ultimately equalize the party balance within the magistracy. In 1846, for example, the Liberals had proposed to double the number of judicial districts in an attempt to create overnight a counter-constituency of Liberal judges among the empire's newest law graduates. This ominous packing bill was defeated, but the passage of time and the opportunism of younger judges would eventually have the same effect.[46] The Conservatives responded in 1850 by passing an ingenious measure designed to guarantee their present advantage and hedge their position against a new generation of magistrates. The new law divided the empire's comarcas into three categories according to their desirability, and prohibited the transfer of any judge to a comarca of category inferior to the one he held when the law was passed. Judges would work their way up in steps from the most isolated, poorest districts, to the most attractive. The measure ostensibly regulated the transfer of magistrates, but in effect it froze proven Conservative judges into the most important districts of the empire. (The Conservative minister of justice had made over seventy strategic transfers the year before he sent this bill to the Chamber of Deputies.)[47] For all its cleverness, however, the measure was only a stopgap.

Regardless of party, Brazilian ministries were also concerned with the absenteeism caused by the election of large numbers of practicing judges to the imperial legislature. Judges who won election to the Chamber of Deputies had to abandon their judicial posts for most of the year, thus failing to carry out their essential role as government intermediaries in the districts of the country. In Bahia, for example, the provincial president complained in 1841 that government effectiveness in that province was compromised because only "two or three" district judges were presently active in the fifteen Bahian comarcas. "The rest are in the Chamber of Deputies or on leaves-of-absence in Rio de Janeiro."[48] A measure of judicial absenteeism was of course an inevitable concomitant of a political judiciary, but in its extreme form absenteeism vitiated the first principles of the political system by leaving the government with no agent at the local level. As a result, Conservative ministries were not always averse to Liberal plans to bar magistrates from the legislature, and occasionally proposed such legislation themselves.[49]

The cohesive faction of professional judges in the legislative branch was perhaps the ultimate expression of the magisterial oligarchy referred to by contemporaries, for these judges, unlike their individual colleagues in the provinces, were disquietingly independent. Working magistrates gained their powers as a function of their dual dependence upon local elites and the central government, but the esprit-de-corps and legislative potency of the magistrates in Parliament defied party and ministerial discipline on the one hand and overcame a judge-deputy's sense of constituency on the other. The judicial legislative faction, for instance, was responsible for the fact that no major reform of the legal system, no matter how innocuous or beneficial, could be passed in the empire before 1871.[50] When such legislation was proposed, whatever its partisan origins, discussions quickly bogged down in wrangling between the judges, who always suspected a disguised attack, and their opponents, frustrated at this invincible corporate obstructionism. So furiously defensive were the judges in Parliament that they came to be known collectively as the "hornet's nest."[51] Legislation which disturbed this *casa de maribondos* (hornet's nest) invariably suffered a long, slow, and rhetorical death.

Epilogue

A form of judicial politics characterized the Brazilian empire in its maturity, and to describe it is to identify an important component of the state. Yet the influence of the professional judges was in part a self-limiting phenomenon, for their very successes as political integrators also tended to obviate their political roles. During the course of the nineteenth century, understandings were reached among the political classes, and communications improved dramatically. In a stable, integrated empire the judicial intermediate was a less crucial factor, and as district judges became more dispensable their sources of independent power also tended to dry up. Then, as Brazilian society grew more complex and broadly politicized, the judicial oligarchy found itself under attack by rival groups at a time when its corporate defenses were crumbling.[52] The substantial decline in the number of magistrates in the Chamber of Deputies after mid-century may be symptomatic of this type of more general decline. The waning of the judicial bloc in Congress was probably due primarily to ministerial discouragement of candidacy in order to lessen the problem of absenteeism, and it need not have affected the system of judicial brokerage at the district level, but there are some collateral indications that it also reflects a more general pattern of breakdown of magisterial politics.

Because the political magistracy was a career that held out the prospect of great rewards, destructive pressures were generated very early within the magistracy itself. Corporate solidarity was an essential ingredient of the system here described, but after mid-century the overproduction of candidates for the magistracy jeopardized the tight esprit-de-corps that had characterized the judiciary in the first half of the century. The problem arose because the semiformalization of the magistrates' political role in 1841 had sustained a rush on the law schools and caused a subsequent glut on the market. As one of Brazil's most acute social observers remarked in 1842, "Nowadays there is scarcely a young man, no matter how poor, who does not pursue legal studies. They think that if they have law degrees the government is rigorously obliged to employ them." The steady upward percolation of senior judges into high political posts was insufficient to relieve the mounting pressure from below; vacant positions were few in comparison to the ambitious graduates who clamored over them like "a thousand dogs after one bone."[53] In 1851 the ex-minister of justice wrote to his son, then studying law in São Paulo: "We have piles of bacharéis around here and no one pays them any mind."[54] Increasingly, graduates of the law schools sank into what Edward Shils has aptly termed "the nether regions of the bar."[55]

As competition mounted, the clubby atmosphere of the early law schools diminished. Ever-smaller percentages of the ever-larger graduating classes were able to enter the magistracy, and in consequence, the legal faculties became less geared to the production of jurists. For those who did enter the magistracy, however, the deterioration of the law schools and the relentless political involvements of judgeship must have been factors of professional demoralization. Before mid-century, attacks on the professional competence of judges and the political appointment process were largely reserved for oppositionists and hecklers, but by the 1860s at least one magistrate had publicized in pamphlet form his concern over what he called "the decadence of the magistracy," blaming it on the politicization of judges and the deficiencies of their education.[56] By the end of the empire the term *bacharel* had completely lost its earlier denotation of judgeship, and the increased use of the inflated title *doutor* (doctor) further attested to the devaluation of the university degree. The great Portuguese novelist Eça de Queiroz commented acidly in 1888 that one scarcely met a Brazilian of any occupation who did not call himself "doutor."[57]

The rhetoric of those who resented the magistracy never changed much in the course of the empire, although increasingly it broadened its reference to include the hordes of *bacharéis*—law graduates with no magisterial status—that swarmed in the machinery of the empire in its last years. Opponents never quite gave up their criticism of the "state within the state," or stopped warning against reducing Brazil to a "fiefdom of the magistracy."[58] But the familiar criticism carried more weight later in the century because it was more solidly grounded in emerging social groups who felt themselves disenfranchised by the judicial "oligarchy." As the century progressed, new professional groups arose to challenge judicial supremacy in the political system. The professional resentments and attacks of military officers, physicians, and engineers betrayed the growing complexity of Brazilian society in the late nineteenth century and were probably as great a threat to the judiciary as internal demoralization. The increasingly self-conscious military officers of the empire led the corporate opposition to the bacharéis and judges, and it may be no coincidence that the single major judicial reform of the post-1841 period was passed the year after the end of the Paraguayan War (1871), when military pride was at its height.[59] And as the numbers of professional magistrates in Congress declined after 1860, their places were taken by men of other professions. In 1867, for the first time, physicians outnumbered judges in the Chamber of Deputies.[60]

Conclusion

Contemporary students of Brazil generally have two complementary perspectives on the history of independence and the early empire. Perhaps because they are conditioned by a more or less militant concern for apparent lack of change in the present, they posit rather static models of Brazilian sociopolitical development at the crucial juncture of the early nineteenth century. First, historians are apt to see the independence movement itself as an essentially conservative episode in which the status quo was, in effect, guaranteed against a recolonizing Portugal. Second, they are in general agreement that the primary Brazilian beneficiaries of this preservation were the large landowners, whose needs it presumably met. Economic evidence is then adduced to show that monoculture and export agriculture continued to be the dominant economic realities, and the nineteenth century becomes a time of "neo-colonialism."[1] Or social evidence of the continuation of slavery and archaic social relations is presented to show the partial survival of a corporate or quasi-feudal society.[2] This sort of analysis gains support from the later political history of the empire whose obscurity (for it is superficially studied) and fundamental stability also suggest a system characterized by handshakes exchanged within a national elite basically in agreement over most issues. Hence the common characterization of the Chamber of Deputies as a gentlemen's debating society. Hence also the popularity of the aphorism that remains the political epitaph of the empire: "Nothing so resembles a Conservative as a Liberal in power."

An alternative interpretation has recently questioned some of these assumptions. While not doubting the existence of a socioeconomic elite of landowners, the Brazilian historian Raymundo Faoro has suggested that there was no necessary correspondence between this group and the level at which the business of state was carried on. Recognizing that the static, landowner-dominated model could not account for the heated controversy over centralization and decentralization in the early empire, Faoro went almost to the other extreme, depicting a rural elite traditionally oppressed by an autonomous "bureaucratic estate."[3] Faoro argued that the early localizing reforms were indeed inspired by the landowners who shared a "natural ideology" of local isolation from the central government. The centralizing policies that followed and triumphed, however, signaled the end of landowner hegemony and the victory of the bureaucratic estate. Whatever the flaws of this argument, it enlarged the debate over the early formation of the empire to admit the possibility of conflict over goals at the elite level, and at the same time underscored the need to be more specific about defining the groups involved and their interests. Implicitly Faoro framed a question for other synthesizers: Was Brazilian sovereignty guaranteed at the public or at the private level? And the answer framed yet another question for the empirically minded: How did this come about?

This book has sought to explore these difficult questions of sociopolitical articulation, using the judicial structure as a point of departure. Although the analysis presented here cannot offer a complete paradigm of Brazilian society, it does suggest revisions in the stereotypes now current. The proposition that a landed elite ultimately dominated the empire is not specifically challenged, but partially explicated in light of common assumptions. The landed groups of colonial Brazil were not, and did not suddenly become, a monolithic elite at the time of independence; indeed, during those transitional years it would be hard even to demonstrate the existence of an economic base for an identifiable and coherent landed interest. Given the diffuse nature of landed society in Brazil, it is impossible to show how its representatives could have guided the first years of independence. The most active figures of the early liberal movement were in fact priests, journalists, and bureaucrats who struggled to conceive of Brazilian society in terms of simple consensus—not of class—and who cannot in any event be shown to have consciously articulated the desires of a "landed class," however defined. The nearest approach to such a demonstration is Faoro's deduction that the landed classes' interests *must* have been supreme during the liberal period because during those years their alleged natural isolationism was satisfied by localizing reforms such as the justice of the peace. Yet it seems contradictory that a group all-powerful at the national level would seek parochial self-isolation as a favored policy. The standard social categories break down at the level of political participation.

Brazilian society of the early national period was evidently too unstable and complex to justify mechanistic assumptions about relationships between its components and a political system which was itself unformed. Early national Brazil was a country poised on multiple thresholds—political, economic, and regional frontiers—and the most satisfactory explanation of political sociology is one which evaluates actors in terms of their "social location" with respect to those frontiers.[4] Regional, economic or occupational "marginality" have been found to characterize those who favored localistic and democratic institutions because they breached the exclusivistic patterns of traditional society. In early national Brazil such men called themselves liberals. Established groups, on the other hand, were more inclined to favor reforms which validated traditional patterns by rewarding known quantities with systemic predictability and order. These were conservative goals. Such a scheme has the virtue of allowing free passage from one group to another in a transitional socioeconomic context. It also encompasses the particularities of the Brazilian case: for example, political marginality caused by place of birth (nativism), or personal resentment of colonial rule.

When applied to a fluid sociopolitical scheme such as this, the present study of institutional change and performance gains its explanatory value. The justice of the peace and the jury system were extremely localistic institutions of the kind that could be expected to appeal to "liberals" as defined above: economic frontiersmen, urban social climbers, declassé priests, or political oppositionists. And the new institutions were extremely popular in the early transitional years, but only for about as long as it took for vested interests to be created, or, put politically, for the opposition to find itself in government. At that point of sociopolitical consolidation—whether occurring in space or time—the liberal institutions outlived their usefulness, and the reaction against them at last gives us precise information about the nature of the imperial elite in formation. As might have been expected, established local elites were antidemocratic; but for largely unanticipated reasons. Elections posed no class threat but they conferred no prestige. Juries were not too independent; on the contrary, they were too open to local influence of all types and therefore prone to acquittal. A somewhat less expected insight exposed by the local institutions is the extreme lack of elite cohesiveness. Because juries and lay magistrates were unpredictable and required frequent renewal, both institutions promoted disruptive instability within the bosom of the elite itself. Least expected of all, perhaps, is the attitude of local elites who objected to extreme local autonomy because it severed their ties to the central administration. In fact, contrary to the stereotype of the self-isolating landowner, the local institutions became unpopular precisely because they increased local isolation; they turned the concept of political integration on its head.

Local institutions might continue to thrive in peripheral or frontier areas, but newly established groups had no use for administrative isolation or local disruption. After 1837, therefore, judicial policy evolved in a very different direction. As an imperial elite gained substance and identity, a new type of judicial connection between public and private interests—and in this case it was a true connection—arose in the form of a professional district magistracy. The professional judges had institutional ties to the central government and prospective social ties to local elites. They served as political integrators, brokers, and middlemen. So although there is probably much truth in the statement that landowners ultimately dominated the empire after 1841, the judicial connection again offers a significant twist. The empire did indeed possess a de facto form of corporate representation, but not in the sense usually employed by those who see landed groups as the dominant "estate." A planter elite may have embodied the spirit and served as the political bedrock of the empire, but in functional terms one can speak more precisely of a judicial oligarchy than of one made up of landowners.

All this can be stated schematically as an instance of statebuilding, but the constant centrality of judicial policy in the Brazilian case is too remarkable to be merely one research perspective among many. In the national period, as in the colonial, those who ruled Brazil assumed that judges were a government's political caretakers and agents of force, as well as (ideally) the disinterested representatives of the law. The even hand of justice wore the iron glove of police. The liberal reformers fervently believed that their local judge and compatible institutions would both weaken central authority and improve the administration of justice. The reactionaries who followed them had profoundly antagonistic political goals, but they pursued them through yet another judicial reform of analogous conception. Whatever their social position or ideological predilections, Brazilian political actors looked instinctively to the reform of the judicial system for solutions to their problems. In judicial policy they invested both their ideals and their pragmatism, both their altruism and ulterior political concerns, and in this they showed the true potency of their colonial inheritance.

Is the importance of the judiciary unique to Brazil? The state of our knowledge of nineteenth-century Latin America does not permit definitive comparisons, but at first glance the development of a judicial oligarchy, at least, seems as great an anomaly within the Latin American context as were Brazil's political stability and form of government. And yet, viewed from a perspective of corporate political solutions, there is much to suggest possible parallels. It is not surprising that the newly independent countries of Latin America, given their racial and social divisions and inevitably low levels of politicization, should have developed some sort of politics by oligarchy. Nor is it surprising that such national oligarchies might rest very substantially upon preexisting entities whose cohesiveness and compactness gave them disproportionate influence at a time of general political disorganization. Thus, in Spanish America the church and the military have long been known to have played fundamental roles in the political life of the nineteenth century. For a variety of reasons, however, in Brazil the church's influence was a pale reflection of its counterpart in, say, nineteenth-century Mexico. And in the absence of extended wars of liberation, the Brazilian army likewise never achieved the commanding position that it occupied in many of the former Spanish American colonies. This left Brazil's imperial judiciary to fill the vacuum in the 1830s, and it is perhaps to the religious and military corporations elsewhere that the Brazilian judiciary can most profitably be compared.

Immaculate political vacuums and pure institutional variables do not truly exist in the affairs of men, however, so the hypothesis might alternatively be stated in a more human way: Of all Latin American liberals faced with the problem of state formation, none had more difficulty in defining plausible enemies than those of Brazil. The weakness of the church and army, and the absence of a true aristocracy allowed power to fall into liberal hands easily, but it also deprived the new rulers of the external enemies—symbolic or real—that gave shape to liberal movements elsewhere. Brazilian reformers, as a result, had to seek the reasons for their failures internally. Eventually they found the blame in the fabric of their own society, and this doleful conclusion left them mortally vulnerable to any challenge on principle. It was the judicial corporation—a group with no need of enemies and only an instrumental concern with society—that made the challenge and then picked up the pieces of Brazilian liberalism. The process is especially clear in Brazil since it took place on two planes: first at the local level, where the justice of the peace shouldered aside municipal councils, priests, and militia commanders; then at the national level, where the district judges and professional magistrates supplanted the elective magistracy and all competing powers and eventually captured the state. It would be perfectly incorrect to suggest that the magistracy took up this political prominence without opposition, but, lacking the independent wealth of the church or the disposition to violence of the army, it did so without provoking the tumult that characterized the former Spanish American colonies. And since there was much historical continuity in the Brazilian solution, there was also the legitimacy of tradition.

If stability as an end is accepted as justifying oligarchy and force as means, then it could be argued that this was a fortunate outcome for independent Brazil. The inclination to make the argument is reinforced by a certain tendency to view the building of a state in normative terms—as something good and progressive. But a political system is not created without values which rationalize its application, and certainly in the case of Brazil changes in political structures were paralleled by radical changes in attitudes toward society. The building of a nation of shared values properly accompanies the building of a state with its shared deference to authority, but in Brazil the two processes worked out of phase. The decentralizing experimentation of the liberal period rested intellectually upon those optimistic, universalistic, and even egalitarian images of Brazilian nationality which enjoyed such an extraordinary vogue just after independence. The emergence of an effective Brazilian state after 1837, by contrast, correlated directly with the adoption of a darkening popular attitude toward Brazilian society that emphasized its hopeless fragmentation into class, corporate, racial or factional parts. What had been thought of as a nation was redefined as a problem. By mid-century Brazilians had conceptualized and built a state to deal with the problem, but in doing so had sacrificed a larger sense of their nationhood.

Notes

Abbreviations Used

ACB	Arquivo do Associação Comercial da Bahia.
AEG	Arquivo do Estado da Guanabara.
ANRJ	Arquivo Nacional, Rio de Janeiro.
AMS	Arquivo Municipal de Salvador, Bahia.
APBa	Arquivo Público do Estado da Bahia.
B-CDA	Brazil, Câmara dos Deputados, *Anais*.
B-CLB	Brazil, *Coleção das Leis do Brasil*.
B-SA	Brazil, Senado, *Anais*.
BNRJ	Biblioteca Nacional, Rio de Janeiro.
HAHR	*Hispanic American Historical Review*.
HGCB	*História Geral da Civilização Brasileira*, ed. Sérgio Buarque de Holanda (São Paulo, 1968-).
PEQ	Papers of Eusébio de Queiroz, Arquivo Nacional.
PVU	Papers of Visconde de Uruguai, Niterói.
RIHGB	*Revista do Instituto Histórico e Geográfico Brasileiro*.

Preface

1. The distinction between the terms *state* and *nation* used here is basically a Weberian one, briefly stated in Juan Linz, "Early State-Building and Late Peripheral Nationalisms against the State: The Case of Spain," in *Building States and Nations,* ed. S. N. Eisenstadt and Stein Rokkan, 2: 33-34. *State* refers to a "compulsory political organization [claiming] the monopoly of the legitimate use of force in the enforcement of its order." *Nation* refers to "a specific sentiment of solidarity in the face of other groups . . . the concept belongs in the sphere of values."

Chapter 1: Liberalism in a Time of Transition

1. See, for example Tulio Halperín-Donghi, *Historia contemporánea de América Latina,* pp. 68-71; Maria Odila Silva Dias, "A interiorização da metrópole (1808-1853)," in *1822: Dimensões,* ed. Carlos Guilherme Mota, pp. 171, 174.

2. Richard M. Morse, "Some Themes of Brazilian History," *The South At-lantic Quarterly*, 61: 2 (Spring 1962), 159-182; Stanley J. Stein, "The Historio-graphy of Brazil, 1808-1889," *HAHR* 40 (May 1960): 234-278 (see list of ab-breviations); Sérgio Buarque de Holanda, *Raízes do Brasil;* Francisco José de Oliveira Vianna, *Evolução do povo brasileiro*, pp. 117-118.

3. See Tobias do Rego Monteiro, *História do império: A elaboração da inde-pendência;* Francisco Adolfo de Varnhagen, *História da independência do Brasil até o reconhecimento pela antiga metrópole;* Manuel de Oliveira Lima, *O movi-mento da independência*, and *D. João VI no Brasil.*

4. On Latin American liberalism and political thought in the early nine-teenth century, see Charles A. Hale, *Mexican Liberalism in the Age of Mora, 1821-1853;* Simon Collier, *Ideas and Politics of Chilean Independence, 1808-1833.* Frank Safford discusses political formation from a complementary per-spective in his "Bases of Political Alignment in Early Republican Spanish Amer-ica," in *New Approaches to Latin American History,* ed. Richard Graham and Peter H. Smith, pp. 71-111.

5. Monteiro, *História do império*, chap. 6.

6. Pedro Octávio Carneiro da Cunha, "A fundação de um império liberal," in *HGCB*, vol. 2, pt. 1, p. 243 (see list of abbreviations).

7. *Ibid.,* pp. 252-260. On the Constitution of 1824, see João Camilo de Oliveira Torres, *A democracia coroada: Teoria política do império do Brasil.* The text of the Constitution is given on pp. 479-496.

8. Octávio Tarquínio de Sousa, *A vida de D. Pedro I,* vol. 2; John Armitage, *The History of Brazil . . . ,* 1: 159-204.

9. The liberal reformer's point of view is best expressed in the pages of the newspaper *Aurora Fluminense,* founded in 1827. An early statement of prin-ciples may be found in the issue of 12 May 1828.

10. Some of the liberal reforms are described in Thomas W. Palmer, Jr., "A Momentous Decade in Brazilian Administrative History, 1831-1840," *HAHR* 30 (May 1950): 209-217.

11. The authoritative works on the Brazilian Regency are João Manuel Pereira da Silva, *História do Brasil de 1831 a 1840;* Alfredo Valladão, *Da aclamação à maioridade, 1822-1840.* Also of basic importance are the biographies written by Octávio Tarquínio de Sousa: *A vida de D. Pedro I; Diogo Antônio Feijó (1784-1843); José Bonifácio; Bernardo Pereira de Vasconcelos e seu tempo;* and *Evaristo da Veiga.*

12. Joaquim Nabuco, *Um estadista do império, Nabuco de Araújo,* 1: 31-32.

13. Paulo Pereira Castro, "A experiência republicana, 1831-1840," in *HGCB,* vol. 2, pt. 2, p. 25.

14. On institutional roles and weakness, see José Murilo de Carvalho, "Elite and State-Building in Imperial Brazil" (Ph.D. diss.); Michael Charles McBeth, "The Politicians vs. the Generals: The Decline of the Brazilian Army during the First Empire, 1822-1831" (Ph.D. diss.); João Dornas Filho, *O padroado e a igreja brasileira.*

15. The economic cycles are described in Caio Prado, Jr., *História econômica*

do Brasil; Celso Furtado, *The Economic Growth of Brazil;* Roberto C. Simonsen, *História econômica do Brasil, 1500-1800.* For the nineteenth century specifically, see Virgílio Noya Pinto, "Balanço das transformações econômicas no século XIX," in *Brasil em perspectiva,* ed. Carlos G. Mota, pp. 141-164.

16. An example is the demand for cotton boosted by the Napoleonic Wars and the War of 1812. Cotton prices peaked in 1816, and by 1821 had fallen almost by half. Noya Pinto, "Balanço das transformações," pp. 146-149.

17. Marques de Queluz (João Severiano Maciel da Costa) to Junta do Comércio, Agricultura, Fábricas, etc., Bahia, 6 May 1826, APBa (see list of abbreviations), Presidente da Província/Correspondência para o governo imperial, vol. 676, 1826, f. 115.

18. The continuity of elites has been illustrated in another context by Warren K. Dean in "The Planter as Entrepreneur: The Case of São Paulo," *HAHR* 46 (May 1966), 138-152. A theoretical formulation is Lester G. Seligman, "Elite Recruitment and Political Development," in *Political Development and Social Change,* ed. Jason L. Finkle and Richard W. Gable, pp. 240-249.

19. José Maria dos Santos has discoursed acerbically on this aspect of the pathology of liberalism in Latin America and Brazil. "What is essential is that every child of the New World believes himself legally enabled to one day exercise tyranny over his fellow citizens. This is the egalitarian principle in which are contained all the fundaments of the idea of liberty in America" (*A política geral do Brasil,* p. 6).

20. Nabuco, *Um estadista do império,* 1: 23. The following discussion owes something to concepts formulated by Everett V. Stonequist, *The Marginal Man: A Study in Personality and Culture Conflict.* See also, Bert F. Hoselitz, *Sociological Aspects of Economic Growth;* Everett E. Hagen, "A Framework for Analyzing Economic and Political Change," in *Development of the Emerging Countries. An Agenda for Research,* ed. Robert E. Asher.

21. Sousa, *Evarista da Veiga.*

22. For something of the social flavor of high society in Rio de Janeiro during the period, see José Wanderley de Araújo Pinho, *Salões e damas do segundo reinado,* pp. 15-25.

23. Nabuco, *Um estadista do império,* 1: 23.

24. Nelson Werneck Sodré, *A história da imprensa no Brasil,* pp. 57-69, 113 and passim. Luis Augusto May, liberal editor of *A Malagueta,* was a Portuguese immigrant; Francisco Sales Torres Homem, a mulatto, was a protegé of Evaristo da Veiga; Justiniano José da Rocha, though he cast his lot with the conservatives, was also a mulatto.

25. Sousa, *Diogo Antônio Feijó;* Alfredo Ellis, Jr., *Feijó e a primeira metade do século XIX.*

26. Nabuco, *Um estadista do império,* 1: 23. Feijó's personality has inspired attempts at psychohistory. See Luiz Gonzaga Novelli, Júnior, *Feijó: Um paulista velho.*

27. Sousa, *Diogo Antônio Feijó,* p. 153.

28. On Brazilian liberalism, the clerical question, and priests in politics, see

Emília Viotti da Costa, "Introdução ao estudo da emancipação política do Brasil," in *Brasil em perspectiva*, ed. Mota, pp. 104-105; Paulo Castro, "A experiência republicana," pp. 43-44; João Capistrano de Abreu, "O Brasil no século XIX," in *Ensaios e estudos*, p. 136.

29. Sousa, *Bernardo Pereira de Vasconcelos*, pp. 7-18.

30. Vasconcelos was mainly responsible for the original drafts of the Brazilian Criminal Code and the Additional Act. See chapters 6 and 9.

31. Vasconcelos baffled contemporaries. John Armitage was put off by his physical appearance and inscrutable ambition; Reverend Walsh found him an affable man of simple habits (Armitage, *History of Brazil*, 2: 17-19; Robert Walsh, *Notices of Brazil in 1828 and 1829*, 2: 121-123, 243). See also the description in Sousa, *Bernardo Pereira de Vasconcelos*, pp. 31-41.

32. See Vasconcelos' comments on national needs in his *Carta aos senhores eleitores da província de Minas Gerais em 1828* and his *Comentário à lei dos juízes de paz*. An image of Vasconcelos' liberalism may be gleaned from the pages of his newspaper, *O Sete de Abril*, in 1833 and 1834.

Chapter 2: Reformist Thought

1. On the Enlightenment in Portugal and Brazil, see Alexander Marchant, "Aspects of the Enlightenment in Brazil," in *Latin America and the Enlightenment*, ed. Arthur P. Whitaker, pp. 95-118; João Cruz Costa, *Contribuição à história das idéias no Brasil*, pp. 45-62, and "As novas idéias," in *AGCB*, vol. 2, pp. 179-180; E. Bradford Burns, "The Role of Azeredo Coutinho in the Enlightenment of Brazil," *HAHR* 44 (May 1964), 145-160; Kenneth R. Maxwell, "The Generation of the 1790's and the Idea of Luso-Brazilian Empire," in *Colonial Roots of Modern Brazil*, ed. Dauril Alden, pp. 107-144; João Lúcio de Azevedo, *O Marques de Pombal e a sua época;* José Ferreira Carrato, *Igreja, iluminismo e escolas mineiras coloniais*, pp. 123-178.

2. José da Silva Lisboa (Visconde de Cairu), *Refutação das declamações contra o comércio inglês, extraída de escritores eminentes, por José da Silva Lisboa;* Manuel Pinto de Aguiar, *A abertura dos portos: Cairu e os ingleses;* Alan K. Manchester, "The Transfer of the Portuguese Court to Rio de Janeiro," in *Conflict and Continuity in Brazilian Society*, ed. Henry Keith and S. F. Edwards, pp. 148-183.

3. Manuel de Oliveira Lima, *D. João VI no Brasil*, vol. 2, chap. 18; Emília Viotti da Costa, "Introdução ao estudo da emancipação política do Brasil," in *Brasil em perspectiva*, ed. Carlos Guilherme Mota, pp. 96-102.

4. Nelson Werneck Sodré, *A história da imprensa no Brasil*, pp. 57-69, 113; Hélio Vianna, *Contribuição à história da imprensa brasileira (1812-1869)*.

5. *O Carapuceiro*, 11 May 1837.

6. *O Par de Tetas: Jornal Satírico e Político*, 10 April 1833.

7. Students of this period in Spanish America have found a similar faith in documents and institutions as "efficient in themselves." See Simon Collier, *Ideas and Politics of Chilean Independence, 1808-1833*, pp. 184-188; Charles A. Hale, *Mexican Liberalism in the Age of Mora, 1821-1853*, pp. 105-106.

8. Again, comparisons may be found in the rest of Latin America. See Daniel Cosío Villegas, *American Extremes*, pp. 154-176; Collier, *Ideas and Politics*, pp. 183-184.

9. President of Province of Bahia (Marques de Queluz) to Junta do Comércio, Agricultura, e Fábricas, Bahia, 6 May 1826, APBa, Presidente da Província/ Correspondência para o governo imperial, vol. 676, 1826, ff. 114v-115.

10. "Conselhos desinteressados de Mylord Rostbeaf aos senhores eleitores da paróquia," *O Sete de Abril*, 26 February 1833. Similar satirical articles published after 1827 in *O Echo*. See Octávio Tarquínio de Sousa, *Evaristo da Veiga*, p. 76.

11. See, for example, Hipólito da Costa Pereira, *Diário de minha viagem para Filadélfia (1798-1799)*, pp. 96-97; João Francisco Lisboa, *Obras de João Francisco Lisboa, natural do Maranhão; precedidas de uma notícia biográfica pelo Dr. Antonio Henriques Leal*, 1: 155-157.

12. Quoted in Emília Viotti da Costa, "Introdução ao estudo da emancipação," in *Brasil em perspectiva*, ed. Mota, pp. 96-97.

13. *O Astro de Minas*, 20 March 1832 (reprint from *O Federalista*).

14. On Bentham, rich comparative inferences can be derived from Hale's study of utilitarianism in Mexico, *Mexican Liberalism*, chap. 5. On Puritan political and social thought, see the discussion in Kenneth A. Lockridge, *A New England Town: The First Hundred Years*, pp. 52-56. For the effect of this ethic on North American legal thought, see William E. Nelson, *Americanization of the Common Law: The Impact of Legal Change on Massachusetts Society, 1760-1830*.

15. *Aurora Fluminense*, 22 April 1829.

16. Ibid., 5 January 1831, 8 June 1832.

17. Ibid., 8 June 1832.

18. Ibid., 17 January 1831, 11 February 1831.

19. Aureliano Cândido Tavares Bastos, *A província: Estudo sobre a decentralização no Brasil*, pp. 162-163.

20. *A Malagueta*, 13 February 1829.

21. *O Despertador*, 22 February 1839.

22. B-CDA (see list of abbreviations), 1857, 1: 586 (speech of Nabuco de Araújo). See also, Joaquim Nabuco, *Um estadista do império, Nabuco de Araújo: Sua vida, suas opiniões, sua época*, 1: 297.

23. *Aurora Fluminense*, 24 October 1828. Evaristo himself used the term *classe média*, literally, "middle class."

24. *O Jornal do Comércio*, 27 October 1828.

25. This attitude is present in most right-wing writings of the period. See the unsigned pamphlets *Considerações sobre as causas de nossos males* and *O gênio do Brasil mostrando em scenas interessantes o espelho de verdades para o desengano dos homens*. The regional disturbances are described in greater detail in chapter 8.

26. *O Jornal do Comércio*, 2 June 1834.

27. A good discussion of the slavery issue at the turn of the century is

included in Maxwell, "The Generation of the 1790's," in *Colonial Roots,* ed. Alden, pp. 127-130. For a synthesis of attitudes toward slavery in the 1820s, see Emília Viotti da Costa, *Da senzala à colônia,* pp. 333-339. Contemporary economic and social arguments against slavery are summarized in *O Jornal do Comércio,* 22 August and 24 August 1833 (reprints from *O Carapuceiro*), and in *O Carapuceiro,* 16 August 1834.

28. Cited in Emília Viotti da Costa, *Da senzala à colônia,* pp. 337-338.

29. See Gilberto Freyre, *Casa grande & senzala: Formação da família brasileira sob o regime patriarcal,* 2: 472, 487-489, 515-522; *O Carapuceiro,* 16 August 1834, 11 May 1837.

30. Maxwell, "The Generation of the 1790's," in *Colonial Roots,* ed. Alden, p. 129, and Emília Viotti da Costa, *Da senzala à colônia,* p. 338.

31. *O gênio do Brasil,* p. 12.

32. *Aparição extraordinária, e inesperada do velho venerando ao roceiro: Diálogo havido entre eles sobre a atual situação política do Brasil.*

33. See *Nova Luz Brasileira,* 5 February and 9 March 1830; *Aurora Fluminense,* 28 February and 15 April 1831.

34. See *Aurora Fluminense,* 11 November and 11 January 1832; 21 January, 25 October, and 22 November 1833; 1 April, 6 April, and 6 November 1835. See also *O Astro de Minas,* 14 April 1832. Some examples of exaltado or Caramuru papers that provoked *Aurora* with their irresponsible "Haitianism" were *O Filho da Terra,* 28 October 1831; *O Mulato, Ou, O Homem da Cor,* 28 September and 23 October 1833; *O Exaltado,* 10 January 1833; and *O Brasileiro Pardo,* 21 October 1833. On Haitianism and the race issue, see Jeanne Berrance de Castro, "O negro na guarda nacional brasileira," *Anais do Museu Paulista,* 23 (1969), 154-162; Hélio Vianna, *Contribuição,* p. 223.

35. See for example Maciel da Costa's remarks quoted in Emília Viotti da Costa, *Da senzala à colônia,* p. 335.

36. Ibid.

37. *O Carapuceiro,* 16 August 1834, 17 June 1837.

38. *O Brasil império e o Brasil república: Reflexões políticas oferecidas aos brasileiros amantes da sua pátria,* pp. 41-42.

39. *O Jornal do Comércio,* 2 June 1834.

40. *Aurora Fluminense,* 29 October 1828, 12 January 1829.

41. Ibid., 12 May 1828, 26 January 1835.

42. For examples of similar attitudes toward the colonial period, see Hale, *Mexican Liberalism,* p. 107; Collier, *Ideas and Politics,* pp. 189-201.

43. *Sentinela do Serro* (Minas Gerais), 25 June 1831 (cited in Teófico B. Ottoni, "Circular dedicado aos srs. eleitores de senadores pela província de Minas Gerais no quatriêno atual," in Basílio de Magalhães, "A 'Circular' de Teófilo Ottoni," *Revista do Instituto Histórico e Geográfico Brasileiro,* 78: (1916), 71.

44. *Aurora Fluminense,* 12 January 1829.

45. *O Jornal do Comércio,* 22 August 1833 (reprint from *O Carapuceiro*). Similar though even more extreme estimates of the long-term effects of colonialism

were made elsewhere in Latin America at about this time. See Collier, *Ideas and Politics*, p. 267.

46. *Aurora Fluminense*, 26 Janaury 1835, 6 June 1838; *O Astro de Minas*, 7 March 1829, 4 July 1835.

47. Speech of 3 May 1823, quoted in João Cruz Costa, "As novas idéias," in *HGCB*, vol. 2, pt. 1, p. 184.

48. *O Jornal do Comércio*, 27 October 1828.

49. *Aurora Fluminense*, 16 May 1828, 9 Janaury 1829. Evaristo da Veiga believed the organization of the local regime to be "perhaps the basis of all the practical improvement that Brazil hopes for, because it extends its benefits to the most remote twigs of the tree of society."

50. *B-CDA*, 1827, 5: 94-95.

51. Ibid., pp. 94-96; *A Malagueta*, 27 January, 13 February, and 5 June 1829.

52. May's model parish plan was accused in the Chamber of Deputies of being too "Jesuitic," and unconstitutional as well. Nevertheless, in 1836 an attempt was made to revive interest in the scheme. (*A Malagueta*, 5 June 1829; *O Atlante*, 10 June 1836.)

53. See the proposals of Feijó and Vergueiro in *B-CDA*, 1826, 3: 127-131; 313-316.

54. See, for example Felipe Alberto Patroni (Martins Maciel Parente), *A bíblia do justo meio da política moderada, ou prolegômenos do direito constitucional da natureza explicada pelas Leis físicas do mundo.*

Chapter 3: The Judicial Legacy

1. Stuart B. Schwartz, *Sovereignty and Society in Colonial Brazil: The High Court of Bahia and Its Judges, 1609-1751*, pp. 3-4. On bureaucracy and empire, see S. N. Eisenstadt, *The Political Systems of Empires*. The sections on the Spanish empire are perhaps more relevant than others.

2. Schwartz, *Sovereignty and Society*, pp. 9-12; Aurelino Leal, "História judiciária do Brasil," *Dicionário histórico geográfico e etnográfico do Brasil*, 1: 1118-1120; Alfredo Pinto Vieira de Mello, "O poder judiciário no Brasil, 1532-1871," *RIHGB*, special issue (1916), pt. 4, p. 111 (see list of abbreviations).

3. Leal, "História judiciária," *Dicionário*, 1: 1120.

4. Schwartz, *Sovereignty and Society*, pp. 284, 375-379. For a late colonial case, see Afonso Ruy, *A primeira revolução social brasileira (1798)*, pp. 110-113.

5. Schwartz, *Sovereignty and Society;* see also his "Magistracy and Society in Colonial Brazil," *HAHR* 50 (November 1970): 715-730.

6. Leal, "História judiciária," *Dicionário*, 1: 1112-1113; John Armitage, *The History of Brazil . . .* , pp. 2-3.

7. Dauril Alden, *Royal Government in Colonial Brazil . . .* , pp. 422-424. See the example of the creation of a *juiz de fora* in Bahia in 1696 in Charles Ralph Boxer, *Portuguese Society in the Tropics: The Municipal Councils of Goa, Macau, Bahia and Luanda, 1510-1800*, pp. 74-75.

8. David Davidson, "How the Brazilian West Was Won: Freelance and State

on the Matto Grosso Frontier, ca. 1737-1752," in *Colonial Roots of Modern Brazil*, ed. Dauril Alden, pp. 85-87. See also the complaints of Brazilian delegates to the Cortes of 1821, M. E. Gomes de Carvalho, *Os deputados brasileiros nas cortes gerais de 1821*, pp. 177-196.

9. Schwartz, *Sovereignty and Society*, p. 299.

10. Ibid., p. 174.

11. A good example of the argument is to be found in Antônio Pereira Rebouças, *Recordações da vida parlamentar*, 2: 14-15. There were colonial precedents for this sentiment. Kenneth Maxwell holds that the appointment of local magnates to high offices was a conscious policy of the Pombaline government. Examples are provided in his *Conflicts and Conspiracies: Brazil and Portugal, 1750-1808*, pp. 46, 64, 68-69.

12. Luísa da Fonseca, "Bacharéis brasileiros: Elementos biográficos (1635-1830)," *Anais do IV Congresso de História Nacional* (1951), 11: 109-407.

13. See Luis Augusto May's description of the corporate spirit of the magistracy in *A Malagueta*, 27 January 1829. In his study of the 1789 conspiracy in Minas Gerais, Kenneth Maxwell found that professional loyalties among the magistrates proved even stronger than family ties in determining solidarity among the conspirators (*Conflicts and Conspiracies*, p. 202).

14. The available data do not permit us to know whether the Brazilian predominance in these figures was a conscious policy, or whether it represents a departure from pre-1808 practices. Taken together with Schwartz' work on the High Court during the colonial period, however, they suggest that the creole-peninsular rivalries over office-holding in late colonial Spanish America may have had a different material basis in Brazil. For a brief summary of the debate in Spanish American historiography, see D. A. Brading, "Government and Elite in Late Colonial Mexico," *HAHR* 53 (August 1973): 400-402.

15. Manuel de Oliveira Lima, *O movimento da independência*, pp. 185-189.

16. Desembargo do Paço, Registro de Consultas, ANRJ (see list of abbreviations), cód. 17, L° 12, ff. 8v-12. The magistrate in question, Antônio de Almeida Silva Freire da Fonseca, was named juiz de fora in 1820. See Magistratura, Decretos de doação de cargos, 1821, ANRJ, cód. 239, L° 1. Similar occurrences in Bahia are described in Braz do Amaral, *História da Bahia do império à república*, pp. 80-81.

17. See Gomes de Carvalho, *Os deputados brasileiros*, pp. 27-28, 177-196, 205-206; *A Malagueta*, 23 March 1822; *A Astréia*, 31 July 1828.

18. *A Astréia*, 31 July 1828. For a description of judicial venality just before independence, see L. F. de Tollenare, *Notas dominicaes tomadas durante uma viagem em Portugal e no Brasil em 1816, 1817 e 1818*, pp. 352-353.

19. Brazil, Assembléia Constituinte, *Anais*, 1823, 5: 151.

20. Minister of the Empire to Provincial President of Bahia, 8 August 1827, APBa, Ministérios Imperiais, vol. 757, f. 310.

21. Robert Walsh, *Notices of Brazil in 1828 and 1829*, 1: 268. For the salaries of Rio judges, see Chanceler da Casa de Suplicação to Minister of Justice, 11 March 1829, ANRJ, Magistratura/Ofícios com anexos, IJ^{4}284. John Luccock,

more cold-blooded than Walsh, estimated that judicial salaries were insufficient and regarded the sale of justice as part of the structure emoluments (*Notes on Rio de Janeiro* . . . , pp. 566-567).

22. Walsh, *Notices of Brazil,* 1: 156, 268-269. See also Tollenare, *Notas dominicaes,* pp. 352-353; Luccock, *Notes on Rio de Janeiro,* pp. 484-485, 566-567; Francisco de Sierra y Mariscal, "Idéias gerais sobre a revolução do Brasil e suas consequências," *Anais da Biblioteca Nacional do Rio de Janeiro,* 43-44 (1931): 61.

23. *Aurora Fluminense,* 8 March and 2 April 1830; Armitage, *History of Brazil,* 2: 94-95.

24. *A Malagueta,* 23 March 1822. See also *B-CDA,* 1828, 1: 76; *O Jornal do Comércio,* 27 October 1828.

25. Clóvis Bevilaqua, *História da faculdade de direito do Recife,* 1: 11-24.

26. *O Carapuceiro,* 1 July 1837.

27. Identical complaints were current in Portugal (Gomes de Carvalho, *Os deputados brasileiros,* pp. 27-28). In Brazil the decree of 17 November 1824 ordered that no new litigation be brought by parties who had not first tried all means of conciliation (*B-CLB,* 1824, pt. 2, pp. 83-84; see list of abbreviations). The justice of the peace (juiz de paz) provided for in the constitution and created by statute in 1827 was to be a judge of conciliations.

28. *O Carapuceiro,* 1 July 1837.

29. The best description of the lower reaches of the legal profession is Luccock's Dickensian account of Rio's lawyers (*Notes on Rio de Janeiro,* pp. 102-103). Another description of the courthouse milieu on the eve of independence is included in Tollenare, *Notas dominicaes,* pp. 352-353. An early Brazilian novel whose action revolves around courthouse personnel and judicial corruption in Rio de Janeiro is Manuel Antônio de Almeida, *Memórias de um sargento de milícias.*

30. *A Malagueta,* 23 March 1822.

31. Luccock, *Notes on Rio de Janeiro,* p. 103.

32. *Aurora Fluminense,* 8 March 1830.

33. *O Jornal do Comércio,* 5 February 1836.

34. Apparently the obscure system of emoluments also encouraged the prolongation of trials (Desembargador João Rodrigues de Brito, *Cartas econômico-políticas sôbre a agricultura e comércio da Bahia, dadas à luz por I. A. F. Benavides,* p. 51.

35. *Correspondência oficial das províncias* . . . , p. 57.

36. *A Astréia,* 31 July 1828.

37. Ibid., 17 May 1828.

38. Brazil, *Falas do Trono desde o ano de 1823 até o ano de 1889; acompanhadas dos respectivos votos de graças.* See Falas do Trono of 1827, p. 132; 1828, p. 142; 1829, p. 166; voto de graças, 1829, p. 169.

39. In the years following independence an extraordinary amount of the official correspondence of the minister of justice dealt with the requesting and granting of leaves. See Ministérios Imperiais, 1822-1823, APBa, vol. 754.

40. See the discussion of this problem in Brazil, Assembléia Constituente, *Anais*, 1823, 5: 90-93.

41. Ministérios Imperiais, 1822-1823, 1824, APBa, vols. 754-1.

42. Brazil, Assembléia Constituinte, *Anais*, 1823, 5: 91. To some extent the scarcity of judges predated formal independence; see Junta provisória do governo da província de Pernambuco to king, 17 May 1822, quoted in *Correspondência oficial das províncias*, p. 238. Yet an imperial decree of 9 January 1825 blamed the "notorious" lack of candidates on independence. Primitivo Moacyr, *A instrução e o império, 1823-1853*, I: 320.

43. Provincial President of Bahia to Minister of Finance (Fazenda), 9 June 1826, APBa, Presidente da Província/Correspondência para o governo imperial, vol. 676.

44. Antônio Calmon du Pin e Almeida to Provincial President of Bahia, 1 June 1826, APBa, Juizes de Paz, maço 2687.

45. *The Rio Herald*, 15 March 1828.

46. Brazil, Assembléia Constituinte, *Anais*, 1823, 1: 167.

47. João Paulo de Melo Barreto Filho and Hermeto Lima, *História da polícia do Rio de Janeiro. Aspectos da cidade e da vida carioca, 1565-1831* 1: 159-161, 179-196. On the improvement of the Rio police from 1808 to 1818, see Luccock, *Notes on Rio de Janeiro . . .* , pp. 135-137, 250, 548.

48. *O Jornal do Comércio*, 9 August 1830; *The Rio Herald*, 15 March 1828; and *Aurora Fluminense*, 28 May 1828. On the extinction of the Intendência Geral de Polícia, see *Aurora Fluminense*, 16 May 1828.

49. Walsh, *Notices of Brazil*, 1: 269.

50. Brazil, Minister of Justice, *Relatório*, 1831, p. 3.

51. Ibid., p. 5.

52. *O Jornal do Comércio*, 20 October and 21 October 1829.

53. *O Astro de Minas*, 24 April 1828; *Aurora Fluminense*, 12 May 1828; *A Astréia*, 17 June 1830.

Chapter 4: The Imperial Justice of the Peace

1. M. E. Gomes de Carvalho, *Os deputados brasileiros nas cortes gerais de 1821*, pp. 179-183, 206. Faustino José de Madre de Deus, *A Constituição de 1822, comentada e desenvolvida na prática*, pp. 98-100.

2. Law of 15 October 1827, *B-CLB*, 1827, pp. 67-70.

3. Aurelino Leal, "História judiciária do Brasil," *Dicionário histórico geográfico e etnográfico do Brasil*, 1: 1126-1128. See also chapter 3 above.

4. *B-CDA*, 1830, 1: 98. See also *B-CDA*, 1827, 4: 259.

5. Ibid., 1827, 1: 128. See the Baron of Cairú's criticism of this approach in *B-SA*, 1827, II, 51 (see list of abbreviations).

6. Stuart B. Schwartz, *Sovereignty and Society in Colonial Brazil*, pp. 3-21. See also chapter 3 above.

7. Law of 15 October 1827, art. 5, sec. 2, *B-CLB*, 1827, p. 67; José Joaquim dos Santos, *Manual prático das conciliações . . .* , pp. 5-6.

8. When Evaristo da Veiga made voting recommendations he usually des-

cribed an ideal candidate that closely resembled him and his colleagues. *Aurora Fluminense,* 24 October 1828, 3 September 1832, 15 February 1833.

9. Cf. Bernardo Pereira de Vasconcelos, *Carta aos senhores eleitores da província de Minas Gerais em 1828,* pp. 76-78. Paulo Pereira Castro, "A experiência republicana, 1831-1840," in *HGCB,* vol. 2, pt. 2, p. 27.

10. Provincial President of Bahia to Minister of Justice, Bahia, 15 April 1829, APBa, Correspondência expedida, vol. 678, f. 83; Jerônimo José Albernaz et al. to Provincial President of Bahia, Cachoeira, 1 April 1829, APBa Judiciária/ Revolução, maço 2855; *A Astréia,* 31 July 1828; *Aurora Fluminense,* 16 February 1829, 2 May 1832.

11. *A Malagueta,* 13 February 1829.

12. Brazil, *Falas do Trono desde o ano de 1823 até o ano de 1889 acompanhados dos respectivos votos de graças,* pp. 142, 153; Paulo Pereira Castro, "A experiência republicana," p. 27.

13. The best source for Portuguese judicial structure is Cândido Mendes de Almeida's edition, *Código filipino ou ordenações e leis do Reino de Portugal.* All subsequent descriptions merely repeat Cândido Mendes but several are adequate and considerably more accessible. The discussion here is taken largely from Edmundo Zenha, *O município no Brasil, 1532-1700,* pp. 56-59; Aurelino Leal, "História judiciária," *Dicionário,* 1: 1108-1111; Santos, *Manual prático,* p. 5.

14. In 1827 a free construction worker in Rio de Janeiro earned close to one milrei per day (Eulália Maria Lahmeyer Lôbo, "Evolução dos preços e do padrão de vida no Rio de Janeiro, 1820-1930—resultados preliminares," *Revista Brasileira de Economia,* 25, no. 4 [1971]: 254 n. 26). After 1824 a yearly income of 100 milreis was required to vote in primary elections; 200 milreis, to vote in secondary elections. See also the discussion of incomes in Emílio Willems, "Social Differentiation in Colonial Brazil," *Comparative Studies in Society and History,* 12 (January 1970): 31-49.

15. *B-SA,* 1826, 4: 125-126.

16. *B-CDA,* 1827, 1: 142.

17. *B-CDA,* 1827, 1: 129-130, 133-134; *Aurora Fluminense,* 9 January 1829; Zenha, *O município,* pp. 58-59; Dauril Alden, *Royal Government in Colonial Brazil . . . ,* pp. 422-424.

18. Santos, *Manual prático,* p. 5.

19. *B-CDA,* 1828, 1, 27.

20. An intriguing study of local law-enforcement practices is Patricia Ann Aufderheide, "Order and Violence: Social Deviance and Social Control in Brazil, 1780-1840" (Ph.D. diss., 1976).

21. The authorities are unanimous on the decline of the municipal council (*Câmara municipal*) and the effect of the law of 1 October 1828. See Aureliano Cândido Tavares Bastos, *A província: Estudo sobre a descentralização no Brasil;* João Batista Cortines Laxe, *Regimento das câmaras municipaes, ou Lei de 1 de Outubro de 1828;* Zenha, *O município.*

22. Law of 1 October 1828; *B-CLB,* 1828, 1: 74-89.

23. *B-CDA,* 1827, 1: 143. The Philippine Ordinances was the body of law

under which colonial Brazil had been ruled since 1603.

24. Philip Dawson, *Provincial Magistrates and Revolutionary Politics in France, 1789-1795*, pp. 243-244.

25. *B-CDA*, 1827, 1: 150-152.

26. *B-CDA*, 1827, 2: 176. The complete Chamber of Deputies version can be found in *B-CDA*, 1827, 3: 94-95.

27. *B-SA*, 1827, 1: 413-416; *B-SA*, 1827, 2: 84-85, 154, 215.

28. *B-CDA*, 1827; 4: 256-259.

29. *B-CLB*, 1822, pt. 2, pp. 23-24. The decree of 18 June 1822 stipulated that press offenses were to be tried before a jury in Rio de Janeiro and in provinces where there was a High Court.

30. *A Malagueta*, 13 February 1829.

31. *A Astréia*, 8 July 1830.

32. *O Jornal do Comércio*, 21 October 1829.

33. See, for example, *O Astro de Minas*, 7 March and 3 December 1829; 6 March, 18 September, and 25 September 1830.

34. *Recopilador Cachoeirense*, December 1832.

35. Diogo Antônio Feijó, *Guia dos juizes de paz;* Bernardo Pereira de Vasconcelos, *Comentário à lei dos juizes de paz;* and *Vade-mecum dos juizes de paz, suplentes, fiscaes, e escrivães para a província do Rio de Janeiro.* In 1833 the publishing firm of Seignot-Plancher advertised in *O Jornal do Comércio* six different manuals for use by justices of the peace.

36. Vasconcelos, *Comentário*, pp. 31-33; *Vade-mecum dos juizes*, p. iii.

37. *Aurora Fluminense*, 19 October 1832.

38. Law of 15 October 1827, art. 5, secs. 1, 5, 14.

39. Ibid., art. 5, sec. 2.

40. Ibid., art. 5, secs. 3, 6, 7, 8, 10.

41. Ibid., art. 5, secs. 4, 5.

42. Ibid., art. 5, secs. 12, 13, 15.

43. A good explanation of the labor contracts jurisdiction at a time when its importance had become quite obvious is included in Santos, *Manual prático*, pp. 7-8, 49-50, 55-60. See also Carlos Antônio Cordeiro, *Diretor do juizo de paz*, pp. 43-127.

44. *O Astro de Minas*, 7 March 1829; *Aurora Fluminense*, 16 July 1830.

45. There are scattered and infrequent references to juizes de paz browbeating humble citizens into conciliations unfair to them. See Brazil, Minister of Justice, *Relatório*, 1831, p. 51; Câmara de Belmonte (Bahia) to Assembléia Legislativa da Bahia, 2 April 1835, APBa/Seção legislativa, Ofícios à Assembléia Legislativa.

46. In 1835 a Rio de Janeiro newspaper complained that the conciliatory responsibilities of the juizes de paz had become "just a formula that no one thinks about anymore" (*Aurora Fluminense*, 26 January 1835). Years later the Commercial Association of Bahia said that the candidates for conciliation no longer showed up to be reconciled. The Association recommended the abolition of conciliation court as a waste of time that delayed justice in the regular courts.

Associação Comercial da Bahia to Assembléia Legislativa da Bahia, 4 April 1843, APBa/Seção legislativa, Ofícios à Assembléia Legislativa.

47. Brazil, Ministério da Justiça, *Notícia histórica dos serviços, instituições e estabelecimentos pertencentes a esta repartição, elaborada por ordem do respectivo ministro, Dr. Amaro Cavalcante* (Rio de Janeiro, 1898), pt. 7, p. 72; Santos, *Manual prático*, p. 45.

48. A discussion of Brazil's electoral laws can be found in "Exposição e Projeto de Eleições," 18 April 1842, ANRJ, Conselho de Estado/Pareceres, 1842-1844, códice 49, vol. 1. See also, Francisco Belisário Soares de Sousa, *O sistema eleitoral do Brasil, como funciona, como tem funcionado, e como deve ser reformado.*

49. Tobias do Rego Monteiro, *História do império: A elaboração da independência*, 2: 328. On the justices of the peace as the agents responsible for maintaining order in the capital at the time of abdication, see Brazil, Minister of Justice, *Relatório*, 1831, pp. 3 ff.

50. Jean Baptiste Debret, *Viagem pitoresca e histórica ao Brasil*, 2: 280-281, pl. 51.

51. See especially the decree of 6 June 1831 in *B-CLB*, 1831, pp. 103; also Aurelino Leal, "História judiciária," p. 1139.

52. See, for example, the petitions of city juizes de paz to the Brazilian parliament regarding the resignation of the regents and requesting a general amnesty for political criminals (*O Jornal do Comércio*, 1 August 1832, 4 September 1833).

53. The Código do Processo Criminal de Primeira Instância can be found in *B-CLB*, 1832, pp. 186-242.

54. Ibid., chap. 2, sec. 1; chap. 4. See also the exceptionally lucid analysis of the early accumulation of police and criminal powers in *B-CDA*, 1870, 4: 155-157 (speech of Teodoro da Silva).

55. Câmara Municipal of Feira de Santana to Assembléia Legislativa da Bahia, 18 August 1843, APBa/Seção legislativa, Ofícios à Assembléia Legislativa.

56. Eusébio de Queiroz to Minister of Justice, 25 April 1838, PEQ, cód. 1004 (see list of abbreviations).

57. Rio de Janeiro, Presidente da Província (Paulino José Soares de Souza), *Mensagem à Assembléia Legislativa*, 1840, p. 22. See also Oliveira Torres, *A democracia coroada: Teoria política do império do Brasil*, p. 234, n. 10.

58. *O Astro de Minas*, 4 July 1835. See also ibid., 7 March 1829; *Aurora Fluminense*, 26 January 1835, 6 June 1838.

59. See, for example, the complaints of the provincial president of Rio de Janeiro (Rio de Janeiro, Presidente da Província, *Mensagem à Assembléia Legislativa*, 1836, pp. 8-9; 1839, p. 2; 1840, p. 22).

60. Decree of 20 March 1829, *B-CLB*, 1829, pt. 2; Decree of 17 July 1832, *B-CLB*, 1832, pt. 1; Juiz de Paz of Guaratiba (Rio de Janeiro) to Minister of Justice, 9 November 1833, ANRJ, IJ4311.

61. This point has been advanced by Paulo Pereira Castro in "A experiência republicana," p. 27.

62. See Rio de Janeiro, Presidente da Província, *Mensagem à Assembléia Legislativa*, 1840, p. 26. In 1842 one newspaper reported that in Rio no justice of the peace had ever been convicted after suspension (*O Brasil*, 10 February 1842).

63. Of the eighteen juiz de paz suspensions in the province of Rio de Janeiro between 1832 and 1842, twelve were ordered in 1832 and 1833 alone. See Magistratura/Suspenções (1828-1865), ANRJ, IJ434.

64. *B-CLB*, 1841, vol. 4, pt. 1, pp. 75-95.

Chapter 5: Judicial Personnel

1. For Rio de Janeiro, the only existing list of juizes de paz of the city parishes was published in *Vade-mecum dos juizes de paz, suplentes, fiscaes, e escrivães para a província do Rio de Janeiro*. The only accessible list for the city of Bahia is that of 1828, copied out of the Atas da Câmara of that year by Braz do Amaral (Ignácio Accioli de Cerqueira e Silva [notes by Braz do Amaral], *Memórias históricas e políticas da província da Bahia*, 4: 244-245). For Rio de Janeiro the *Almanack Laemmert* lists city juizes by parish beginning in 1844, and those of some of the interior municípios beginning in 1847.

2. John Norman Kennedy, "Bahian Elites, 1750-1822," *HAHR*, 53 (August 1973): 420-421.

3. Inventory of Pedro Rodrigues Bandeira, 14 October 1835, APBa, Inventários/Capital, maço 146; Will of Pedro Rodrigues Bandeira, 28 June 1835, APBa, Testamentos/Capital, L° 23, ff. 233v-246v.

4. Afonso Ruy, *História da câmara municipal da cidade do Salvador*, p. 368. Cezimbra's only prior involvement with municipal government was service as almotacel in 1826 (Atas da Câmara Municipal do Salvador, AMS, 1826, vol. 37 [see list of abbreviations]).

5. Arnoldo Wildberger, *Os presidentes da província da Bahia, efectivos e interinos, 1824-1889*, pp. 84-88.

6. Ibid., p. 88; Associação Comercial to President of Province, 28 October 1841, ACB, "Registro de Ofícios, 1840-1850," pp. 78-79 (see list of abbreviations).

7. Livros de Notas de Escrituras (hereafter cited as Notas)/Capital, 7 October 1820, APBa, L° 202, ff. 177v-178; 23 February 1827, APBa, L° 222, f. 44; 23 September 1839, APBa, L° 268, ff. 131-131v; 25 August 1840, APBa, L° 269, ff. 34v-35; Associação Comercial to Cezimbra e Filhos, 17 July 1843, ACB, "Registro de Ofícios, 1840-1850, p. 130.

8. Ruy, *História da câmara*, p. 368.

9. Wildberger, *Os presidentes*, pp. 315-335.

10. Accioli de Cerqueira e Silva, *Memórias históricas*, 4: 241; João Ladislau's pharmacy was said to be the best in Bahia; his daughters were known for the quality of the medical advice they dispensed. João Rodrigues de Brito, *Cartas econômico-políticas sobre a agricultura e comércio da Bahia, dadas à luz por I. A. F. Benavides*, p. 64.

11. *Livro de matrícula de engenhos desta Capitania pelos dízimos Reaes*

administrados pela Junta de Real Fazenda de Julho de 1807 em diante, APBa, 1818; Will of José Barbosa Madureira, 10 May 1839, APBa, Testamentos/Capital, L° 26, f. 141v; Notas/Capital, 15 March 1834, APBa, L° 246, ff. 15v-16; Minister of Império to Provincial President of Bahia, 14 May 1834, APBa, Presidência da Província, vol. 853, 5.44.

12. Francisco Marques de Góes Calmon, *Elementos para a história da vida econômico-financeira da Bahia de 1808-1889,* pp. 18, 47. The active small-time speculation in roça lands east of the city is amply documented in contemporary notarial records, Notas/Capital, APBa, L°ˢ 236-270.

13. Notas/Capital, 5 May 1834, APBa, L° 241, f. 8v.

14. Juiz de Paz of Freguesia da Sé to Provincial President of Bahia, 22 March 1832, APBa, Juizes de Paz da Primeira Vara, maço 2682.

15. The sugar mill was purchased from another justice of the peace, Lázaro José Jambeiro. Notas/Capital, 10 June 1839, APBa, L° 268, f. 91v; 29 March 1842, APBa, L° 275, ff. 181v-182.

16. Juiz de Paz of Freguesia da Sé to Provincial President of Bahia, 24 January 1835, APBa, Juizes de Paz da Primeira Vara, maço 2684.

17. Notas/Capital, 3 September 1834, APBa, L° 246, ff. 129v-130; 6 June 1839, L° 265, ff. 62v-63; *Livro de matrícula,* 1835.

18. Provincial President (Gordilho de Barbuda) to Minister of Império, 27 November 1828, APBa, Presidência da Província/Correspondência para o Governo Imperial, vol. 678, ff. 24v-25.

19. Ruy, *História da câmara,* p. 368. He had served as almotacel in 1826 (Atas da Câmara Municipal do Salvador, AMS, 1826, vol. 37).

20. Ruy, *História da câmara,* p. 368.

21. Notas/Capital, 15 January 1825, APBa, L° 214, ff. 44-44v; 9 October 1835, L° 257, f. 40v; 21 August 1833, L° 239, ff. 194v-195; 9 October 1835, L° 257, f. 40v; 10 June 1839, L° 268, f. 91v; Inventory of Lázaro Manuel Muniz Medeiros, 27 August 1836, APBa, Inventários/Capital, maço 830.

22. Notas/Capital, 29 July 1836, APBa, L° 254, ff. 177-177v; 5 December 1836, ff. 239-240. For a list of the great trapiches of Bahia, see Góes Calmon, *Elementos para a história,* p. 40.

23. The procedural code of 1832 authorized the subdivision of the original parishes into single-judge districts (Código do Processo Criminal, 1835, chap. 1, arts. 1, 2).

24. Notas/Capital, 7 August 1832, APBa, L° 238, ff. 122-122v; 15 March 1834, L° 246, ff. 15v-16; Will of Maria Clara Rofino de Argolo, 4 April 1840, APBa, Testamentos/Capital, L° 27, f. 188v.

25. Notas/Capital, 16 March 1822, APBa, L° 207, f. 150v; 14 October 1823, L° 212, f. 10; 13 March 1835, L° 241a, ff. 88-88v; 26 June 1837, L° 255, f. 182v; *Livro de matrícula,* 1838.

26. Notas/Capital, 16 February 1828, APBa, L° 223, f. 13v; 4 February 1831, L° 234, ff. 6v-7; 14 June 1831, L° 242, ff. 4v-5v.

27. Carvalho Câmara was juiz de paz in 1835 and 1837. Notas/Capital, 17 September 1839, APBa, L° 226, ff. 13v-14.

28. José de Cerqueira Lima served as juiz de paz of Vitória in 1831. Pereira dos Matos was an executor of João Cerqueira Lima's will, in which he is referred to as "amigo e compadre." Inventory of João Cerqueira Lima, 1851, APBa, Inventários/Capital, maço 865, vol. 4; Notas/Capital, 15 July 1835, APBa, L° 245, ff. 239v-240; 10 May 1839, APBa, L° 268, ff. 82-82v.

29. Emílio Willems gives a discussion of the two-class stereotype and offers evidence of considerable social variety in rural São Paulo, ca. 1822, in "Social Differentiation in Colonial Brazil," *Comparative Studies in Society and History* 12 (January 1970): pp. 31-49.

30. Will of Francisco Antônio Fernandes Pereira, 20 March 1837, APBa, Testamentos/Cachoeira, L° 17, ff. 49v-54.

31. Juiz de Paz of Cachoeira to Provincial President of Bahia, 26 August 1829, 28 March 1830, 29 April 1830, APBa, Judiciário/Juizes de Cachoeira, maço 2270.

32. Jerônimo José Albernaz et al. to Provincial President of Bahia, Cachoeira, 1 April 1829, APBa, Judiciária/Revolução/Cachoeira e São Felix, maço 2855.

33. Rollie E. Poppino, *Feira de Santana* (Bahia, 1868), pp. 23-24.

34. Will of Col. Joaquim José Bacelar e Castro, 5 December 1834, APBa, Testamentos/Cachoeira, L° 16, ff. 86-87; Will of Capt. Manuel Xavier de Miranda, n.d., APBa, Testamentos/Cachoeira, L° 13, ff. 98-98v; Câmara de Cachoeira, maço 1270; *Livro de matrícula,* 1818.

35. An identical pattern of juiz de paz recruitment is found in the sugar parishes of Pernambuco. Peter L. Eisenberg, *The Sugar Industry in Pernambuco: Modernization without Change, 1840-1910,* p. 133.

36. APBa, Judiciário/Juizes de Cachoeira, maço 2270.

37. Tibúrcio José de Barros to Provincial President of Bahia, 16 April 1841, 17 April 1841, APBa, Judiciário/Eleições, maço 2794.

38. Câmara Municipal of Cachoeira to Provincial President of Bahia, 8 November 1844, APBa, Câmara da Cachoeira, 1836-1844, maço 1270. On the Vieira Tostas in Outeiro Redondo, see Inventory of Sebastião Vieira Tosta, n.d. [1800?], APBa, Inventários/Capital, maço 1168, vol. 6; Will of Manuel Vieira Tosta, 10 September 1823, APBa, Testamentos/Cachoeira, L° 11, ff. 25v-26v.

39. "Marquês de Muritiba" (obituary in *Revista do Instituto Geográfico e Histórico da Bahia,* vol. 3, no. 7 [1896]: pp. 118-121).

40. See, for example, *Aurora Fluminense,* 15 February and 25 February 1833; *O Sete de Abril,* 23 February 1833.

41. Manuel Caetano dos Matos to Câmara Municipal of Rio de Janeiro, n.d., AEG, cód. 45-2-51, f. 116; Juiz de Paz of Iguassú to Minister of Justice, 13 October 1832, ANRJ, Rio/Eleições, LJJ9564.

42. *Almanack Laemmert* (Rio de Janeiro, 1847-1848).

43. The judges so labeled were João Evangelista Teixeira Leite and Antônio Torquato Leite Brandão.

44. The analogous case is that of the sugar cane farmers (*lavradores de cana*) of Bahia. Stuart B. Schwartz, "Free Labor in a Slave Economy: The *Lavradores de Cana* of Colonial Bahia," in *Colonial Roots of Modern Brazil,* ed. Dauril Alden, pp. 175-182.

Chapter 6: World of the Justice of the Peace

1. Juiz de Paz of Cachoeira to Provincial President of Bahia, 26 August 1829, APBa, Judiciário/Juizes de Cachoeira, maço 2270; *Aurora Fluminense,* 16 February 1829. See also chapter 4 above.

2. See one professional judge's recollection of conflicts between elective and professional magistrates in the 1830s, *B-CDA,* 1870, 4: 156.

3. Eul-Soo Pang and Ron L. Seckinger, "The Mandarins of Imperial Brazil," *Comparative Studies in Society and History,* 14 (March 1972): 215-244.

4. Provincial President of Bahia (Visconde de Camamú) to Minister of Justice, 15 April 1829, APBa, Presidência da Província/Correspondência para o Governo Imperial, vol. 678, f. 83.

5. *B-CDA,* 1870, 4: 156.

6. Provincial President of Bahia (Visconde de Camamú) to Minister of Império, 27 November 1828, APBa, Presidência da Província/Correspondência para o Governo Imperial, vol. 678, ff. 24v-25.

7. The troublesome history of counterfeit coinage in Bahia is best described in Luis Afonso d'Escragnolle, "O Visconde de Camamú e o derrame de moedas falsas de cobre na Bahia," *Anais do primeiro congresso de história da Bahia* (Bahia, 1950), 4: 143-171.

8. Fernandes Pereira is one of the magistrates profiled in chapter 5.

9. Some of the activities of juiz de fora Antônio Vaz de Carvalho in Cachoeira are described in the correspondence contained in APBa, Câmara de Cachoeira/1823-1835, maço 1269; and APBa, Judiciário/Juizes de Cachoeira, maço 2270. For a description of the "riot" of 1829 see Jerônimo José Albernaz et al. to Provincial President of Bahia, Cachoeira, 1 April 1829, APBa, Judiciária/Revolução/Cachoeira e São Felix, maço 2855.

10. *B-CDA,* 1828, 1: 27.

11. Ibid., 1829, 3: 13.

12. Ibid., 1828, 1: 74.

13. Ibid., 1828, 1: 80; II, 104.

14. *A Astréia,* 31 July 1828.

15. *A Malagueta,* 27 January 1829. See also *O Astro de Minas,* 6 March 1830.

16. See chapter 3.

17. *Aurora Fluminense,* 8 March 1830.

18. *O Carapuceiro,* 1 July 1837.

19. See Jacinto Ferreira de Paiva to Câmara Municipal of Rio de Janeiro, 17 December 1833, AEG, cód. 45-2-55; José Ribeiro da Cruz Portugal to Câmara Municipal of Rio de Janeiro, 21 January 1831, AEG, cód. 45-2-54; Braz Carneiro Leão to Câmara Municipal of Rio de Janeiro, 26 March 1831, AEG, cód. 45-2-54 (see list of abbreviations).

20. For abuses by the scribes of juizes de paz, see Juiz de Direito of Vassouras to Provincial President of Rio de Janeiro, 3 August 1846, ANRJ, IJ1449; Suspension of juiz de paz of São João da Barra, 23 June 1834, ANRJ, Magistratura/suspenções (1826-1865), IJ434; Câmara of Cachoeira to Provincial President of Bahia, 29 May 1841, APBa, Câmara de Cachoeira, maço 1270; Eusébio

de Queiroz to Minister of Justice, 12 October 1836, PEQ, cód. 1004; *O Despertador,* 23 May 1841.

21. Quoted in *O Jornal do Comércio,* 8 June 1847.

22. Câmara Municipal of Nova Boipeba to Assembléia Legislativa of Bahia, 14 November 1842, APBa, Seção Legislativa, Ofícios à Assembléia Legislativa. See also Paulino José Soares de Souza, *Estudos práticos sobre a administração das províncias no Brasil,* 1: vi-xxvii; João de Azevedo Carneiro Maia, *O município: Estudos sobre administração local,* p. 189 and passim.

23. See chapter 5.

24. *O Jornal do Comércio,* 18 April 1831.

25. Juiz de Paz of Brejo do Salgado to Minister of Justice, 11 May 1831, ANRJ, IJ4308; Juiz de Paz of Piraí to Minister of Justice, 22 June 1832, ANRJ, IJ4319; Juiz de Paz of Engenho Velho to Minister of Justice, 30 September 1833, ANRJ, IJ4306; President of Province of Bahia (Pinheiro de Vasconcelos) to Minister of Justice, 3 August 1833, APBa, Presidência da Província/Correspondência para o Governo Imperial, vol. 681, ff. 11-11v.

26. Câmara Municipal of Cabo Frio to Ministro do Império, 22 May 1833 and 23 May 1833, ANRJ, IJJ9561; Juiz de Paz of Cabo Frio to Câmara Municipal of Cabo Frio, 22 May 1833, ANRJ, IJJ9561.

27. Câmara Municipal of Belmonte to Assembléia Legislativa of Bahia, 2 April 1835, APBa, Seção Legislativa, Ofícios à Assembléia Legislativa.

28. Law of 15 October 1827, art. 5, secs. 3, 6, *B-CLB,* 1827.

29. Law of 18 August 1831, art. 6, *B-CLB,* 1831, 1ª parte.

30. The question of whether militiamen or officers enjoyed legal privileges is hard to answer. The Ministry of Justice was consistent in its denial of such privileges, but questions arose so often that they must have been observed in practice in many places. See Feijó's clarifications of 1832: Minister of Justice to Manuel da Fonseca Lima e Silva, 17 January 1832, 31 March 1832, in Brazil, *Decisões do governo do Império do Brasil,* 1832, pp. 37, 139.

31. Provincial President of Bahia to Juiz de Paz of Iguape, 3 October 1828, APBa, Presidência da Província/Correspondência expedida, vol. 1627, ff. 133v-134; Juiz de Paz of Penha to Provincial President of Bahia, 11 August 1835, APBa, Juizes de Paz da Primeira Vara, maço 2684; Juiz de Paz de Pirajá to Provincial President of Bahia, 8 September 1832, APBa, Juiz de Paz da Primeira Vara, maço 2682; Juiz de Paz of Conceição da Praia to Provincial President, 9 August 1832, APBa, Juizes de Paz da Primeira Vara, maço 2682; Juiz de Paz de São Pedro to Provincial President of Bahia, 16 September 1832, APBa, Juizes de Paz da Primeira vara, maço 2682; Juiz de Paz de Iguape to Provincial President of Bahia, 9 December 1840, APBa, Juizes de Paz, maço 2691; Juiz de Direito of Cachoeira to Provincial President of Bahia, 19 November 1838, APBa, Judiciário/Juizes de Cachoeira, maço 2273; Juiz de Paz of Lagoa (Rio de Janeiro) to Minister of Justice, 15 November 1833, ANRJ, IJ4306.

32. In 1827 the militia regiment of Iguape, Bahia, with its great slave population possessed only twelve arms in fireable condition. The National Guard usually inherited this dangerous and obsolete equipment after 1832. Juiz de

Direito of Cachoeira to Provincial President of Bahia, 17 January 1827, APBa, Judiciário/Juizes de Cachoeira, maço 2270.

33. Jeanne Berrance de Castro, "A Guarda Nacional," in *HGCB*, vol. 2, no. 4, pp. 280-281.

34. Juiz de Paz of Penha to Provincial President of Bahia, 28 August 1831, APBa, Juizes de Paz da Primeira Vara, maço 2680. See also Juiz de Direito of Ilhéus to Provincial President of Bahia, 15 February 1837, APBa, Seção legislativa/Ofícios à Assembléia Legislativa, 1837.

35. Juiz de Paz of Pilão Arcado to Provincial President of Bahia, 10 December 1832, APBa, Judiciária/Juizes de Pilão Arcado, maço 2533. As late as 1838 there were whole comarcas in the Bahian interior where the juizes de paz had failed to take the first steps toward establishing the National Guard. *Correio Mercantil*, 3 April 1838 (message of Provincial President to Provincial Assembly). See also Bahia, Presidente da Província, *Mensagem à Assembléia Legislativa*, 1840, pp. 5-6; Brazil, Minister of Justice, *Relatório*, 1832, p. 4.

36. Juiz de Paz of Guaratiba to Minister of Justice, 17 June 1833, ANRJ, IJ4311. Brazil, Minister of Justice, *Relatório*, 1832, p. 4. See also related concerns expressed in *Aurora Fluminense*, 28 November 1831; *O Astro de Minas*, 14 Jan. 1832; and warnings of social inversion in *O Brasil*, 11 May 1841; *Correio Mercantil*, 19 Oct. 1839; *O Carapuceiro*, 24 Aug. 1833; *B-CDA*, 1843, 3: 400.

37. See, for example, Rio de Janeiro, Presidente da Província, *Mensagem à Assembléia Legislativa*, 1835, p. 13; 1836, p. 10; 1837, p. 15; 1845, pp. 28-29; 1848, p. 9; Brazil, Minister of Justice, *Relatório*, 1832, p. 4; 1834, p. 10; 1838, p. 25; 1841, pp. 30-32; *Correio Mercantil*, 3 April 1838 (message of Provincial President of Bahia to Provincial Assembly); Bahia, Presidente da Província, *Mensagem à Assembléia Legislativa*, 1840, p. 5; Provincial President of Bahia to Minister of Justice, 9 May 1845, APBa, Presidência da Província/Correspondência para o Governo Imperial, vol. 688, ff. 191-191v; Patricia Ann Aufderheide, "Order and Violence: Social Deviance and Social Control in Brazil, 1780-1840" (Ph.D. diss., 1976), pp. 128-129.

38. *O Jornal do Comércio*, 5 February 1840.

39. Juiz de Paz of São Pedro to Provincial President of Bahia, 4 June 1833, APBa, Juizes de Paz da Primeira Vara, maço 2683; Juiz de Paz of Conceição da Praia to Provincial President of Bahia, 26 May 1835, APBa, Juizes de Paz da Primeira Vara, maço 2685; Juiz de Paz of Guaratiba (Rio de Janeiro) to Minister of Justice, 9 November 1833, ANRJ, IJ4311. In Rio one publication dedicated to the interests of the National Guard complained that in the capital preference in the hiring of commercial clerks was given to foreigners because Brazilians in the National Guard were too often called away from their work (*O Guarda Nacional*, 13 February 1836).

40. In 1838 the parish of São Pedro Velho, Bahia, counted slightly more than two thousand *fogos* (hearths) and forty-four block inspectors—an average of approximately one per fifty *fogos*. The parish of Conceição da Praia, with a similar population had only nineteen inspectors. Thales de Azevedo, *Povoamento da cidade do Salvador*, p. 233; Juiz de Paz of Conceição da Praia to

Provincial President of Bahia, 26 September 1838, and Juiz de Paz of São Pedro Velho to Provincial President, 11 October 1838, APBa, Juizes de Paz da Primeira Vara, maço 2689. Block inspectors, it appears, were also used to get out the vote in their districts (*O Brasil*, 18 December 1848).

41. Juiz de Paz of Second District of Sé to Provincial President of Bahia, 2 May 1836, APBa, Juizes de Paz da Primeira Vara, maço 2686.

42. Brazil, Minister of Justice, *Relatório,* 1835, pp. 32-33.

43. Provincial President to Major Comandante Interino de Cachoeira, 4 December 1834, APBa, Presidência da Província/Correspondência expedida, vol. 1650, ff. 204v-205. See also Provincial President of Rio de Janeiro to Minister of Justice, 10 June 1829, ANRJ, IJ1935. A typical magistrate's point of view is expressed in Juiz de Paz of Paty do Alferes to Provincial President of Rio de Janeiro, 20 September 1838, ANRJ, IJ1860.

44. Juiz de Paz of Second District of Sé to Provincial President of Bahia, 2 May 1836, Juiz de Paz of Second District of Vitória to Provincial President, 4 May 1836, and Juiz de Paz of Second District of Brotas to Provincial President, 5 May 1836, APBa, Juizes de Paz da Primeira Vara, maço 2686. The situation in Bahia remained unchanged until at least 1840. Bahia, Presidente da Província, *Mensagem à Assembléia Legislativa,* 1839, p. 7; 1840, p. 5.

45. See, for example, Juiz de Paz of Iguape to Provincial President of Bahia, 24 December 1840, APBa, Juizes de Paz, maço 2690. This document describes how Cachoeira's Guarda Nacional commander, in his attempt to intimidate voters and influence elections in Cachoeira, rode at the head of a force of "armed rabble" and even slaves, thus "staining the honor of his class."

46. It is unclear whether justices of the peace had the legal right to carry out unauthorized conscription, but many did so. See the doubts expressed by Juiz de Direito of Cachoeira to Provincial President of Bahia, 28 November 1840, APBa, Judiciária/Juizes de Cachoeira, maço 2273.

47. Juiz de Paz of Paty do Alferes to Provincial President of Rio de Janeiro, 13 November 1838, ANRJ, IJ1860. José Antônio Soares de Souza "O efêmero quilombo de Paty do Alferes em 1838," *RIHGB,* no. 295 (April-June, 1972): 33-69.

48. Bede Anthony Dauphinee, O.F.M., "Church and Parliament in Brazil during the First Empire, 1823-1832," (Ph.D. diss., 1965), pp. 7-11, 53-82.

49. Newspapers like *O Astro de Minas* which carried many references to individual juizes de paz show a high proportion of priests serving in 1829.

50. *B-CDA,* 1829, 5: 31-32.

51. Ibid., 85.

52. Decree of 18 September 1829, *B-CLB,* 1829.

53. Provincial President of Bahia to Câmaras Municipaes of Bahia, 12 May 1824, APBa, vol. 1621, ff. 98-99.

54. Ata de eleição of Freguesia of Nossa Senhora da Conceição da Angra dos Reis, 21 July 1822, ANRJ, Eleições, IJJ9563. Other elections in the interior of Rio showed the same pattern. Those electors who were not priests were usually militia captains.

55. Brazil, Ministério da Justiça, *Organizações e programas ministeriaes: Regime parlamentar no império,* pp. 279-283.

56. "Exposição e Projeto de Eleições," 18 April 1824, ANRJ, Conselho de Estado/Pareceres, 1842-1844, cód. 49, vol. 1.

57. *O Astro de Minas,* 10 March 1829. See also *O Astro de Minas,* 29 March 1832, 2 October 1832.

58. Fernando de Azevedo, *Canaviais e engenhos na vida política do Brasil,* pp. 80 ff.

59. *Aurora Fluminense,* 15 November 1830.

60. Citizens of Arrozal to Provincial President of Rio de Janeiro, 29 September 1840, ANRJ, IJ1446.

61. See, for example, Juiz de Paz of Iguape to Provincial President of Bahia, 24 December 1840, APBa, Juizes de Paz, maço 2690.

62. For a brief but suggestive description of the reasons for antagonism between magistrates and clergymen, see Paulo Pereira Castro, "A experiência republicana, 1831-1840," *HGCB,* vol. 2, pt. 2, p. 43.

63. Rio de Janeiro, Presidente da Província, *Mensagem à Assembléia Legislativa,* 1839, pp. 1-4; 1840, pp. 23 ff.

64. See note 7 above. Also, Joaquim Nabuco, *Um estadista do império, Nabuco de Araújo: Sua vida, suas opiniões, sua época,* 1: 266. In Pernambuco, too, Juizes de Paz collected protection money from counterfeit operations. *O Jornal do Comércio,* 15 March 1833 (reprint from *O Carapuceiro*).

65. George Gardner, *Travels in the Interior of Brazil . . . ,* p. 16.

66. *O Maiorista,* 20 November 1841. The "Código Criminal Prático da Simi-República de Passamão na Oceania" published in this number of *O Maiorista* was the creation of the great satirist Padre Miguel do Sacramento Lopes Gama of Recife.

67. Brazil, Minister of the Empire, *Relatório,* May 1835, p. 7. See also Leslie Bethell, *The Abolition of the Brazilian Slave Trade: Britain, Brazil, and the Slave Trade Question, 1807-1869,* p. 77; Beatriz Westin de Cerqueira, "Um estudo de escravidão em Ubatuba," *Estudos Históricos,* no. 5 (1966), pp. 54-58.

68. Pinto Bulhões to Provincial President of Rio de Janeiro, 15 July 1840, ANRJ, IJ1446; Alberto Ribeiro Lamego, "A aristocracia rural do café na província fluminense," *Anuário do museu imperial,* 3 (1946): 65-69; Rio de Janeiro, Presidente da Província, *Mensagem à Assembléia Legislativa,* 1840, p. 25.

69. *B-CDA,* 1841, 1: 140-144.

70. The procedure for judicial inquests into cases of slave smuggling remained largely unchanged since colonial times (Dauril Alden, *Royal Government in Colonial Brazil . . . ,* pp. 403-408).

71. Provincial President of Bahia (Pinheiro de Vasconcelos) to Juiz de Paz of Conceição da Praia, 3 June 1834, APBa, Presidência da Província/Correspondência expedida, vol. 1649, ff. 49v-50; Provincial President of Bahia (Pinheiro de Vasconcelos) to Minister of Justice, 26 June 1834, 24 July 1834, 22 September 1834, APBa, Presidência da Província/Correspondência para o Governo Imperial, vol. 681, f. 99v, f. 108, ff. 128-128v; Provincial President of Bahia

(Francisco de Sousa Martins) to Minister of Justice, 14 February 1835, APBa, vol. 682, ff. 9v-11.

72. *B-CDA,* 1846, 2: 655.

73. *O Cronista,* 3 May 1837; *A Lanterna Mágica,* no. 5 [n.d.].

74. *B-CDA,* 1839, 3: 279.

75. Bethell, *The Abolition of the Brazilian Slave Trade,* p. 78.

76. Fairly sober analyses of electoral manipulation are to be found in Francisco Belisário Soares de Souza, *O sistema eleitoral do Brasil, como funciona, como tem funcionado, como deve ser reformado;* "Exposição e Projeto de Eleições," 18 April 1842, ANRJ, Conselho de Estado/Pareceres, 1842-1844, cód. 49, vol. 1; Vitor Nunes Leal, *Coronelismo: Enxada e voto.*

77. Juiz de Paz of Iguape to Provincial President of Bahia, 21 December 1840, 24 December 1840, APBa, Juizes de Paz, maço 2690; Provincial President of Bahia to Juiz de Paz of Iguape, 15 January 1841, APBa, Presidência da Província/Correspondência expedida, vol. 1684, ff. 71-71v.

78. Provincial President of Bahia (Pinheiro de Vasconcelos) to Ministro do Imperio, 18 November 1842, APBa, Presidência da Província Correspondência para o Governo Imperial, vol. 686, ff. 1-9v.

79. Provincial President (Pinheiro de Vasconcelos) to Minister of Justice, 26 August 1841, APBa, Presidência da Província/Correspondência para o Governo Imperial, vol. 685, ff. 215-217.

80. *O Jornal do Comércio,* 11 September 1835; *Aurora Fluminense,* 6 March 1833; *O Brasil,* 15 September 1840; Antônio Pereira Rebouças, *Recordações da vida parlamentar,* 1: 428.

81. Luis Carlos Martins Pena, *Teatro de Martins Pena,* ed. Darcy Damaceno and Maria Filgueiras, pp. 29-56.

82. Most of the early nineteenth-century farces have been lost. See references to *O Novo Desertor, O Muleiro Maqueado,* and *O Recrutamento na Aldéia* in *O Jornal do Comércio,* 28 September 1830. Bento José Rodrigues, *O Juiz Eleito,* 1856 (copy in Biblioteca Nacional/Manuscript Collection). This play takes place in Portugal. See review of *O Juiz de Paz Abdicando* in *O Jornal do Comércio,* 18 October 1840.

83. See Rio's humorous magazine *Lanterna Mágica,* 1844-1845, and Pernambuco's great satirical tabloid *O Carapuceiro,* 1834-1843; *O Jornal do Comércio,* 1 February 1840.

84. Juiz de Paz of Pirajá to Provincial President of Bahia, 8 September 1832, APBa, Juizes de Paz da Primeira Vara, maço 2682.

85. For a description of the juiz's role in civic celebrations, see Francisco de Paula Ferreira de Rezende, *Minhas recordações,* pp. 68-69. See also *O Astro de Minas,* 2 October 1832; Câmara of Cachoeira to Provincial President of Bahia, 22 May 1839, APBa, Câmara of Cachoeira, maço 1270.

86. Carlos Drummond de Andrade, "O Juiz de Paz," *Jornal do Brasil,* 8 February 1973, p. 5; João Camilo de Oliveira Torres, *A democracia coroada: Teoria política do império do Brasil,* pp. 224-234, 273-283.

87. Raymundo Faoro, *Os donos de poder: Formação do patronato político*

brasileiro.
88. Ibid., pp. 169, 178-179.

Chapter 7: Legal Codes and the Jury System
1. The nativist position is best expressed in the pages of *Nova Luz Brasileira*, 1829-1831.
2. *B-CDA*, 1826, 4: 16-17.
3. *B-CDA*, 1827, 4: 130-131.
4. The debates on the death penalty in the Chamber of Deputies began in mid-September, 1830. *B-CDA*, 1830, 2. See also João Camilo de Oliveira Torres, *A democracia coroada: Teoria política do império do Brasil*, pp. 224-225; John Armitage, *The History of Brazil . . . ,* 2: 85-87.
5. *Aurora Fluminense*, 26 November 1830.
6. Capital punishment was reserved only for specific cases, including slave insurrection and homicide with "aggravating" circumstances. See Código Criminal, *B-CLB*, 1830, pt. 1, pp. 142-200.
7. Ibid.; Armitage, *History of Brazil*, 2: 86. Aurelino Leal, "História judiciária do Brasil," in *Dicionário histórico geográfico e etnográfica do Brasil*, 1: 1136-1137.
8. *Aurora Fluminense*, 25 April 1834.
9. Armitage, *History of Brazil*, 2: 87. *Aurora Fluminense*, 25 April 1834.
10. *Aurora Fluminense*, 2 July 1832, 25 April 1834, 14 March 1839; *O Jornal do Comércio*, 22 August 1833.
11. Código Criminal, *B-CLB*, 1830, pt. 1.
12. Armitage, *History of Brazil*, 2: 101.
13. Ibid., p. 291.
14. Código do Processo Criminal de Primeira Instancia, *B-CLB*, 1832, pt. 1, pp. 186-242.
15. *B-CDA*, 1829, 3: 97-98, 125; *B-SA*, 1831, 1: 251-254, 320-324; 1832, 2: 28-29, 430 ff.; Oliveira Torres, *A democracia coroada*, p. 226.
16. See, for example, Oliveira Torres, *A democracia coroada*, p. 226; Paulo Pereira Castro, "A experiência republicana," in *HGCB*, vol. 2, pt. 2, p. 27.
17. A list of the members of this committee can be found in *O Jornal do Comércio*, 8 October 1833. The revision of defects and lacunae in the Code was the purpose of the committee, according to the instructions of the minister of the empire. Special attention was to be paid to laws relating to the police and National Guard, the Juizado de Paz, and the judiciary in general. Minister of the empire to Paulino José Soares de Souza, 3 October 1833, PVU.
18. *B-SA*, 1831, 2: 320-321.
19. For other examples, see *O Jornal do Comércio*, 20 October 1829, 28 April 1832.
20. *B-SA*, 1831, 2: 320-321.
21. *Aurora Fluminense*, 2 July 1832.
22. B-SA, 1832, 1: 28-29.
23. Joaquim Nabuco, *Um estadista do império: Nabuco de Araújo: Sua vida,*

suas opiniões, sua época, 1: 146; Paulino José Soares de Souza, *Ensaio sobre o direito administrativo,* 2: 218.

24. Código do Processo, *B-CLB,* 1832, pt. 1, p. 192.

25. Ibid., p. 193.

26. Soares de Souza, *Ensaio sobre o direito,* 2: 205.

27. *B-CLB,* 1832, pt. 1, pp. 194-195; Brazil, Ministério da Justiça, *Notícia histórica dos serviços, instituições, e estabelecimentos pertencentes a esta repartição, elaborada por ordem do respectivo ministro, Dr. Amaro Cavalcante,* pp. 63-64.

28. The Cortes decree of 12 July 1821 created the jury system to adjudicate press offenses in Portugal (*B-CLB,* 1821-1822, pt. 1, pp. 19-28). This law was extended to Brazil on 18 June 1822 (*B-CLB,* 1822, pt. 2, pp. 23-24).

29. *B-CLB,* 1822, pt. 2, p. 24.

30. Ibid., 1823, pt. 2, pp. 89, 90-94. According to this law, jurors would be elected from among the homens bons of the comarca.

31. Brazil, *Assembléia Constituinte, Anais,* 1823, 5: 12-13.

32. Ibid., pp. 21-22, 151-154.

33. Ibid., p. 150.

34. Ibid., pp. 151-152.

35. Ibid., pp. 150-151, 154, 160-161, 174-175, 177-181.

36. Ibid., p. 153.

37. Brazil, *Constituição política do império do Brasil,* 1824, title VI, art. 151.

38. *Aurora Fluminense,* 26 October 1835.

39. *O Sete de Abril,* 26 January, 1833. Even much later the jury system continued to irritate the professional magistrates. One juiz de direito complained in 1862 that "[the jury] dulled the splendor that in other times [the magistracy] radiated." He charged that the judges had lost the "holy priesthodd of Justice" and that the "cult of the Laws" because of the jury's influence. José Antônio de Magalhães Castro, *Decadência da magistratura brasileira: Suas causas e meios de restabecê-la,* p. 4.

40. See, for example, *Nova Luz Brasileira,* 4 May 1830 ("Deus te salva ó Instituição Santa. Desça ja dos ceus: acode aos míseros opressos brasileiros . . ."). See also *A Malagueta,* 27 January 1829, 23 March 1822; *Aurora Fluminense,* 19 October 1832; *O Carapuceiro,* 17 May 1834.

41. *O Jornal do Comércio,* 3 July 1835. The books advertised, in addition to that of Sir Richard Phillips, were: I. D. M. Ferraz, *Exame sobre o jury; Código dos jurados; Guia dos jurados;* Francisco de Paula Almeida, *Manual do jury,* 2 vols. Also: João Pereira Batista Vieira Soares, *Catecismo político dos jurados,* (Rio de Janeiro, 1832). The political attack is Justiniano José da Rocha, *Considerações sobre a administração da justiça criminal no Brasil e especialmente sobre o jury.*

42. *B-CLB,* 1832, pt. 1, pp. 190-191; Oliveira Torres, *A democracia coroada,* pp. 253-254; Rocha, *Considerações,* p. 23.

43. Rocha, *Considerações,* p. 23.

44. *B-CLB,* 1832, pt. 1, pp. 191-192.

45. Ibid., pp. 222-223, 233.
46. Ibid., pp. 223-226.
47. Ibid., pp. 223-228.
48. Ibid., p. 228.
49. Brazil, Assembléia Constituinte, *Anais*, 1823, 5: 160-161.
50. Ibid., p. 174.
51. *Nova Luz Brasileira*, 4 May 1830.
52. Ibid., 7 January 1831.
53. Francisco José de Oliveira Vianna, *Instituições políticas brasileiras*, 1: 365. A similar analysis was offered by an anonymous writer as early as 1831. *Explicações breves e singelas sobre o que é a federação*, p. 35.
54. *O Atlante*, 21 June 1836; Paulino José Soares de Souza Neto, "O visconde de Uruguai e a consolidação da ordem em 1842," *Anuário do Museu Imperial*, 1945, 4: 112.
55. "O Progressivo do Ceará," *O Sete de Abril*, 8 August 1835. In 1836 Feijó wrote that one of Brazil's major problems was the lack of personnel to fill offices. "Correspondência Passiva do Senador Alencar," *Anais da Biblioteca Nacional*, 86 (1966): 231.
56. "O Lavrador do Recôncavo," *Correio Mercantil*, 7 February 1839; Rocha, *Considerações*, p. 23.
57. Eusébio de Queiroz to Minister of Justice, 19 June 1838, PEQ, cód. 1004.
58. Bahia, Presidente da Província, *Mensagem à Assembléia Legislativa*, 1848, p. 20. In 1839 Francisco Gonçalves Martins claimed that two to three years had passed in his town of Santo Amaro without any meeting of the jury. *B-CDA*, 1839, 2: 91; Brazil, Minister of Justice, *Relatório*, 1838, pp. 17-18.
59. "Apolinário de Jaboatão," *Correio Mercantil* (Bahia), 19 October 1839.
60. *O Carapuceiro*, 14 January 1840 (also reprinted in *O Despertador*, 8 March 1840).
61. Brazil, Minister of Justice (Aureliano de Sousa e Oliveira Coutinho), *Relatório*, 1834, pp. 21-22.
62. *O Astro de Minas*, 24 January 1835 (reprint from *O Justiceiro* of São Paulo); Rocha, *Considerações*, pp. 40-42.
63. *O Carapuceiro*, 6 April 1836.
64. *Aurora Fluminense*, 26 January 1835; *O Despertador*, 20 August 1839; Rocha, *Considerações*, pp. 23-24; Brazil, Minister of Justice, *Relatório*, 1840, p. 16; Juiz de Direito of Niterói (Ignácio Manuel Álvares de Azevedo) to Presidente of Province of Rio de Janeiro, 15 February 1840, ANRJ, IJ1446.
65. *O Carapuceiro*, 22 August 1833. See also Rio de Janeiro (province), Presidente da Província, *Mensagem à Assembléia Legislativa*, 1840, p. 25.
66. Eusébio de Queiroz to Minister of Justice, 19 June 1838, PEQ, cód. 1004.
67. Nabuco, *Um estadista do império*, 1: 45, 89.
68. *B-CDA*, 1836, 2: 254.
69. Eusébio de Queiroz to Minister of Justice, 17 May 1838, PEQ, cód. 1004.
70. See, for example, Brazil, Minister of Justice, *Relatório*, 1840, p. 19;

Nabuco, *Um estadista do império*, 1: 89-90.

71. For other examples of jury leniency, see Juiz de Direito of Cabo Frio to Minister of Justice, 27 February 1838, ANRJ, IJ1860; Juiz de Direito of Niterói to President of Province of Rio de Janeiro, 15 February 1840, ANRJ, IJ1446; *O Sete de Abril*, 8 August 1835. For a general statement of the problem, see Bahia, Presidente da Província, *Mensagem à Assembléia Legislativa*, 1842, p. 4. Patricia Aufderheide provides additional evidence in "Order and Violence: Social Deviance and Social Control in Brazil, 1780-1840" (Ph.D. diss., 1976), pp. 280-282.

72. Provincial President of Rio de Janeiro to Minister of Justice, 7 June 1841, ANRJ, IJ1446.

73. An exchange of correspondence giving different versions of the Arrozal incident appeared in the pages of *O Despertador*, 23 May, 26 May, 11 June, 13 June, 28 June, and 4 July 1841.

74. Juiz de Direito of Vassouras (Sayão Lobato) to Provincial Presidente of Rio de Janeiro, 16 October 1841, ANRJ, IJ1446. It appears that the protector of the jailbreak defendants in this incident was Joaquim José de Sousa Breves. See Sousa Breves to Emperor, n.d., ANRJ, IJ1862.

75. See, for example, Rocha, *Considerações*, pp. v-5, 25-71. Rocha contended that the jury was a misguided concept to begin with and tried to show that the jury system was defective in all the countries where it existed. England, he advanced, only preserved its jury system because Englishmen were innately terrified of all innovation.

76. Brazil, Assembléia Constituinte, *Anais*, 1823, 5: 174.

77. José Antônio Pimenta Bueno (Marques de São Vicente), *Direito público brasileiro e análise da constituição do império*, p. 321.

Chapter 8: Reactionary Thought

1. The classic application of Rocha's formula is his 1855 pamphlet, "Ação, reação, transação: Duas palavras acerca da atualidade política do Brasil," in Raymundo Magalhães, Jr., *Tres panfletários do segundo império*, pp. 163-218. Earlier versions appeared in *O Brasil*, 19 September 1843, 25 January 1848.

2. Joaquim Nabuco, *Um estadista do império, Nabuco de Araújo: Sua vida, suas opiniões, sua época*, 1: 31-32. See also Paulo Pereira Castro, "A experiência republicana, 1831-1840," in *HGCB*, vol. 2, pt. 2, pp. 9-67.

3. Juiz de Paz of Guaratiba to Minister of Justice, 9 November 1833, ANRJ, IJ4311; Juiz de Paz of São Salvador dos Campos to Minister of Justice, 22 December 1833, ANRJ, IJ4309. On the restoration fear, see also *O Astro de Minas*, 3 April and 14 April 1832.

4. Clarence H. Haring, *Empire in Brazil: A New World Experiment with Monarchy*, pp. 46-47; Caio Prado, Jr., *Evolução política do Brasil e outros estudos*, pp. 61-75.

5. Manuel Correia de Andrade, *Movimentos nativistas em Pernambuco;* Haring, *Empire in Brazil*, p. 46.

6. Stanley J. Stein, *Vassouras: A Brazilian Coffee County, 1850-1900*, p.

53; Virgílio Noya Pinto, "Balanço das transformações econômicas no século XIX," in *Brasil em perspectiva,* ed. Carlos G. Mota, p. 152.

7. The best description of life and labor in the Paraíba Valley is to be found in Stein's *Vassouras.* See also Alberto Ribeiro Lamego, "A aristocracia rural do café na província fluminense," *Anuário do Museu Imperial,* 3 (1946): 53-123.

8. Nabuco, *Um estadista do império,* 1: 326-327.

9. *O cortesão e o homem da aldéia,* p. 8; *O Brasil império e o Brasil república: Reflexões políticas oferecidas aos brasileiros amantes da sua pátria,* pp. 78-79; *Considerações sobre as causas de nossos males.*

10. See especially, A. M. C., *Diálogo entre dous cidadãos do Reino de Zilbra acerca do estado político do mesmo* (Rio de Janeiro, 1833); *O gênio do Brasil, mostrando em scenas interessantes o espelho de verdades para o desengano dos homens; Aparição extraordinária e inesperada do velho venerando ao roceiro: Diálogo havido entre eles sobre a atual situação política do Brasil.*

11. *O Astro de Minas,* 9 July 1836.

12. *Aurora Fluminense,* 15 February and 25 February 1833. See also *O Sete de Abril,* 23 February 1833.

13. *O Carapuceiro,* 1834; *O Sete de Abril,* 30 March 1836 (reprint from *O Carapuceiro*).

14. "Correição aos Juizes de Paz," *O Sete de Abril,* 20 August 1833.

15. See, for example, *O Brasil,* 23 September 1841; Brazil, Minister of Justice, *Relatório,* 1836, p. 30.

16. The Procedural Code called for the juiz de paz elections to be held every four years, as was the practice under the regulatory law of 1827. But rather than choosing one man for a four-year term, four men would be chosen—one to serve in each year of the term. On the problems of multiplicity of juizes, see *Correio Mercantil,* 3-4 April 1838 (Mensagem do Presidente da Província da Bahia).

17. *Correio Mercantil,* 29 May 1838, 13 March 1839 (reprint from *O Jornal do Comércio*). The lack of *instrução* (education) of many juizes de paz disturbed liberals, and *Aurora Fluminense* especially regretted the accumulation of duties. See for example, *Aurora Fluminense,* 18 May 1835; and *O Astro de Minas,* 3 April 1832.

18. Brazil, Minister of Justice (Manuel José de Sousa França), *Relatório,* 1831, p. 5. At the same time that Sousa França advocated putting the juizes de paz on salary, it is well to note that he also affirmed his belief that part of the juiz de paz problem would be solved by the passage of such complementary liberal reforms as the jury system.

19. Brazil, Minister of Justice (Diogo Antônio Feijó), *Relatório,* 1832, pp. 5-6. In the same *relatório,* the frustrated Feijó insulted the professional magistrates in such scathing terms that he was censured in the Chamber of Deputies (*B-CDA,* 1831, 1: 17).

20. Brazil, Minister of Justice (Manuel Alves Branco), *Relatório,* 1835, pp. 16-21. Alves Branco seems to have been most impressed by the abortive slave

revolt of 1835 in Bahia. At the time he wrote to the provincial president of his dismay "at seeing the incredible negligence and carelessness . . . of so many block inspectors, juizes de paz, and other authorities in allowing a . . . long premeditated revolt almost to erupt . . . and bury the province in the greatest calamity" (Minister of Justice [Alves Branco] to Provincial President of Bahia, 27 February 1835, APBa, Presidência da Província/Ministro da Justiça, vol. 890, f. 74). The Minister of Justice of 1833 and 1834 also called attention to the juiz de paz and police problem. See Brazil, Minister of Justice (Honório Hermeto Carneiro Leão), *Relatório,* 1833; and (Aureliano de Sousa e Oliveira Coutinho), *Relatório,* 1834.

21. Brazil, Minister of Justice (Antônio Paulino Limpo de Abreu), *Relatório,* May 1836.

22. See, for example, B-CDA, 1834, 1: 144.

23. Brazil, Minister of Justice (Paulino José Soares de Souza), *Relatório,* 1841, p. 19.

24. Rio de Janeiro, Presidente da Província (Paulino José Soares de Souza), *Mensagem à Assembléia Legislativa,* 1840, pp. 23-25. As minister of justice, Paulino continued this sensationalism (Brazil, Minister of Justice, *Relatório,* 1841, pp. 9-16). See also his speeches in the Senate session of 16 June 1840, in *O Despertador,* 17 June 1840.

25. Brazil, Minister of Justice (Francisco Ramiro de Assis Coelho), *Relatório,* 1840, p. 15.

26. Rio de Janeiro, Presidente da Província (Paulino José Soares de Souza), *Mensagem à Assembléia Legislativa,* 1839, p. 3; Brazil, Minister of Justice (Paulino José Soares de Souza), *Relatório,* 1841, p. 20. See also Brazil, Minister of Justice (Francisco Ramiro de Assis Coelho), *Relatório,* 1840, p. 22; Brazil, Minister of Justice (Bernardo Pereira da Vasconcelos), *Relatório,* 1838, p. 14; Justiniano José da Rocha, *Considerações sobre a administração da justiça criminal do Brasil e especialmente sobre o jury,* pp. 11, 18.

27. Rocha, *Considerações.*

28. Brazil, Minister of Justice, *Relatório,* 1843, p. 8.

29. Rocha, *Considerações,* p. v.

30. Ibid., pp. 25-35, 59.

31. *O Cronista* (Justiniano José da Rocha, ed.), 30 July 1836.

32. Luis Viana Filho, *A sabinada (A república bahiana de 1837),* pp. 186-192.

33. The editor of *Correio Mercantil,* João Antônio Sampaio Viana, exercised the post of interim probate judge in Bahia at the same time he conducted his journalistic attack on the liberal legal system. *Correio Mercantil,* 2 January 1840.

34. *Correio Mercantil,* 26 May 1838, 2 April 1838, 17 January 1839, 7 February 1839, 19 July 1839.

35. *O Sete de Abril,* 6 February 1836 (reprint from *O Universal*).

36. Brazil, Minister of Justice (Francisco Ramiro de Assis Coelho), *Relatorio,* 1840, p. 19.

37. *Aurora Fluminense*, 15 June 1838.
38. *O Despertador*, 20 August 1839. The paper advocated a requirement of at least 800 milreis in provincial capitals and 600 milreis in the interior.
39. *O Carapuceiro*, 6 April 1836. See also Rocha, *Considerações*, p. 23.
40. *O Sete de Abril*, 6 February 1836 (reprint from *O Universal*).
41. Rocha, *Considerações*, p. 11; *O Carapuceiro*, 30 March 1836; *O Brasil*, 23 September 1841.
42. *Aurora Fluminense*, 15 June 1838.
43. "O Nosso Gôsto Por Macaquear," *O Carapuceiro*, 14 January 1840 (reprinted in *O Despertador*, 8 March 1840).
44. *Correio Mercantil*, 29 May 1838.
45. *O Brasil*, 21 September 1843.
46. *Aurora Fluminense*, 26 January 1835 (reprinted from *O Justiceiro* of São Paulo).
47. Ibid.
48. The article of 26 January provoked correspondents of *Aurora Fluminense* to attack the paper for the "defamatory libel against Brazil . . . quite derogatory to the national character and having a terrible effect on [Brazil's] credit in foreign nations" (*Aurora Fluminense*, 6 February 1835).
49. The foremost paid Conservative Party journalist was Justiniano José da Rocha, editor of *O Cronista* (1836-1839), *O Atlante* (1836), and *O Brasil* (1840-1848). See Elmano Cardim, *Justiniano José da Rocha;* Raymundo Magalhães, Jr., *Tres panfletários do segundo império*, p. 127-159.
50. *O Sete de Abril*, 30 March 1836 (reprinted from *O Carapuceiro*). See also *O Carapuceiro*, 24 August 1833, 17 May and 16 August 1834, 11 May 1837, 14 July 1838, 4 June and 25 October 1839.
51. *O Carapuceiro*, 17 January 1838.
52. Amaro Quintas, *O Padre Lopes Gama, político.*
53. *B-SA*, 1839, 4:297. See also *Correio Mercantil*, 23 September 1839, 15 October 1839, 17 January 1840.
54. "O Lavrador do Recôncavo," *Correio Mercantil*, 28 January 1829, 7 February 1839, 19 July 1839, 12 September 1839.
55. *Correio Mercantil*, 1 June and 21 June 1839.
56. Brazil, Minister of Justice (Antônio Paulino Limpo de Abreu), *Relatório*, 1836, p. 31.
57. *A Astréia*, 3 September 1829.
58. *B-CDA*, 1841, 1: 127. In 1840 the *Jornal do Comércio* had offered a similar plan (*O Jornal do Comércio*, 24 January 1840).
59. *O Astro de Minas*, 3 May 1836.
60. See, for example, "Soliloquy of a voter of good faith," *Aurora Fluminense*, 15 February 1833. See also *Aurora Fluminense*, 24 October 1828, 3 September 1832, 3 October 1834; *O Astro de Minas*, 14 January 1832.
61. *Aurora Fluminense*, 26 October 1835.
62. Ibid.
63. Ibid., 6 June 1838.

64. The same was not true of some priests. Padre Feijó and Padre Lopes Gama were especially critical of ignorant, immoral, and negligent Brazilian priests. See Octávio Tarquínio de Sousa, *Diogo Antônio Feijó*, pp. 70, 79-89; *O Carapuceiro*, 11 May 1837, 18 July 1838.

65. See especially *O gênio do Brasil.*

66. *O Brasil*, 19 September 1843.

67. *O Astro de Minas*, 11 May 1839 (reprinted from *Aurora Fluminense*). On immorality and religion, see also *O Carapuceiro*, 11 May 1837.

68. *O Astro de Minas*, 30 April 1835.

69. *O Jornal do Comércio*, 22 August 1833 (reprinted from *O Carapuceiro*).

70. *A Astréia*, 24 January 1832.

71. *O Carapuceiro*, 11 May 1837.

72. *Aurora Fluminense*, 26 January 1835 (reprint from *O Justiceiro*).

73. *Aurora Fluminense*, 26 January 1835. See also Brazil, Minister of Justice, *Relatório*, 1840.

74. *O Carapuceiro*, 16 August 1834.

75. *Aurora Fluminense*, 13 August 1838.

76. *O Brasil*, 16 June 1840; *O Jornal do Comércio*, 22 August 1833 (reprint from *O Carapuceiro*); Rocha, "Ação, reação, transação," in Magalhães, *Tres pan panfletários*, p. 191; Antônio Carlos de Andrada e Silva to Evaristo da Veiga, quoted in Nabuco, *Um estadista do império*, 1: 24.

77. Brazil, Minister of Justice, *Relatório*, 1841, p. 25.

78. Rio de Janeiro, Presidente da Província (Paulino José Soares de Souza), *Mensagem à Assembléia Legislativa*, 1839, pp. 2-3 and table 1, and 1840, pp. 23-26.

79. Brazil, Minister of Justice (Diogo Antônio Feijó), *Relatório*, 1832, pp. 12-13.

80. Brazil, Minister of Justice (Paulino José Soares de Souza), *Relatório*, 1841, pp. 18-19.

81. *O Sete de Abril*, 19 November 1838.

82. Quoted in Nabuco, *Um estadista do império*, 1: 31.

83. *O Brasil*, 16 June 1840, 19 September and 21 September 1843.

84. *O Sete de Abril*, 6 February 1836 (reprint from *O Universal*).

85. *Correio Mercantil*, 14 April 1838. For a critique of political materialism, see *Aurora Fluminense*, 6 June 1838.

86. "A política dos interesses industriais," *O Despertador*, 5 August 1839.

87. Ibid.

88. "A classe conservadora," *O Sete de Abril*, 19 November 1838.

89. *O Jornal do Comércio*, 24 January 1840; *O Cronista*, 23 September 1827; *O Brasil*, 27 September 1842.

90. *O Cronista*, 23 September 1837, 27 January 1837.

91. *O Sete de Abril*, 31 January 1838.

92. See, for example, *Aurora Fluminense*, 24 October 1828 and 16 February 1829.

93. *Aurora Fluminense*, 6 March, 22 March, and 29 March 1833, 3 October

1834; *O Sete de Abril,* 23 February and 2 April 1833.

94. *O Jornal do Comércio,* 5 September 1840. The review is of the first performance of Martins Pena's *A família e a festa da roça.*

95. *O Brasil,* 3 October, 5 November, and 24 November 1840.

96. Quoted in *O Brasil,* 13 May 1843 (speech of Antônio Pereira Rebouças in the Chamber of Deputies on 11 May 1843).

97. *Aurora Fluminense,* 14 March 1839.

98. Brazil, Minister of Justice (Paulino José Soares de Souza), *Relatório,* 1841, pp. 19-20.

99. *O Sete de Abril,* 2 March 1836 (reprinted from *O Diário de Pernambuco,* [Recife]). See also *O Brasil,* 21 September 1843, 10 January 1848.

100. The following discussion is taken from *O Brasil,* 19 September, 23 September, and 26 September 1843.

101. Rocha's proposal that landowners utilize a free labor force held in quasi-feudal bondage foreshadowed the first plans for sharecropping using free immigrant labor and reflected the impending labor crisis as the inevitable end of the Atlantic slave trade approached.

102. Aureliano Cândido Tavares Bastos, *A província: Estudo sobre a descentralização no Brasil,* p. 163.

Chapter 9: Justice, Police, and Patronage

1. *Correio Mercantil,* 1 October 1839.

2. In addition to the yearly reports of the ministers of justice previously cited, see Brazil, Minister of the Empire (Nicolau Pereira de Campos Vergueiro), *Relatório,* 1833, p. 3. Vergueiro's "secondary agents" would be a kind of intendant. See also Brazil, Minister of the Empire (Antônio Pinto Chichorro da Gama), *Relatório,* 1834, p. 7.

3. The classic view of the Additional Act is stated in Aureliano Cândido Tavares Bastos, *A província: Estudo sobre a descentralização no Brasil.* See also Francisco José de Oliveira Vianna, *Evolução do Povo Brasileiro,* pp. 303-304.

4. See, for example, João Batista Cortines Laxe, *Regimento das câmaras municipaes, ou Lei de 1° de Outubro de 1828,* p. xxvi: "The idea [of the Additional Act] was to inaugurate a decentralized administrative system; the result was in fact an oppressive centralization." See also João de Carneiro Maia, *O município: Estudos sobre a administração local,* p. xv; Paulino José Soares de Souza, *Estudos práticos sobre a administração das províncias no Brasil,* p. ix. For a good example of local-level practical complaints against the Additional Act, see Câmara of Caetité (Bahia) to Assembléia Legislativa of Bahia, 7 March 1838, APBa, Seção Legislativa, Ofícios à Assembléia Legislativa, 1838; Câmara of Vila de Minas do Rio das Contas (Bahia) to Assembléia Legislativa of Bahia, 6 March 1839, APBa, Seção Legislativa, Ofícios à Assembléia Legislativa, 1839.

5. See the text of the Additional Act (Lei de 12 de Agôsto de 1834) in João Camilo de Oliveira Torres, *A democracia coroada: Teoria política do império do Brasil,* pp. 497-501, art. 10, secs. 3-6.

6. Ibid., art. 10, sec. 7.

7. Ibid., art. 10, sec. 4.

8. During the liberal years after the Procedural Code was passed, plans for reforming the Code to allow more governmental control were common. See especially, *B-CDA*, 1833, 2: 265; 1835, 2: 41-49, 216-218, 267-270; 1836, 1: 126.

9. For a lucid contemporary statement of this view of the Additional Act, see *O Astro de Minas*, 9 July 1836 (reprint from *O Atlante*).

10. Vitor Nunes Leal, *Coronelismo, enxada e voto*, p. 141.

11. Tavares Bastos, *A província*, p. 166.

12. Ibid., p. 167.

13. Ibid., pp. 167-170; Nunes Leal, *Coronelismo*, p. 141; *B-CDA*, 1837, 2:69.

14. *Correio Mercantil*, 18 June 1838. The proposed legislation was never passed, probably because by 1838 conservative reforms were already being discussed at the national level.

15. Tavares Bastos, *A província*, pp. 181-182. See also Jeanne Berrance de Castro, "A Guarda Nacional," in *HGCB*, vol. 2, pt. 4, pp. 279-281. Castro suggests that most provinces modified the electoral principles of the original National Guard law.

16. Juiz de Direito Interino of Inhambupe (Bahia) to Assembléia Legislativa of Bahia, 26 March 1841, Seção Legislativa, Ofícios à Assembléia Legislativa, 1841.

17. *O Carapuceiro*, 19 July 1839.

18. See Clarence H. Haring, *Empire in Brazil: A New World Experiment with Monarchy*, pp. 46-47; João Wanderley de Araújo Pinho, "A Bahia, 1808-1856," in *HGCB*, vol. 2, pt. 2, pp. 273-285.

19. See the discussion of whether provincial assemblies could legally change the elective process of juiz de paz selection in *B-CDA*, 1837, 1: 94.

20. *O Atlante*, 21 June 1836; *O Astro de Minas*, 9 July 1836.

21. Paulino José Soares de Souza, *Ensaio sobre o direito administrativo*, 2: 205.

22. Ibid., p. 216.

23. Ibid.

24. Ibid., p. 217.

25. See *O Despertador*, 11 June 1839. Even the liberal *Aurora Fluminense* agreed that the Additional Act should be "interpreted" (*Aurora Fluminense*, 5 June 1839).

26. Justiniano José da Rocha, "Ação, reação, transação: Duas, palavras acer-acerca da atualidade política do Brasil," in Raymundo Magalhães, Jr., *Tres panfletários do segundo império*, pp. 195-196.

27. Oliveira Torres, *A democracia coroada*, pp. 440-441. In 1835 and 1836 formal initiatives were taken by those who wished to clarify some of the articles of the Additional Act.

28. Ibid., p. 441.

29. See "Lei de 12 de Maio de 1840 Interpretando alguns Artigos da Reforma da Constituição," in Oliveira Torres, *A democracia coroada*, pp. 502-503.

30. *B-CDA,* 1837, 2: 68-73; 1838, 2: 384-385, 389. See also the speech of Manuel Vieira Tosta defending the interpretation bill, *B-CDA,* 1838, 2: 408.

31. *B-CDA,* 1839, 3: 278.

32. *B-SA,* 1839, 2: 176-178.

33. When president of the province of Ceará in 1835, Alencar had promoted laws giving provincial presidents the right to transfer district judges, fire provincial employees, restrict the competence of the jury system, and alter juiz de paz elections. Joaquim Inácio da Costa Miranda to Senator Alencar (n.d., probably 1835) in "Correspondência passiva do Senador Alencar," *Anais da Biblioteca Nacional,* 86 (1966): 82.

34. Alencar was of course referring to the proposals to reform the Procedural Code.

35. *B-SA,* 1839, 2: 176.

36. Ibid., p. 199.

37. Ibid., p. 234.

38. Ibid., pp. 290-291.

39. Alencar's tally was probably an exaggeration. The terms *bacharel* and *magistrado* were used interchangeably in these debates. The official lists of deputies are inconsistent in giving the representatives' professions, but even this flawed listing names 47 out of 101 deputies in 1839 as bacharéis or magistrates, Brazil, Ministério da Justiça, *Organizações e programas ministeriaes: Regime parlamentar no império,* pp. 292-295.

40. *B-SA,* 1839, 2: 308.

41. Haring, *Empire in Brazil,* p. 57.

42. Under the conservative governments from 1837 to 1840 there had been no uniform policy governing who named district judges. Provinces with "prefect laws" usually named their own judges, while other provinces either accepted district judges appointed by the central government or "recommended" candidates to the minister of justice, who routinely appointed the suggested magistrate. See *B-SA,* 1839, 2: 329.

43. *O Brasil,* 29 April 1841. See also *O Jornal do Comércio,* 7 December 1840.

44. Miguel Arcanjo Galvão, *Relação dos cidadãos que tomaram parte no governo do Brasil no período de Março de 1808 a 15 de Novembro de 1889* (Rio de Janeiro, 1969), pp. 80, 207.

45. *Correio Mercantil,* 21 October and 4 November 1840.

46. *B-CDA,* 1840, 1: 468-469. Such manipulation of the Guard officer corps for electoral ends was initiated by the Conservatives but was adopted by the Liberals in 1840. See also *Correio Mercantil,* 27 March 1841.

47. The infamous elections of 1840 were in fact three elections: the first, held in Rio on 7 September 1840, was to choose council members and juizes de paz for the next four years; the second, and most tumultuous and corrupt, was that of 25 October that designated parochial electors. The last, held on 15 November, was the actual election for provincial deputies. In the capital, this election's outcome had already been decided by the selection of pro-government

electors. *O Brasil,* 3 September, 15 September, 13 October, 27 October, 5 November, and 7 November 1840.

48. See Francisco Belisário Soares de Souza, *O sistema eleitoral do Brasil: Como funciona, como tem funcionado, como deve ser reformado,* p. 47. Before reforms were introduced in 1842, the electoral board was chosen by popular voice vote on names presented by the juiz de paz and the four other members of the board.

49. *O Brasil,* 10 September and 27 October 1840.

50. Ibid., 3 October and 24 November 1840.

51. *Correio Mercantil,* 5 January 1841.

52. *O Brasil,* 10 September 1840.

53. *Correio Mercantil,* 19 December 1840.

54. *O Brasil,* 12 November 1840, 30 March 1841.

55. Ibid., 30 March and 14 August 1841.

56. *B-CLB,* 1841, vol. 4, pt. 1, pp. 75-95. See also Rocha, "Ação, reação, transação," in Magalhães, *Tres panfletários,* pp. 207-208; Oliveira Torres, *A democracia coroada,* p. 236.

57. *B-CLB,* 1841, vol. 4, pt. 1, pp. 75-77.

58. Ibid., p. 91. The junta de paz provided for in the original law was a dead letter from its creation, and no one mourned its passing.

59. Ibid., p. 89; Rocha, "Ação, reação, transação," in Magalhães, *Tres panfletários,* p. 206. The major structural change wrought in the jury system by the reformed code was the abolition of the grand jury (Jury de Acusação). This uncontroversial simplification eliminated what was generally thought to be an unnecessary procedural step.

60. *B-CLB,* 1841, vol. 4, pt. 1, p. 81. See also José Marcelino Pereira de Vasconcelos, *Roteiro dos delegados e subdelegados de polícia.*

61. *B-CLB,* 1841, vol. 4, pt. 1, p. 81.

62. Ibid., pp. 89-90.

63. Rocha, "Ação, reação, transação," in Magalhães, *Tres panfletários,* p. 206.

64. *O Jornal do Comércio,* 18 October 1841. The bill was introduced in the Senate, where its debate lasted for an unparalleled 125 days.

65. *O Brasil,* 24 December 1842.

66. For the conservative view of this impasse, articulated by the Conservative ministry recommending the dissolution of the Chamber of Deputies of 1842, see the report of the ministry to Pedro II on 1 May 1842, in Brazil, *Falas do Trono,* pp. 251-255.

67. *O Brasil,* 23 October 1841.

68. *B-CDA,* 1841, 3: 660.

69. Ibid., pp. 660, 687.

70. Ibid., pp. 641, 660, 705.

71. Ibid., p. 704.

72. Ibid., p. 707.

73. *O Maiorista,* 24 August 1841.

74. *B-CDA,* 1841, 1: 73.

75. *O Maiorista,* 24 August 1841.

76. The Liberal minority in the Chamber of Deputies vainly tried to limit the number of judges on the new Relações in Minas and São Paulo. Efforts by Liberals to limit the number of supernumerary desembargadores and assure a seniority system of promotion to desembargador also failed. *B-CDA,* 1841, 2: 595; *O Maiorista,* 24 August 1841.

77. *B-SA,* session of 24 June 1840, in *O Despertador,* 25 June 1840.

78. *O Maiorista,* 24 August and 2 September 1841.

79. *B-SA,* session of 10 August 1841 (in *O Despertador,* 12 August 1841), session of 14 August 1841 (in *O Despertador,* 18 August 1841). See also *B-CDA,* 1841, 3: 734.

80. Provincial President of Rio de Janeiro (João Caldas Viana) to Minister of the Empire, 5 May 1843, ANRJ, IJJ9378. The situation was identical in Bahia; see Bahia, Presidente da Província, *Mensagem à Assembléia Legislativa,* 1845, pp. 12-19.

81. The regulatory law was promulgated on 31 January 1842. *B-CLB,* 1842, vol. 4, pt. 2, pp. 31-128.

82. *B-SA,* session of 7 August 1841 (in *O Despertador,* 10 August 1841); session of 9 August 1841 (in *O Despertador,* 11 August 1841); session of 13 August 1841 (in *O Despertador,* 16 August 1841).

83. The cultivating of political support through sinecures continued to be identified with the Conservative Party for the rest of the empire. See, for example, Tito Franco de Almeida, *A grande política. Balanço do império no reinado atual. Liberaes e Conservadores. Estudo político financeiro,* pp. 172-173.

84. "Código Criminal Prático da Simi-República de Passamão na Oceania" in *O Maiorista,* 20 November 1841. For equally inspired sarcasm expressed officially, see Bahia, Presidente da Província, *Mensagem à Assembléia Legislativa,* 1845, p. 17.

85. *B-CDA,* 1841, 3: 822.

86. *O Jornal do Comércio,* 18 February 1842.

87. See the Conservative ministry's report to the emperor on the fraudulent elections of 1840 and its consequent request for dissolution of the legislature of 1842, in Brazil, *Falas do Trono,* pp. 351-355.

88. Cônego José Antônio Marinho, *História do movimento político que no ano de 1842 teve lugar na província de Minas Gerais,* pp. 66-73.

89. Francisco Belisário Soares de Souza, *O sistema eleitoral,* pp. 51-52. These changes in Brazil's electoral procedures were determined by the "instructions" of 4 May 1842. See also Marinho, *História do movimento,* p. 80.

90. Marinho, *História do movimento;* Aluísio de Almeida [pseud.], *A revolução liberal de 1842;* Octávio Tarquínio de Sousa, *Diogo Antônio Feijó;* Paulo Pinheiro Chagas, *Teófilo Ottoni, ministro do povo.*

91. The deputy sheriffs were also juizes de paz in some 80 percent of the twenty-four parishes in the interior of the province of Rio in 1848. *Almanack Laemmert* (Rio de Janeiro, 1848).

92. James C. Fletcher and Daniel P. Kidder, *Brazil and the Brazilians Portrayed in Historical or Descriptive Sketches,* pp. 263-264.

Chapter 10: The Politics of Justice
    1. Provincial President of Rio de Janeiro (Manuel de Jesus Valdetaro) to Minister of the Empire, "Reservado," 4 May 1848, ANRJ, IJJ9378.
    2. Quoted in Joaquim Nabuco, *Um estadista do império: Nabuco de Araújo: Sua vida, suas opinões, sua época,* 1: 140.
    3. Quoted in ibid., p. 139.
    4. In late 1841 Justiniano José da Rocha feared that Liberals would try to prevent the reform of the Procedural Code by making propaganda among the artisans and workers (*ofícios mecânicos*) in hopes of organizing "popular movements." *O Brasil,* 18 November 1841. For an identical fear of political manipulation of racial fears, see "O Sr. Antônio Carlos e os Mulattos," in *O Brasil,* 11 September 1841.
    5. See the discussion in José Murilo de Carvalho, "Elite and State-Building in Imperial Brazil" (Ph.D. diss., 1975), pp. 448-450; also Warren K. Dean, "Latifundia and Land Policy in Nineteenth-Century Brazil," *HAHR,* 51 (November, 1971): 606-625.
    6. Paulino José Soares de Souza, *Ensaio sobre o direito administrativo,* 2: 217-218.
    7. Speech of Francisco Álvares Machado, *B-CDA,* 1841, 3: 734. Parts of the subsequent discussion appeared in a different form in Thomas Flory, "Judicial Politics in Nineteenth-Century Brazil," *HAHR,* 55 (November, 1975): 664-692.
    8. *O Brasil,* 29 April 1841, 20 June 1844; Francisco Belisário Soares de Souza, *O sistema eleitoral do Brasil: Como funciona, como tem funcionado, como deve ser reformado,* p. 53.
    9. Provincial President of Rio de Janeiro (Aureliano de Sousa e Oliveira Coutinho) to Minister of Justice, 19 June 1844, 3 August 1844, ANRJ, IJ1862.
    10. B-CDA, 1850, 2: 338-339.
    11. Francisco Gonçalves Martins to Eusébio de Queiroz, Bahia, n.d., PEQ, gavetão 11.
    12. "Circular aos juizes de direito do Rio de Janeiro," 19 July 1849, and Provincial President of Rio de Janeiro to Minister of Justice, 13 December 1849, ANRJ, IJ1864.
    13. ANRJ, Magistratura/Ofícios, 1848-1860, Caixa 775, Pasta 3. Provincial Presidents furnished most such political intelligence.
    14. Registro de Informações Reservadas de Magistrados, 1846-1862 (Informações Reservadas, Livro 3º.), ANRJ, IJ423. The party division was almost even in this sample, with eleven Conservative magistrates, ten Liberals, and three unknown.
    15. *B-CDA,* 1841, 1: 71; see also the analysis of another judge-deputy, D. Manuel de Assis Mascarenhas, who believed that ministries demanded political service as the price for not being transferred: "I believe that judges have taken

up politics principally in order to keep their jobs." Ibid., 1850, 2: 193; also on electioneering judges, ibid., 1850, 2: 373.

16. The private correspondence of political figures often contains statements by a correspondent that his own letters of recommendation should be uniformly disregarded. See, for example, Bernardo Pereira de Vasconcelos to Paulino José Soares de Souza, n.d. (1841), PVU; Justiniano José da Rocha to Firmino Rodrigues Silva, 20 January 1843, quoted in Nelson Lage Mascarenhas, *Um jornalista do império, Firmino Rodrigues Silva*, p. 87.

17. Chichorro da Gama to Antônio Pereira Rebouças, Nazareth, Bahia, 13 October 1847, BNRJ, seção de manuscritos, Coleção Antônio Pereira Rebouças; Joaquim da Silva Santiago to José Martiniano de Alencar, 9 July 1844, *Anais da Biblioteca Nacional*, 86 (1966), pp. 40-41.

18. *B-CDA*, 1854, 4: 31.

19. *B-SA*, session of 26 August 1841 (in *O Despertador*, 29 August 1841). For confirmation of the prediction, see *B-CDA*, 1843, 1: 418.

20. *B-SA*, session of 21 August 1841 (in *O Despertador*, 2 August 1841); session of 26 August 1841 (in *O Despertador*, 29 August 1841; *O Maiorista*, 2 September 1841).

21. *B-CDA*, 1841, 3: 814-822. The minister of justice was Paulino José Soares de Souza; his speech was delivered on 3 November, the day before the reform's passage in the Chamber of Deputies.

22. Chief of Police (Ignácio Manuel Álvares de Azevedo) to Minister of Justice, Rezende, 25 June 1842, ANRJ, IJ1862.

23. *Almanack Laemmert* (Rio de Janeiro, 1847-1848).

24. Provincial President of Rio de Janeiro (Honório Hermeto Carneiro Leão) to Minister of Justice, 4 December 1841, ANRJ, IJ1446. See also Rio de Janeiro, Presidente da Província, *Mensagem à Assembléia Legislativa*, 1 March 1842. That the conscription referred to was meant to be applied selectively to the followers of Liberal boss Joaquim José de Sousa Breves is clear in Honório's private correspondence with the minister of justice.(Honório Hermeto Carneiro Leão to Paulino José Soares de Souza, 10 December 1841, PVU). For a dramatic example of the fear of conscription, see Juiz de Paz of Campo Grande (Rio de Janeiro) to Provincial President, 30 April 1847, ANRJ, IJ4310.

25. Mascarenhas, *Um jornalista*, pp. 53, 110; Nabuco, *Um estadista do império*, 1: 60-81.

26. Mascarenhas, *Um jornalista*, pp. 53, 59-60, 104-109, 153. On Sampaio Vianna's appointment and transfer, see *Correio Mercantil*, 2 January, 21 October, 4 November 1840. On Caravelas, see Albino José Barbosa de Oliveira, *Memórias de um magistrado do império*, p. 127.

27. There are examples of judges becoming violently involved in local affairs. (see Brazil, Minister of Justice, *Relatório*, 1835, p. 18). The occasional murder of a district judge also indicates an overstepping of limits. Provincial President of Bahia to Minister of Justice, 6 September 1836, APBa, Correspondência para o Governo Imperial, vol. 683, f. 45v; Interim district judge of Paraíba do Sul to Provincial President of Rio de Janeiro, 30 July 1839, ANRJ, IJ1861.

28. Information on these judge-politicians has been taken from: José Antônio Soares de Souza, *A vida do Visconde do Uruguai, 1807-1866;* Manuel de Queiroz Matoso Ribeiro, "Apontamentos sobre a vida do conselheiro Eusébio de Queiroz," *Revista Americana,* January 1919, pp. 48-80; Octávio Tarquínio de Sousa, *Bernardo Pereira de Vasconcelos e seu tempo;* Nabuco, *Um estadista do império;* Maurílio de Gouvéia, *O marques do Paraná, um varão do império;* Hélio Viana, *O Visconde de Sepetiba;* Mascarenhas, *Um jornalista;* Barão de Muritiba, "Marquês de Muritiba," *Revista do Instituto Histórico e Geográfico da Bahia,* 49 (1924): 183-193; Arnold Wildberger, *Os presidentes da província da Bahia, efetivos e interinos, 1824-1889,* pp. 315-335. Unfortunately, the published lists of Brazilians who graduated from the University of Coimbra in the late colonial and early independence periods rarely give background information more specific than the birthplace and parents' names of the bacharéis. Luísa da Fonseca, "Bacharéis Brasileiros: Elementos biográficos (1635-1830)," *Anais do IV Congresso de História Nacional* 11 (1951): 113-405; Manuel Xavier de Vasconcelos Pedrosa, "Letrados do século XVIII," *Anais do Congresso Comemorativo do Bicentenário da Transferência da Sêde do Governo do Brasil* (1967), 4: 293-312.

29. Stuart B. Schwartz, *Sovereignty and Society in Colonial Brazil: The High Court of Bahia and Its Judges, 1609-1751,* p. 290.

30. José Luis de Almeida Nogueira, *A academia de São Paulo: Tradicões e reminiscências;* Clóvis Bevilaqua, *História de faculdade de direito do Recife;* Carvalho, "Elite and State-Building," pp. 63-82.

31. A fascinating account of a typical legal education and career at this time is given in Barbosa de Oliveira's *Memórias,* see especially pp. 61-65.

32. Ibid., pp. 120-130. See also Albino José Barbosa de Oliveira to Provincial President of Bahia, 7 August 1833, 22 August 1833, APBa, Judiciária/Juizes, maço 2271.

33. Juiz de Direito of Cantagalo (Rio de Janeiro) to Minister of Justice, 17 December 1845, ANRJ, IJ1339.

34. Juiz de Direito of Rezende to Minister of Justice, 9 June 1871, ANRJ, Registro de Fatos Notáveis, IJ432, ff. 26-26v.

35. Juiz de Direito of Sento Sé (Bahia) to Provincial President of Bahia, 10 February 1844, BNRJ, seção de manuscritos, II-33, 23, 18.

36. José Soares de Souza, *A vida do Visconde do Uruguai,* pp. 9-21; Ribeiro, "Apontamentos sobre a vida," pp. 48-50.

37. Barbosa de Oliveira, *Memórias,* pp. 112-114, 118, 122.

38. It should be recalled, too, that many judges came from professional families with shallow roots of their own. Paulino José Soares de Souza, for instance, was the third generation of his family to leave home to follow economic cycles. His grandfather had emigrated from the Azores to the mines of Minas Gerais during the gold rush; a cotton boom had attracted his father to Maranhão in the extreme north; politics and coffee drew Paulino to Rio de Janeiro. José Soares de Souza, *A vida do Visconde do Uruguai,* pp. 9-12.

39. In his study of Vassouras, a coffee county of Rio de Janeiro considered

by contemporaries to be one of the most toothsome judicial assignments in the empire, Stanley Stein has noted that planters rarely sent their own sons to professional schools. On the other hand, "there was a tendency for professional men to become planters by marriage and purchase of land." Stanley J. Stein, *Vassouras: A Brazilian Coffee County, 1850-1900*, p. 125.

40. José Soares de Souza, *A vida do Visconde do Uruguai*, pp. 44-45; Barbosa de Oliveira, *Memórias*, pp. 169-216; Mascarenhas, *Um jornalista*, p. 191. These are only a few examples. Even from the limited data available, many more might be given. The energy with which judges sought marriages in new and promising areas of the empire seems especially significant. More extensive research into the marriage patterns of judges may show them to be something like a second generation of economic pioneers, incorporated through the female line of the first generation.

41. *O Cronista*, 23 September 1837; 27 January 1838; *O Sete de Abril*, 31 January 1838. See also chapter 8 above.

42. Paulino José Soares de Souza, *Ensaio sobre o direito administrativo*, 2: 217-218.

43. Nicolau Pereira de Campos Vergueiro in *B-SA*, 1839, 2: 290-291, 308; *B-CDA*, 1841, 1: 73.

44. *B-CDA*, 1845, 1: 800-801.

45. *B-CLB*, Law of 19 September 1855 (Lei dos Círculos). On the ease of circumventing the law, see José Antônio Pimenta Bueno, *Direito público brasileiro e análise da constituição do império*, pp. 196-200. On "absolute ineligibility" see Aureliano Cândido Tavares Bastos, *Reforma eleitoral e parlamentar e constituição da magistratura*, p. iv.

46. *B-CDA*, 1846, 2: 125-128, 397-401, 409-413.

47. *B-CLB*, Law of 28 June, 1850; *B-CDA*, 1850, 2: 77, 373-374.

48. Provincial President of Bahia to Minister of Justice, 26 August 1841, APBa, Correspondência para o Governo Imperial, vol. 685, fols. 215-217.

49. See, for example, Conservative Nabuco de Araújo's ill-fated plan of 1854 for judicial reform, which originally included a provision that would have severely limited a judge's access to elective political offices. Nabuco, *Um estadista do império*, 1: 136-150.

50. The reform law of 20 September 1871 increased the number of judicial posts and separated police and judicial functions, but it did not provide for absolute ineligibility of judges. Nabuco, *Um estadista do império*, 2: 172-176.

51. *B-CDA*, 1853, 1: 296; *B-CDA*, 1854, 4: 29.

52. Richard Graham, *Britain and the Onset of Modernization in Brazil, 1850-1914*, pp. 32-34.

53. Miguel do Sacramento Lopes Gama in *O Carapuceiro*, 15 June 1842; *O Jornal do Comércio*, 26 July 1843 (reprint from *O Carapuceiro*).

54. Paulino José Soares de Souza to Paulino José Soares de Souza, Jr., 24 April 1851, PVU. The employment crisis for law school graduates is confirmed in Carvalho, "Elite and State-Building," pp. 104, 220-221; and in Roderick and Jean Barman, "The Role of the Law Graduate in the Political Elite of Imperial

Brazil," *Journal of Interamerican Studies and World Affairs,* 18 (November 1976): 423-450.

55. Edward Shils, "The Intellectual in the Political Development of the New States," in *Political Development and Social Change,* ed. Jason L. Finkle and Richard W. Gable, pp. 253-254.

56. José Antônio de Magalhães Castro, *Decadência da magistratura brasileira: Suas causas e meios de restabelecê-la.*

57. Eça de Queiroz, *A correspondência de Fradique Mendes,* in *Obras de Eça de Queiroz,* 4: 526-527.

58. B-CDA, 1850, 2: 226; B-CDA, 1854, 4: 33.

59. The military is specifically set up as a counterpoise to magisterial political influence in an anonymous pamphlet of 1861, *Os bacharéis: Ensaio político sobre a situação.* In a popular novel written shortly after the fall of the empire, the protagonist perceives the major political difference as the change from domination by bacharéis to domination by the military. Alfredo de Escragnolle Taunay, *O encilhamento: Scenas contemporâneas da bolsa em 1890, 1891 e 1892,* pp. 19-20. On the imperial army, see John Schulz, "O exército e o império," in *HGCB,* 2: 4, 248, 252.

60. Brazil, Ministério da Justiça, *Organizações e programas ministeriais. Regime parlamentar no império,* pp. 341-346.

Conclusion

1. Stanley J. Stein and Barbara H. Stein, *The Colonial Heritage of Latin America: Essays on Economic Dependence in Perspective,* pp. 147-150.

2. Caio Prado, Jr., *Evolução política do Brasil e outros estudos,* pp. 84-85; Florestan Fernandes, *A revolução burguesa no Brasil: Ensaio de interpretação sociológica,* pp. 31-85; Gilberto Freyre, *Sobrados e mucambos: Decadência do patriarcado rural e desenvolvimento do urbano,* 3: 951-953 and passim.

3. Raymundo Faoro, *Os donos do poder: Formação do patronato político brasileiro,* pp. 169-181.

4. Frank Safford, "Bases of Political Alignment in Early Republican Spanish America," in *New Approaches to Latin American History,* ed. Richard Graham and Peter H. Smith, pp. 102-111.

Bibliography

Archives and Private Papers
Arquivo da Associação Comercial da Bahia, Salvador (ACB).
Arquivo Municipal de Salvador, Bahia (AMS).
Arquivo do Estado da Guanabara, Rio de Janeiro (AEG).
Arquivo Nacional, Rio de Janeiro (ANRJ).
Arquivo Público do Estado da Bahia, Salvador (APBa).
Biblioteca Nacional, seção de manuscritos, Rio de Janeiro (BNRJ).
Papers of Eusébio de Queiroz (in Arquivo Nacional), Rio de Janeiro (PEQ).
Papers of the Visconde do Uruguai, Niterói (PVU).

Public Documents
Bahia (province). Presidente da Província. *Mensagem à Assembléia Legislativa.*
Title varies.
Brazil. Assembléia Constituinte. *Anais.* 1823-1824.
————. Câmara dos Deputados. *Anais.* 1826-1870.
————. *Constituição política do Império do Brasil.* Rio de Janeiro: Typ.
Nacional, 1834.
————. *Coleção das Leis do Império do Brasil.* 1822-1871.
————. *Decisões do governo do Império do Brasil.* 1824-1838.
————. *Falas do Trono desde o ano de 1823 até o ano de 1889 acompan-
hadas dos respectivos votos de graças.* Rio de Janeiro, 1889.
————. Ministério da Justiça. *Organizações e programas ministeriaes: Re-
gime parlamentar no império.* 2nd. ed. Rio de Janeiro, 1962.
————. ————. *Notícia histórica dos serviços, instituições, e estabeleci-
mentos pertencentes a esta repartição, elaborada por ordem do respectivo
ministro, Dr. Amaro Cavalcante.* Rio de Janeiro, 1889.
————. Minister of Justice. *Relatório.* 1831-1848. Title varies.
————. Minister of the Empire. *Relatório.* 1833-1848. Title varies.
————. Senado. *Anais.* 1826-1848.
Rio de Janeiro (province). Presidente da Província, *Mensagem à Assembléia Le-
gislativa.* Title varies.

Contemporary Newspapers and Periodicals
Almanack Laemmert (Rio de Janeiro).
A Astréia (Rio de Janeiro).
O Astro de Minas (Ouro Prêto).
O Atlante (Rio de Janeiro).
Aurora Fluminense (Rio de Janeiro).
O Brasil (Rio de Janeiro).
O Brasileiro Pardo (Rio de Janeiro).
O Bahiano (Bahia).
O Caramuru (Rio de Janeiro).
O Carapuceiro (Recife).
O Correio da Bahia (Bahia).
Correio Mercantil (Bahia).
O Cronista (Rio de Janeiro).
O Despertador (Rio de Janeiro).
O Exaltado (Rio de Janeiro).
O Federalista (São Paulo).
O Filho da Terra (Rio de Janeiro).
O Guaicurú (Bahia).
O Guarda Nacional (Rio de Janeiro).
O Jornal do Comércio (Rio de Janeiro).
O Justiceiro (São Paulo).
A Lanterna Mágica (Rio de Janeiro).
O Maiorista (Rio de Janeiro).
A Malagueta (Rio de Janeiro).
O Mulato, Ou, O Homem de Cor (Rio de Janeiro).
Nova Luz Brasileira (Rio de Janeiro).
O Par de Tetas: Jornal Satírico e Político (Rio de Janeiro).
O Parlamentar (Rio de Janeiro).
Recopilador Cachoeirense (Cachoeira, Bahia).
The Rio Herald (Rio de Janeiro).
O Sete de Abril (Rio de Janeiro).
O Universal (Ouro Prêto).
A Voz Fluminense (Rio de Janeiro).

Books, Articles, Pamphlets, and Theses
Abreu, João Capistrano de. *Ensaios e estudos (crítica e historia).* Rio de Janeiro: Livraria Briguiet, 1938.
Accioli de Cerqueira e Silva. *Memórias históricas e políticas da província da Bahia.* Notes by Braz do Amaral. Vol. 4. Bahia: Imprensa Oficial, 1933.
Aguiar, Manuel Pinto de. *A abertura dos portos: Cairu e os ingleses.* Bahia: Progresso, 1960.
Alden, Dauril. *Royal Government in Colonial Brazil, with Special Reference to the Administration of Marquis de Lavradio, Viceroy, 1769-1779.* Berkeley: University of California Press, 1968.

Almeida, Aluísio de [pseud.]. *A revolução liberal de 1842.* Rio de Janeiro: José Olympio, 1944.

Almeida, Cândido Mendes de. *Código filipino ou ordenações e leis do Reino de Portugal.* Rio de Janeiro: Typ. do Instituto Philomathico, 1870.

Almeida, Manuel Antônio de. *Memórias de um sargento de milícias.* 4th ed. São Paulo: Livraria Martins, 1941. First published 1854-1855.

Almeida, Tito Franco de. *A grande política. Balanço do império no reinado atual. Liberais e Conservadores. Estudo político financeiro.* Rio de Janeiro: Imperial Instituto Artístico, 1877.

Amaral, Braz do. *História da Bahia do império à república.* Bahia: Imprensa Oficial, 1923.

A. M. C. *Diálogo entre dous cidadãos do reino de Zilbra acerca do estado político do mesmo.* Rio de Janeiro, 1833.

Andrade, Manuel Correia de. *Movimentos nativistas em Pernambuco.* Recife: Universidade Federal de Pernambuco, 1971.

————. "The Social and Ethnic Significance of the War of the Cabanos." In *Protest and Resistance in Angola and Brazil: Comparative Studies,* edited by Ronald H. Chilcote, pp. 91-107. Berkeley: University of California Press, 1972.

Aparição extraordinária, e inesperada do velho venerando ao roceiro: Diálogo havido entre eles sobre a atual situação política do Brasil. Unsigned pamphlet. Rio de Janeiro and Recife, 1831.

Armitage, John. *The History of Brazil from the Period of the Arrival of the Bragança Family in 1808 to the Abdication of Dom Pedro the First in 1831.* 2 vols. London: Smith, Elder and Co., 1836.

Arnisau, José Joaquim de Almeida e. "Memória topográfica, histórica, comercial e política da Vila da Cachoeira da Província da Bahia," *Revista trimensal do Instituto Histórico Geográfico e Etnográfico do Brasil,* 25 (1862): 127-143.

Atos, atribuições, deveres e obrigações dos juizes de paz, por um Bacharel. Rio de Janeiro, 1852.

Aufderheide, Patricia Ann. "Order and Violence: Social Deviance and Social Control in Brazil, 1780-1840." Ph.D. dissertation, University of Minnesota, 1976.

Azevedo, Fernando de. *Canaviais e engenhos na vida política do Brasil.* Rio de Janeiro: Instituto do Açucar do Alcool, 1948.

Azevedo, João Lúcio de. *O Marques de Pombal e a sua época.* 2nd ed. Rio de Janeiro: Anuário do Brasil, 1922.

Azevedo, Thales de. *Povoamento da cidade do Salvador.* Bahia: Editôra Itapuã, 1969.

Os bacharéis: Ensaio político sobre a situação. Rio de Janeiro, 1861.

Baker, John M. *A View of the Commerce between the United States and Rio de Janeiro, Brazil.* Washington: 1838.

Barman, Roderick, and Jean Barman. "The Role of the Law Graduate in the Political Elite of Imperial Brazil," *Journal of Inter-American Studies and World Affairs,* 18 (November 1976): 423-450.

Barreto Filho, João Paulo de Melo, and Hermeto Lima. *História da polícia do Rio de Janeiro: Aspectos da cidade e da vida carioca (1565-1831)*. Vol. 1. Rio de Janeiro: A Noite, 1939.

Bendix, Reinhard. *Nation-Building and Citizenship: Studies of Our Changing Social Order*. New York: Wiley, 1964.

Bethell, Leslie. *The Abolition of the Brazilian Slave Trade: Britain, Brazil, and the Slave Trade Question, 1807-1869*. Cambridge: Cambridge University Press, 1970.

Bevilaqua, Clóvis. *História da faculdade de direito do Recife*. 2 vols. Rio de Janeiro: F. Alves, 1927.

Boxer, Charles R. *The Golden Age of Brazil, 1695-1750: Growing Pains of a Colonial Society*. Berkeley: University of California Press, 1969.

_____. *Portuguese Society in the Tropics: The Municipal Councils of Goa, Macau, Bahia, and Luanda, 1510-1800*. Madison: University of Wisconsin Press, 1965.

Brading, D. A. "Government and Elite in Late Colonial Mexico," *Hispanic American Historical Review*, 53 (August 1973): 389-414.

O Brasil império e o Brasil república: Reflexões políticas oferecidas aos brasileiros amantes de sua pátria. Unsigned pamphlet. Philadelphia, 1831.

Brasiliense, Américo. *Os programas dos partidos do segundo império*. Pt. 1. São Paulo: Typ. de Jorge Seckler, 1878.

Brito, João Rodrigues de. *Cartas econômico-políticas sobre a agricultura e comércio da Bahia, dadas à luz por I. A. F. Benavides*. 2nd ed. Bahia: Imprensa Oficial, 1924. First published in Lisbon, 1821.

Buarque de Holanda, Sérgio (ed.). *História geral da civilização brasileira*. Vols. 1-7. São Paulo: Difusão Européia do Livro, 1963-1972.

_____. *Raízes do Brasil*. 6th ed. Rio de Janeiro: José Olympio, 1971.

Burns, E. Bradford. "The Role of Azeredo Coutinho in the Enlightenment of Brazil," *Hispanic American Historical Review*, 44 (May 1964): 145-160.

Cabral, Osvaldo R. *A organização das justiças na colônia e no império e a história da comarca da Laguna*. Porto Alegre, 1955.

Calógeras, João Pandiá. *A History of Brazil*. Chapel Hill: University of North Carolina Press, 1939.

Cardim, Elmano. *Justiniano José da Rocha*. São Paulo: Companhia Editôra Nacional, 1964.

Carrato, José Ferreira. *Igreja, iluminismo e escolas mineiras coloniais*. São Paulo: Companhia Editora Nacional, 1968.

Carvalho, José Murilo de. "Elite and State-Building in Imperial Brazil." Ph.D. dissertation, Stanford University, 1975.

Castro, Jeanne Berrance de. "A guarda nacional." In *História geral da civilização brasileira*, edited by Sérgio Buarque de Holanda, vol. 2, pt. 4, pp. 274-298. São Paulo: Difusão Européia do Livro, 1963-1972.

_____. "O negro na guarda nacional brasileira," *Anais do Museu Paulista*, 23 (1969): 149-172.

Castro, José Antônio de Magalhães. *Decadência da magistratura brasileira: Suas causas e meios de restabelecê-la.* Rio de Janeiro, 1862.

Castro, Paulo Pereira. "A experiência republicana, 1831-1840." In *História geral da civilização brasileira,* edited by Sérgio Buarque de Holanda, vol. 2, pt. 2, pp. 9-67. São Paulo: Difusão Européia do Livro, 1963-1972.

_____. "Política e administração de 1840 a 1848." In *História geral da civilização brasileira,* edited by Sérgio Buarque de Holanda, vol. 2, pt. 2, pp. 509-540. São Paulo: Difusão Européia do Livro, 1963-1972.

Cerqueira, Beatriz Westin de. "Um estudo de escravidão em Ubatuba." *Estudos Históricos,* nos. 5-6 (1966-1967), pp. 7-58, 9-66.

Chagas, Paulo Pinheiro. *Teófilo Ottoni, ministro do povo.* 2nd ed. Rio de Janeiro: Livraria São José, 1956.

Collier, Simon. *Ideas and Politics of Chilean Independence, 1808-1833.* Cambridge: Cambridge University Press, 1967.

Considerações sobre as causas de nossos males. Unsigned pamphlet. Rio de Janeiro, 1832.

Cordeiro, Carlos Antônio. *Diretor do juizo de paz.* Rio de Janeiro, 1881.

Correspondência oficial das provincias do Brasil durante a legislatura das Cortes Constituintes de Portugal nos annos de 1821-1822, precedida das cartas dirigidas a El-Rei D. João VI pelo Príncipe Real D. Pedro de Alcântara, como regente. 2nd ed. Lisbon, 1872.

"Correspondência passiva do Senador Alencar," *Anais da Biblioteca Nacional,* vol. 86 (1966).

O cortesão e o homem da aldéia. Unsigned pamphlet. Rio de Janeiro, 1832.

Cortines Laxe, João Batista. *Regimento das câmaras municipaes, ou Lei de 1° de Outubro de 1828.* 2nd ed. Rio de Janeiro: B. L. Garnier, 1885.

Cosío Villegas, Daniel. *American Extremes.* Austin: University of Texas Press, 1964.

Costa, Emília Viotti da. "Introdução ao estudo da emancipação política do Brasil." In *Brasil em perspectiva,* edited by Carlos Guilherme Mota, pp. 75-139. São Paulo: Difusão Européia do Livro, 1968.

_____. *Da senzala à colônia.* São Paulo: Difusão Européia do Livro, 1966.

Costa, João Cruz. "As novas idéias." In *História geral da civilização brasileira,* edited by Sérgio Buarque de Holanda, vol. 2, pt. 1, pp. 179-190. São Paulo: Difusão Européia do Livro, 1963-1972.

_____. *Contribuição à história das idéias no Brasil.* 2nd ed. Rio de Janeiro: Civilização Brasileira, 1967.

Cunha, Pedro Octávio Carneiro da. "A fundação de um império liberal." In *História geral da civilização brasileira,* edited by Sérgio Buarque de Holanda, vol. 2, pt. 1, pp. 135-178, 238-262, 379-404. São Paulo: Difusão Européia do Livro, 1963-1972.

Dauphinee, Bede Anthony. "Church and Parliament in Brazil during the First Empire, 1823-1831." Ph.D. dissertation, Georgetown University, 1965.

Davidson, David. "How the Brazilian West Was Won: Freelance and State on the Matto Grosso Frontier, ca. 1737-1752." In *Colonial Roots of Modern Brazil,* edited by Dauril Alden, pp. 61-106. Berkeley: University of California

Press, 1973.

Dawson, John P. *A History of Lay Judges.* Cambridge, Mass.: Harvard University Press, 1960.

Dawson, Philip. *Provincial Magistrates and Revolutionary Politics in France, 1789-1795.* Cambridge, Mass.: Harvard University Press, 1972.

Dealy, Glen. "Prolegomenon on the Spanish American Political Tradition," *Hispanic American Historical Review,* 48 (February 1968): 37-58.

Dean, Warren K. "Latifundia and Land Policy in Nineteenth Century Brazil," *Hispanic American Historical Review,* 51 (November 1971): 606-625.

————. "The Planter as Entrepreneur: The Case of São Paulo," *Hispanic American Historical Review,* 46 (May 1966): 138-152.

Debret, Jean Baptiste. *Viagem pitoresca e histórica ao Brasil.* 2 vols. São Paulo: Livraria Martins Editôra, 1949.

Diálogo entre Basílio mercador e os eleitores de uma freguesia do sertão no ano de 1833. Unsigned pamphlet. Rio de Janeiro: 1834.

Dias, Maria Odila Silva. "A interiorização da metrópole (1808-1853)." In *1822: Dimensões,* edited by Carlos Guilherme Mota, pp. 160-187. São Paulo: Editôra Perspectiva, 1972.

Díaz, Benito. *Juzgados de paz de la campaña de la provincia de Buenos Aires (1821-1854).* La Plata, Argentina: Universidad Nacional de la Plata, 1959.

Dornas Filho, João. *O padroado e a igreja brasileira.* São Paulo: Companhia Editôra Nacional, 1938.

Eisenberg, Peter L. *The Sugar Industry in Pernambuco: Modernization without Change, 1840-1910.* Berkeley: University of California Press, 1974.

Eisenstadt, S. N. *Essays on Comparative Institutions.* New York: Wiley, 1965.

————. *The Political Systems of Empires.* New York: Free Press, 1963.

Ellis, Jr., Alfredo. *Feijó e a primeira metade do século XIX.* São Paulo: Companhia Editôra Nacional, 1940.

Escragnolle, Luis Afonso d'. "O visconde de Camamú e o derrame de moedas falsas de cobre na Bahia," *Anais do 1.° Congresso de História da Bahia,* 4 (1950): 143-171.

Explicações breves e singelas sobre o que é a federação. Rio de Janeiro, 1831.

Faoro, Raymundo. *Os donos do poder: Formação do patronato político brasileiro.* Porte Alegre: Editôra Globo, 1958.

Fernandes, Florestan. *A revolução burguesa no Brasil: Ensaio de interpretação sociológica.* Rio de Janeiro: Zahar Editores, 1975.

Fernandes, Heloisa Rodrigues. *Política e segurança: Força pública do estado de São Paulo, fundamentos histórico-sociais.* São Paulo: Editora Alfa-Omega, 1974.

Feijó, Diogo Antônio. *Guia dos juizes de paz.*

Ferreira de Rezende, Francisco de Paula. *Minhas recordações.* Rio de Janeiro: José Olympio, 1944.

Fletcher, James C., and Daniel P. Kidder. *Brazil and the Brazilians Portrayed in Historical or Descriptive Sketches.* 6th ed. Boston: Little Brown, 1866.

Fonseca, Luísa da. "Bacharéis brasileiros: Elementos biográficos (1635-1830),"

Anais do IV Congresso de História Nacional, 11 (1951): 109-407.

Franco, Maria Sílvia de Carvalho. *Homens livres na ordem escravocrata.* São Paulo: Instituto de Estudos Brasileiros, 1969.

Freyre, Gilberto. *Casa grande & senzala: Formação da família brasileira sob o regime de patriarcal.* 2 vols. 14th ed. Rio de Janeiro: José Olympio, 1969.

_____. *Sobrados e mucambos: Decadência do patriarcado rural e desenvolvimento do urbano.* 3 vols. 2nd ed. Rio de Janeiro: José Olympio, 1951.

Furtado, Celso. *The Economic Growth of Brazil.* Berkeley: University of California Press, 1963.

Galvão, Eneas. "O poder judiciária no império," *Revista do Instituto Histórico e Geográfico Brasileiro,* special issue, pt. 3 (1916): 321-339.

Galvão, Miguel Arcanjo. *Relação dos cidadaõs que tomaram parte no governo do Brasil no período de Março de 1808 a 15 de Novembro de 1889.* Rio de Janeiro: Arquivo Nacional, 1969.

Gardner, George. *Travels in the Interior of Brazil, Principally through the Northern Provinces and the Gold and Diamond Districts during the Years 1836-1841.* London: Reeve Bros., 1846.

O gênio do Brasil, mostrando em scenas interessantes o espelho de verdades para o desengano dos homens. Unsigned pamphlet. Rio de Janeiro, 1831.

Góes Calmon, Francisco Marques de. *Elementos para a história da vida econômico-financeira da Bahia de 1808 a 1899.* Bahia, 1925.

Gomes de Carvalho, M. E. *Os deputados brasileiros nas cortes gerais de 1821.* Porto: Livraria Chardron, 1912.

Gouvéia, Maurílio de. *O Marques do Paraná, um varão do império.* Rio de Janeiro: Biblioteca do Exército Editôra, 1962.

Graham, Richard. *Britain and the Onset of Modernization in Brazil, 1850-1914.* Cambridge: Cambridge University Press, 1968.

Hagen, Everett E. "A Framework for Analyzing Economic and Political Change," In *Development of the Emerging Countries. An Agenda for Research,* edited by Robert E. Asher, pp. 1-38. Washington: Brookings Institution, 1962.

Hale, Charles A. *Mexican Liberalism in the Age of Mora, 1821-1853.* New Haven, Conn.: Yale University Press, 1968.

_____. "The Reconstruction of Nineteenth-Century Politics in Spanish America: A Case for the History of Ideas," *Latin American Research Review,* 8, no. 2 (Summer 1973): 53-74.

Halperín-Donghi, Tulio. *Historia contemporánea de América Latina.* 2nd ed. Madrid: Alianza Editorial, 1970.

Haring, Clarence H. *Empire in Brazil: A New World Experiment with Monarchy.* Cambridge, Mass.: Harvard University Press, 1958.

Hoselitz, Bert F. *Sociological Aspects of Economic Growth.* Glencoe, Ill.: Free Press, 1960.

Kelly, Prado. "A realidade política do município," *Anuário do Museu Imperial,* 20 (1959): 9-25.

Kennedy, John Norman. "Bahian Elites, 1750-1822," *Hispanic American Historical Review,* 53 (August 1973), 415-439.

Lamego, Alberto Ribeiro. "A aristocracia rural do café na província fluminen-se," *Anuário do Museu Imperial,* 3 (1946): 53-123.

Leal, Aurelino. "O ato adicional. Reação conservadora. Bernardo Pereira de Vasconcelos. A lei de interpretação. O golpe de estado da maioridade. O ministério das nove horas," *Revista do Instituto Histórico e Geográfico Bra-sileiro,* special issue, pt. 3 (1916), pp. 105-194.

_____ . "História judiciária do Brasil." In *Dicionaário histórico geográfico e etnográfico do Brasil,* 1: 1107-1187. Rio de Janeiro, 1922.

Leal, Hamilton. *História das instituições políticas do Brasil.* Rio de Janeiro, 1962.

Leal, Vitor Nunes. *Coronelismo, enxada e voto.* Rio de Janeiro, 1948.

Lins, Wilson. *O médio São Francisco: Uma sociedade de pastores e guerreiros.* Bahia: Livraria Progresso, 1952.

Linz, Juan. "Early State-Building and Late Peripheral Nationalisms against the State: The Case of Spain." In *Building States and Nations,* edited by S. N. Eisenstadt and Stein Rokkan, 2: 32-116. Beverly Hills: Sage, 1973.

Lisboa, João Francisco. *Obras de João Francisco Lisboa, natural de Maranhão; precedidas de uma notícia biográfica pelo Dr. Antônio Henriques Leal.* Vol. 1. São Luis: Castro e Leal, 1864.

Lôbo, Eulália Maria Lahmeyer. "Evolução dos preços e do padrão de vida no Rio de Janeiro, 1820-1930–resultados preliminares," *Revista Brasileira de Economia,* 25, no. 4 (1971): 235-265.

Lockridge, Kenneth A. *A New England Town: The First Hundred Years.* New York: Norton, 1970.

Luccock, John. *Notes on Rio de Janeiro and the Southern Parts of Brazil; Taken during a Residence of Ten Years in that Country, from 1808 to 1818.* London: S. Leigh, 1820.

McBeth, Michael Charles. "The Politicians vs. the Generals: The Decline of the Brazilian Army during the First Empire, 1822-1831." Ph.D. dissertation, University of Washington, 1972.

Macedo, Joaquim Manuel de. *Memórias da Rua do Ouvidor.* São Paulo: Com-panhia Editôra Nacional, 1952.

Madre de Deus, Faustino José de. *A Constituição de 1822, comentada e desen-volvida na prática.* 2nd ed. Lisbon: Typ. Maigrense, 1823.

Magalhães, Jr., Raymundo. *Tres panfletários do segundo império.* São Paulo: Companhia Editôra Nacional, 1956.

Maia, João de Azevedo Carneiro. *O município: Estudos sobre administração local.* Rio de Janeiro, 1883.

Manchester, Alan K. *British Preeminence in Brazil, Its Rise and Decline: A Stu-dy in European Expansion.* Chapel Hill: University of North Carolina Press, 1933.

_____ . "The Transfer of the Portuguese Court to Rio de Janeiro." In *Con-flict and Continuity in Brazilian Society,* edited by Henry Keith and S. F. Edwards, pp. 148-183. Columbia: University of South Carolina Press, 1969.

Merchant, Alexander. "Aspects of the Enlightenment in Brazil." In *Latin America and the Enlightenment,* edited by Arthur P. Whitaker, pp. 95-118.

2nd ed. Ithaca, N. Y.: Cornell University Press, 1961.

Marinho, José Antônio. *História do movimento político que no ano de 1842 teve lugar na província de Minas Gerais.* 2nd ed. Conselheiro Lafayete: Typ. Almeida, 1939. First published in 1844.

"Marques de Muritiba" (obituary), *Revista do Instituto Geográfico e Histórico da Bahia,* 3 (March 1896): 118-121.

Martin, Percy Alvin. "Federalism in Brazil," *Hispanic American Historical Review,* 18 (May 1938): 143-163.

Martins, Luis. *O patriarca e o bacharel.* São Paulo: Livraria Martins, 1953.

Mascarenhas, Nelson Lage. *Um jornalista do império: Firmino Rodrigues Silva, 1815-1879.* São Paulo: Companhia Editôra Nacional, 1961.

Mattoso, Kátia M. de Queiroz. *Presença francesa no movimento democrático bahiano de 1798.* Bahia: Editôra Itapuã, 1969.

Maxwell, Kenneth R. *Conflicts and Conspiracies: Brazil and Portugal, 1750-1808.* Cambridge: Cambridge University Press, 1973.

———. "The Generation of the 1790's and the Idea of Luso-Barzilian Empire." In *Colonial Roots of Modern Brazil,* edited by Dauril Alden, pp. 107-144. Berkeley: University of California Press, 1973.

Mello, Alfredo Pinto Vieira de. "O poder judiciário no Brasil, 1532-1871," *Revista do Instituto Histórico e Geográfico Brasileiro,* special issue, pt. 4 (1916), pp. 97-149.

Moacyr, Primitivo. *A instrução e o império, 1823-1853.* Vol. I. São Paulo: Companhia Editôra Nacional, 1936.

Monteiro, Tobias do Rego. *História do império: A elaboração da independência.* Rio de Janeiro: F. Briguiet, 1927.

Moraes, Francisco. "Estudantes da Universidade de Coimbra nascidos no Brasil," *Brasília* (supplement to vol. 4), 1949.

Morse, Richard M. "Some Themes of Brazilian History," *The South Atlantic Quarterly,* 61, no. 2 (Spring 1962): 159-182.

Mota, Carlos Guilherme. *Atitudes de inovação no Brasil, 1789-1801.* Lisbon: Livros Horizonte, n.d.

——— (ed.). *1822: Dimensões.* São Paulo: Editôra Perspectiva, 1972.

———. *Nordeste: 1817.* São Paulo: Editôra Perspectiva, 1972.

Muritiba, Barão de. "Marques de Muritiba," *Revista do Instituto Histórico e Geográfico da Bahia,* 49 (1924): 183-193.

Nabuco, Joaquim. *Um estadista do império, Nabuco de Araújo: Sua vida, suas opiniões, sua época.* 2 vols. Rio de Janeiro: Civilização Brasileira, 1936.

Nelson, William E. *Americanization of the Common Law: The Impact of Legal Change on Massachusetts Society.* Cambridge, Mass.: Harvard University Press, 1975.

Nogueira, José Luis de Almeida. *A academia de São Paulo: Tradições e reminiscências.* São Paulo: Typ. Vanorden, 1907-1912.

Novelli, Júnior, Luiz Gonzaga. *Feijó: Um paulista velho.* Rio de Janeiro: Edições GRD, 1963.

Oliveira, Albino José Barbosa de. *Memórias de um magistrado do império,* edited by Américo Jacobino Lacombe. São Paulo: Companhia Editôra Nacional, 1943.

Oliveira Lima, Manuel de. *D. João VI no Brasil.* 3 vols. Rio de Janeiro: José Olympio, 1909.

_____. *O movimento da independência.* 4th ed. São Paulo: Melhoramentos, 1962.

Osborne, Bertram. *Justices of the Peace, 1361-1848: A History of the Justices of the Peace for the Counties of England.* Shaftesbury: Sedgehill Press, 1960.

Ottoni, Teófilo B. "Circular dedicado aos srs. eleitores de senadores pela província de Minas Gerais no quatriênio atual," in Basílio de Magalhães, "A 'circular' de Teófilo Ottoni," *Revista do Instituto Histórico e Geográfico Brasileiro,* 78 (1916).

Palmer Jr., Thomas W. "A Momentous Decade in Brazilian Administrative History, 1831-1840," *Hispanic American Historical Review,* 30 (May 1950): 209-217.

Pang, Eul-Soo, and Ron L. Seckinger. "The Mandarins of Imperial Brazil," *Comparative Studies of Society and History,* 14, no. 2 (March 1972): 215-244.

Patroni (Martins Maciel Parente), Felipe Alberto. *A bíblia do justo meio da política moderada, ou prolegômenos do direito constitucional da natureza explicada pelas leis físicas do mundo.* Rio de Janeiro, 1835.

Pedrosa, Manuel Xavier de Vasconcelos. "Letrados do século XVIII." In *Anais do Congresso Comemorativo do Bicentenário da Transferência da Sêde do Governo do Brasil.* 4 vols. Rio de Janeiro, 1967.

Pena, Luis Carlos Martins. "O juiz de paz da roça: Farça em um ato com anexos." Ms. Biblioteca Nacional do Rio de Janeiro.

_____. *Teatro de Martins Pena.* Edited by Darcy Damaceno and Maria Filgueiras. Rio de Janeiro: Instituto Nacional do Livro, 1956.

Pereira, Hipólito da Costa. *Diário de minha viagem para Filadélfia (1798-1799).* Rio de Janeiro: Academia Brasileira, 1955.

Pereira da Silva, João Manuel. *História do Brasil de 1831 a 1840.* Rio de Janeiro: D. da Silva, Jr., 1878.

Pimenta Bueno, José Antônio (Marques de São Vicente). *Direito público brasileiro e análise da constituição do império.* Rio de Janeiro: Ministério de Justiça, 1958.

Pinto, Caetano José de Andrade. *Atribuições dos presidentes de província.* Rio de Janeiro, 1865.

Pinto, Luiz de Aguiar. *Lutas de famílias no Brasil.* São Paulo: Companhia Editôra Nacional, 1949.

Pinto, Virgílio Noya. "Balanço das transformações econômicas no século XIX." In *Brasil em perspectiva,* edited by Carlos G. Mota, pp. 141-164. São Paulo: Editôra Perspectiva, 1968.

Poppino, Rollie E. *Feira de Santana.* Bahia: Editôra Itapuã, 1968.

Prado, Jr., Caio. *Evolução política do Brasil e outros estudos.* 5th ed. São Paulo: Brasiliense, 1966.

_____. *História econômica do Brasil.* 8th ed. São Paulo: 1963.

Pye, Lucien W. "The Concept of Political Development." In *Political Development and Social Change,* edited by Jason L. Finkle and Richard W. Gable, pp. 43-50. New York: Wiley, 1971.

Queiroz, Eça de. *Obras de Eça de Queiroz.* Porto: Lello Irmãos, 1957.

Queiroz, Maria Isaura Pereira de. *O mandonismo local na vida política brasileira.* São Paulo: Instituto de Estudos Brasileiros, 1969.

Quintas, Amaro. *O Padre Lopes Gama, político.* Recife, 1958.

Rangel, Alberto. *No rolar do tempo.* Rio de Janeiro: José Olympio, 1937.

Rebouças, Antônio Pereira. *Recordações da vida parlamentar.* 2 vols. Rio de Janeiro: Laemmert, 1870.

Retrospecto sobre os erros da administração do Brasil por um Brasileiro. Niterói, 1848.

Rezende, Astolfo de. "Polícia administrativa. Polícia judiciária. O código do processo de 1832. A lei de 3 de decembro de 1841. A lei de 20 de setembro de 1871," *Revista do Instituto Histórico e Geográfico Brasileiro,* special issue, pt. 3 (1916), pp. 400-422.

Ribeiro, Manuel de Queiroz Matoso. "Apontamentos sobre a vida do conselheiro Eusébio de Queiroz," *Revista Americana,* January 1919, pp. 48-80.

Rocha, Justiniano José da. "Ação, reação, transação: Duas palavras acerca da atualidade política do Brasil." In Raymundo Magalhães, Jr., *Tres panfletários do segundo império.* São Paulo: Companhia Editôra Nacional, 1956.

_____. *Biografia de Manuel Jacinto Nogueira da Gama, Marques de Baependy.* Rio de Janeiro, 1851.

_____. *Considerações sobre a administração da justiça criminal do Brasil e especialmente sobre o jury.* Rio de Janeiro, 1835.

Rodrigues, Bento José. "O juiz eleito." Ms. Biblioteca Nacional do Rio de Janeiro, 1856.

Ruy, Afonso. *História da câmara municipal da cidade do Salvador.* Bahia: Câmara Municipal de Salvador, 1953.

_____. *A primeira revolução social brasileira (1798).* 3rd ed. Rio de Janeiro: Laemmert, 1970.

Safford, Frank. "Bases of Political Alignment in Early Republican Spanish America." In *New Approaches to Latin American History,* edited by Richard Graham and Peter H. Smith, pp. 71-111. Austin: University of Texas Press, 1974.

Santos, José Joaquim dos. *Manual prático das conciliações e processo civil da alçada do juizo de paz.* Bahia, 1854.

Santos, José Maria dos. *A política geral do Brasil.* São Paulo: J. Magalhães, 1930.

Schulz, John. "O exército e o império." In *História geral da civilização brasileira,* edited by Sérgio Buarque de Holanda, vol. 2, pt. 4, pp. 248-252. São Paulo: Difusão Européia do Livro, 1963-1972.

Schwartz, Stuart B. "Free Labor in a Slave Economy: The *Lavradores de Cana* of Colonial Bahia." In *Colonial Roots of Modern Brazil,* edited by Dauril Alden, pp. 147-197. Berkeley: University of California Press, 1973.

_____. "Magistracy and Society in Colonial Brazil," *Hispanic American Historical Review*, 50 (November 1970): 715-730.

_____. *Sovereignty and Society in Colonial Brazil: The High Court of Bahia and Its Judges, 1609-1751.* Berkeley: University of California Press, 1973.

Seligman, Lester G. "Elite Recruitment and Political Development." In *Political Development and Social Change*, edited by Jason L. Finkle and Richard W. Gable, pp. 240-249. New York: Wiley, 1971.

Shils, Edward. "The Intellectual in the Political Development of the United States." In *Political Development and Social Change*, edited by Jason L. Finkle and Richard W. Gable, pp. 253-254. New York: Wiley, 1971.

Sierra y Mariscal, Francisco de. "Idéias gerais sobre a revolução do Brasil e suas consequências," *Anais da Biblioteca Nacional*, vols. 43-44. Rio de Janeiro, 1931.

Silva, Pedro Celestino da. "A Cachoeira e seu município," *Revista do Instituto Geográfico e Histórico da Bahia*, 63 (1937): 3-71.

_____. "Datas e tradições Cachoeiranas," *Anais do Arquivo Público da Bahia*, 29 (1943): 324-401.

_____. "Galeria cachoeirana," *Revista do Instituto Geográfico e Histórico da Bahia*, 68 (1942): 1-91.

Silva Lisboa, José da. *Refutação das declamações contra o comércio ingles, extraída de escritores eminentes, por José da Silva Lisboa.* Rio de Janeiro, 1810.

Simonsen, Roberto C. *História econômica do Brasil, 1500-1800.* 6th ed. São Paulo: Companhia Editôra Nacional, 1969.

Sodré, Nelson Werneck. *A história da imprensa no Brasil.* Rio de Janeiro: Civilização Brasileira, 1966.

Sousa, Octávio Tarquínio de. *A mentalidade da constituinte.* Rio de Janeiro: José Olympio, 1931.

_____. *A vida de D. Pedro I.* 3 vols. Rio de Janeiro: José Olympio, 1952.

_____. *Bernardo Pereira de Vasconcelos e seu tempo.* Rio de Janeiro: José Olympio, 1937.

_____. *Diogo Antônio Feijó (1784-1843).* Rio de Janeiro: José Olympio, 1942.

_____. *Evaristo da Veiga.* São Paulo: Companhia Editôra Nacional, 1939.

_____. *História de dois golpes de estado.* Rio de Janeiro: José Olympio, 1939.

_____. *José Bonifácio.* Rio de Janeiro: José Olympio, 1945.

Souza, Francisco Belisário Soares de. *O sistema eleitoral do Brasil: Como funciona, como tem funcionado, como deve ser reformado.* Rio de Janeiro, 1872.

Souza, José Antônio Soares de. *A vida do visconde do Uruguai (1807-1866).* São Paulo: Companhia Editôra Nacional, 1944.

_____. "O efêmero quilombo de Paty do Alferes em 1838," *Revista do Instituto Histórico e Geográfico Brasileiro*, no. 295 (April-June, 1972): 33-69.

Souza, Paulino José Soares de. *Ensaio sobre o direito administrativo.* 2 vols. Rio de Janeiro: Typ. Nacional, 1862.

_____. *Estudos práticos sobre a administração das províncias no Brasil.* 2 vols. Rio de Janeiro: Typ. Nacional, 1865.

Souza Neto, Paulino José Soares de. "O visconde do Uruguai e a consolidação da ordem em 1842," *Anuário do Museu Imperial,* 6 (1945): 105-129.

Stein, Stanley J. "The Historiography of Brazil, 1808-1889," *Hispanic American Historical Review,* 40, no. 2 (May 1960): 234-278.

_____. *Vassouras: A Brazilian Coffee County, 1850-1900.* New York: Atheneum, 1970.

_____, and Barbara H. Stein. *The Colonial Heritage of Latin America: Essays on Economic Independence in Perspective.* New York: Oxford University Press, 1970.

Stonequist, Everett V. *The Marginal Man: A Study in Personality and Culture Conflict.* New York: Russell & Russell, 1961.

Sturz, J. J. *A Review, Financial, Statistical and Commercial of the Empire of Brazil and Its Resources.* London: E. Wilson, 1837.

Suetônio [pseud.]. *O antigo regimen (homens e cousas).* Rio de Janeiro: Cunha e Irmão, 1896.

Taunay, Alfredo de Escragnolle. *O encilhamento: Scenas contemporâneas da bolsa em 1890, 1891, e 1892.* São Paulo: Melhoramentos, 1923.

Tavares Bastos, Aureliano Cândido. *A província: Estudo sobre a decentralização no Brasil.* 2nd ed. São Paulo: Companhia Editôra Nacional, 1937. First published in 1870.

_____. *Cartas do Solitário.* 3rd ed. São Paulo: Companhia Editôra Nacional, 1938. First published in 1862.

_____. *Os males do presente e as esperanças do futuro.* São Paulo: Companhia Editôra Nacional, 1939. First published in 1861.

_____. *Reforma eleitoral e parlamentar e constituição da magistratura.* Rio de Janeiro, 1873.

Tollenare, L. F. de. *Notas dominicaes tomadas durante uma viagem em Portugal e no Brasil em 1816, 1817 e 1818.* Bahia: Livraria Progresso Editor, 1956.

Torres, João Camilo de Oliveira. *A democracia coroada: Teoria política do império do Brasil.* 2nd ed. Petrópolis: Editôra Vozes, 1964.

_____. *A formação do federalismo no Brasil.* São Paulo: Companhia Editôra Nacional, 1961.

Torres, Maria Celestina T. M. "Um lavrador paulista do tempo do império," *Revista do Arquivo Municipal,* 172 (1968): 191-262.

Vade-mecum dos juizes de paz, suplentes, fiscaes, e escrivães para a província do Rio de Janeiro. Rio de Janeiro, 1830.

Valladão, Alfredo. *Da aclamação à maioridade, 1822-1840.* 2nd ed. São Paulo: Companhia Editôra Nacional, 1939.

Varnhagen, Francisco Adolfo de. *História da independência do Brasil até o reconhecimento pela antiga metrópole.* São Paulo: Melhoramentos, 1957.

Vasconcelos, Bernardo Pereira de. *Carta aos senhores eleitores da província de Minas Gerais em 1828.* 2nd ed. Rio de Janeiro: F. Rodrigues de Paiva, 1899.

_____. *Comentário à lei dos juizes de paz.* Ouro Prêto, 1829.

Vasconcelos, José Marcelino Pereira de. *Roteiro dos delegados e subdelegados de polícia.* 2nd ed. Rio de Janeiro: J. Villeneuve, 1861.

Veiga, Luis Francisco da. *O primeiro reinado estudado à luz da sciencia, ou a revolução de 7 de Abril de 1831 justificada pelo direito e pela história.* Rio de Janeiro: G. Leuzinger & Filhos, 1877.

Viana Filho, Luis. *A sabinada (A república Bahiana de 1837).* Rio de Janeiro: José Olympio, 1938.

Vianna, Francisco José de Oliveira. *Evolução do povo brasileiro.* São Paulo: Companhia Editôra Nacional, 1938.

──────. *Instituições políticas brasileiras.* 2 vols. Rio de Janeiro: José Olympio, 1955.

Vianna, Hélio. *Contribuição à história da imprensa brasileira, 1812-1869.* Rio de Janeiro: Imprensa Nacional, 1945.

──────. "Notável documento da história política do império," *Anuário do Museu Imperial,* 11 (1950): 53-64.

──────. *O Visconde de Sepetiba.* Petrópolis: Typ. Ipirauga, 1943.

Vilhena, Luis dos Santos. *A Bahia no século XVIII.* 3 vols. Bahia, Editôra Irapuã, 1969.

Walsh, Robert. *Notices of Brazil in 1828 and 1829.* 2 vols. Boston: Richard, Lord, and Holbrook, 1831.

Wanderley de Araújo Pinho, José. "A Bahia, 1808-1856." In *História geral da civilização brasileira,* edited by Sérgio Buarque de Holanda, vol. 2, pt. 2, pp. 245-311. São Paulo: Difusão Européia do Livro, 1963-1972.

──────. *Cotegipe e seu tempo: Primeira fase, 1815-1867.* São Paulo: Companhia Editôra Nacional, 1937.

──────. *História de um engenho do Recôncavo.* Rio de Janeiro: Z. Valverde, 1946.

──────. *Salões e damas do segundo reinado.* 4th ed. São Paulo: Livraria Martins, 1970.

Wildberger, Arnoldo. *Os presidentes da província da Bahia, efectivos e interinos, 1824-1889.* Bahia: Typ. Beneditina, 1949.

Willems, Emílio. "Social Differentiation in Colonial Brazil," *Comparative Studies in Society and History,* 12 (January 1970): 31-49.

Zenha, Edmundo. *O município no Brasil, 1532-1700.* São Paulo: Instituto Progresso, 1948.

Index

L 261656/HC

DATE DUE

MAY 31 1989		
AUG 31 1989		
DEC 31 1989		
OCT 12 1989		
GAYLORD		PRINTED IN U.S.A.